Mental Health Initiative

A Grant Funded by the
Southern California Library Cooperative

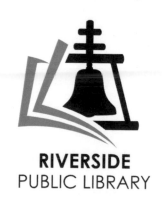

RIVERSIDE
PUBLIC LIBRARY

Encyclopedia of Rape and Sexual Violence

Encyclopedia of Rape and Sexual Violence

Volume 2: S–Z and Primary Documents

MERRIL D. SMITH, EDITOR

An Imprint of ABC-CLIO, LLC
Santa Barbara, California • Denver, Colorado

Library of Congress Cataloging-in-Publication Data

Names: Smith, Merril D., 1956- editor.
Title: Encyclopedia of rape and sexual violence.
Description: Santa Barbara, California : ABC-CLIO, an Imprint of ABC-CLIO, LLC, [2018] | Includes index.
Identifiers: LCCN 2017044792 (print) | LCCN 2018016452 (ebook) | ISBN 9781440844904 (eBook) | ISBN 9781440844898 (set : alk. paper) | ISBN 9781440849169 (volume 1) | ISBN 9781440849176 (volume 2)
Subjects: LCSH: Rape—Encyclopedias. | Sex crimes—Encyclopedias.
Classification: LCC HV6558 (ebook) | LCC HV6558 .E53 2018 (print) | DDC 364.15/303--dc23
LC record available at https://lccn.loc.gov/2017044792

ISBN: 978-1-4408-4489-8 (set)
     978-1-4408-4916-9 (vol. 1)
     978-1-4408-4917-6 (vol. 2)
     978-1-4408-4490-4 (ebook)

22 21 20 19 18   1 2 3 4 5

This book is also available as an eBook.

ABC-CLIO
An Imprint of ABC-CLIO, LLC

ABC-CLIO, LLC
130 Cremona Drive, P.O. Box 1911
Santa Barbara, California 93116-1911
www.abc-clio.com

This book is printed on acid-free paper ∞

Manufactured in the United States of America

Contents

Acknowledgments

It has taken a global village to write and publish this book. I want to thank my husband, Doug Smith, for keeping me supplied with food, wine, and chocolate in the final days of getting this book to press. I also feel deep gratitude to my family and friends for the much-needed love and laughter that gave me breaks from researching and writing on this grim subject. The scholars who came through with such fine entries deserve special accolades—and certainly have my thanks. A big thank you to senior acquisitions editor Kevin Hillstrom, who asked me back in June 2015 if I would be interested in doing this book. Finally, a special thank you to Patrick Hall, who took over as development editor at ABC-CLIO for this project, and who has been unwaveringly patient and gracious despite many delays, and to Erin Ryan, who helped to get the final manuscript into production.

Introduction

The World Health Organization estimates that approximately 30 percent of women worldwide experience physical and/or sexual violence, mainly from an intimate partner. The Rape, Abuse & Incest National Network (RAINN) states, "Every 98 seconds another American is sexually assaulted" (Scope of the Problem: Statistics n.d.) In crime statistics, unreported crimes are known as "the dark figure," and sexual violence has perhaps the darkest of dark figures, as many victims never report incidents because of stigma, shame, and fear of reprisal from their assailants. Although under-reported, the data that are available clearly indicate that sexual violence is a global problem that affects not only women, but men and children, too.

The history of rape is as old as the history of humankind. Although the names and fates of most victims from long ago are unknown, others, real and legendary, can be found in ancient tales: Leda, the Sabine women, Lucretia, and the biblical Dinah are a few examples. The regulation of rape also goes far back in time. The Babylonian Code of Hammurabi (ca. 1789 BCE), a code of laws literally inscribed in stone, included many laws that concerned sexual crimes and accusations. Among them is the declaration that a virgin who is raped is innocent, but her attacker is guilty and must be killed. In contrast, the code states that if a married woman is caught with another man, they are both to be executed—but the husband may choose to pardon his wife. In other words, women belonged to men: first to their fathers, then to their husbands.

The word *rape* comes from the Latin *raptus* or *rapere*, meaning "to seize or carry off by force." The rape of a virgin meant her virtue was taken and her family was disgraced. The rape of a married woman stole her honor; it stole her husband's honor as well, by usurping his exclusive sexual rights to her body and making uncertain the paternity of any child born within nine months of the rape. Such beliefs about women's honor and virtue continue, as can be seen in the number of women still punished for adultery or murdered in so-called honor killings (Gidda 2017). Even today, women often fear to speak about being raped, either because they think they will not be believed or, even worse, because they fear their husbands, fathers, or brothers will abandon them or kill them (Wolfe 2013).

Differences in how rape and sexual crimes have been prosecuted through time and place underscore the fluid definition of the word *rape*. As historian

Estelle B. Freedman has noted, "Historians and feminist scholars ask how its [rape's] definition is continually reshaped by specific social relations and political contexts" (Freedman 2013, 3). Though this encyclopedia focuses on rape in contemporary society, the topics—different categories of rape and sexual assault, examined both in the United States and globally—demonstrate that the word *rape* continues to be redefined over time and place.

Sexual violence is a term that includes rape, sexual abuse, and sexual assault of women, men, and children. Within that broad category are such types of sexual violence as child sexual abuse, intimate partner sexual violence, and drug-facilitated sexual assault. Legal definitions of *sex crimes* and *sex-related violence* are different, however, and they vary from state to state and from country to country. Each of the entries in this book covers a type of sexual violence, although many of the issues, problems, and concerns overlap. Nevertheless, as should be clear from all of them, sexual violence is never the fault of the victim.

The issue of consent is the central focus in American rape law, as well as in legislation throughout most of the world. Following English common law, American rape law defined *rape* as a forced sexual attack on a woman for which she did not give consent and which was "against her will." However, the 17th-century English jurist Matthew Hale specified this: "But the husband cannot be guilty of a rape committed by himself upon his lawful wife; for by their mutual matrimonial consent and contract the wife hath given up herself in the kind unto her husband, which she cannot retract" (Hale 1847, 628). Thus, a wife's consent to all sexual acts with her spouse was assumed to be granted with her wedding vows, and husbands were permitted to rape their wives under what has become known as the marital or spousal exemption.

Most states previously defined *rape* as forcible penetration of the body of a woman who was "not the wife" of the perpetrator. Until the 1990s, some U.S. states still had not criminalized marital rape. That the issues of consent and marital rape are still misunderstood can be seen in the 2015 comment made by Michael Cohen, then special counsel to the Trump Organization, regarding accusations against Donald Trump: "You cannot rape your spouse. And there's very clear case law." Until 1984, however, marital rape was not illegal in New York (Zadrozny and Mak 2015).

In other parts of the world, marital rape has not been criminalized, even in places that have updated their rape laws. For example, despite pressure from citizens, women's rights advocates, and the United Nations, in 2016 India was one of 49 countries that still had not made marital rape illegal. Some Indian leaders have said that such a law would go against Indian culture and societal norms (Sachdev 2016). Figures cited in a 2015 joint Clinton Foundation/ Gates Foundation report demonstrate that many around the world believe men have the right to beat their wives and to demand sex from women, even if the woman has not consented. In the Democratic Republic of the Congo, "62 percent of women and 48 percent of men agreed or partially agreed that a man has the right to sex even if a woman refuses," and 45 percent of women in Ethiopia surveyed between 2009 and 2013 believed a husband was "justified" to beat his wife if she argued with him (though these figures have decreased from 61 percent in 2003–2004) (Clinton Foundation and Bill & Melinda Gates Foundation 2015, 20, 21).

Who can give consent and how that consent is indicated have evolved over time. Most nations have laws stipulating that children cannot give consent, but the age of consent varies from place to place. In most states in the United States, the age of consent is between ages 16 and 18. However, individuals who are younger than the age of consent are permitted to legally marry with the permission of a parent or guardian. Most commonly, the girl is younger than her husband, and recent investigations have uncovered examples of girls as young as 11 or 12 years old who are married. In these cases, the young woman is at risk of sexual violence and abuse, as well as physical and emotional harm. Throughout the world, women who are coerced into early marriages suffer. Among other problems they face, child brides generally must leave school, thus limiting their economic opportunities, and their young bodies face increased risks during childbirth (Kristof 2017).

Child sexual abuse is a problem both within the United States and throughout the world. One 2002 report found that 1 in 12 (82 percent) of children sampled had been subjected to some form of sexual abuse in that year. In addition, most knew their attacker (Finkelhor et al. 2005, 10). All over the world, children living in poverty or in strife-torn regions engage in "survival sex" in order to get food, money, or goods. Children are also exploited by celebrities, coaches, and sex traffickers.

In recent years, the United Kingdom has had several high-profile child sexual abuse cases made public. For example, a 2016 report estimated that Jimmy Savile, a television and radio personality who died in 2011, may have abused as many as 500 children over several decades. His youngest known victim was 10 years old. Other scandals have involved football (soccer) coaches, clergy, and politicians. Moreover, a large child sexual abuse ring operated in Rotherham for over a decade (Manzoor 2017). The perpetrators were British-Pakistani men, and the victims were young, white women. As Sarfraz Manzoor noted in the *New York Times* in 2014, however, this case is not only about race, religion, class, or gender. The Pakistani men got away with their sexual abuse for as long as they did, Manzoor writes, "because they targeted a community even more marginal and vulnerable than theirs, a community with little voice and less muscle: white working-class girls" (Manzoor 2014).

Consent is also an issue if a person, female or male, is intoxicated, drugged, unconscious, mentally ill, mentally challenged, or physically challenged (for example, unable to speak or move). In the United States, a number of cases in which women consumed several glasses of alcoholic beverages at parties and then were raped have received media attention. In some cases, the women did not find out what had happened to them until they saw photographs on social media. This was what happened to the young woman who was raped by Brock Allen Turner while she was unconscious. Turner was found guilty of sexual assault in 2016, but he was not sentenced to any prison time. His sentence spurred California to revise rape laws in 2017 so that individuals convicted of sexually assaulting a person who was unconscious or incapable of giving consent must now serve prison time.

Throughout history, rape has been a part of everyday domestic life—the rape of wives, concubines, children, servants, and slaves by husbands, uncles, brothers, masters, friends, and neighbors. Rape has been a companion of soldiers and explorers as they conquered new lands, subdued their enemies, and took spoils of war or revenge. Through rape, soldiers then and now have proven their masculinity and strengthened their bonds with comrades.

In conflict zones, both women and men are at risk of sexual violence. When the Japanese army captured the Chinese city of Nanking in December 1937, they began to commit mass murder, torture, mutilation, and rape. It is estimated that hundreds of thousands were murdered, and 20,000 women were raped, including schoolgirls, nuns, and elderly women. Thousands of other Chinese women were forced into sexual slavery as "comfort women." The survivors are still seeking reparations from Japan.

During the Holocaust, though technically forbidden by race laws to do so, Nazis raped Jewish women, as well as sexually humiliating them by forcing them to stand or dance naked. Sometimes women or girls were raped as part of looting, or as part of a bargain so that the woman could receive food or other necessities. Jewish women were also sexually abused by fellow prisoners and by those who helped them when they were in hiding (Wolfe 2012).

The Holocaust sought to wipe out the entire Jewish population. Other conflicts since then have also tried to eradicate various ethnic or religious groups. In addition to murder, policies of ethnic cleansing also target women's bodies by raping them so that they are forced to bear their oppressors' offspring, or by forcing them to have abortions or to undergo sterilization (Wolfe 2012). In more recent times, sexualized violence as part of a policy of ethnic cleansing has taken place in Bosnia, the Congo, Rwanda, South Sudan, and Syria. Survivors of this sexualized violence often suffer additionally because they are stigmatized by their families or communities. Furthermore, they or their families may not accept babies born of these rapes. Women in refugee camps face additional risks, including sexual violence. Men are also raped, and sometimes they are forced to watch as their family members are raped, or they are forced to commit rape themselves.

Within the United States, rape has been intertwined with perceptions about gender and race. Slavery, "our peculiar institution," as well as permitting 18th-century and 19th-century Americans to rape, beat, and torture their slaves with impunity, left a lasting legacy of racial conflict and myths. From the 16th century onward, many white Americans believed black women (and Native American women) were loose, licentious, and sexually insatiable. Even after slavery was abolished, some white men believed black women were promiscuous. In addition, the "myth of the black beast" has led to black men being falsely arrested, tortured, or lynched for raping white women. For example, in the notorious Scottsboro Boys case of the 1930s, nine African American teenagers were falsely accused of raping two white women on a train near Scottsboro, Alabama.

Issues of class and gender, and beliefs about how men and women should behave, have precipitated acts of sexual violence or have complicated how the acts have been perceived. Some men have considered women of any race "fair game" if they lived in particular areas, worked in or frequented bars or taverns, or were known to be sexually active. As recent news reports indicate, this belief is still held by both men and women. In numerous cases, witnesses, the accused, and the general public have indicated a belief that a young woman should not dress a certain way, or that she should not go to a party and get drunk. For example, in the 2013 Steubenville rape case, photos and videos of the young woman who was assaulted were posted on social media, some eliciting comments implying that the victim was to blame. Steubenville citizens were divided over the reports, especially after the story began to receive wide media coverage. In a *Rolling Stone* magazine article, tennis star Serena Williams made comments that blamed the victim; her statements received national attention, forcing her to apologize for what she had said.

Yet, as Abigail Rine pointed out in a July 2013 article in *The Atlantic* magazine, male victims are also blamed. In a case in Norwood, Colorado, three high-school wrestlers anally raped a 13-year-old boy with a pencil. After the perpetrators were finally arrested, other students in school and on social media blamed and harassed the victim. Some parents even encouraged this victim-blaming. As some studies have shown, many believe men are supposed to remain silent and stoic about such assaults. Moreover, those who believe most strongly in gender stereotypes or ideals are more likely to blame the victim. Both men and women who appear to have violated gender norms are often blamed if they become victims of sexual violence (Rine 2013).

Studies of sexual violence with the U.S. military indicate that while more men than women are abused, fewer men than women report the incidents (though sexual assaults on both women and men are under-reported). In addition to being perceived as weak or not "masculine," some men fear being labeled as gay. In fact, *GQ* magazine undertook to report on the subject in a long form article in 2014 entitled "Son, Men Don't Get Raped." In surveys and studies, military men often report that they considered the acts to be "hazing." Many men who have been sexually assaulted indicate that the acts were intended to humiliate them. In addition, military culture has a definite power structure, and those within it are taught to obey authority. Sexual acts are often demanded as a show of power.

A 2015 U.S. Government Accountability Office report on sexual assaults on male military service members described a common scenario:

> . . .victim advocates and prosecutors at one installation described a series of escalating incidents that began with hitting the victim in the crotch, then throwing objects at the victim's crotch, and ultimately then saying the hazing would stop if the victim performed oral sex on the assailants. These service officials added that training on hazing-type activities and their relationship to sexual assault would be particularly beneficial to males in that it might lead to increased reporting and fewer inappropriate incidents. However, they stated that they have not seen this addressed in the training. (Government Accountability Office 2015, 47)

Throughout the world, LGBTQ (Lesbian, Gay, Bisexual, Transgender, and Queer) individuals face greater risks of sexual violence. In some cases, the cases are reported as hate crimes; as with all sexual violence crimes, though, the victims often do not report them. In the case of LGBTQ individuals, there may also be fears of gender orientation or sexual orientation being revealed. RAINN reports that 21 percent "of TGQN (transgender, genderqueer, nonconforming) college students have been sexually assaulted, compared to 18% of non-TGQN females, and 4% of non-TGQN males" (Victims of Sexual Violence: Statistics 2017). Worldwide, some LGBTQ individuals are raped in hate crimes known as "corrective rape." The United Nations has spoken out against hate crimes and transphobia and homophobia in such documents as the 2008 UN Human Rights Council Resolution on Sexual Orientation and Gender Identity.

Prisoners are another group that faces a higher chance of sexual violence. Prisoners are at risk from both inmates and staff. Efforts have been made within the United States to address the problem, but inmates are often fearful of reporting rape because they fear retaliation by staff or other prisoners. All sexual contact between incarcerated men and women and staff is illegal. Even if a prisoner agrees to sexual activity, the power that a prison staff member has over an inmate makes the act coercive. RAINN estimates that annually 80,600 prisoners experience sexual violence, and that in 60 percent of the cases the perpetrator is a jail or prison staff member (Victims of Sexual Violence: Statistics n.d.). LGBTQ prisoners, those with mental health problems, minors, and those who seem vulnerable are most likely to be targets of sexual violence.

Both within the United States and in other parts of the world, many believe that prisoners do not deserve assistance, or that rape might even be an appropriate punishment for their crimes. However, when those prisoners are released, they bring their trauma back into the world and into their homes. Sexual trauma, both physical and emotional, may make it difficult for ex-prisoners to adjust to life outside of prison. In addition, shame may keep them from telling sexual partners about their sexual assaults, thus exposing the partners to sexually transmitted diseases.

Including all victims of rape, female and male, has been an important goal of recent laws and studies. From 1927 until 2012, the FBI's Uniform Crime Report defined *forcible rape* as "the carnal knowledge of a female, forcibly and against her will." In 2013, a new, broader definition was put into place, and it allows for victims and perpetrators to be of any gender: "The penetration, no matter how slight, of the vagina or anus with any body part or object, or oral penetration by a sex organ of another person, without the consent of the victim" (Federal Bureau of Investigation 2013).

Studies indicate that most rapes are committed by a person known to the victim. Only 28 percent of rapes are committed by a stranger, while acquaintances commit 45 percent of rapes, and 25 percent are committed by current or former boyfriends, girlfriends, or spouses (The remaining percent are nonspouse relatives, more than one person, or someone the victim cannot remember.) (Perpetrators of Sexual Violence: Statistics 2017).

The Centers for Disease Control and Prevention (CDC) reports that teen dating violence—also known by such terms as relationship abuse, dating abuse, and intimate partner violence—is a widespread problem. It includes stalking and harassment, and it may take place in person or electronically. In a 2013 national survey of high-school students, 10 percent reported that they had been physically assaulted and 10 percent had experienced sexual victimization from a dating partner within the previous year. Studies indicate that teens who experience sexual victimization are often at risk for experiencing it again. Often, they are afraid to tell their families or friends about what has happened, and the teens may experience depression and anxiety, may begin abusing drugs or alcohol or engaging in other unhealthy behaviors, and may have thoughts of suicide (Centers for Disease Control and Prevention n.d.).

Despite these statistics, the typical image of a rapist in popular culture is of someone unknown to the victim. Many people still consider acquaintance rape, date rape, and spousal rape to be lesser or insignificant crimes. Missouri representative Todd Akin was much maligned for his use of the term "legitimate rape" in 2012. In addition, Akin said that pregnancy could not result from a rape, because "the female body has ways to try to shut the whole thing down" (Moore 2012). Despite the science and the evidence, Akin is not alone in his beliefs. The belief goes back centuries. A widely used 17th-century judicial manual, Michael Dalton's *The Country Justice*, stated that "if a Woman at the time of the supposed Rape, do conceive with Child by the Ravisher, this is no Rape; for a Woman cannot conceive with Child except she doth consent" (Dalton 1690, 392). One has only to look at the numbers of enslaved women who became pregnant after being raped or the pregnancies that resulted from wartime rapes to realize that this belief has no validity. In fact, scientific studies have demonstrated that pregnancy from rape occurs at the same rate as pregnancy from consensual sex. Most reports, including those from RAINN, estimate the figure as about 3.1–5 percent (Clancy 2012).

Though rape is an age-old crime, modern technology has created new forms of sexual violence. The Internet and social media have made cyberstalking possible, and they have also permitted victims of sexual assaults to be revictimized through the posting of photos and videos of their attacks. Web sites, often sites on the "dark web" that are accessible only through special software and authorization, display pornography, including child pornography and pornography made by those held in sexual slavery. In addition, violence, including sexual violence, is frequently found in television shows, movies, and video games. Sociologist Laura Finley notes that "more than 1,000 studies have confirmed that television contributes in various ways to violent behavior." For example, it can increase aggression and fear in viewers. Importantly, frequent watching of violent media desensitizes viewers to real-world violence. Finally, consumers of violent media develop an increased appetite for violence (Finley 2016, 27–28). This violent media—in games, television, music videos, and movies—tends to portray hypersexualized characters and may present violent sex as acceptable.

Yet in recent decades, reformers, legislators, and the media have brought attention to the problem of rape and sexual violence. Laws such as the Clery Act (first passed in 1990) and the Campus Sexual Assault Victims' Bill of Rights (1992) have been enacted to combat sexual violence on college campuses. State and federal rape shield laws, which limit how much of the victim's prior sexual history can be admitted into court testimony, help shield the victim's identity. Other important laws have been the Violence Against Women Act—passed in 1994 and reauthorized most recently in 2013—and the Justice for Victims of Trafficking Act of 2015. During the Yugoslav and Rwanda tribunals following the wars there, the courts enforced the idea that rape is a war crime and a crime against humanity, and in the 1990s the International Criminal Court's Rome Statute expanded the list of sex-based crimes included in the crimes against humanity. In 2016, for the first time, the International Criminal Court at The Hague passed a guilty sentence for the perpetration of rape as an act of war: The court declared Jean-Pierre Bemba, the former vice president of the Democratic Republic of the Congo and the commander in chief of the Movement for the Liberation of Congo, guilty of crimes against humanity, including rape, murder, and pillage, for acts carried out in 2002 and 2003. Nevertheless, 113 of the 276 Chibok schoolgirls who were abducted from a boarding school in 2014 remain in captivity. In October 2016, 21 girls were released, and in May 2017, 82 of them were released after the Nigerian government negotiated with the Boko Haram terrorists and released five of their commanders in exchange. In conflict areas of the world, the abduction and rape of women and girls happens routinely and openly.

As some of the stigma against speaking out against rape loosens, victims worldwide have come forward to accuse their attackers. In the United States in 2016, more than two dozen women accused Roger Ailes, creator of Fox News, of sexual harassment. Comedian and television actor Bill Cosby was prosecuted for drugging and sexually assaulting Andrea Constand in 2004, as well as a woman identified as "Jane Doe," who also claims to have been drugged and assaulted. More than 50 women have accused Cosby of sexual assault, though only these two faced him in this trial. Judge Steven T. O'Neill declared a mistrial after the jury could not reach a decision. A new trial is expected to take place in March 2018 (Bowley 2017).

In October 2017, numerous women accused movie producer Harvey Weinstein of sexual assault and harassment. He was fired from the Weinstein Company, which he cofounded with his brother. Following these allegations, a social media hashtag, #MeToo, went viral, as women all over the world began to chime in with their experiences of sexual assault and harassment. The *New York Times* reported that as of December 18, 2017, 47 powerful men had been accused of sexual misconduct and had lost their jobs. The names include chef and TV celebrity Mario Batali; Garrison Keillor, former host of the radio show, "A Prairie Home Companion"; actor Kevin Spacey; and Senator Al Franken. An additional 26 men have been suspended for allegations of sexual misconduct (Almukhtar, Gold, and Buchanan 2017).

In 2016, the *Washington Post* obtained an "Access Hollywood" tape of then presidential candidate Donald Trump talking to television personality Billy Bush. Trump made several vulgar comments about women, including saying that stars "can do anything" to women and suggesting he can "Grab 'em by the p***y" (New York Times Staff 2016). Trump dismissed the remarks as "locker room talk." However, many professional athletes condemned the remarks and denied that such talk was common in locker rooms (Blau 2016).

It seems that rape cases are still too often viewed as a matter of "he said, she said," and victims often fight to have their stories believed, especially when the perpetrator is well known or powerful. In the 17th century, the British barrister, judge, and legal scholar Matthew Hale wrote, "It is true rape is a most detestable crime, and therefore ought severely and impartially to be punished with death;

but it must be remembered that it is an accusation easily to be made and hard to be proved, and harder to be defended by the party accused, tho never so innocent" (Hale 1736, 635). This idea still seems pervasive though it is a rape myth. In fact, studies indicate that false reports happen only between 2 and 10 percent of the time (National Sexual Violence Resource Center 2012, 2–3).

In 2004, in the introduction to my *Encyclopedia of Rape,* I wrote that "depictions and coverage of rape permeate U.S. culture. Some people will say that it is too much . . . the idea of an *Encyclopedia of Rape* is controversial, if not unnecessary. I would argue otherwise. It is all the more necessary" (Smith 2004, xi). I still believe this. With the proliferation of "fake news," it seems even more important to educate people about rape and to give them facts, instead of myths. In 2017, too many survivors remain afraid to come forward, fearing they will not be believed or that they will be harmed in retaliation for revealing an attack. Too many people across the world believe it is acceptable to force others to have sex. Perhaps some minds will be changed, as well as informed, by reading the entries in this volume. My hope is that some people will also be energized to fight against sexual violence.

Further Reading

Almukhtar, Sarah, Michael Gold, and Larry Buchanan. 2017. "After Weinstein: 47 Men Accused of Sexual Misconduct and Their Fall from Power." *New York Times,* December 18. Accessed December 20, 2017. https://www.nytimes.com/interactive/2017/11/10/us/men-accused-sexual-misconduct-weinstein.html?_r=0

Blau, Max. 2016. "Not 'Locker Room' Talk: Athletes Push Back against Trump's Remark." *CNN Politics,* October 10. Accessed December 20, 2017. http://www.cnn.com/2016/10/10/politics/locker-room-talk-athletes-respond-trnd/index.html/.

Bowley, Graham, and Richard Pérez-Peña. 2017. "In Tears, First Trial Witness Says Cosby Drugged and Assaulted Her." *New York Times*, June 5. Accessed December 20, 2017. https://www.nytimes.com/2017/06/05/arts/television/bill-cosby-trial-day-1.html.

Centers for Disease Control and Prevention. n.d. "Teen Dating Violence." Accessed June 2, 2017. https://www.cdc.gov/violenceprevention/intimatepartnerviolence/teen_dating_violence.html.

Clancy, Kate. 2012. "Here Is Some Legitimate Science on Pregnancy and Rape." *Scientific American*, August 20. Accessed June 1, 2017. https://blogs.scientificamerican.com/context-and-variation/here-is-some-legitimate-science-on-pregnancy-and-rape/.

Clinton Foundation and Bill & Melinda Gates Foundation. 2015. "No Ceilings: The Full Participation Report." Accessed August 31, 2017. http://www.noceilings.org/.

Dalton, Michael. 1690. *The Country Justice.* London: William Rawlins and Samuel Roycroft.

Federal Bureau of Investigation. 2013. "Crime in the United States 2013." Accessed May 31, 2017. https://ucr.fbi.gov/crime-in-the-u.s/2013/crime-in-the-u.s.-2013/violent-crime/rape.

Finkelhor, David, Richard Ormrod, Heather Turner, and Sherry L. Hamby. 2005. "The Victimization of Children and Youth: A Comprehensive, National Survey." *Child Maltreatment* 10 (1): 5–25.

Finley, Laura L. 2016. *Domestic Abuse and Sexual Assault in Popular Culture*. Santa Barbara, CA: Praeger.

Freedman, Estelle B. 2013. *Redefining Rape: Sexual Violence in the Era of Suffrage and Segregation*. Cambridge, MA: Harvard University Press.

Gidda, Mirren. 2017. "Women Are Dying in Overseas Honor Killings, and No One Knows How Bad the Problem Is." *Newsweek*, May 13. Accessed May 31, 2017. http://www.newsweek.com/2017/05/12/honor-killings-violence-against-women-seeta-kaur-india-pakistan-593691.html.

Government Accountability Office. 2015. "Military Personnel: Actions Needed to Address Sexual Assaults of Male Servicemembers." Report to the Committee on Armed Services, House of Representatives. GAO-15-284. Accessed June 1, 2017. http://www.gao.gov/assets/670/669096.pdf.

Hale, Matthew. 1736. *Historia Placitorum Coronae: The History of the Pleas of the Crown*, edited by Sollum Emlyn. Vol. 1. London: In the Savoy.

Hale, Matthew. 1847. *History of the Pleas of the Crown*. Vol. 1. Philadelphia: R. H. Small.

Kristof, Nicholas. 2017. "11 Years Old, a Mom, and Pushed to Marry Her Rapist in Florida." *New York Times*, May 26. Accessed November 28, 2017. https://www.nytimes.com/2017/05/26/opinion/sunday/it-was-forced-on-me-child-marriage-in-the-us.html?mcubz=3.

Manzoor, Sarfraz. 2014. "The England That Is Forever Pakistan: Multiculturalism and Rape in Rotherham." *New York Times*, September 15. Accessed June 1, 2017. https://www.nytimes.com/2014/09/16/opinion/multiculturalism-and-rape-in-rotherham.html.

Manzoor, Sarfraz. 2017. "Britain's Soccer Sex Abuse Scandal." *New York Times*, January 19. Accessed June 1, 2017. https://www.nytimes.com/2017/01/19/opinion/britains-soccer-sex-abuse-scandal.html.

Moore, Lori. 2012. "Rep. Todd Akin: The Statement and the Reaction." *New York Times*, August 20. Accessed June 1, 2017. http://www.nytimes.com/2012/08/21/us/politics/rep-todd-akin-legitimate-rape-statement-and-reaction.html.

National Sexual Violence Resource Center. 2012. "False Reporting: Overview." Accessed June 2, 2017. http://www.nsvrc.org/sites/default/files/Publications_NSVRC_Overview_False-Reporting.pdf.

New York Times Staff. 2016. "Transcript: Donald Trump's Taped Comments about Women." *New York Times*, October 8. Accessed June 2, 2017. https://www.nytimes.com/2016/10/08/us/donald-trump-tape-transcript.html.

Penn, Nathaniel. 2014. "Son, Men Don't Get Raped." *GQ*, September 7. Accessed June 2, 2017. http://www.gq.com/long-form/male-military-rape.

RAINN Staff. 2017. "Perpetrators of Sexual Violence: Statistics." Rape, Abuse & Incest National Network (RAINN). Accessed May 31, 2017. https://www.rainn.org/statistics/perpetrators-sexual-violence.

RAINN Staff. 2017. "Scope of the Problem: Statistics." Rape, Abuse & Incest National Network (RAINN). Accessed June 1, 2017. https://www.rainn.org/statistics/scope-problem.

RAINN Staff. 2017. "Victims of Sexual Violence: Statistics." Rape, Abuse & Incest National Network (RAINN). Accessed May 31, 2017. https://www.rainn.org/statistics/victims-sexual-violence.

Rine, Abigail. 2013. "No Rape Victim, Male or Female, Deserves to Be Blamed." *The Atlantic*, July 8. Accessed June 1, 2017. https://www.theatlantic.com/sexes/archive/2013/07/no-rape-victim-male-or-female-deserves-to-be-blamed/277598/.

Sachdev, Chhavi. 2016. "Rape Is a Crime in India—But There Are Exceptions." *Goats and Soda: Stories of Life in a Changing World. NPR*, April 13. Accessed November 28, 2017. http://www.npr.org/sections/goatsandsoda/2016/04/13/473966857/rape-is-a-crime-in-india-with-one-exception.

Smith, Merril D. 2004. *Encyclopedia of Rape*. Santa Barbara, CA: Greenwood Press.

WHO Media Centre. n.d. "Violence against Women." World Health Organization. Accessed June 1, 2017. http://www.who.int/mediacentre/factsheets/fs239/en/.

Wolfe, Lauren. 2012. "Holocaust." Women Under Siege Conflict Profile. *Women's Media Center*, February 8. Accessed November 28, 2017. http://www.womensmediacenter.com/women-under-siege/conflicts/holocaust.

Wolfe, Lauren. 2013. "The Legacy of Silence: Why We Ignore the Rape of Women from Guatemala to Syria." Women Under Siege Project (blog), May 13. Women's Media Center. Accessed June 1, 2017. http://www.womenundersiegeproject.org/blog/entry/the-legacy-of-silence-why-we-ignore-the-rape-of-women-from-guatemala-to-syr.

Zadrozny, Brandy, and Tim Mak. 2015. "Ex-Wife: Donald Trump Made Me Feel 'Violated' during Sex." *Daily Beast*, July 27. Accessed June 1, 2017. http://www.thedailybeast.com/ex-wife-donald-trump-made-me-feel-violated-during-sex.

Chronology of Selected Rape and Sexual Violence Events

1736   Posthumous publication of Sir Matthew Hale's *History of the Pleas of the Crown*. This work influenced rape law in the United States and the United Kingdom into the late 20th century, including the idea that husbands cannot be guilty of marital rape.

1765–1769   Sir William Blackstone writes *Commentaries on the Laws of England*. Until the 20th century, this work influenced how rape was prosecuted and how rape victims were treated—both in the United States and the United Kingdom.

1930s–1945 Thousands of women in Japanese-occupied territories are forced into sexual slavery as "comfort women."

1931   In the Scottsboro Boys case, two white women accuse nine African American men of raping them on a freight train near Scottsboro, Alabama. The accusations were false.

            In the Massie Rape-Murder case, Thalia Massie, wife of a U.S. Navy officer, accuses several Hawaiian men of raping her in Honolulu, Hawaii. After the rape trial ends in a deadlocked jury, Massie's husband, mother, and other accomplices are arrested and tried for murdering one of the alleged rapists. The murder trial is widely publicized.

1937   The Japanese Imperial Army takes Nanking, China, and rapes and massacres thousands of people.

1968   In My Lai, Vietnam, U.S. soldiers rape, murder, and pillage.

1972   The first rape crisis center opens in Berkeley, California.

            Title IX, part of the Educational Amendments Act of 1972, is passed.

1975   Susan Brownmiller's landmark book on rape, *Against Our Will,* is published.

1977   Nebraska becomes the first state to include marital rape in its rape laws.

1978   John Rideout is acquitted of raping his wife, Greta, in Salem, Oregon, in what is credited as the first trial of a marital rape case. He is convicted of raping two other women in 2017.

1980   In *Alexander v. Yale,* plaintiffs Ronni Alexander, Margery Reifler, Pamela Price, Lisa Stone, and Ann Olivarius claim that Yale failed to provide adequate sexual discrimination and harassment-reporting procedures. This is the first time Title IX is used in a suit of sexual harassment against a college or university.

1983   Cheryl Araujo is gang-raped on a pool table in a bar in New Bedford, Massachusetts. The case becomes known as the Big Dan's Tavern case and receives much publicity. Four of the six men in the case are convicted.

1986   College student Jeanne Ann Clery is raped and murdered in her dormitory room at Lehigh College in Bethlehem, Pennsylvania.

            The Federal Sexual Abuse Act is passed. The act amends the federal criminal code to include several types of sexual offenses, including aggravated sexual abuse, sexual abuse, sexual abuse of a minor, and abusive sexual conduct. It also criminalizes marital rape on all federal lands, including tribal lands.

1987   Tommie Lee Andrews becomes the first American convicted on the strength of DNA evidence. He is convicted of raping a Florida woman in her home.

1988   Barbara Blaine founds the Survivors Network of those Abused by Priests (SNAP) in Chicago.

1990s   A number of cases of sexual abuse by Catholic clergy come to light in the United States. The survivors pursue civil litigation.

1990   The Crime Awareness and Campus Security Act of 1990 (Clery Act) is passed. It requires federally funded institutions of higher education to publicly report all campus crimes, including rape.

1990   The Victims of Child Abuse Act of 1990 is passed.

                In California, the first antistalking bill is passed.

1991   In *Michigan v. Lucas*, the U.S. Supreme Court upholds the state's rape shield law, which protects rape victims' prior sexual history and prevents their names from being published.

                Male naval aviators sexually harass and molest female officers and nonmilitary personnel during nightly gauntlets at the Tailhook Convention at the Las Vegas Hilton Hotel.

1991–1995   Thousands of women are raped and impregnated during the Balkans Wars.

1992   The Campus Sexual Assault Victims' Bill of Rights is passed as part of the reauthorization of the Clery Act and supplement to Title IX. Institutions must disclose policies on sexual assault, including victims' rights, disciplinary procedures, and educational programming regarding sexual violence.

                U.S. Catholic bishops approve guidelines on how to handle sex abuse cases, but the guidelines are not binding, and many ignore them.

1993   North Carolina and Oklahoma become the last U.S. states to eliminate the spousal exemption clauses in rape laws.

1994   New Jersey passes Megan's Law, requiring convicted sex offenders to register and notifying residents when sex offenders move into their communities. Other states pass similar laws.

                The federal Violence Against Women Act (VAWA) is first passed. The act also establishes the Office on Violence Against Women within the U.S. Department of Justice.

                The federal version of Megan's Law is passed.

1995   The United Nations Fourth World Conference on Women meets in Beijing. Delegates from 189 nations call for a platform for "full and equal participation of women in political, civil, economic, social and cultural life."

1996   The Drug-Induced Rape Prevention and Punishment Act is passed.

1997–2013   More than 1,400 children are sexually abused in a sex ring in Rotherham, England.

1998   The Rome Statute creates an International Criminal Court.

      During the Rwandan war trials, the United Nations declares rape a war crime.

2000   The Campus Sex Crimes Prevention Act is passed.

2002   The *Boston Globe* begins an extensive Spotlight series on clerical sexual abuse in the Catholic Church.

      Pope John Paul II meets with U.S. cardinals in Rome to discuss clergy sex abuse.

      The UN convenes a special court in Sierra Leone to prosecute war crimes, including rape.

2003   The Prison Rape Elimination Act of 2003 (PREA) (Pub.L. 108-79) is passed, becoming the primary federal law pertaining to prison rape.

2004   The International Criminal Court begins investigating war crimes committed during conflicts in the Democratic Republic of the Congo.

2005   The Mental Capacity Act of England and Wales is passed. This legislation includes guidelines to consider for determining whether an individual is capable of giving consent.

2008   South African football player and LGBT activist Eudy Simelane is gang-raped and murdered. The crime brings attention to the issue of "corrective rape."

2009   The Matthew Shepard and James Byrd, Jr., Hate Crimes Prevention Act (the Matthew Shepard Act) is passed. The law modifies existing hate crimes legislation to include crimes committed because of a person's gender (or perceived gender), gender identity, sexual orientation, or disability.

      Prosecutor v. Issa Hassan Sesay, Morris Kallon and Augustine Gbao, a case tried before the Residual Special Court for Sierra Leone, becomes the first international conviction for sexual slavery and forced marriage as a crime against humanity.

2010   In the Luvungi mass rape, the Mai Mai Sheka militia rape 387 civilians in the Democratic Republic of the Congo.

The clerical abuse scandal of the Catholic Church widens to include cases in Germany, Brazil, and elsewhere.

2011   Yale University bans activity by Delta Kappa Epsilon for five years after the 2010 fraternity pledges march through the campus chanting "No means yes, yes means anal."

The U.S. Office for Civil Rights sends a "Dear Colleague Letter" to all federally funded educational institutions, to remind them of the Title IX requirements regarding sexual harassment.

All over the world, women (and men) march in "Slut Walks" to protest the idea that what women wear and how they behave make them targets of rape. The demonstrations begin in Toronto, Canada, in response to a police officer telling students that to avoid rape, they shouldn't dress like "sluts." The demonstrations then spread worldwide, including cities throughout the United States, Canada, Sweden, and South Africa.

2011–present   Conflict in Syria includes mass rapes by ISIS and other groups.

2012   The Federal Bureau of Investigation updates its definition of *rape* from "forcible rape against a woman" to include all genders and forms of sexual assault.

During a Naval Academy "yoga and toga" party, a female midshipman allegedly is gang-raped. In the Article 32 proceedings in 2013, she is brutally cross-examined about her sexual behavior and her underwear.

In the United Kingdom, the police investigation named Operation Yewtree is a criminal investigation looking into the abuse of children by the British media personality Jimmy Savile, but it expands to include others. Since 2012, several men have been convicted.

2013   The European Parliament approves a bill allowing victims of stalking, as well as victims of other types of sexual violence, to receive the same protections from country to country within the European Union.

2013   Following the Verma Report, the Indian Penal Code on sexual assault is updated to cover stalking and cyberstalking, to increase penalties for gang rape, and to expand the definition of *rape*. The update does not include marital rape.

The Campus Sexual Violence Elimination Act (Campus SaVE Act) is an amendment to the Clery Act, enacted as part of the Violence Against Women Act in 2013, and intended to act as a companion to Title IX.

The Violence Against Women Act is reauthorized.

In a case that receives national attention, two high-school football players are convicted of raping a 16-year-old girl at a party in Steubenville, Ohio. Much of the evidence comes from text messages, photos, and social media.

2014   President Barack Obama creates a task force to investigate and protect students from sexual abuse. The resulting report is entitled "Not Alone."

More than 250 schoolgirls are abducted in Chibok, Nigeria, by the militant Islamist group Boko Haram.

The "Yes means Yes" bill passed in California requires definitive affirmation of consent before sexual activity.

A report commissioned by Rotherham Metropolitan Borough in Rotherham, England, describes children as young as 11 who have been sexually abused and trafficked since 1997.

2015   Two Vanderbilt University football players are convicted of raping an unconscious woman in 2013. The verdicts are subsequently thrown out. In a new trial in April 2016, one of the men, Cory Batey, is convicted, and a second man, Brandon Vandenburg, is convicted later that year. A third man, Brandon E. Banks, is convicted in 2017. The fourth man accused, Jaborian "Tip" McKenzie, testified against the others and has yet to be tried.

The Hunting Ground, a documentary film, is released. It takes an intense look at sexual assault on American college campuses.

The Justice for Victims of Trafficking Act of 2015 is passed to curb domestic sex trafficking—and in particular, to help child survivors of sex trafficking.

2016   In *The Prosecutor v. Jean-Pierre Bemba Gombo* (ICC-01/05-01/08), the International Criminal Court convicts Jean-Pierre Bemba as the commander of forces that committed murder, rape, and pillage in the Central African Republic in 2002–2003.

Stanford University swimmer Brock Allen Turner is convicted of sexually assaulting an unconscious woman, but there is a public outcry when he receives a sentence of only six months in county jail and three years of probation instead of a prison sentence.

The *Boston Globe*'s Spotlight team reports on sexual abuse in private schools in New England. In nearly all of the cases, going back decades, school administrators did not report sexual misconduct to the police.

2017   Following the conviction and sentencing of Brock Allen Turner, California passes two laws that make prison time mandatory for sexual assault convictions.

Of the more than 250 Chibok schoolgirls kidnapped in 2014 by Boko Haram in Nigeria, 82 are released after negotiation with the government of Nigeria.

The *Indianapolis Star* breaks the story of ongoing sexual abuse of U.S. gymnasts by coaches, a doctor, and other adults working for USA Gymnastics. The president and CEO of the organization, Steve Penny, resigns amid allegations that the organization ignored reports.

Choate Rosemary Hall, an elite private boarding school in Connecticut, releases a report detailing decades of sexual abuse by teachers and school staff.

#MeToo begins spreading virally on social media in October after a tweet by actress Alyssa Milano in support of all those who have been victims of sexual harassment and sexual assault and to demonstrate the extent of the problem. This follows allegations of sexual misconduct against movie producer Harvey Weinstein. The phrase had previously been used in 2006 by social activist Tarana Burke.

SEXUAL ASSAULT IN THE MILITARY

Although the U.S. military has faced many scandals involving a number of issues, of significant concern is the sexual violence that occurs within the different branches of the service when the victims and the offenders are both members of the military. One of the first incidents that brought attention to this issue was the Tailhook scandal of 1991 in Las Vegas, during which male aviator officers assaulted 83 women and 7 men during nightly gauntlets. This was the 35th annual conference held to acknowledge the best of the military's fighter pilots. Similar behavior had taken place in previous years, but this time naval lieutenant Paula Coughlin, one of the women who were sexually assaulted, spoke out. The Inspector General of the Department of Defense and the Naval Investigative Service (NIS) launched an investigation, which led to some disciplinary actions, though both the Navy's and Pentagon's inquiries were later criticized. Among the items cataloged in the investigation were misogynistic photographs with derogatory comments about the women photographed.

The second incident occurred at the Aberdeen Proving Ground's (APG) Ordnance Center in Maryland. The 1996 Aberdeen scandal displayed the same lack of attention to the issue of sexual violence as had been seen in earlier incidents. In this incident, 12 officers (commissioned and noncommissioned) were charged with assaulting female trainees. In September 1996, a female trainee complained that she had been sexually harassed by her superior. Soon after, 34 women reported being victims of rape, sexual assault, or sexual harassment. A hotline was set up by the Army for other victims. By the end of November 1996, the Army had received more than 6,000 calls. The Army discovered that they had a significant problem, not just at Aberdeen, but at all their military bases around the world.

In January 2003, an anonymous email was sent detailing the widespread sexual violence at the U.S. Air Force Academy in Colorado Springs, Colorado. After this report, the Air Force created the Sexual Assault Services Committee. This working group released a report in June 2004 indicating that they did not find any systematic acceptance of sexual assault at the academy. What they did find, however, is that the attention to sexual assault issues had lessened over time, resulting in a poor environment for the appropriate response to sexual assaults at the academy. The cases that were investigated did not result in any criminal charges.

The military faced another scandal in 2012 at Lackland Air Force Base in San Antonio, Texas. This scandal involved basic military training instructors and recruits at the base, and it is considered one of the worst sex scandals in military history. By the end of the investigation, 62 recruits were identified as having been abused, and 35 basic military training personnel were court-martialed. In a more recent 2016 incident, hundreds of Marines used social media to solicit and share hundreds of photographs of naked women servicemembers and veterans. The photographs were posted on Facebook in a private group called "Marines United." This group appears to have in excess of 30,000 followers, who made obscene comments about many of the photographs. Senior officials within the Marine Corps investigated this incident and discovered that photographs of women soldiers were also being circulated through links to a Google Drive and on image-sharing message boards, and these continued to operate after the Facebook site had been shut down. In March 2017, reports indicated that the scandal involved other branches of the armed services as well (Szoldra 2017).

Experts believe these are a few visible instances of an inherent problem within the military. The culture of the military has attempted to change, or has been been forced to change—a clear example being the repeal of the "Don't Ask, Don't Tell" (DADT) policy. This compromise policy, first introduced in the 1990s by President Bill Clinton, removed the question concerning sexual orientation from all military recruitment forms. Prior to this legislation, any openly gay or lesbian individual was denied entrance into the military. Despite the policy, however, there was still blatant discrimination, and any credible evidence of homosexual activity by a servicemember could still be investigated. Don't Ask, Don't Tell was repealed in 2011 by President Barack Obama. Although this change allowed LGBTQ+ individuals to serve openly in the military, studies suggest that they have not been welcomed into the established military culture. Experts have recognized that the military is still struggling to understand the connections among homophobia, misogyny, and the widespread acceptance of sexual violence—against both men and women—within military ranks (Aosved and Long 2006).

Many authorities believe a lax policy on sexual assault can be viewed as a threat to military readiness. In addition, they believe the public health threat and the effect of sexual assault on performance represent an issue that must be addressed. The U.S. military has demonstrated only sporadic success in its attempts to end sexual assault, and the methods used to address this problem appear to be erratic (Buchhandler-Raphael 2014). To successfully address the issue of sexual violence within the military, experts say a policy that addresses the issues and aspects of sexual violence must be enacted. This policy must consider the underlying causes and myths surrounding sexual violence, and such a strategy would address the part that the military subcultural factors play in contributing to sexual violence. Lastly, this policy would address difficult issues of sexual violence that have been ignored, such as the amount of male sexual assault within the military (Buchhandler-Raphael 2014).

The Uniform Code of Military Justice (UCMJ) is the source for all military law (United States Code 2010). The UCMJ was established by the U.S. Congress in accordance with the authority given by the U.S. Constitution in Article I, Section 8. The Department of Defense (DoD) Directive 6495.01 describes the policies and practices for the Sexual Assault Prevention and Response Office (SAPR), which were developed in response to the needs of victims. The directive defines *sexual assault* as "Intentional sexual contact characterized by use of force, threats, intimidation, or abuse of authority or when the victim does not or cannot consent. The term includes a broad category of sexual offenses consisting of the following specific UCMJ offenses: rape, sexual assault, aggravated sexual contact, abusive sexual contact, forcible sodomy (forced oral or anal sex), or attempts to commit these acts" (U.S. Department of Defense 2017d, 20).

The United States

Prevalence

As with cases of rape in civilian life, it is hard to nail down the numbers for sexual assault within the military because a majority of cases are never reported. However, the percentage of nonreporting in military service is considerably higher than that in the civilian system. The Pentagon estimates that one in three servicewomen are sexually assaulted. This rate is significantly higher than the civilian rate, where 1 in 5 women and 1 in 71 men will be raped at some point in their lives. It is estimated that 70 percent of the soldiers who experience sexual violence never report these crimes (National Sexual Violence Resource Center 2015).

Section 1631 of the Ike Skelton National Defense Authorization Act for Fiscal Year 2011 (Pub.L. 111-383) requires the Department of Defense to provide Congress with an annual report on sexual assaults involving members of the Armed Forces. The Sexual Assault Response and Prevention reports meet the requirements of the annual reporting. In addition, the Pentagon publishes the Department of Defense Report to the President of the United States on Sexual Assault Prevention and Response. In the 2010 report, the Pentagon identified 19,000 instances of unwanted sexual contacts, of which only 3,158 were recorded by the military. There were 575 processed, with only 96 resulting in a court-martial (Lawrence and Peñaloza 2013).

In the 2012 report, the Pentagon determined that the instances of unwanted sexual contact had increased to 26,000, of which 3,374 were reported and 302 went to trial (Gillibrand n.d.). Reports indicate sexual violence, especially within the military, is a display of power and domination. Often, perpetrators target those who appear most vulnerable. The victims of these crimes are not just female; male-on-male rape is also a problem. Studies reveal that the majority of perpetrators of male-on-male sexual assault identify themselves as heterosexual. Under DADT, however, male victims of sexual assault by other men were especially reluctant to speak out or report a crime for fear of being labeled as homosexual. Other male victims do not want to appear weak, while both male and female victims often fear losing their career and military benefits in retaliatory measures (Ellison 2011).

The most recent data on the number of rapes in the military was collected for fiscal year 2016. In this year, the DoD received 6,172 reports of sexual violence involving soldiers. This number, which includes all those in military service as either victims or perpetrators, is a 1.5 percent increase from reports made in the previous fiscal year. These reports were for incidents during military service. Of the 6,172 sexual assault accounts, 5,350 were made by servicemembers. DoD initially received 1,995 Restricted Reports involving servicemembers as either victims or subjects. Of these, 414 (21 percent) Restricted Reports converted to Unrestricted Reports in fiscal year 2016 (Sexual Assault Prevention and Response Office 2017, 9).

Major Laws

The U.S. Constitution gives Congress the power to regulate the military. In 1950, Congress first passed, and President Harry S. Truman signed into law, the Uniform Code of Military Justice (UCMJ). The UCMJ addresses what behaviors are considered violations by individuals in the Armed Forces against individuals in or outside of the Armed Forces. The UCMJ is simply a complete set of criminal laws. It identifies the elements and punishments associated with crimes punishable under civilian law—for example murder, sexual assault, drug offenses, or even drunk driving. In addition, it includes crimes that are specific to the military.

Just as other laws are modified to address changing issues, so has the UCMJ been modified over time. In 2007, in Article 120 of the UCMJ, the military revised its definition of *sexual assault* from one that focused on rape to a broader definition that included a wide variety of sexual offenses. Consequently, based on the new Article 120, the DoD updated its definition of sexual assault to the following:

> [I]ntentional sexual contact, characterized by use of force, physical threat or abuse of authority or when the victim does not or cannot consent. It includes

rape, nonconsensual sodomy (oral or anal sex), indecent assault (unwanted, inappropriate sexual contact or fondling), or attempts to commit these acts. Sexual assault can occur without regard to gender or spousal relationship or age of victim. "Consent" shall not be deemed or construed to mean the failure by the victim to offer physical resistance. Consent is not given when a person uses force, threat of force, coercion, or when the victim is asleep, incapacitated, or unconscious. (Sexual Assault Prevention and Response Office 2008, 16)

The National Defense Authorization Act (NDAA) is a federal law that addresses issues of funding for the DoD. Each year, revisions are made to existing provisions. When the NDAA was modified for fiscal year 2014, the changes resulted in the need for significant revisions to the UCMJ, which Congress enacted on December 26, 2013. Although these changes addressed a number of offenses, there were significant changes that affected the rights of victims of sexual assault in court, the rights of convening authorities, sentencing, and the investigations leading to trial (National Defense Authorization Act 2014). Several provisions of the UCMJ were rewritten under the NDAA for fiscal year 2014, most significantly, Articles 32, 60, 120, and 125. The changes made to the UCMJ also addressed the statute of limitations for rape. Prior to the 2014 NDAA, there was a five-year statute of limitations on rape and sexual assault under Article 120 cases, which was eliminated under Section 551 of the act (National Defense Authorization Act 2014).

Article 32 relates to a preliminary investigation to determine reasonable grounds to go forward in a general court-martial, which is the highest military court. In Article 32 hearings, rules of evidence do not apply, and in some cases, this is the first time that the victim testifies in court. Under changes to Article 32, judge advocates—trained lawyers—are required to be used as investigating officers (IOs). Article 32 also involves hearings to determine if there is enough evidence to warrant a general court-martial. It is convened for felony-level cases, such as rape or murder. There are also new requirements for a special victims' counsel, to provide services to victims—for example, to notify the victim of upcoming hearings, trials dates, and other events in the legal proceedings. In addition, special victims' counsels help to ensure that victim's rights are not violated during hearings.

One aspect identified in the UCMJ is the character of the victim. Military Rule of Evidence (MRE) 412 discusses how the victim's character can be addressed. Federal rape shield laws were created under the Violence Against Women Act of 1994 (states have had rape shield laws since 1980). Rape shield laws are designed to limit or prohibit the use of rape victims' past sexual history as evidence to smear their character and creditability. Some authorities believe that when victims must testify in court, the experience can often be equated to a second victimization. By prohibiting defense attorneys from cross-examining victims about their past sexual history, emotional distress for victims can be minimized. With the passage of NDAA 2014, rape and sexual assault victims are no longer subject to the type of interrogation that had been previously allowed during the Article 32 hearing (National Defense Authorization Act 2014). Before passage of NDAA 2014, victims were ordered to attend Article 32 hearings and commonly were required to provide testimony.

Other changes made by NDAA 2014 were the provisions of Article 60, which covers pretrial agreements and powers of the convening authority, "a commander who exercises significant control over courts-martial." Convening authorities could make decisions on "whether to approve charges for trial, select the jury and negotiate plea deals, and they can overturn guilty verdicts or reduce recommended sentences" (Savage 2013). The revisions came about after a public outcry, particularly from advocates for victims of military sexual assault, following Air Force Commander Lt. Gen. Craig A. Franklin's dismissal of Lt. Col. James Wilkerson's conviction of aggravated sexual assault.

The case of Lt. Col. Wilkerson brought other attempts at reform. Senate Bill 1752, more commonly referred to as the Military Justice Improvement Act (MJIA), was introduced by U.S. Senator Kirsten Gillibrand (D-NY) in 2013. Senator Gillibrand wanted to change the way in which the military justice

---

The Case That Modified Article 60

In 2012, Kim Hanks, a civilian, accepted Lt. Col. James Wilkerson and his wife Beth's invitation to stay in their guest room following a small party the couple had hosted after a USO concert at Aviano Air Base. Hanks woke to find Wilkerson in her bed, digitally penetrating her. As she struggled with him, his wife appeared in the doorway and yelled at Hanks to leave the house. The military court jury found Wilkerson guilty. He was sentenced to a year's imprisonment and given a dishonorable discharge. A few months later, General Craig Franklin, who had been the convening authority for the trial, overturned the verdict. Wilkerson was released from prison and his military rank was reinstated.

Colonel Don Christensen, the prosecutor in the case, told Hanks, "You're about to become an agent for change." He met with Defense Secretary Chuck Hagel to recommend that Article 60 of the Uniform Code of Military Justice be modified so that this type of situation could no longer happen. Congress passed the measure, which was signed by President Obama.

Source: Draper, Robert. 2014. "The Military's Rough Justice on Sexual Assault." *New York Times*, November 26. Accessed December 21, 2017. https://www.nytimes.com/2014/11/30/magazine/the-militarys-rough-justice-on-sexual-assault.html?_r=0.

system addresses the prosecution of certain crimes. The bill focused on the way in which the U.S. military had been reporting sexual assaults, as well as how it had been conducting investigations. The act, which was designed to amend the NDAA, would have restructured the way in which reporting was required and to whom the criminal offense would be reported. This act would also have significantly changed the manner in which the military tried servicemembers for criminal offenses; it would have required that an outside officer be brought in to determine if a court-martial should be pursued for serious felonies, such as sexual violence. Gillibrand believed that victims of rape within the military did not report their crimes because they did not "trust the chain of command not to retaliate against them for doing so" (Bassett 2015). Although the bill had bipartisan support, it did not have enough votes to pass the Senate.

Previously, the Sexual Assault Training Oversight and Protection Act (STOP Act) was introduced by Representative Jackie Speier (D-CA) on November 16, 2011 (GovTrack.us 2011). To address the reports of sexual assault in the military that do not reach prosecution, this bill proposed the formation of the Sexual Assault Oversight and Response. The bill also looked to create a new method of reporting rather than having the report go through the chain of command. The bill died in Congress. Representative Speier reintroduced the bill (H.R. 1593) in April 2013, but no movement has been made on it.

Fiscal year 2015 brought additional changes to the UCMJ, particularly in reference to Article 32 hearings. In particular, more rights are provided for victims. Under MRE 412, victims who believe "the military judge erred in a ruling pertaining to rape shield evidence" or who violated privileged between the victim and healthcare professionals, may file a writ of mandamus, "an order from a superior court to a subordinate government court to do or refrain from doing something" (Vergun 2015). Moreover, the military courts are now no longer able to consider "the general military character of the accused." Furthermore, all sexual assault cases that are not brought to court-martial are sent for review, and victims of sexual assault who were discharged from the service without an honorable discharge may "challenge the characterization of their discharge on the grounds that it was adversely affected by the individual being the victim of a sex-related offense" (Vergun 2015).

Maximum Punishments

For rape convictions in military courts, the following punishments apply: dishonorable discharge, death or confinement for life, and forfeiture of all pay and allowances. This is one area where the military diverges significantly from the civilian world. The U.S. Supreme Court stated in *Coker v. Georgia* that the death penalty was grossly disproportionate and excessive punishment for rape (U.S. Supreme Court 1977). With the case of *Kennedy v. Louisiana* (U.S.

Supreme Court 2008), the Court expanded the *Coker* ruling, stating that the death penalty could not be imposed for anything except murder or crimes against the state.

The death penalty as a punishment is generally reserved for instances when rape has been committed during wartime. Only one soldier has been put to death for a rape charge: In 1961, John A. Bennett was hanged for the rape and attempted murder of a young girl in Austria.

Reporting Procedures for Rape

Sexual violence is a significant problem in the United States. As with the rapes that occur outside of the military, sexual assaults are underreported within the military. Rape is, in fact, the most underreported crime in civilian and military areas. According to the 2014 National Victimization Survey (Rape, Abuse & Incest National Network n.d.), only 344 out of every 1,000 sexual assaults are reported to police In simpler terms, about two out of three rapes go unreported in the civilian population. DoD figures indicate that only 43 percent of female victims of sexual assault in the military report the crime, while the figure is even smaller for male victims at 10 percent (Rape, Abuse & Incest National Network n.d.). Over- and underreporting of sexual violence within the military services was investigated by the RAND Corporation in 2014. The RAND Corporation had surveyed the military during 2006, 2010, and 2012. The initial research tool (Workplace and Gender Relations Survey) was revised to better assess the issue of sexual violence. The follow-up Military Workplace Study addressed the issues of under- and overreporting of sexual assaults. The RAND Corporation determined that not only had the participants in the RAND survey not overreported, but also the statistics provided by the initial RAND study (Workplace and Gender Relations Survey) had underestimated the number of soldiers who experienced sexual violence. Instead, the estimates established by the RAND Corporation suggest that the prior measures and methods slightly underestimated the proportion of servicemembers who experienced a sexual assault during the survey period (National Defense Research Institute et al. 2014).

The reporting of sexual assault follows different procedures in the military than in the civilian world. Military reports are classified as either Unrestricted or Restricted in nature. Victims can make a Restricted Report to such personnel as a Sexual Assault Response Coordinator (SARC), a Sexual Assault Prevention and Response (SAPR) Victim Advocate (VA), or a healthcare provider. Restricted Reports are for victims who want to report the assault but maintain their confidentiality. The DoD does not investigate Restricted Reports. In this reporting method, the soldier is not required to communicate all the specifics about the sexual violence. SARCs record only the most important facts about these victims and the alleged offenses in the Defense Sexual Assault Incident

Database (DSAID). Furthermore, the DoD does not keep the soldier's identity. A soldier can choose to reclassify a Restricted Report to an Unrestricted Report at any time during the process (Sexual Assault Prevention and Response Office 2017).

Unrestricted Reports of sexual violence differ from Restricted Reports in a number of ways. Whereas Restricted Reports are not subject to an investigation, Unrestricted Reports, which are made by one soldier implicating one or more other soldiers, are referred for investigation to a specific branch of service. The DoD collects data on Unrestricted Reports; this information is recorded within the DSAID by the SARCs. Additionally, criminal investigators have created an interface with the DSAID in order to incorporate subject and investigative case information into the records. The length of an investigation may vary, from a few months to over a year, depending on several specific variables:

1. The offense or offenses reported: The more serious the offense, the more likely it is that the investigation will be lengthy.
2. The logistics of an investigation: If all parties involved (victim, defendant, and witnesses) are located in close proximity—for example, on the same military base—then an investigation may take less time. If they are stationed a significant distance apart from each other, then the investigation will take more time.
3. The type of physical evidence that was collected during the initial investigation: In many instances, rape victims do not immediately report the assault, and as a result, physical evidence is lost. In the absence of physical evidence, the time needed for the investigation may be lengthened.
4. The need for laboratory tests: Laboratory tests can take a significant amount of time, resulting in significant delays.

A Senate subcommittee chaired by Senator Barbara S. Jones visited military sites in the United States and Asia to investigate and assess sexual assault investigations. The committee's February 17, 2017, report made a number of recommendations to improve the way investigations are conducted and to reduce the time involved. For example, they recommended that military criminal investigative organizations (MCIOs) use some non-MCIO resources because "MCIOs are spread too thin" (Subcommittee of the Judicial Proceedings Panel 2017, 5). The subcommittee recommended that many policies be re-evaluated, including a review of forensic laboratory "resources, staffing, procedures, and policies (Subcommittee of the Judicial Proceedings Panel 2017, 6).

During the reporting period for 2016, the average time it took to complete an investigation was 4.3 months (U.S Department of Defense 2017b, 14). Each year, the DoD compiles a report to address a number of issues within the military organizations—including the number of sexual assaults reported—with the report generally covering the months from October to September. The annual reports also identify the status of all Restricted and Unrestricted rape reports, the entire investigation status, and any case dispositions. Congress requires the DoD to provide reports on the results of any sexual violence cases housed within the Unrestricted Reports database that were filed against servicemembers. During 2016, only a minimum number of reports resulted in the accused (302) facing any type of penalty or honorable or dishonorable discharge; further, only 2.5 percent of the reported instances of sexual violence resulted in any form of disciplinary action. One reason that is cited for making a report is that doing so allows the victim to receive support services. As was noted above, Restricted Reports are never investigated if they remain within the Restricted group. Victims may change a Restricted Report to an Unrestricted Report at any time. A Restricted Report can be made only to certain non–law enforcement agencies, such as medical providers. If a report is made to anyone other than those specifically identified as able to take Restricted Reports, the report immediately is recorded as Unrestricted. As such, the case will then be put forward for investigation by one of the military's criminal investigation units. After an investigation is completed, the agency provides a Report of Investigation (ROI) to the suspect's immediate commander and to the legal office of the special court-martial convening authority (SPCMA). The ROI is also reviewed by the chief of justice (COJ), who coordinates with the SPCMA's staff judge advocate (SJA); the COJ then recommends to the immediate commander whether the suspect should be charged. The immediate commander (who may be a man or a woman) may not dismiss the charges (this was a result of the changes made by NDAA 2014). If the commander prefers to charge the suspect (now the accused), the commander forwards the charges to the SPCMA with a recommendation of how the charges should be processed. There are significant differences between the military justice system and the civilian system.

Several research efforts have detailed the adverse effects of sexual assault on the female soldier. A 2015 Human Rights Watch report, "Embattled: Retaliation against Sexual Assault Survivors in the US Military," discussed many of the reasons why victims did not report the crime. Many feel that there is a significant lack of support from the leadership when reporting sexual assault. This lack of support is compounded by problematic work situations in which victims must continue to work with their assaulter, especially if the assaulter is in a position of power over the victim. Additionally, victims have commonly expressed the possible negative effects on their career if they report assaults. Others find that after reporting they are unable to progress professionally within the military (Human Rights Watch 2015).

In 2014, a government report of the Pentagon noted that only 25 percent of sexual assault victims in the military made a formal report to their superior regarding the assault (Yuhas 2014). This report identified the structural and cultural elements of the military that keep victims from coming forward. One of the biggest issues identified and continually addressed in the literature is the chain of command. According to a 2003 report from the *American Journal of Industrial Medicine*, 25 percent of soldiers who were sexually assaulted indicated that they did not file a report because the offender was the ranking officer. One-third did not report rape because the rapist was a friend of the ranking officer (Sadler et al. 2003, 266). And clearly, if the individual to whom the victim is to report the assault is the offender, there is a significant problem. The external method of reporting rape in the military is not available, unless it is reported to a civilian authority. When rapes are committed by commanding officers, victims are much less likely to report, given the current reporting system.

Sexual violence has many damaging effects, and these effects can often interfere with victim-soldiers' ability to do their jobs. This, in turn, is often a reason why the soldiers eventually leave the service. If victims do report the violence, their colleagues and superiors may doubt them and may question the validity of the report. The judgment and effectiveness of reporting soldiers can be questioned. Reporting may also affect the soldiers' ability to advance within the military. In addition to the soldiers' concerns about their career, the military has created a culture of doubting victims' claims of sexual assault. This culture leads to the victims' stories being questioned not only by the investigators, but also by the victims' colleagues and superiors (Yaeger et al. 2006). Female veterans who experience sexual assaults often develop PTSD at a rate that is significantly higher than that of other veterans (Kang et al. 2005).

In the formal reporting system, the statistics do not differentiate gender. The Pentagon estimated (Yuhas 2014) that most incidents of sexual violence involved attacks on men by other men. Male victims in the military are faced with many more challenges as sexual assault victims. Studies indicate that as the result of the assault men begin questioning their sexual orientation and identity as well as their masculinity. If the perpetrator is male and the victim is homosexual, male victims often believe (just as women do) that the violence is a form of punishment. They believe that they are being punished for their sexuality and for being open about how they identify.

Originally, the Uniform Code of Military Justice concerning sexual violence was limited to women as victims. These rules have changed. However, the myths surrounding sexual violence remain, and surveys reveal that many believe that a man cannot be raped. The anger concerning sexual violence in the military has focused largely on women soldiers. There is support for this, as women in uniform are much more likely to be targets of violence than their male counterparts. But because men greatly outnumber women in the military, officials believe that the majority of victims may be men. This remains an unknown due to underreporting of male soldiers.

SAPRO is responsible for the management of the DoD's sexual assault policy. The DoD has created a comprehensive policy to address the needs of victims. This policy was the result of a task force report in 2004. The Care for Victims of Sexual Assaults Task Force was created to address the issue of sexual assault and victim services. Changes in policy and procedures were proposed by the task force and undertaken by the DoD. One of the policy recommendations was to provide a central point of contact for all policy involving sexual assault. This policy recommendation resulted in the formation of the Sexual Assault Prevention and Response Office. In addition to the SAPRO, the military has developed a special victims unit (SVU) whose sole purpose is to investigate instances of sexual violence. The military has established policies that require all unit commanders to record and report sexual violence allegations and forward this information up the chain of command. The problem with this current model is the apparent weakness within the chain of command. SAPRO also has a helpline for those who have been affected by sexual violence.

The film *The Invisible War* (Dick 2012) looked at the amount and types of sexual violence within the military. The film followed a number of veterans who spoke about their experiences with sexual violence in the military and their struggle to take legal action. After seeing the film, then Secretary of Defense Leon Panetta ordered that all sexual violence allegations be handled by individuals with a rank of colonel or higher. This was an effort to take the case disposition out of the hands of unit commanders. Many believe that the current leadership structure within the military provides a strong incentive for commanders to avoid following through on sexual violence investigations in their ranks. Often, if the allegations are kept within the unit, commanders see them as problematic and as something that can hurt their careers. Commanders are responsible for keeping their troops disciplined and in good order. Despite the directive, however, there are still a significant number of cases that

---

Department of Defense Safe Helpline

The Rape, Abuse & Incest National Network (RAINN) runs Safe Helpline for the Department of Defense's (DoD) Sexual Assault Prevention and Response Office (SAPRO). The helpline is available worldwide, 24 hours a day, seven days a week. It is open to all members of the DoD community, including those who have been victimized and those who know someone who has been victimized. The helpline's services are confidential. It provides live and anonymous crisis support and intervention, one-to-one, and it provides information and resources as well. The helpline is available on the Internet at www.SafeHelpline.org or via telephone at 877-995-5247.

do not get forwarded up for investigation. Advocates are trying to prevent the problems associated with chain of command. Many have suggested that these investigations should be taken out of the hands of commanders or the military altogether. It is believed that if this were done, the investigations and subsequent trials would be conducted fairly. Other countries have already done this within their militaries. England and Canada, for example, rely on outside agencies to conduct investigations. Senator Kirsten Gillibrand, as was noted above, has fought for a bill to separate sexual assault cases from the military's chain of command.

The military has attempted to explain why sexual assault is such a significant problem within their ranks. The first explanation offered by the U.S. military includes the idea that there is a higher percentage of "sexual predators" in the military than in civilian society. Another explanation is the current structure of the military. Reporting sexual assaults and protecting personnel from such assaults have been identified as a problem for the military. This was illustrated by the scandal at the U.S. Air Force Academy in 2003, involving allegations of sexual assault as well as allegations that the events had been ignored by the academy's leadership. Military commanders not only tolerated the sexual assault of cadets, but also were identified as being complicit in covering up the incidents. When the issue was investigated, 12 percent of the women who graduated from the Air Force Academy in 2003 acknowledged that they were victims of sexual assault or attempted assault while at the academy (Schemo 2003).

Studies have found that the current structure of reporting sexual assaults has in fact resulted in commanders punishing victims and exonerating perpetrators. If a sanction is imposed, it has amounted to a "boys will be boys" slap on the wrist. Unlike the civilian reporting system, the current military system (although changes have been recommended) allows commanding officers to stop an investigation or reduce a sentence at any time. The commanding officer even has the power to set aside a conviction (Lucero 2015).

The structure of the military has resulted in an occupational subculture that, again, differs from civilian culture. Like other occupations, the military has created a code of conduct applicable to the occupation. It has a unique legal system, which includes police and courts. It has its own form of higher education, its own mechanisms for conducting research on problems, and, lastly, its own medical system. The military's occupational subculture has its own norms and values, which have become a central part of the training that recruits receive in basic training.

Even though this occupational subculture is in place to help teach soldiers, experts note some of the same value structures that make up the military's occupational subculture create an environment that is tolerant of sexual violence. Several components of the military's occupational subculture that can foster sexual violence are such actions as sexualized and violent language and the general acceptance of violence. Thus, some experts believe the culture of violence that is present within the military may contribute to the increased risk for sexual victimization. In addition, many general cultural considerations have been tied to explanations for sexual violence. Among these are the gender stereotypes that exist all over the world. Although not limited to the military, gender stereotypes play a significant part in the perpetration of sexual violence in the military environment. Group cohesion and deindividuation (loss of self-awareness in groups) are powerful elements of the training process. Recruits are trained in a manner that reinforces the negative gender and sexual beliefs. The male-dominated nature of the military has fostered an inability to handle the needs of women. Military subcultural values can create an environment that promotes hypermasculinity and rigid sex roles. ("Hypermasculinity" is a form of masculinity based on views that serve to polarize gender roles.) These views endorse the stereotypical gender roles, while placing a high value on control, power, and mandatory heterosexuality (Hunter 2007). Studies show that men who report hypermasculine values also have a rape-supportive attitude. These individuals commit more acts of sexual aggression. Research indicates an established link between men's negative attitudes toward women, acceptance of violence, and the tolerance of attitudes towards sexual violence (Castro et al. 2015).

Studies demonstrate that training in the military maintains an adherence to the chain of command and respect for the chain of command. Soldiers are taught that they must protect the service (Buchhandler-Raphael 2014). In the military, the chain of command places great value on being able to resolve problems at the lowest levels. The military structure also requires teamwork on the part of soldiers. This reliance on team allegiance provides an environment where individuals fear that they may be vulnerable if they report an incident or support those who do report it. The military structure demands that individuals rely on each other. Authorities believe that this rigid structure combined with an emphasis on us-against-them (that those outside of the military will not recognize normal actions within this environment) is likely to produce individuals who will not report or will not be believed by others if they do report.

Studies on military culture have identified these and other cultural values that promote sexual violence. For example, the military places a premium value on performance. The value on an individual's performance can lead to the rejection or minimization of reports of sexual violence. This is significant when the soldier who is accused is identified as a high performer or when the accuser is a low performer. Studies note the structure of the military is one that remains a male-dominated institution, and within it men assume more leadership positions than women, which in turn creates a power gap. This value system provides fertile ground for sexual violence. Scholars explain that sexual violence is about power—whether it occurs in the military or in civilian life. Those who commit sexual violence do so because they can, and the military chain of command, experts say, does little to stop it (Castro et al. 2015).

Obstacles

According to recent studies, almost 40 percent of female soldiers who reported incidences of sexual violence indicated that the perpetrator was a superior officer (U.S. Commission on Civil Rights 2013, 7). Due to the hierarchical structure and adherence to the chain of command, victims can feel that they cannot report the wrongdoing because of the position held by the perpetrator. One-third of victims indicated that the offending soldier was a ranking officer's friend, making reporting just as difficult (Turchik and Wilson, 2010).

Reprisals and retaliation are specifically prohibited under the sexual assault regulations, and under the Military Whistleblower Protection Act (Military Whistleblower Protection Act 2010, 2013; DoD Directive 7050.06). Nonetheless, these problems are common. Reprisals can range from informal harassment by the assaulter's friends or the command, to poor performance evaluations, involuntary psychiatric evaluations, loss of promotions, and even involuntary discharges (Human Rights Watch 2015).

The 2015 Military Investigation and Justice Experience Survey (MIJES) investigated how soldiers who made Unrestricted Reports were treated. The survey employed a new measure of retaliation that brings it into line with the new policy and laws addressing retaliation. The results showed that 68 percent of those who were surveyed experienced at least one negative experience associated with their report of sexual assault. Although the participants identified these events as retaliation, once the events were analyzed with the policy requirement, only 38 percent of the responses equaled the circumstances prohibited by that military law. This does not minimize the experiences of victims, as these behaviors (although not meeting the military law) do concern reprisal, ostracism, and maltreatment (Defense Manpower Data Center 2016).

In 2016, the survey indicated that the majority of respondents indicated that they were satisfied with the process and resources provided within the military justice system. However, most were more positive about sexual assault services, such as Sexual Assault Response Coordinators (SARC), Uniformed Victim Advocates, and those who provided them with legal counsel, and less satisfied with their military commanders and supervisors (Office of People Analytics 2017). As with the 2015 MIJES, the 2016 survey asked questions to determine if respondents experienced "reprisal, ostracism, and maltreatment in the

Uniform Code of Military Justice (UCMJ) and military policies and regulations" (Office of People Analytics 2017, v). In fact, additional questions were added to the 2016 survey to better measure such behavior, and using this new metric, "38% of respondents indicated experiencing perceived professional reprisal, ostracism, and/or maltreatment. Specifically, 28% of respondents indicated experiencing perceived professional reprisal, while 27% perceived experiencing ostracism/maltreatment (17% perceived experiencing ostracism and 24% perceived experiencing maltreatment)" (Office of People Analytics 2017, vi). However, most of those who experienced these behaviors chose to continue with the process of filing a complaint.

Due to the military's significant restrictions on an individual's behavior, a sexual assault report or investigation may disclose that the victim violated some regulation or local ordinance prior to the assault (illegal drinking, for example, or violation of barracks rules). A result of this is fear that the retaliation could result in the loss of a soldier's career. If a victim is married and reports a sexual assault, military codes allow for the victim to be punished for adultery. Retaliation is also seen as a factor through which soldiers could lose their job. Persons reporting an assault might face court-martial or a charge of "conduct unbecoming an officer," might lose rank, or might be accused of "having set up" the perpetrator. It is a system designed for abuse by the commander. Of the female soldiers who reported sexual violence in 2012 (data on men was not included), 62 percent were met with retaliation (Schwellenbach 2013). Studies have also reported a form of retaliation that involves diagnosing victims as having a psychological illness or disorder. An examination of 1,200 soldiers who sought help at the Military Rape Crisis Center found that 90 percent of victims who had reported their rape were involuntarily discharged. These individuals were also subject to a diagnosis with mental disorders, resulting in a discharge from the service (King 2013). This remains a problem, despite the Military Whistleblower Protection Act and Statute Prohibiting the Use of Mental Health Evaluations in Reprisal Act (2013). The military mind-set has also been seen as an obstacle to change. The military's emphasis on strength, toughness, and emotional resilience has made addressing its sexual violence problem difficult.

According to Shawn Woodham (2013), the military's strategy to change the current responses to sexual assault should involve a number of strategic changes. The first priority would be to address the characteristics of the military occupational subculture. Of particular importance is a change in the way women are viewed and treated within the service. The second priority is education and training. Training that addresses the cultural misconception must become part of the military curriculum. The military must also identify and fix the problems that have been identified in the reporting procedures for sexual violence. The victim must be an active member of the investigation and be able to maintain total control throughout the entire process, including the prosecution phase. Changes in the reporting procedures should address perpetrators' ability to manipulate the law to obtain acquittals. Sexual violence within the military is not simply a problem for the U.S. military. Studies demonstrate that any military organization in which the culture has grown out of a patriarchal historical perspective is subject to these problems. The militaries around the world face problems similar to those in the United States.

Worldwide

Canada

In the United States, women make up 14 percent of the military's 1.4 million active members. The makeup of the Canada Armed Forces mirrors that of the U.S. military; women comprise 12 percent of the Canadian Armed Forces' 68,000 regular and reserve members. Although only a select number of females are assigned to combat positions (Lorincz 2013), since 1989, the Canadian military has allowed women to serve in combat roles. Canada's first female soldier killed was Captain Nichola Goddard, who was killed in Afghanistan in 2006. Journalist Valerie Fortney, who wrote a biography of Captain Goddard, *Sunray: The Death and Life of Captain Nichola Goddard* (2010), described Captain Goddard's time in Afghanistan. Goddard wrote letters to her husband detailing multiple instances of sexual harassment and assault of military women on Canadian bases. One letter noted that six rapes occurred in one week, making an escort system for female soldiers necessary. The Canadian military noted that from 2004 to 2010, only five reports of sexual assault in Afghanistan were investigated. This difference between what was reported by Captain Goddard and what was contained in the military's formal reports illustrates that issues regarding sexual violence in the military are not exclusive to any one country.

The Survey on Sexual Misconduct in the Canadian Armed Forces in 2016 was based on a voluntary survey of active-duty and Primary Reserve members. The survey found that 27.3 percent of women had been sexually assaulted or were subject to being touched sexually against their will since joining the Canadian Armed Forces. These assaults occurred while the women were either deployed on a Canadian Forces operation or at a Canadian Forces Workplace (Statistics Canada 2016).

Canadian soldiers are adjudicated for sexual assault charges by service tribunals. Canada has limited the role of military commanders in the adjudication process. The Canadian system has tried to use an independent system to investigate and try these cases. The current Canadian system relies on the Canadian Military Prosecution Service to determine which cases should move forward to court-martial and which cases should result in a criminal prosecution. If a soldier reports sexual misconduct, the commanding officer must immediately contact the military police. It is up to the military police to determine if civilian law enforcement should be notified (Library of Congress Canada 2015).

France

Unlike in many foreign military groups (with the exception of Israel), women occupy one in seven places in the French military and a fifth of posts in the French Air Force. Across the British and German armed forces, the figure is one in ten. In 2014, the French Defense Ministry (FDM) made a significant effort to address sexual harassment and sexual abuse in the French Armed Forces. The defense minister, Jean-Yves Le Drian, took action against sexual assault and harassment in the military as a result of a book published in 2014. In *La Guerre Invisible* ("The Invisible War"), Leila Minano and Julia Pascual documented 35 cases of sexual abuse—ranging from alleged constant sexual harassment to alleged rape—that are currently being investigated by the French military.

In France, according to the *La Guerre Invisible,* the scale of the problem has been systematically concealed. Until now, no statistics have been kept. Units were not obliged to report incidents to their military hierarchy or to the Defense Ministry (Lichfield 2014). A controller-general of the French Armed Forces who helped to draw up the official report remarked that the silence must end. In a news conference, the controller-general emphasized the need to encourage women to talk (Lichfield 2014). The great majority of cases involve relatively young recruits—both male and female—from relatively poor and uneducated backgrounds. Many of the young men are surprised that sexually loaded comments or aggressive behavior toward women is unacceptable. Many of the young women are attracted to the military by choice rather than because of a lack of other jobs. The women feel lucky to have obtained a position, so they are reluctant to complain because they don't want to seem fragile. Many women in the French military service believe that they have entered a masculine environment and must conform.

The French military justice system changes depending on the country's current standing of being at war or being in peacetime. In addition, the administration of military justice depends on a number of factors. For example, different actions are taken if an offense was committed by a servicemember, or if the offense was committed on French soil versus foreign soil. Whether the servicemember was on duty or off duty will also result in different actions.

Australia

As of February 2017, women personnel made up 20 percent of the Australian Defence Force. The Defence Abuse Response Taskforce was created to address sexual misconduct in the defense service before 2011. The task force reported on the problems within the defense service, identifying factors that contributed to the risk of assault in cases that occurred between 2000 and 2011.

1. The location and/or physical environment. (For example, a remote location, aboard a ship, or on deployment.) The location might also involve working where alcohol was consumed and/or being the only woman or one of few women present.
2. "The lack of adequate supervision of young people." This was a particular problem on weekends and a night,
3. "The influence of hierarchy and authority." The chain of command favored not reporting and did not discourage superiors from abusing the soldiers in their command.
4. Certain social and environmental factors related to military service were involved—an environment where alcohol is used and where those involved are often young individuals at risk of becoming intoxicated or taken advantage of, and where many complainants felt "under considerable pressure to acquiesce out of fear of repercussions for rejecting advances by work colleagues or superiors" (Defense Abuse Response Taskforce 2016 ,30).

The Australian Defence Force's Sexual Misconduct Prevention & Response Office (SeMPRO) was launched in July 2013. SeMPRO's key objectives are to respond to and support victims of sexual misconduct and other personnel impacted by sexual misconduct incidents and offences; to be the single point of sexual misconduct data collection and analysis within the Defence Force; and to provide education, primary prevention tools, and advice about sexual misconduct in the Defense Force. The number of reports of sexual violence is significantly lower than that reported by the U.S. military, with an average of only 80 reports each year. In the 2015–2016 annual report, SeMPRO reported that 63 members of the military service sought support or case management for sexual assault. The report found that a total of 298 personnel sought help for any kind of sexual misconduct between 2013 and 2016. This number represents those that have reported (Australian Defence SeMPRO Annual Report 2015–2016, 7–8).

The reporting system used in Australia is like that in the United States. Soldiers who have been sexually assaulted can file either a Restricted Report or an Unrestricted Report. There is no need to report through the chain of command. In Australia, serious crimes such as sexual assault are immediately referred to the civilian authorities. While the military commanders have repeatedly expressed reservations about their lack of input into the decision-making, the system effectively minimizes command influence in the criminal process to maintain fuller accountability and impartiality in meting out punishment.

In 2006, Australia established a standing military court, which allowed for all proceedings for sexual assault to be removed from the chain of command. Following a revision of the court system in 2009, the system now requires offenses to go before the Defense Force magistrates. An independent Director of Military Prosecutions (DMP) is also involved, to determine whether to initiate prosecutions for the offenses. Sexual assault complaints are always referred to the DMP. The DMP is required to report certain alleged offenses to civilian prosecution authorities. As a result of the mandatory reporting, these cases often go through the civilian justice system, rather than within the military justice system (Library of Congress Australia 2016).

United Kingdom

The statistics concerning sexual violence in the United Kingdom are very similar to those in the other countries identified here. Between 2001 and 2011, the Ministry of Defence (MoD) figures show that 56 members of the Armed Forces were court-martialed for sexual offences. In 2012, an internal investigation found that all 400 female soldiers questioned at a base reported that they had been subjected to unwanted sexual attention at some point in their careers (Rainey 2014). In addition to the showing of the film *The Invisible War*, the attention to sexual violence in the British Armed Forces was increased by the suicide of a female soldier and a suit brought by a female sailor stating she was sexually assaulted by a British soldier in Afghanistan while guarding a terrorist.

Despite the Ministry of Defence's insistence on a zero-tolerance policy for this type of behavior, there are still significant concerns. E-mails sent by a servicemember just prior to her suicide point to the feeling that nothing was being done, nor would be done, about her attacks. The United Kingdom has operated a system of military courts-martial similar to that of the United States. In 2009, all military criminal prosecutions were centralized and occur within the Service Prosecuting Authority. This was an attempt by the British military to make sure that all criminal cases were given unbiased and consistent consideration. Commanding officers still have the authority to punish all minor offenses and can still confer with the prosecuting attorneys in sexual assault cases.

In 2009, the Ministry of Defence created a permanent court (Court Martial) to address military matters. As in the United States, U.K. law provides that a large number of offenses are disciplined from within the military structure's chain of command. Legislative acts have changed or limited a commander's authority to discipline some serious crimes. For example, prosecutions of sexual assault have been removed from the military chain of command and placed in a civilian system. These cases are now prosecuted by the independent Director Service Prosecutions, who may be a civilian lawyer. Specially trained prosecutors are tasked with prosecuting any rape cases (Library of Congress United Kingdom 2015).

Israel

The "Military Justice: Adjudication of Sexual Offenses" report includes studies of the many systems of military justice across the world. Of the countries surveyed, Israel is the only one where men and women are equally subject to a military draft system. This results in a system with significantly more females than any other defense service around the world. This diversity in the service means addressing sexual crimes is essential for maintaining military morale and improving performance. In Israel's military justice system, the decision to adjudicate sexual offenses within a disciplinary proceedings can be made only by the Military Advocate General's attorneys. This process has removed commanding officers. As a result, only officers with special training can preside over sexual assault cases. Sexual assault offenses within the IDF are generally investigated by the Military Investigative Police and decided by court-martial (Library of Congress Israel 2015).

Deborah Laufersweiler-Dwyer

Further Reading

Anderson, Pat. 2010. "Late Soldier's Letter Tell of Rapes at Camp." *Deceived World* (blog), October 5. Accessed June 1, 2017. http://deceivedworld.blogspot.com/2010/10/late-soldiers-letters-tell-of-rapes-at.html.

Aosved, Allison, and Patricia Long. 2006. "Co-occurrence of Rape Myth Acceptance, Sexism, Racism, Homophobia, Ageism, Classism, and Religious Intolerance." *Sex Roles* 55 (7–8): 481–92.

Australian Government. 2015. "Australian Government Response to the Foreign Affairs, Defence and Trade References Committee Report: Processes to Support Victims of Abuse in Defence." Accessed June 1, 2017. http://www.defence.gov.au/publications/docs/government_response_sscfadt_report_on_processes_to_support_victims_of_abuse_in_defence.pdf.

Australian Government Department of Defence. 2016. "SeMPRO Annual Report 2015–2016 Supplementary." Accessed July 2, 2017. http://www.defence.gov.au/annualreports/15-16/Downloads/SeMPRO-Supplementary-Report-2015-16-online-only.pdf.

Australian Government Department of Defence. 2017. "Sexual Misconduct Prevention & Response Office: Improving Services and Responses for Male ADF Members." Accessed June 1, 2017. http://www.defence.gov.au/sempro/Default.asp.

Bassett, Laura. 2015. "Military Rape Cases Will Stay within the Chain of Command." *HuffPost News*, June 16. Accessed July 5, 2017. http://www.huffingtonpost.com/2015/06/16/gillibrand-military-sexual-assault_n_7597386.html.

Baugher, Shannon, Jon Elhai, James Monroe, and Matt Gray. 2010. "Rape Myth Acceptance, Sexual Trauma History, and Posttraumatic Stress Disorder." *Journal of Interpersonal Violence* 25 (11): 2036–53.

Brissenden, Michael. 2014. "Defence Abuse Response Taskforce: Report Recommends Royal Commission into Abuse." *ABC News*, November 26. Accessed June 1, 2017. http://www.abc.net.au/news/2014-11-26/report-recommends-royal-commission-adfa-abuse/5918206.

Buck, Christopher. "Legacy of Tailhook." Retro Report. *New York Times* video, 12:41. Accessed June 1, 2017. https://nyti.ms/2rtrenV.

Buchhandler-Raphael, Michael. 2014. "Breaking the Chain of Command Culture: A Call for an Independent and Impartial Investigative Body to Curb Sexual Assaults in the Military." *Wisconsin Journal of Law, Gender & Society* 29 (3): 342–76.

Castro, Carl, Sara Kintzl, Ashley Schuyler, Carrie Lucas, and Christopher Warner. 2015. "Sexual Assault in the Military." *Current Psychiatry Report* 17 (7): 54. doi: 10.1007/s11920-015-0596-7.

Corbet, Sylvie. 2014. "French Military Launches Its First-Ever Plan to Battle Sexual Assault, Harassment in the Ranks." *US News & World Report*, April 15. Accessed June 1, 2017. https://www.usnews.com/news/world/articles/2014/04/15/for-1st-time -france-tackles-military-sex-assaults.

Defense Abuse Response Taskforce. 2016. "Final Report." Accessed December 17, 2017. http://apo.org.au/system/files/67232/apo-nid67232-40656.pdf.

Defense Manpower Data Center. 2013. "2012 Workplace and Gender Relations Survey of Active Duty Members Tabulations of Responses." DMDC Report No. 2012-065. Alexandria, VA: Defense Manpower Data Center. Accessed June 1, 2017. http:// www.sapr.mil/public/docs/research/WGR_ActiveDuty_2012_Report.pdf.

Defense Manpower Data Center. 2016. "2015 Military Investigation and Justice Experience Survey." DMDC Report No. 2016-008. Alexandria, VA: Defense Manpower Data Center. Accessed June 1, 2017. http://sapr.mil/public/docs/reports/FY15_Annual /Annex_3_2015_MIJES_Report.pdf.

Deschamps, Marie. 2015. "External Review into Sexual Misconduct and Sexual Harassment in the Canadian Armed Forces." National Defence and the Canadian Armed Forces. Accessed June 1, 2017. http://www.forces.gc.ca/en/caf-community-support -services/external-review-sexual-mh-2015/summary.page.

Dick, Kirby, Regina K. Scully, Jennifer S. Newsom, Tanner K. Barklow, Amy Ziering, Thaddeus Wadleigh, . . . Derek Boonstra. 2012. *The Invisible War*. Sausalito, CA: Roco Films Educational.

Ellison, Jesse. 2011. "The Military's Secret Shame." *Newsweek*, April 3. Accessed June 1, 2017. http://www.newsweek.com/militarys-secret-shame-66459.

Fortney, Valerie. 2010. *Sunray: The Death and Life of Captain Nichola Goddard*. Toronto, Canada: Key Porter Books.

Gillibrand, Kirsten. 2014. "Snapshot Review of Sexual Assault Report Files at the Four Largest U.S. Military Bases in 2013." Kirsten Gillibrand Senate Website. Accessed June 1, 2017. https://www.gillibrand.senate.gov/imo/media/doc/Gillibrand_Sexual %20Assault%20Report.pdf.

Gillibrand, Kirsten. n.d. "Stats from SAPRO Report." Kirsten Gillibrand Senate Website. Accessed July 4, 2017. https://www.gillibrand.senate.gov/mjia/stats-from-sapro -report.

GovTrack.us. 2011. "H.R. 3435 (112th Congress): Sexual Assault Training Oversight and Prevention Act." www.GovTrack.us. 2011. Accessed June 17, 2017. https:// www.govtrack.us/congress/bills/112/hr3435.

GovTrack.us. 2014. "H.R. 4310 (112th Congress): National Defense Authorization Act for Fiscal Year 2013." Accessed June 1, 2017. http://www.govtrack.us/congress/bills /112/hr4310.

GovTrack.us. 2017a. "S. 967 (113th Congress): Military Justice Improvement Act of 2013." Accessed June 1, 2017. https://www.govtrack.us/congress/bills/113/s967.

GovTrack.us. 2017b. "S. 1081 (113th Congress): Military Whistleblower Protection Enhancement Act of 2013." Accessed June 1, 2017. https://govtrack.us/congress/bills/113/s1081.

Horzepa, Hayley R. 2011. "Victim Blaming: An All-Too-Common Response to Sexual Assault." *HuffPost News*, April 22. Accessed June 1, 2017. http://www.huffington post.com/hayley-rose-horzepa/victim-blaming_b_847310.html.

Hoyt, Tim, Jennifer Klosterman Reilage, and Lauren F. Williams. 2013. "Military Sexual Trauma in Men: A Review of Reported Rates." *Journal of Trauma Dissociation* 12 (3): 244–60.

Human Rights Watch. 2015. "Embattled: Retaliation against Sexual Assault Survivors in the US Military." Accessed June 1, 2017. https://www.hrw.org/sites/default/files /report_pdf/us0515militaryweb.pdf.

Hunter, Mic. 2007. *Honor Betrayed: Sexual Abuse in the Military*. New York: Barricade Books.

Kang, Han, Nancy Dalager, Clare Mahan, and Erick Ishii. 2005. "The Role of Sexual Assault on the Risk of PTSD among Gulf War Veterans." *Annals of Epidemiology* 15 (3): 191–95.

King, Karisa. 2013. "Military Often Betrays Sex-Assault Victims." *SFGate*, May 18. Accessed July 5, 2017. http://www.sfgate.com/nation/article/Military-often-betrays -sex-assault-victims-4528669.php.

Koons, Jennifer. 2013. "Sexual Assault in the Military: Can the Pentagon Stem the Rise in Incidents?" *CQ Researcher* 23 (29): 693–716. http://library.cqpress.com/cqre searcher/document.php?id=cqresrre2013080906.

Lawrence, Quil, and Marisa Peñaloza. 2013. "Sexual Violence Victims Say Military Justice System Is 'Broken.'" *NPR*, March 21. Accessed June 1, 2017. http://www.npr .org/2013/03/21/174840895/sexual-violence-victims-say-militaryjustice-system -is-broken.

Library of Congress Australia. 2016. "Military Justice System: Adjudication of Sexual Offenses: Australia." Accessed July 5, 2017. https://www.loc.gov/law/help/military justice/australia.php.

Library of Congress Canada. 2015. "Military Justice System: Adjudication of Sexual Offenses: Canada." Accessed July 5, 2017. https://www.loc.gov/law/help/military justice/canada.php.

Library of Congress Israel. 2015. "Military Justice System: Adjudication of Sexual Offenses: Israel." Accessed July 5, 2017. https://www.loc.gov/law/help/military justice/israel.php.

Library of Congress United Kingdom. 2015. "Military Justice System: Adjudication of Sexual Offences: United Kingdom." Accessed July 5, 2017. https://www.loc.gov /law/help/militaryjustice/unitedkingdom.php.

Lichfield, John. 2014. "France Battles Sexual Abuse in the Military: Female Generals Are at Record High, Yet Cases of Harassment among New Recruits Are Common." *Independent*, April 19. http://www.independent.co.uk/news/world/europe/france -battles-sexual-abuse-in-the-military-9271383.html.

Lorincz, Tamara. 2013. "Canada's Invisible War: Violence against Women in the Canadian Armed Forces." Canadian Voice of Women for Peace. Accessed July 5, 2017. http://vowpeace.org/wp-content/uploads/2013/03/Canadas-Invisible-War-Fact -Sheet.pdf.

Lucero, Gabrielle. 2015. "Military Sexual Assault: Reporting and Rape Culture." *Sanford Journal of Public Policy* 6 (1): 1–32.

Marquis, Jeff, and RAND Corporation. 2017. "Improving Oversight and Coordination of Department of Defense Programs That Address Problematic Behaviors among Military Personnel: Final Report." Santa Monica, CA: RAND Corporation. Accessed June 1, 2017. https://www.rand.org/pubs/research_reports/RR1352.html.

Military Whistleblower Protection Act. 2010. Title 10 U.S.C., § 1034.

Minano, Leila, and Julia Pascual. 2014. *La Guerre Invisible*. Paris: Les Arènes.

National Defense Authorization Act for Fiscal Year 2014. Public Law 113-66. Accessed December 17, 2017. https://www.congress.gov/113/plaws/publ66/PLAW-113pub l66.pdf

National Defense Research Institute et al. 2014. "Sexual Assault and Sexual Harassment in the U.S. Military: Top-Line Estimates for Active-Duty Service Members from the 2014 RAND Military Workplace Study." Santa Monica, CA: RAND Corporation. https://www.rand.org/pubs/research_reports/RR870.html.

National Sexual Violence Resource Center. 2015. "Statistics about Sexual Violence." Accessed June 1, 2017. http://www.nsvrc.org/sites/default/files/publications_nsvrc _factsheet_media-packet_statistics-about-sexual-violence_0.pdf.

Office of People Analytics (OPA). 2017. "2016 Military Investigation and Justice Experience Survey (MIJES): Overview Report." Defense Technical Center. Ft. Belvoir, VA. Accessed December 17, 2017. http://www.sapr.mil/public/docs/reports /FY16_Annual/Annex_2_2016_MIJES_Report.pdf.

Rainey, Sarah. 2014. "'Military Rape Is Like Being Abused by Your Family.'" *The Telegraph*, February 7. Accessed July 5, 2017. http://www.telegraph.co.uk/news/uknews /defence/10624398/Military-rape-is-like-being-abused-by-your-family.html.

Rape, Abuse & Incest National Network. n.d. "The Criminal Justice System: Statistics." Accessed July 5, 2017. https://www.rainn.org/statistics/criminal-justice-system.

Rumble, Gary A., and Melanie McKean. 2011. *Report of the Review of Allegations of Sexual and Other Abuse in Defence: Facing the Problems of the Past*. Commonwealth of Australia. Volume 1. Accessed July 2, 2017. http://www.defence.gov.au/pathway tochange/Docs/DLAPiper/DefenceDLAPiperReview-FullReport.pdf.

Sadler, Anne G., Brenda M. Booth, Brian L. Cook, and Bradley N. Doebbeling. 2003. "Factors Associated with Women's Risk of Rape in the Military Environment." *American Journal of Industrial Medicine* 43 (3): 262–73.

Savage, Charlie. 2013. "Amid Criticism, Pentagon Seeks Overhaul of the Court-Martial System." *New York Times*, April 8. Accessed July 5, 2017. http://www.nytimes.com /2013/04/09/us/politics/pentagon-to-ask-congress-to-overhaul-court-martial-system .html.

Schemo, Diane. 2003. "Rate of Rape at Academy Is Put at 12% in Survey." *New York Times*, August 29. Accessed June 1, 2017. https://www.nytimes.com/2003/08/29 /national/29ACAD.html?th.

Schwellenbach, Nick. 2013. "Fear of Reprisal: The Quiet Accomplice in the Military's Sexual-Assault Epidemic." *Time*, May 9. http://nation.time.com/2013/05/09/fear of reprisal-the-quiet-accomplice-in-the-militarys-sexual-assault-epidemic/.

Sexual Assault Prevention and Response Office. 2008. "Department of Defense FY07 Report on Sexual Assault in the Military." Washington, DC: U. S. Department of Defense. Accessed July 5, 2017. http://www.sapr.mil/public/docs/reports/2007-annual -report.pdf.

Sexual Assault Prevention and Response Office. 2017. "Annual Report on Sexual Assault in the Military Fiscal Year 2016." Washington, DC: U.S. Department of Defense. Accessed July 4, 2017. http://www.sapr.mil/public/docs/reports/FY16 _Annual/FY16_SAPRO_Annual_Report.pdf.

Skinner, Kathrine, Nancy Kressin, Susan Frayne, Tara Tripp, Cheryl Hankin, Donald Miller, and Lisa Sullivan. 2002. "The Prevalence of Military Sexual Assault among Female Veterans' Administration Outpatients." *Journal of Interpersonal Violence* 15 (3): 291–310.

Statistics Canada. 2016. "Survey on Sexual Misconduct in the Canadian Armed Forces, 2016." Accessed June 1, 2017. http://www.statcan.gc.ca/daily-quotidien/161128 /dq161128a-eng.htm.

Subcommittee on the Judicial Proceedings Panel. 2017. "Report on Sexual Assault Investigations in the Military. Accessed December 17, 2017. http://jpp.whs.mil /Public/docs/08-Panel_Reports/JPP_SubcommReport_Investigations_Final_2017 0224.pdf.

Szoldra, Paul. 2017. "The Marine Corps' Nude-Photo-Sharing Scandal Is Even Worse Than First Realized." *Business Insider*, March 9. Accessed July 2, 2017. http://www .businessinsider.com/nude-photo-marine-corps-pentagon-scandal-2017-3.

Turchik, Jessica A., and Susan Wilson. 2010. "Sexual Assault in the U.S. Military: A Review of the Literature and Recommendations for the Future." *Aggression and Violent Behavior* 15 (4): 267–77.

U.S. Code. 2010. *Title 10—Armed Forces: Chapter 47—Uniform Code of Military Justice*. Washington, DC: U.S. Government Publishing Office. Accessed June 1, 2017. https://www.gpo.gov/fdsys/pkg/USCODE-2010-title10/html/USCODE-2010-title10 -subtitleA-partII-chap47.htm.

U.S. Commission on Civil Rights. 2013. "Statutory Enforcement Report: Sexual Assault in the Military." Accessed June 1, 2017. http://www.usccr.gov/press/2013/FinalPress Release_SexualAssaultMilitaryRept.pdf.

U.S. Department of Defense. 2016. "DoD Retaliation Prevention and Response Strategy: Regarding Sexual Assault and Harassment Reports." Accessed June 1, 2017. http://sapr.mil/public/docs/reports/Retaliation/DoD_Retaliation_Strategy.pdf.

U.S. Department of Defense. 2017a. "Annual Report on Sexual Harassment and Violence at the Military Service Academies. Academic Program Year 2015–2016." Accessed June 1, 2017. http://sapr.mil/public/docs/reports/MSA/APY_15-16/APY _15_16_MSA_Report_v2.pdf.

U.S. Department of Defense. 2017b. "Appendix B: Statistical Date on Sexual Assault." 2017. Department of Defense. Accessed December 17, 2017. http://sapr.mil/public /docs/reports/FY16_Annual/Appendix_B_Statistical_Section.pdf.

U.S. Department of Defense. 2017c. "Sexual Assault Prevention and Response Program Procedures." Instruction Number 6495.02. Accessed June 1, 2017. http://www.vi .ngb.army.mil/html/sapr/docs/DoD%20Instruction%206495.02.pdf.

U.S. Department of Defense 2017d. "Sexual Assault Prevention and Response (SAPR) Program." Directive Number 6495.01. Accessed July 3, 2017. http://www.esd.whs .mil/Portals/54/Documents/DD/issuances/dodd/649501p.pdf.

U.S. Senate Committee on Armed Services. 2003. "Allegations of Sexual Assault at the U.S. Air Force Academy." Senate Hearing 108-652. Accessed July 2, 2017. https:// www.gpo.gov/fdsys/pkg/CHRG-108shrg89536/html/CHRG-108shrg89536.htm.

U.S. Supreme Court. 1977. *Coker v. Georgia*. No. 75-5444. http://caselaw.findlaw.com /us-supreme-court/433/584.html.

U.S. Supreme Court. 2008. *Kennedy* **v.** *Louisiana*. No. 07-343. http://caselaw.findlaw .com/us-supreme-court/554/407.html.

Vergun, David. 2014. "New Law Brings Changes to Uniform Code of Military Justice." *Army News Service*, February 20. Accessed June 1, 2017. https://www.army.mil /article/120622/New_law_brings_changes_to_Uniform_Code_of_Military_Justice/.

Vergun, David. 2015. "Legislation Changes UCMJ for Victims of Sexual Assault." *Army News Service*, January 7. Accessed July 5, 2017. https://www.army.mil/article /140807.

Woodham, Shawn. 2013. *Sexual Assault in the Military: Analysis, Response, and Resources*. Hauppauge, NY: Nova Science.

Yaeger, Deborah, Naomi Himmelfarb, Alison Cammack, and Jim Mintz. 2006. "DSM-IV Diagnosed Posttraumatic Stress Syndrome in Women Veterans with and without Military Sexual Trauma." *Journal of General Internal Medicine* 21 (S3): S65–69.

Yuhas, Alan. 2014. "Pentagon: Rape Reports Increase among 19,000 Estimated Military Victims." *The Guardian*, December 4. Accessed June 1, 2017. https://www.theguard ian.com/us-news/2014/dec/04/pentagon-rape-assault-reports-increase-military.

SEXUAL HARASSMENT

In "A Short History of Sexual Harassment," the introduction in the book *Directions in Sexual Harassment Law*, Reva B. Siegel tracks sexual harassment back to the era of chattel slavery. According to Siegel, the abusive treatment of females in domestic service was largely unrecognized as a social problem, and those involved in domestic service often suffered repeatedly from sexual coercion. As industrialization began in the 19th century, some women worked in factories and sweatshops, where they endured sexual harassment from bosses and foremen. During this period, paid work outside the home became distinct from domestic work. In wartime, particularly during the two world wars in the 20th century, women took over jobs that traditionally had been male; but when peace returned, women were forced out of many jobs. Those women who did remain at businesses and factories were often relegated to jobs requiring less skill, and they were more liable to be harassed. Because many women worked out of need, they believed they could not challenge men or push off men's advances, since they might lose employment or suffer reduced wages. On the other hand, accepting the advances of men could brand women as "loose" and make the possibility of finding a husband less likely.

In 1964, the United States Congress passed the Civil Rights Act. The act, designed to protect and enforce various constitutional rights of individuals, was a significant step. Title VII of this act applies specifically to the prohibition of discrimination based on race, color, religion, sex, or national origin. The Equal Employment Opportunity Commission (EEOC) is the organization tasked with enforcing the Civil Rights Act. The EEOC was designed to investigate and create policy regarding workplace sexual discrimination. Title VII is applicable to businesses that employ 15 or more employees—including all federal, state, and local governments and private businesses. Also required to follow these provisions are all employment agencies and labor organizations.

In 1980, the EEOC began to apply Title VII to the act of sexual discrimination. In 1981, with *Bundy v. Jackson* (641 F.2d 934), the U.S. Court of Appeals for the District of Columbia evaluated the EEOC's enforcement of Title VII and held that insults and propositions of a sexual nature can create a hostile working environment. In 1986, in *Meritor Savings Bank v. Vinson* (477 U.S. 57), the U.S. Supreme Court continued evaluating instances in the workplace and established that sexual harassment is a form of sex discrimination and is prohibited by Title VII.

Title VII was meant to address any form of discrimination on the job, although sexual harassment was not covered initially. The issue of sexualized treatment in the workplace was finally given a name—sexual harassment—in the late 1970s. Social movements and women's organizations created public awareness of this issue. Like other social causes, sexual harassment has historical figures who were instrumental in making the problem known. Activists Lin Farley, Susan Meyer, and Karen Sauvigné are the founders of the Working Women United Institute. This institute, in conjunction with the Alliance Against Sexual Coercion (AASC), brought sexual harassment into the public forum. AASC was founded in 1976 by Freada Kapor Klein, Lynn Wehrli, and Elizabeth Cohn-Stuntz. Their efforts helped to raise public awareness of a significant problem that many women were encountering.

The term *sexual harassment* became commonly known in 1991, during the hearings to confirm Clarence Thomas as a justice of the U.S. Supreme Court. During the public hearings, Anita Hill alleged that Thomas had sexually harassed her. Hill testified that while she was employed with the Department of Education and EEOC, Thomas, her supervisor, made sexually charged and often explicit comments to her. Though Thomas was confirmed, Hill's testimony brought attention to the problems women faced, and it encouraged some

Table 1. Sexual Harassment Charges: EEOC & FEPAs Combined, FY 1997–FY 2011

	FY 1997	FY 1998	FY 1999	FY 2000	FY 2001	FY 2002	FY 2003	FY 2004	FY 2005	FY 2006	FY 2007	FY 2008	FY 2009	FY 2010	FY 2011
Receipts	15,889	15,618	15,222	15,836	15,475	14,396	13,566	13,136	12,679	12,025	12,510	13,867	12,696	11,717	11,364
Percent of Charges Filed by **Males**	11.60%	12.9%	12.1%	13.6%	13.7%	14.9%	14.7%	15.1%	14.3%	15.4%	16.0%	15.9%	16.0%	16.4%	16.3%
Resolutions	17,333	17,115	16,524	16,726	16,383	15,792	14,534	13,786	12,859	11,936	11,592	11,731	11,948	12,772	12,571
Resolutions by Type															
Settlements	1,178	1,218	1,361	1,676	1,568	1,692	1,783	1,646	1,471	1,458	1,571	1,525	1,382	1,417	1,367
	6.80%	7.1%	8.2%	10.0%	9.6%	10.7%	12.3%	11.9%	11.4%	12.2%	13.6%	13.0%	11.6%	11.1%	10.9%
Withdrawals with Benefits	1,267	1,311	1,299	1,389	1,454	1,235	1,300	1,138	1,146	1,175	1,177	1,183	1,285	1,195	1,150
	7.30%	7.7%	7.9%	8.3%	8.9%	7.8%	8.9%	8.3%	8.9%	9.8%	10.2%	10.1%	10.8%	9.4%	9.1%
Administrative Closures	6,908	6,296	5,412	4,632	4,306	3,957	3,600	3,256	2,808	2,838	2,804	2,618	2,835	2,907	2,635
	39.90%	36.8%	32.8%	27.7%	26.3%	25.1%	24.8%	23.6%	21.8%	23.8%	24.2%	22.3%	23.7%	22.8%	21.0%
No Reasonable Cause	7,172	7,243	7,272	7,370	7,309	7,445	6,703	6,708	6,364	5,668	5,273	5,718	5,695	6,393	6,658
	41.40%	42.3%	44.0%	44.1%	44.6%	47.1%	46.1%	48.7%	49.5%	47.5%	45.5%	48.7%	47.7%	50.1%	53.0%
Reasonable Cause	808	1,047	1,180	1,659	1,746	1,463	1,148	1,037	1,070	797	767	687	751	860	761
	4.70%	6.1%	7.1%	9.9%	10.7%	9.3%	7.9%	7.5%	8.3%	6.7%	6.6%	5.9%	6.3%	6.7%	6.1%

Successful Conciliations	298	357	383	524	551	455	350	311	324	253	282	234	254	308	288
	1.70%	2.1%	2.3%	3.1%	3.4%	2.9%	2.4%	2.3%	2.5%	2.1%	2.4%	2.0%	2.1%	2.4%	2.3%
Unsuccessful Conciliations	510	690	797	1,135	1,195	1,008	798	726	746	544	485	453	497	552	473
	2.90%	4.0%	4.8%	6.8%	7.3%	6.4%	5.5%	5.3%	5.8%	4.6%	4.2%	3.9%	4.2%	4.3%	3.8%
Merit Resolutions	3,253	3,576	3,840	4,724	4,768	4,390	4,231	3,821	3,687	3,430	3,515	3,395	3,418	3,472	3,278
	18.80%	20.9%	23.2%	28.2%	29.1%	27.8%	29.1%	27.7%	28.7%	28.7%	30.3%	28.9%	28.6%	27.2%	26.1%
Monetary Benefits (Millions)*	$49.50	$34.3	$50.3	$54.6	$53.0	$50.3	$50.0	$37.1	$47.9	$48.8	$49.9	$47.4	$51.5	$48.4	$52.3

* Does not include monetary benefits obtained through litigation.

Total number of charge receipts filed and resolved under Title VII alleging sexual harassment discrimination as an issue.

The data in the sexual harassment table reflect charges filed with EEOC and the state and local Fair Employment Practices agencies around the country that have a work-

sharing agreement with the commission.

The data are compiled by the Office of Research, Information and Planning from data compiled from EEOC's Charge Data System and, from FY 2004 forward, EEOC's Integrated Mission System.

Source: U.S. Equal Employment Opportunity Commission. 2011. "Sexual Harassment Charges: EEOC & FEPAs Combined, FY 1997–FY 2011." Accessed December 20, 2017. https://www.eeoc.gov/eeoc/statistics/enforcement/sexual_harassment.cfm.

women—who may not have had the confidence to do so prior to the hearing—to speak out about their own experiences.

In 1991, the Civil Rights Act was amended to allow for jury trials. These trials would also allow victims to seek compensatory and punitive damages. After 1991, the number of sexual harassment cases increased significantly. Damages awarded to victims increased as well

Definition of Sexual Harassment

Scholars and experts use the following terms when discussing sexual harassment. The first term is *sexism*—an attitude, held by an individual or a group of individuals, of one sex toward another sex. This attitude often displays a sense of superiority that the person has regarding his or her own sex. Examples include a belief that all women are bad drivers or that men are not good caregivers. *Sex discrimination* occurs when decisions concerning an individual's employment are made on the basis of sex or gender, or when an individual is treated differently because of his or her sex. Examples of this type of behavior include a woman supervisor tasking only male employees to carry heavy material, or an employer not hiring women because they could become pregnant. Sexual harassment also includes unwelcome behavior of a sexual nature; it can take many forms—for example, catcalls by men to women on the street, and discrimination inside the workplace.

Sexual harassment has been identified as instances of unwelcome sexual behavior; examples include suggestive comments on one's dress, inappropriate looks, and inappropriate touching. If these behaviors make individuals uncomfortable, then they are examples of sexual harassment. If the behavior can be identified as offensive, hostile, and/or intimidating in nature, and it can negatively affect the ability of employees to do their job, it creates a hostile work environment. The threshold is the measure of whether the identified behavior creates a hostile work environment or interrupts employees' ability to perform their work.

Sexual harassment can be quid pro quo, and/or it can create a hostile work environment. *Quid pro quo* is a Latin term that translates loosely to "this for that" or "something for something." In the venue of sexual harassment, the term has been clearly interpreted as an exchange. This exchange—between employees or between employer and employee—involves sex in return for such work-related advantages as preferential treatment or favorable duty assignments. It can also be a condition of employment that, if not done, can result in a loss of one's job. A boss, supervisor, or someone with power over an employee may indicate that employees can be given a promotion or assigned desirable work only if they grant sexual favors.

A *hostile work environment* is created when employees express their desire for unwanted sexual comments or jokes to end but that request is ignored. What differentiates quid pro quo from a hostile work environment is that quid pro quo involves a tangible economic injury. This is not the case for hostile workplace harassment. Instances that can create a hostile or abusive work environment include employees hanging pornographic pictures or cartoons, or telling offensive jokes (of a sexual nature) or making sexual remarks. When businesses and institutions have been found to have hostile work environments—often through research by psychologists on the effects of the harassment—courts have held the institutions liable for damages.

Sexual harassment can occur anywhere. From the local factory to the halls of the U.S. Congress, instances of sexual harassment can occur wherever the sexes interact within a business setting. Often, experts who have analyzed sexual harassment see a power differential, with the harasser in a position of power or control over the victim. This power differential can take many forms within the workplace. Additional examples of relationships where sexual harassment can occur are when a customer, a teacher, or a legal guardian is the harasser; even a fellow student, a friend, or a stranger can be a harasser. In the case of a hostile work environment, more than one individual may be the target of the harassment: If a coworker is a witness and is affected by the behavior, he or she can also be a victim of harassment, and any person who finds the behavior offensive would be considered a victim. Harassment can occur in almost any arena—at school, within a government office, or within a business of any size.

Harassers might not understand that what they are doing could be considered harassment. Also, the victim may view the behavior as something obnoxious or bothersome but not as harassment. For harassment to meet the legal threshold for a case, it must be frequent or severe enough to cause a hostile workplace, or to have a negative effect on the victim's employment or position. Sexual harassment is not confined to one gender. Harassers can be men or

Sexual Harassment or Sexual Assault?

Sexual harassment is connected to a person's employment and/or work performance. It may come in the form of unwelcome sexual advances or requests for sexual favors in return for an offer of employment or advancement, and it creates a hostile workplace environment. It is a civil rights issue. *Sexual assault* includes unwanted sexual contact—from penetrating the mouth, vagina, or anus to touching, forced kissing, and other activity—performed without an individual's consent. It is a criminal act. Sexual harassment may lead to sexual assault, but it does not always. Individuals may also be harassed on the street through catcalling, groping, sexual advances, and even being followed. Each state has different laws for these types of behaviors.

women. The law recognizes that harassment is not a gender-based phenomenon. Harassment can occur out of a misunderstanding, which might come from generalizations about gender and gender roles; in such cases, the harasser might not understand an explicit message from the victim to stop (Heyman 1994).

Examples of unwelcome behaviors include being in a work environment where sexually charged speech or "dirty" jokes are common. What is most important is that the victim must indicate that the behaviors are unwelcome. Many behaviors, such as displaying sexually inappropriate images or posters, can cause a hostile workplace environment. Inappropriate sexual gestures, touching, or comments about clothing are additional behaviors that are considered harassment. Questioning individuals about their sexual history or sexual orientation, or making sexual advances to individuals who have indicated that they are not interested, is harassment. If the behavior continues after the victim has made it known that the behavior is problematic, a hostile workplace has been created. Although research tends to refer to females as the victims, both the victim and the harasser can be male or female. Furthermore, the two people involved may be of the same sex.

Although employees may not actively object to or report harassment, an employer who permits these behaviors to continue may, in fact, be tacitly allowing a hostile workplace. Frequently, employees do not feel strong or safe enough to come forward when incidents make them uncomfortable. Many times, a power differential exists, and victims who are in a subordinate position may appear to consent to the actions of their supervisor. Because the victims appear to consent, however, does not mean that harassment has not occurred.

A hostile work environment can be difficult to understand. Comments must be—either implicitly or explicitly—of a sexual nature. Situations in which the victim is not appointed to important committees, does not receive information about training opportunities, or is not considered for promotion because of family responsibilities are types of sexual harassment and are often hard to articulate. A hostile work environment can be one that has reached the point where individuals find it difficult to do their jobs because the behavior of a boss or coworker goes beyond rude or obnoxious.

There are several theories that analyze the way in which women are treated in general, as well as the treatment of women within the workplace. These theories closely align harassment with violence against women, gender stereotypes, and economic disparity. For example, a Rand Corporation study (Morrall et al. 2014) found that "U.S. military women who had been sexually harassed in the past year were 14 times more likely to have also been sexually assaulted in the same period (compared to women who had not been sexually harassed)." The comparable figure for men was 49 times higher (Chalabi 2016).

Martha Chamallas reports that the law addressing sexual harassment in the United States has been only minimally successful, and that even after decades the results are decidedly mixed. Chamallas notes that those who have been targets of harassment are now able to label the behavior they experienced. In addition, they no longer have to remain in the shadows; nor do they need to fear that they will be seen as having craved attention, or that their clothing or behavior caused the offenders to make advances (Chamallas 2003).

In a 1990 study, Billie Dziech and Linda Weiner divided harassers into two general types. The first group is public harassers, who are blatant in their attitudes, and their actions/attitudes are always seductive or sexist in nature. Private harassers are more difficult to identify: They have created a self-possessed and reputable outward image, and they act out only when they are alone with their intended victim.

Martha Langelan (1993) describes four types of harassers:

- Predatory harassers—These individuals get sexual thrills from humiliating others. They sexually extort or harass targets to gauge how the victim will react.
- Dominance harassers—These individuals engage in the behavior as a means of boosting their self-esteem. This type of harassment is considered the most common.
- Strategic or territorial harassers—These individuals wish to retain the position they hold over the victim. They may choose a job where the victim pool is significant.
- Street harassers—These individuals make unwanted comments and participate in catcalling or wolf-whistles. They are generally strangers to their victims, and the harassment occurs in public places. The types of remarks made are almost always of a sexual nature. Street harassment can also include nonverbal behavior (Bowman 1993).

United States

Prevalence

The Equal Employment Opportunity Commission (EEOC) provides some general statistics about sexual harassment in the United States. In 2015, the EEOC investigated 6,822 cases of alleged sexual harassment. Men filed 17.1 percent of these charges. Nearly 52 percent of the total charges were found to have no reasonable cause. Many cases are withdrawn or closed for various administrative reasons. Of the total charges, 25 percent, or 1,829 cases, were reported as "merit resolutions," and $46 million was awarded in monetary benefits, which does not include sums obtained through litigation. The figures were roughly similar for 2014 and 2016 (Equal Employment Opportunity Commission 2016).

A 2013 YouGov/*Huffington Post* poll of 1,000 adults found that 13 percent had been sexually harassed "at work by a boss or other superior" (3 percent declined to answer); 19 percent had been sexually harassed "at work by a coworker who was NOT a boss or superior." Of those who said they had been sexually harassed at work, 70 percent did not report it. When they saw others being sexually harassed, 61 percent did not report what they saw (Huffington Post Staff 2013). A survey in 1994 reported similar statistics: 72 percent of the individuals polled said they did not report workplace sexual harassment (Chalabi 2016).

A 2011 study examined both EEOC data and U.S. census data. According to this study, published by the *American Economic Review,* the group most likely to be sexually harassed was women between the ages of 25 and 34. Breaking down the figures by industry, the highest rates of sexual harassment occurred in the construction industry; transportation and utilities were the next highest (Chalabi 2016).

A 2015 survey of women in technology (91 percent of whom lived in Silicon Valley) found that 60 percent had "reported unwanted sexual advances." Of the women who had reported, 60 percent were not satisfied with the course of action that was taken after they reported. Of the women who did not report the sexual harassment they had experienced, 39 percent chose not to report because they were afraid it would have a negative effect on their career, 30 percent did not report "because they wanted to forget," and 29 percent had "signed a non-disparagement agreement" (Vassallo et al. 2016).

In 2014, the PEW Research Center addressed online harassment and found that 40 percent of adults who use the Internet had experienced some harassment. This ranged from such incidents as name-calling, which many ignored, to more severe incidents that involve threats, harassment, and even stalking. Of all who had been harassed, 18 percent reported the "more severe" type. Young adults were more likely to be harassed, but young women were more at risk for the sexual and more severe harassment. Of women ages 18–24, 26 percent experienced more severe online harassment, with 26 percent of those subjected to online stalking and 25 percent experiencing online sexual harassment. Harassment by a stranger was reported by 38 percent, while 26 percent did not know the real identity of those who harassed them. Of the online harassment, 66 percent occurred on social network sites. While 60 percent chose to not respond to the harassment, of the 40 percent who did respond, 47 percent confronted their attackers online, 44 percent blocked or "unfriended" their harassers, 22 percent reported the harassment to the Web site or service, and 5 percent reported the harassment to law enforcement. The rest withdrew or stopped attending online events, changed their usernames or profiles, or tried to gain online support from others (Duggan 2014).

The 2016 Select Task Force on the Study of Harassment in the Workplace Report found that defining *sexual harassment* made a difference in how individuals responded in surveys. For example, in random samples, when asked if they had experienced sexual harassment in the workplace (without the term defined), approximately one in four women said they had. This figure is found in a number of surveys. However, when women are asked about more specific behaviors, the figure rises. In a survey in which women were asked about "unwanted sexual attention or sexual coercion" and also about "sexist or crude/offensive behavior" called "gender harassment," nearly 60 percent of women said they had experienced it (Feldblum and Lipnic 2016). The task force also looked at surveys of LGBTQ+ employees. Such surveys reveal a variety of responses, with 7–41 percent reporting verbal or physical abuse. In general, transgender individuals experienced "higher rates of harassment than LGB people" (Feldblum and Lipnic 2016).

There are a number of jobs/occupations in which sexual harassment occurs at a higher rate: sales and marketing, the business industry (primarily trade, banking, and finance), the hospitality industry, civil service, and education. Women face different obstacles depending on the profession, and they either leave the job or stay and put up with the harassment. For instance, according to a 2014 report on sexual harassment in the restaurant industry, "while seven percent of American women work in the restaurant industry, more than a third (an eye-opening 37 percent) of all sexual harassment claims to the Equal Employment Opportunity Commission (EEOC) come from the restaurant industry" (Restaurant Opportunities Centers United 2014, 1). Women servers must often accept the harassment as their income is often dependent on tips. If they do not, they run the risk of a significant impact on their income. The study indicated that restaurant workers reported 66 percent of harassment coming from management, 80 percent from coworkers, and 78 percent from customers. Women and transgender workers reported more sexual harassment than male workers did, while "60% of transgender, 50% of women, and 47% of men reported experiencing 'scary' or 'unwanted' sexual behavior" (Restaurant Opportunities Centers United 2014, 2).

Male-dominated occupations or ones where a gender gap is clearly evident report having higher levels of harassment. Traditionally, in occupations where males dominate, such as policing, harassment is a significant issue. Sexual harassment complaints are being filed in greater numbers by female police officers against their male counterparts. Studies that have examined the frequency of harassing behavior in law enforcement have determined that female officers all reported that they had encountered some form of harassment—from being insulted to being the target of dirty jokes or stories. However, most female officers stated that they were not necessarily bothered by these comments. This was identified as a phenomenon that exists in occupations where trust is essential (Seklecki and Paynich 2007).

Sexual harassment also occurs in educational settings. In 2001, the American Association of University Women (AAUW) conducted a study entitled "Hostile Hallways: Bullying, Teasing, and Sexual Harassment in School." The study found that 83 percent of girls and 79 percent of boys reported having been sexually harassed at school; the figure was 85 percent and 76 percent in 1993 (American Association of University Women 2001, 20–21).Comparing both sets of data (1993 and 2001) showed that a total of 81 percent of respondents (boys and girls) indicated that they had experienced sexual harassment; however, in 1993 girls were more likely to have been sexually harassed than boys (American Association of University Women 2001, 20–21). In general, girls report being more negatively affected by harassment, and to be afraid more often and less confident about themselves. In high schools, sexual harassment for students most commonly occurs in the hallways. The students who are harassed identify inappropriate jokes, looks, or gestures as the most common forms of harassment. Sexually suggestive touching, grabbing, or pinching was the second most common complaint of high-school students. The AAUW report notes that high-school students often find it difficult to understand if behavior is sexual harassment or simply immature behavior. Students report being unable to understand when normal flirting turns into sexual harassment. Other researchers have found similar indications that many students do not understand what constitutes sexual harassment. For example, Nan Stein (2001), of the Wellesley Center for Research on Women, suggests that students should be given a list to help them differentiate between normal behavior and sexual harassment.

Sexual harassment is also a common problem on college campuses across the United States. A Campus Climate Survey on sexual violence and misconduct (Association of American Universities 2017) examined the prevalence of sexual harassment on college campuses. The survey, studying sexual harassment at several institutions of higher education, found that 47.7 percent of students, men and women, were targets of sexual harassment, but those who identify as women or as transgender, genderqueer, questioning or not listed (TGQN) reported the highest rates of sexual harassment. Nearly 62 percent of female undergraduate college students and 61 percent of male college students report having been sexually harassed, while 75.2 percent of undergraduates identifying as TGQN reported being sexually harassed (Association of American Universities 2017, xvl).

In a 2006 study done by the AAUW, 80 percent of students who reported being sexually harassed were harassed by another student or a former student (American Association of University Women 2006, 20). A small percentage (10 percent or fewer) reported their experiences to a university employee (American Association of University Women 2006, 2). More than one-third of students who experienced sexual harassment did not tell anyone (American Association of University Women 2006, 4). In the study, nearly half of all males admitted to sexually harassing someone in college, and one-third of the females admitted to harassing someone in college (American Association of University Women 2006, 3). Women reported suffering as a result of the sexual harassment at higher rates that did male students.

Major Laws

Federal law defines *sexual harassment* as any unwelcome sexual advance, requests for sexual favors, and other verbal or physical conduct of a sexual nature. This definition provides specific criteria that must be met for the actions to be considered sexual harassment:

1. Submitting to these behaviors is either explicitly or implicitly a term or condition of employment.
2. Agreeing to submit or refusing to submit is used as the basis for decisions made in the workplace.
3. The behavior has the intention or effect of disrupting the individual's work performance. The behavior can also create an intimidating, hostile, or offensive working environment.

The law can be found in Code of Federal Regulations (CFR), Title 29, Subtitle B, Chapter XIV, section 1604, part 1604, 1604.11.

In 1991, the Civil Rights Act was amended to give victims the ability to be awarded both compensatory and punitive damages.

Most harassment complaints are filed at the federal level, although many states have their own version of civil rights laws to allow for a complaint to be filed at the state level. These state laws cover much the same issues as Title VII, providing an additional path for addressing a claim of sexual harassment. Most states specify that complaints must first be addressed before a particular board or court. In 2017, 35 states had civil rights laws prohibiting discrimination.

For example, in South Carolina, the South Carolina Human Affairs Commission (SCHAC) defines *sexual harassment* within the same framework as the federal government does. Under South Carolina law, harassment need not be of a sexual nature. It includes offensive comments in general about either gender. As with federal law, both men and women can harass, and they can both be victims of harassment. In addition, the victim and harasser can be of the same sex. According to the SCHAC, it is not considered harassment if an individual is simply obnoxious. An isolated incident or incidents that are not very serious (*seriousness* is not clearly defined) do not constitute harassment. To be identified as harassment, the behavior must be frequent or severe enough to meet the threshold for a hostile workplace, or the behavior must lead to "an adverse employment decision (such as the victim being fired or demoted)" (South Carolina Human Affairs Commission 2017).

California is one of the few states that have legislated training as it applies to sexual harassment. Assembly Bill No. 1825 (AB 1825) was added to California's Fair Employment and Housing Act (FEHA) in 2004. As of 2006, the law began requiring California businesses with 50 or more employees to train their supervisors on sexual harassment every two years. This bill also requires employers to meet specific standards as applied to sexual harassment training. Employees, whether full-time or part-time, must undergo training; supervisors must undergo training as well.

In New York, the law provides protection for third parties. These third parties may file complaints if they know of any form of sexual harassment. The Civil Rights Bureau of the New York State Office of the Attorney General (OAG) examines behavior and decides whether a pattern exists and if the actions meet the threshold for sexual harassment. The state will initiate an investigation and determine what, if any, further legal action should be pursued.

Court Cases

Many of the women who experience a hostile work environment choose not to take legal action. One reason for this is that fewer than half of the cases that are brought to court result in a finding for the plaintiff. In addition, many women do not feel that they will be taken seriously due to stereotypes, such as the "oversensitive woman." Many times, such attitudes keep workers from trusting their instincts and coming forward. Workplaces continue to be places where women do not always feel safe or comfortable. These environments are ones in which employees do not feel as if they will be taken seriously.

Barnes v. Train (1974) was the first adjudicated sexual harassment case in the United States. This case occurred before the use of the term *sexual harassment*. Just two years later, *Williams v. Saxbe* (1976) established that sexual harassment is a form of sex discrimination. In its decision, the U.S. District Court for the District of Columbia stated that by making sexual advances, a male manager could effectively create a barrier to employment. In 1980, the EEOC finally prohibited sexual harassment by placing it under the Civil Rights Act of 1964 as a form of sexual discrimination. Although other cases established that sexual harassment was a form of discrimination, no case had specifically identified that sexual harassment should be part of Title VII. *Meritor Savings Bank v. Vinson* (1986) became the case where the U.S. Supreme Court identified sexual harassment as a violation of Title VII of the Civil Rights Act of 1964. The Court established standards for determining whether conduct was unlawful and when an employer would be liable.

In *Burlington Industries, Inc. v. Ellerth* (1998), Kimberly Ellerth was subjected to emotional and mental abuse because of the sexual harassment by her immediate supervisor. Ellerth never reported the harassment. The U.S. Supreme Court ruled that even if the harassment was not reported, career workers can still bring sexual harassment charges against employers.

Oncale v. Sundowner Offshore Services (1998) involved a man being harassed while employed on an oil rig. The plaintiff stated that he was constantly subjected to various forms of sexual harassment by his male coworkers. He additionally claimed that his employer knew about the harassment and failed to act. Oncale initially lost his case. However, when the case was appealed to the U.S. Supreme Court, the decision was reversed. The Court established in its decision that Title VII protects victims of discrimination even when the harasser is someone of the same sex. The Court went further and specified that Title VII does not mean that everyone must be civil; colleagues who are simply mean do not meet the threshold for sexual harassment. The federal law does not oversee mocking or ugly comments. Instead, the behavior must be clearly offensive, so as to inherently affect an individual's workplace and that person's ability to do work. The conditions within the workplace must be affected in such a way that there is tangible evidence of a change in the workplace, or it must be shown behavior is severe and pervasive.

In *Burlington Northern & Santa Fe Railway Co. v. White* (2006), the standards against retaliation in a sexual harassment cases were established. Sheila White reported harassment to her supervisor. Soon after making this report, White was demoted to a less desirable job. In addition, she was suspended for 37 days. A federal jury determined that White had not suffered sexual harassment, but that she had been retaliated against for making complaints, and they awarded her damages of $43,000. Burlington Northern appealed, and the case eventually went to the Supreme Court, where the question was whether White had suffered retaliatory discrimination for her complaints for which her employer was liable under Title VII of the Civil Rights Act of 1964. The Supreme Court unanimously agreed that she had.

Reeves v. C.H. Robinson Worldwide, Inc. (2010) was heard before the U.S. Court of Appeals for the Eleventh Circuit. The court ruled that a hostile work environment can be created through the accepted use of sexually explicit language and the presence of pornography. If this behavior is the accepted norm, it could create a hostile work environment. The court made it clear that a hostile workplace may exist even when a specific person is not targeted.

Sexual harassment has also been examined within the education environment. Title IX of the Education Amendments of 1972 addresses sexual harassment within primary, secondary, and higher education. Title IX addresses discrimination based on sex; specifically, individuals cannot be excluded from participation in, denied the benefits of, or subjected to discrimination under any education program or activity that receives federal financial assistance (U.S. Department of Labor n.d.).

Franklin v. Gwinnett County Public Schools

Between 1986 and 1988, Christine Franklin, a high-school student in the Gwinnett County Public School District in Georgia, was sexually harassed and abused by teacher Andrew Hill. The behavior included sexually explicit conversations, inappropriate touching, and sexual intercourse. Franklin claimed that other students, teachers, and administrators were aware of the situation but did nothing to stop it. Though the district finally began an investigation, it discontinued the inquiry after Hill resigned in 1988. Franklin sued for monetary damages under Title IX. A federal district court dismissed her case, but the U.S. Supreme Court reversed the district court's decision and allowed for monetary damages to be awarded under Title IX.

The educational system has been at the center of the sexual harassment issue due to the unique relationships that are created in the educational setting. In *Franklin v. Gwinnett County Public Schools* (1992), the U.S. Supreme Court allowed individuals to collect awards for damages when teachers are found liable for sexually harassing their students. Additional cases have gone to court that directly address sexual harassment within the education system. The Department of Education determined that school districts were responsible for the actions of educators if the educator as the harasser "was aided in carrying out the sexual harassment of students by his or her position of authority with the institution" (U.S. Department of Education 1997). In *Davis v. Monroe County Board of Education* (1996) and *Murrell v. School Dist. No. 1* (1999), schools were ultimately responsible for sexual harassment of students by students. This responsibility is applicable only if the school or employees of the school knew about the harassment and showed a deliberate indifference.

Obstacles

Much of the research on sexual harassment has centered on the "indirect evidence" that clarifies the causes of the harassment. These efforts have included determining the motives of harassers when they are targeting victims. Various studies have examined the authoritarian personality to see if there was a connection between such characteristics and sexual harassment. Some of the studies have found that highly authoritarian personalities are less likely to respect women (Begany and Milburn 2002). Men with authoritarian personalities may also exhibit a penchant for hypermasculine behavior and adhere strictly to old-fashioned culture norms.

Two types of sexism have been identified as mediating factors between authoritarianism and sexual harassment: hostile sexism and benevolent sexism.

These forms of sexism allow for men to rationalize their power over women. Men who display benevolent sexism see themselves as protectors of women; they often prefer women to remain in such traditional gender roles as wife, mother, or homemaker. Hostile sexism supports the idea that men are superior to women and the idea that men should sexually dominate women. This combination of authoritarian personality and hostile sexism results in a higher incidence of sexual harassment.

In their 2002 study, John Begany and Michael Milburn hypothesized that men were likely to sexually harass women who challenge traditional gender roles. The study found that women who possess masculine personality traits are likely to be seen as a threat by men who hold hostile sexist views, and thus the men harass them. In contrast, women who display more feminine characteristics are more likely to be harassed in a quid pro quo environment.

Women display several behaviors to manage sexual harassment or the harasser. Several studies have tried to identify how women strategize in traditionally male occupations to manage the sexual harassment. A 1991 study by Kristen Yount identified three dominant strategies developed by women in a traditionally all-male occupation: "ladies," "flirts," and "tomboys."

- The "ladies" disengaged themselves by keeping away from the male employees. They tended to be older, and they avoided any behavior that could be seen as encouraging the male employees. In addition, they relied on such traditional norms as passivity, nurturing, and subordination.
- Women who used the "flirt" strategy were generally single younger women who pretended to be flattered by the sexual comments. This defense mechanism often worked against the women, as they would be identified as flighty and they lost opportunities to move upward within the organization. They were not taken seriously in their chosen career paths.
- The women who used the "tomboy" defense mechanism attempted to remove themselves from the female stereotype. They were older than the flirts, and they were also generally single. These women would focus on their status within the chosen occupation. Their response to the harassment was often humor, comebacks, sexual talk of their own, or reciprocation. This worked to their disadvantage, as they were labeled as "easy" or "sluts." Rather than minimizing the harassment, this increased the instances of it (Yount 1991).

A number of negative effects can result from sexual harassment. Individuals can suffer psychologically and socially; some may have relationship issues, including issues with their sexual life, and if they are married the result could be divorce. Victims have their sense of trust taken away from them, and they often do not feel safe. Victims can suffer significant stress and all the psychological symptoms that can result from stress. The psychological effects can include depression, anxiety, loss of motivation, panic attacks, sleeplessness, nightmares, and feelings of shame or guilt. The health effects can include head-aches and fatigue. Victims can suffer from stomach problems and weight loss or weight gain. They can also abuse alcohol or drugs as an unhealthy cop-ing mechanism. Victims of sexual harassment can suffer financially, if they are fired or are denied promotions. Victims may hesitate to go in to work; some believe they are being scrutinized, or they may feel as though groups of people are evaluating them. They feel that their worth is being measured in a sexual manner. Like victims of other crimes, victims of harassment can suffer from post-traumatic stress disorder (PTSD), and they may have thoughts of suicide or may even attempt suicide.

Employers are accountable for what their employees do, and this account-ability extends to protecting employees from harassment by the organization's other employees, as well as harassment by anyone who interacts with the employees in the business setting. Although having a formal policy is a good start in addressing harassment, it is not the sole means of preventing sexual harassment. Experts note that training also plays a key part in making sure that employees understand what constitutes sexual harassment. A formal pol-icy must clearly stress the illegality of sexual harassment and should outline the procedures employees must follow in response to such harassment. Also important to address is what individuals should do if they witness harassment; for example, witnesses or victims should be encouraged to report the behav-ior immediately. Most experts note that effective policies should also address retaliation against persons who report harassment. Suggested strategies often include requiring attendance at seminars or workshops on sexual harassment to promote companywide knowledge of the policy. State agencies also offer guidance and prevention policies for employers to use. The federal government provides employers with resources through the EEOC.

In the book *Back Off! How to Confront and Stop Sexual Harassment and Harass-ers*, Martha Langelan (1993) recommends that agencies consider a number of strategies for both individuals and businesses. The first strategy is to call out the behavior. By acknowledging—when the behavior occurs—that the behavior is problematic, both the victim and administrators can take proactive moves to keep the behavior from being repeated. Langelan recommends addressing the harasser bluntly and naming the inappropriate behavior. She advises victims to respond at an appropriate level; that is, if the harassment is physical, then a combined verbal and physical response is needed. Victims must also under-stand that they may file an internal complaint through the appropriate avenues offered by the agency. One additional option is available if the employee—whether victim or perpetrator—is a member of a union. Unions are required to represent members involved in sexual harassment complaints; they are obli-gated to represent both the victim and the perpetrator.

For victims, documentation of all actions is essential to support any claim made by the employee. Experts recommend such measures as keeping a journal and sharing experiences with coworkers or family in order to provide evidence for addressing the action with either management or any other outside agency.

Hasiao Fang and Brian Kleiner (1999) created a list of components for an effective organizational policy statement. The components include (a) stating that sexual harassment will not be tolerated, (b) clearly defining what *harassment* is, (c) offering an effective procedure to find resolution, (d) directing the employee to a neutral party, (e) emphasizing action, (f) mentioning the consequences, and (g) committing to nonretaliation. Fang and Kleiner also state that continual training is necessary to ensure that the policy is understood.

Experts recommend that policies be made clear and easy to understand. Management should establish their commitment by ensuring that the company has made clear what the prohibited behaviors are. The possible sanctions, as well as the reporting procedures, should be included in the company's policy. The supervisors' responsibility should be clearly outlined within the policy (Silva and Kleiner 2001). First-line supervisors should be trained to identify and stop behaviors that are harassing. Finally, those who work on these issues state emphatically that company executives must be supportive and employees must be free to confront harassing behavior.

All countries that prohibit sexual harassment have some form of procedure to guide individuals who wish to file a complaint. These policies are designed to inform employees that the behaviors violate policy but also may be a violation of criminal law. When these policies are violated, the victim has several avenues through which to address the behavior. Many of these procedures separate the internal reporting process from any state or federal actions. Mediation is often the first step taken in trying to resolve issues in the workplace and keep both parties out of court. If these efforts do not prove successful, the victim has a number of legal options. In the United States, the first of these is to file a complaint with the federal government through the EEOC. Filing a claim with a state agency under a state Fair Employment Practices (FEP) statute is another option. Finally, the victim can file a common law tort in a civil court.

When discrimination is a significant factor in the case, the victim is generally entitled to compensation. Depending on the severity of the sexual harassment complaints and the findings of the investigator, remedial actions for sexual harassment may include being rehired, getting back pay, receiving a promotion, or—if the victim missed out on a promotion or a particular assignment—being provided financial compensation. In civil cases, victims may be compensated for any injury to their dignity.

Individuals who do not believe the issue has not been adequately addressed can file a claim with the EEOC under Title VII of the 1964 Civil Rights Act.

The EEOC requires that an individual file a claim within 180 days of the last documented incident of sexual harassment. If a complaint was made to a state or local agency first, then the 180-day filing limit is extended to 300 days. Title VII covers all public and private employers in the United States. As was noted above, only companies with 15 or more employees are covered under the Civil Rights Act. It is important for individuals to look to their state laws and file complaints with their Fair Employment Practices Agencies (FEPAs). Due to the complicated nature of sexual harassment, many states provide guidance that is easily accessible to victims. An example of this is the Tennessee Employment Law Center (TELC), which provides guidance on how to file a claim against an employer.

Individual steps are outlined by these state groups. In Tennessee, the TELC provides guidance on the first step of contacting one's employer. The victim must file a grievance through the employer. Most states require this first step to be attempted prior to any federal action. If the individual decides to file a claim, this must be done within the federally mandated 180 days. If an employee is given a "right-to-sue" letter (see below), a suit must be filed within 90 days.

If the state does not have a FEPA, a complainant will go to the EEOC to file a complaint. The EEOC will conduct its own investigation, in which it will determine whether harassment occurred, whether harassment is provable in court, and whether other employees may also have suffered from sexual harassment. Upon finishing the investigation, the EEOC makes a determination if the complaint is founded or unfounded. If the EEOC finds in the favor of the victim (agrees that the individual was harassed), the EEOC can pursue (settle) the case for the employee (this happens in less than 1 percent of cases filed) or issue the employee a right-to-sue letter so the employee can file a lawsuit independently. If the investigation determines that the alleged sexual harassment did not occur, the individual can appeal the EEOC's finding.

Because the investigation by the EEOC can be a drawn-out process, sometimes taking more than a year, the employee may skip the EEOC investigation. Employees wishing to file a civil suit must first file a claim with their agency. This complaint will result in a right-to-sue letter. For the cases that make it to federal court, the remedies are varied. Among these are reimbursement for attorney's fees, payment of lost or back wages, compensatory damages to address any pain and suffering, or punitive damages designed to punish the employer's action. In addition, the judge may provide injunctive relief (changes in workplace policy and practice to prevent future harassment).

Popular Culture and Sexual Harassment

A number of movies have been made highlighting some of the most significant cases about sexual harassment. *Jenson v. Eveleth Taconite Co* (1997) was made into the 2005 movie *North Country*, starring Charlize Theron as mining employee Lois Jenson. During the 1970s and 1980s, Jenson and other miners were victims of constant harassment by their male coworkers. The coworkers would speak to the women in a sexual and threatening manner. Retaliation was problematic when the women complained, and Jenson had her car tires slashed. The trial lasted for a number of years; Jenson and the other plaintiffs eventually settled with the company for $3.5 million.

The television movie *Hostile Advances: The Kerry Ellison Story* was based on the 1991 case of *Ellison v. Brady*. This case created the "reasonable woman" precedent in sexual harassment law. This law allows for cases to be analyzed from the perspective of the complainant/victim and not the defendant. In evaluating sexual harassment complaints, the "reasonable person" standard is a perception-based standard based on an imaginary, reasonable person. Using this standard in sexual harassment cases, the judge would ask whether a person in the victim's place (a reasonable person) would feel that the behavior met the threshold for sexual harassment. The "reasonable woman" standard is different in that it considers the difference between how a woman might feel and how a man might feel. Men and women have different perceptions of words or acts, and women historically have been more vulnerable to sexually related violence. It is now believed that the proper perspective for evaluating a claim of sexual harassment is that of the reasonable woman.

Sexual harassment has also been the theme of movies made outside of the United States. A movie by Mohamed Diab entitled *678* focused on the plight of three women fighting sexual harassment in Egypt. Released in 2010, the film received a number of international awards. However, it also sparked controversy: Some within Egypt requested that the film be banned for the way it portrayed Egypt, while others feared that the film would incite women to physically attack men.

Worldwide

Definition

Despite the effort to eliminate sexual harassment, it must be noted that no single definition of *sexual harassment* exists. Further, there is no consensus on what constitutes prohibited behavior. When the international statutes are reviewed, any well-defined definition of *sexual harassment* broadly includes violence against women and any discriminatory behavior. All definitions, however, agree that the conduct that occurs is unwelcomed and produces harm.

In 1979, the UN General Assembly adopted the Convention on the Elimination of All Forms of Discrimination against Women, defining *discrimination against women* as "any distinction, exclusion or restriction made on the basis of sex which has the effect or purpose of impairing or nullifying the recognition, enjoyment or exercise by women, irrespective of their marital status, on a basis of equality of men and women, of human rights and fundamental freedoms in the political, economic, social, cultural, civil or any other field" (UN Women 1979). The declaration, which is often described as an international bill of rights for women, defines what constitutes discrimination against women and sets up an agenda for international action to end such discrimination. The United Nations refined the definition of *sexual harassment* to include any unwelcome behavior, such as any physical advances, sexual innuendo or remarks, or sexual demands (whether by words or by actions). In addition, the organization has sought to express how this conduct is not only a problem for women but also a considerable problem for health and safety. In 2008, it defined *sexual harassment* further:

> Sexual harassment is any unwelcome sexual advance, request for sexual favour, verbal or physical conduct or gesture of a sexual nature, or any other behaviour of a sexual nature that might reasonably be expected or be perceived to cause offence or humiliation to another, when such conduct interferes with work, is made a condition of employment or creates an intimidating, hostile or offensive work environment. While typically involving a pattern of behaviour, it can take the form of a single incident. Sexual harassment may occur between persons of the opposite or same sex. Both males and females can be either the victims or the offenders. (UN Women 2008)

The International Labor Organization (ILO) was created in 1919, following World War I (1914–1918), to promote peace through social justice. Following World War II (1939–1945) and the founding of the United Nations in 1945, the ILO became UN's first specialized agency, in 1946. The ILO works with governments, workers, and employers. In 1958, it adopted the Discrimination (Employment and Occupation) Convention (No. C111).

The European Union, the Council of Europe, and the European Commission each agree on the three distinct categories of sexual harassment: physical, verbal, and nonverbal. In its 1991 recommendation, the European Commission also identified the unacceptable behaviors as conduct that is unwanted, improper, or offensive. The commission added that if refusal or acceptance of a behavior influences decisions concerning the victim's employment, it is harassment. Finally, if the conduct has created an intimidating, hostile, or humiliating working environment, it is sexual harassment. These definitions serve as the framework for the international laws that specific what is sexual harassment. The international and regional definitions have been the foundation for international law that prohibits sexual harassment. Both the European Union and the Council of Europe categorize sexual harassment as a crime.

United Kingdom

The United Kingdom replaced the Sex Discrimination Act 1975, the Race Relations Act 1976, and the Disability Discrimination Act 1995 with one act: the Equality Act 2010. The act defines *sexual harassment* clearly. The definition describes conduct that is aimed at an individual because of the person's sex. The act refers to conduct that has the aim of violating a person's dignity.

The Sex Discrimination Act 1975 provided for the creation of the Equal Opportunities Commission (EOC), whose main duties are to address discrimination, to create and protect equal opportunity for the sexes, and to revise the Sex Discrimination Act as needed. The EOC helped individuals bring cases against formal organizations outside of their employment. The EOC is now part of the Equality and Human Rights Commission (EHRC).

The Equality Act 2010 outlines the options for employees if they are harassed. Guidelines suggest that employees first try to work out problems informally. If this does not work, they should first speak to their supervisor or manager, human resources department, or trade union representative. Employees can also make a formal complaint through an employment grievance process. A further step involves taking legal action at an employment tribunal, independent of the government. Such tribunals listen to both sides before making a judgment. Settlement generally involves compensating employees or giving them back their jobs.

As a result of the Equality Act 2010, a number of organizations have attempted to survey the problem of sexual harassment. For example, in 2015 the Royal Navy and Royal Marines surveyed men and women in these services and compared the findings to those of a 2009 survey. The 2015 survey found that one in six (16 percent) "believe there is a problem with sexual harassment in the RN/RM." Female respondents (34 percent) were more likely to believe this than were male respondents (14 percent). However, 98 percent responded that they believe "the RN/RM tries to prevent sexual harassment," though the belief that it is done "to a large/very large extent" decreased significantly among female respondents from 2009 to 2015—only 43 percent stated that they believed this in 2015. Of the respondents, 92 percent said they would attempt to stop sexual harassment happening to someone else (Gov.UK 2015, 4).

Canada

According to Canadian labor standards, "everyone is entitled to protection from harassment while on the job." Employees are required to post their sexual harassment policies. Individuals may file complaints with the Canadian Human Rights Commission, though most are required to go through their provinces. Each province within Canada has its own code and responses to sexual harassment. For example, Article 9.1 of the Ontario Human Rights Code, first enacted in 1962, codifies sexual harassment as a human right, and the Ontario Human Rights Commission (OHRC) outlines the procedures for filing complaints. In 2015, the government of Ontario announced its "Action Plan to Stop Sexual Violence and Harassment," which outlined concrete measures to stop sexual harassment. Bill 132, "Sexual Violence and Harassment Action Play Act (Supporting Survivors and Challenging Sexual Violence and Harassment)" was passed in 2016.

In the United States, there have been several high-profile cases of sexual harassment, such as the spate of lawsuits against Roger Ailes, former head of Fox News. Though Ailes died in 2017, cases against him are being continued. There have been recent allegations against prominent men in Canada as well. For example, sexual harassment charges have been brought against David Peterson, former Ontario premier and chair of the Toronto 2015 Pan Am Games, who was sued for sexual harassment in 2015. The case was still active in 2017. Another case that received a great deal of publicity involved a pastry chef who alleged that she endured sexual comments and inappropriate touching by chefs at Weslodge restaurant, a high-profile Toronto establishment. Her case sparked a 2015 conference called "Kitchen Bitches: Smashing the Patriarchy One Plate at a Time." This case was settled in 2015 through mediation, after the woman filed with the Ontario Human Rights Tribunal (Henry 2015).

Australia

In 1984, the Australian government instituted the Sex Discrimination Act. The definitions used in the act—such as "unwelcome sexual advances" and "circumstances in which a reasonable person would be offended, humiliated, or intimidated"—are similar to those used in other countries. Statistics from a 2012 telephone survey about sexual harassment in Australia show that 33 percent of women and 9 percent of men experienced sexual harassment in their lifetime. A significant number of Australians (13 percent) indicate that they either have personally viewed an incident of sexual harassment or have been told about such an incident. Men make up 4 out of 5 perpetrators of sexual harassment. However, men who are victims are more likely to receive sexually explicit text or emails. The largest number of complaints (88 percent) came from the workplace. Despite these statistics, only one out of five of those who have experienced sexual harassment filed a claim (Australian Human Rights Commission 2012, 4, 12).

India

"Eve Teasing" is the slang term used in India to refer to sexual harassment. In India, as in other countries, any unwelcome sexual gestures or behavior, sexual remarks or physical contact, demands for sexual favors, and verbal or nonverbal conduct that is sexual in nature is seen as sexual harassment. The critical factor for India's definition is that the behavior must be unwelcome. According to the Indian constitution, the fundamental rights of women are impacted by sexual harassment. In 1997, the Supreme Court of India established a specific definition for sexual harassment in the workplace. While providing a clear definition, the Court also provided specific preventive measures and policies for addressing these violations. The judgment is popularly known as the Vishaka Judgement (Gopalakrishnan, Solanki, and Shroff 2013). In April 2013, India enacted its own law on sexual harassment. The Sexual Harassment of Women at Workplace (Prevention, Prohibition and Redressal) Act, 2013 finally addressed everything that the Supreme Court of India desired in the Vishaka Judgement. The act has identified sexual harassment as a violation of the Constitution of India. The act also recognized the right of a woman to be protected against sexual harassment. The amended act introduced changes to the Indian Penal Code. The specifics can be found in the Criminal Law (Amendment) Act, 2013, Section 354. Criminal sanctions can range from one to three years imprisonment and/or a fine. Making sexual harassment a criminal offense requires that all employers must report offenses. The Indian government made sexual harassment an expressed offense, which is punishable by up to three years imprisonment. Statistics on sexual harassment show that 17 percent of women in urban areas have experienced sexual harassment. Furthermore, 95 percent of women believe they are vulnerable in public places. Many women are afraid to go out alone after dark, and 21 percent of the women do not go out at all (Gopalakrishnan, Solanki, and Shroff 2013).

Japan

In Japan, the term for sexual harassment was *seiteki iyagarase*, which translates loosely to "sex trouble" or "sexual unpleasantness." This changed in 1989 as the media in Japan adopted *sekuhara* to describe sexual harassment. *Sekuhara* comes from the English by combining the words sexual (*seku*) and harassment (*hara*). In 1992, a court in Fukuoka ruled in favor of a woman who was the victim of sexual rumors started by a coworker. The court awarded her damages in the first successful sexual harassment lawsuit in Japanese history. Two forms of sexual harassment emerged from this case: *daisho*, which refers to rewards or penalties linked to sexual acts, and *kankyo*, which identifies a hostile environment.

Japan's Constitution includes a prohibition against discrimination based on sex. The Ministry of Health, Labour and Welfare has tried to educate the public through a campaign describing what constitutes sexual harassment. The ministry also provides guidance to business owners in addressing sexual harassment in the workplace. In 2013, the Equal Employment office conducted 9,230 sexual harassment investigations. Of those investigations 56 percent were made by women. The government identified that 5 percent of the sexual harassment consultations/reports were made by men (Japan Gender Equality Bureau Cabinet Office 2013). In Japan's first survey of sexual harassment, released in 2016, 30 percent of the respondents said they had experienced sexual harassment. For full-time workers, the number increased to 35 percent. Of the women surveyed, 24 percent experienced harassment from their bosses. Many reported having been pressured to have sex or having experienced inappropriate touching. A majority of women (63 percent) did not report harassment. Working women in Japan also experience "maternity harassment." Few women in Japan hold senior roles in large companies (McCurry 2016).

Deborah Laufersweiler-Dwyer

Further Reading

American Association of University Women. 2001. "Hostile Hallways: Bullying, Teasing, and Sexual Harassment in School." AAUW Educational Foundation. Accessed July 7, 2017. http://www.aauw.org/files/2013/02/hostile-hallways-bullying-teasing -and-sexual-harassment-in-school.pdf.

American Association of University Women. 2006. "Drawing the Line: Sexual Harassment on Campus." AAUW Educational Foundation. Accessed June 1, 2017. http:// www.aauw.org/files/2013/02/drawing-the-line-sexual-harassment-on-campus.pdf.

Association of American Universities. 2017. "Report on the AAU Campus Climate Survey on Sexual Assault and Sexual Misconduct." Accessed December 18, 2017. https:// www.aau.edu/sites/default/files/AAU-Files/Key-Issues/Campus-Safety/AAU-Cam pus-Climate-Survey-FINAL-10-20-17.pdf.

Australian Human Rights Commission. 2012. "Working Without Fear: Results of the Sexual Harassment National Telephone Survey." Accessed July 8, 2017. https:// www.humanrights.gov.au/sites/default/files/content/sexualharassment/survey/SHSR _2012%20Web%20Version%20Final.pdf.

Avina, Claudia, and William O'Donohue. 2002. "Sexual Harassment and PTSD: Is Sexual Harassment Diagnosable Trauma?" *Journal of Traumatic Stress* 15 (1): 69–75. doi:10.1023/A:1014387429057.

Begany, Joseph J., and Michael Milburn. 2002. "Psychological Predictors of Sexual Harassment: Authoritarianism, Hostile Sexism and Rape Myths." *Psychology of Men & Masculinity* 3 (2): 119–26. http://dx.doi.org/10.1037/1524-9220.3.2.119.

Beiner, Theresa. 2004. *Gender Myths v. Working Realities: Using Social Science to Reformulate Sexual Harassment Law*. New York: New York University Press.

Blomfield, Adrian. 2008. "Sexual Harassment Okay as It Ensures Humans Breed, Russian Judge Rules." *The Telegraph*, July 29. Accessed July 7, 2017. http://www.telegraph .co.uk/news/worldnews/europe/russia/2470310/Sexual-harrassment-okay-as-it-en sures-humans-breed-Russian-judge-rules.html.

Boland, Mary L. 2002. *Sexual Harassment: Your Guide to Legal Action*. Naperville, IL: Sphinx Publishing.

Bowman, Cynthia Grant. 1993. "Street Harassment and the Informal Ghettoization of Women." *Harvard Law Review* 106 (3): 517–80. http://scholarship.law.cornell.edu /facpub/142.

Catalyst Staff. 2015. "Sexual Discrimination and Sexual Harassment." Accessed June 1, 2017. http://www.catalyst.org/knowledge/sex-discrimination-and-sexual-harassment -0#footnote5_4hmwea9.

Chalabi, Mona. 2016. "Sexual Harassment at Work: More than Half of Claims in US Result in No Charge." *The Guardian*, July 22. Accessed July 7, 2017. https://www.theguard ian.com/money/2016/jul/22/sexual-harassment-at-work-roger-ailes-fox-news.

Chamallas, Martha. 2003. *Introduction to Feminist Legal Theory.* New York: Wolters Kluwer Law & Business.

Crouch, Margaret A. 2001. *Thinking about Sexual Harassment: A Guide for the Perplexed.* New York: Oxford University Press.

Duggan, Maeve. 2014. "Online Harassment: Summary of Findings." Pew Research Center. Accessed June 1, 2017. http://www.pewinternet.org/2014/10/22/online-harassment.

Dziech, Billie W., and Linda Weiner. 1990. *The Lecherous Professor: Sexual Harassment on Campus.* 2nd ed. Chicago: University of Illinois Press.

EOC.org.uk. 2010. "Sexual Harassment: What the Law Says." Accessed June 1, 2017. http://www.eoc.org.uk/?s=sexual+harassment.

Fang, Hasiao, and Brian H. Kleiner. 1999. "Examples of Excellent Sexual Harassment Policies," *Equal Opportunities International* 18 (2/3/4): 8–12. Accessed December 17, 2017. 2017. https://doi.org/10.1108/02610159910785718.

Feldblum, Chai R., and Victoria A. Lipnic. 2016. "Select Task Force on the Study of Harassment in the Workplace, Report of Co-Chairs Chai R. Feldblum and Victoria A. Lipnic." Equal Employment Opportunity Commission. Accessed July 7, 2017. https://www.eeoc.gov/eeoc/task_force/harassment/report.cfm.

Fitzgerald, Louise, Suzanne Swan, and Karla Fischer. 1995. "Why Didn't She Just Report Him? The Psychological and Legal Implications of Women's Responses to Sexual Harassment." *Journal of Social Issues* 51:117–38. doi:10.1111/j.1540-4560.1995 .tb01312.x.

Gallop, Jane. 1997. *Feminist Accused of Sexual Harassment.* Durham, NC: Duke University Press.

Gopalakrishnan, Veena, Ajay Singh Solanki, and Vikram Shroff. 2013. "India's New Labor Law—Prevention of Sexual Harassment at the Workplace." *Lexology*, April 30. Accessed June 1, 2017. http://www.lexology.com/library/detail.aspx?g=cb74f2ac -f7c5-44f8-b607-aea2f735cef4.

Gov.UK. 2015. "Royal Navy and Royal Marines Survey." Accessed July 7, 2017. https:// www.gov.uk/government/uploads/system/uploads/attachment_data/file/522906 /20160512_RN_RM_2015_Sexual_Harassment_Report.pdf.

Gov.UK. n.d. "Equality Act 2010: Guidance. Accessed July 7, 2017. https://www.gov .uk/guidance/equality-act-2010-guidance#history.

Gregory, Raymond F. 2003. *Women and Workplace Discrimination: Overcoming Barriers to Gender Equality.* New Brunswick, NJ: Rutgers University Press.

Haidin, Mane. 2002. *The Law of Sexual Harassment: A Critique.* Selinsgrove, PA: Susquehanna University Press.

Henry, Michele. 2015. "Pastry Chef Kate Burnham Settles Sexual Harassment Case Against Weslodge Restaurant." *The Star.com*, September 15. Accessed July 7, 2017. https://www.thestar.com/life/food_wine/2015/09/15/pastry-chef-kate-burnham -settles-sexual-harassment-case-against-weslodge-restaurant.html.

Heyman, Richard. 1994. *Why Didn't You Say That in the First Place?* San Francisco: Jossey-Bass.

Hill, Catherine, and Elena Silva. 2005. "American Association of University Women Educational Foundation Drawing the Line: Sexual Harassment on Campus." Accessed June 1, 2017. http://www.aacc.nche.edu/Advocacy/Pages/ResourcesforTitleIX.aspx.

Huen, Yuki. 2007. "Workplace Sexual Harassment in Japan: A Review of Combating Measures Taken." *Asian Survey* 47 (5): 811–27.

Huffington Post Staff. 2013. "YouGov Poll." Accessed July 7, 2017. http://big.assets .huffingtonpost.com/toplines_harassment_0819202013.pdf.

Jaffe, Eric. 2014. "The New Subtle Sexism toward Women in the Workplace." Fast Company. Accessed June 1, 2017. https://www.fastcompany.com/3031101/the-new -subtle-sexism-toward-women-in-the-workplace.

Japan Gender Equality Bureau Cabinet Office. 2013. "Elimination of All Forms of Violence against Women." *Women and Men in Japan: Chapter 7*. Accessed June 1, 2017. http://www.gender.go.jp/english_contents/pr_act/pub/pamphlet/women-and-men13 /pdf/2-7.pdf.

Langelan, Martha. 1993. *Back Off: How to Confront and Stop Sexual Harassment and Harassers.* New York: Fireside.

Lenhart, Sharyn Ann. 2004. *Clinical Aspects of Sexual Harassment and Gender Discrimination: Psychological Consequences and Treatment Interventions.* New York: Brunner-Routledge.

McCurry, Justin. 2016. "Nearly a Third of Japan's Women 'Sexually Harassed at Work.'" *The Guardian*, March 2. Accessed July 8, 2017. https://www.theguardian.com/world /2016/mar/02/japan-women-sexually-harassed-at-work-report-finds.

Ministry of Law and Justice. 2013. "The Protection of Women Against Sexual Harassment Workplace Bill." Accessed June 1, 2017. http://wcd.nic.in/act/2314.

Morral, Andrew R., et al. 2014. *Sexual Assault and Sexual Harassment in the U.S. Military: Volume 1. Design of the 2014 RAND Military Workplace Study.* Santa Monica, CA: RAND Corporation. https://www.rand.org/pubs/research_reports/RR870z1.html.

National Coalition for Women and Girls in Education. 1997. "Title IX at 25: Report Card on Gender Equity." Washington, DC: National Women's Law Center. http:// www.ncwge.org/PDF/TitleIXat25.pdf.

National Coalition for Women and Girls in Education. 2002. "Title IX at 30: Report Card on Gender Equity." Washington, DC: National Women's Law Center. http:// www.ncwge.org/PDF/TitleIXat30.pdf.

Ontario Human Rights Commission. 2013. "Policy on Preventing Sexual and Gender-Based Harassment." Accessed June 1, 2017. http://www.ohrc.on.ca/en/policy-pre venting-sexual-and-gender-based-harassment-0.

Paludi, Michele, and Carmen Paludi Jr., eds. 2003. *Academic and Workplace Sexual Harassment: A Handbook of Cultural, Social Science, Management, and Legal Perspectives.* Westport, CT: Praeger.

Petrocelli, William, and Barbara Kate Repa. 1999. *Sexual Harassment on the Job: What It Is & How to Stop It.* 4th ed. Berkeley, CA: NOLO Press.

Restaurant Opportunities Centers United. 2014. "The Glass Floor: Sexual Harassment in the Restaurant Industry." Accessed July 7, 2017. http://rocunited.org/wp-content /uploads/2014/10/REPORT_TheGlassFloor_Sexual-Harassment-in-the-Restaurant -Industry.pdf.

Saguy, Abigail. 2003. *What Is Sexual Harassment? From Capitol Hill to the Sorbonne.* Berkeley: University of California Press.

Seklecki, Richard, and Rebecca Paynich. 2007. "A National Survey of Female Police Officers: An Overview of Findings." *Police Practice and Research* 8 (1): 17–30. https:// doi.org/10.1080/15614260701217941.

Shuy, Roger. 2012. *The Language of Sexual Misconduct Cases.* New York: Oxford University Press.

Siegel, Reva B. 2004. "Introduction: A Short History of Sexual Harassment." In *Directions in Sexual Harassment Law*, edited by Catharine MacKinnon and Reva B. Siegel, 1–8. New Haven, CT: Yale University Press.

Silva, Julia, and Brian Kleiner. 2001. "Sexual Harassment in City Government." *Equal Opportunities International* 20 (5/6/7): 82–87. https://doi.org/10.1108/026101501 10786796.

Smithson, Isaiah. 1990. "Investigating Gender, Power, and Pedagogy." In *Gender in the Classroom: Power and Pedagogy*, edited by Isaiah Smithson and Susan Gabriel, 127. Chicago: University of Illinois Press.

South Carolina Human Affairs Commission. 2017. "Sexual Harassment." Accessed June 1, 2017. http://www.schac.sc.gov/ed/Pages/SexualHarassment.aspx.

Stampler, Laura. 2014. "66% of Female Restaurant Workers Report Being Sexually Harassed by Managers." *Time*, October 7. Accessed June 1, 2017. http://time.com /3478041/restaurant-sexual-harassment-survey/.

Stein, Laura W. 1999. *Sexual Harassment in America: A Documentary History.* Westport, CT: Greenwood Press.

Stein, Nan. 2001. "Sexual Harassment Meets Zero Tolerance: Life in K-12 Schools." In *Zero Tolerance: Resisting the Drive for Punishment in Our Schools: A Handbook for Parents, Students, Educators, and Citizens*, edited by William Ayers, Rick Ayers, and Bernardine Dohrn, 143–54. New York: New Press.

Stop Violence Against Women. 2007. "Effects of Sexual Harassment." Last Updated May 9, 2007. Accessed December 18, 2017. http://www.stopvaw.org/effects_of _sexual_harassment.html.

Street, Amy E., et al. 2008. "Sexual Harassment and Assault Experienced by Reservists during Military Service: Prevalence and Health Correlates." *Journal of Rehabilitation Research & Development* 45 (3): 409–19. https://www.ncbi.nlm.nih.gov /pubmed/18629749.

Trotter, Richard, and Susan Zacur. 2012. "Investigating Sexual Harassment Complaints: An Update for Managers and Employers." *SAM Advanced Management Journal* 77 (1): 28–37. Accessed December 18, 2017. http://www.freepatentsonline.com/article /SAM-Advanced-Management-Journal/289834350.html.

UN Women. 1979. "Convention on the Elimination of all Forms of Discrimination Against Women." United Nations Entity for Gender Equality and the Empowerment of Women. Accessed June 1, 2017. http://www.un.org/womenwatch/daw/cedaw.

UN Women. 2008. "Prohibition of Discrimination, Harassment, including Sexual Harassment, and Abuse of Authority." United Nations Entity for Gender Equality and the Empowerment of Women. Accessed July 8, 2017. https://www.un.org/womenwatch /osagi/fpsexualharassment.htm.

U.S. Department of Education. 1997. "Sexual Harassment Guidance 1997." Last updated October 16, 2015. Accessed July 7, 2017. https://www2.ed.gov/about/offices/list /ocr/docs/sexhar01.html.

U.S. Department of Education. n.d. "Sex Discrimination." Accessed June 1, 2017. https:// www2.ed.gov/policy/rights/guid/ocr/sex.html.

U.S. Department of Labor. n.d. "Title IX, Education Amendments of 1972." Accessed June 1, 2017. https://www.dol.gov/oasam/regs/statutes/titleix.htm.

U.S. Equal Employment Opportunity Commission. 2016. "Charges Alleging Sex-Based Harassment (Charges filed with EEOC) FY 2010–FY 2016." Accessed July 7, 2017. https://www.eeoc.gov/eeoc/statistics/enforcement/sexual_harassment_new.cfm.

U.S. Equal Employment Opportunity Commission. 2017a. "EEOC Online Inquiry and Appointment System." Accessed December 7, 2017. https://publicportal.eeoc.gov /portal/Login.aspx?ReturnUrl=%2fPortal%2f.

U.S. Equal Employment Opportunity Commission. 2017b. "Sexual Harassment Charges: EEOC & FEPAs Combined: FY 1997–FY 2011." Accessed June 1, 2017. https://www.eeoc.gov/eeoc/statistics/enforcement/sexual_harassment.cfm.

U.S. Equal Employment Opportunity Commission. n.d. "Facts about Sexual Harassment." Accessed June 1, 2017. https://www.eeoc.gov/eeoc/publications/fs-sex.cfm.

Vassallo, Trae, et al. 2016. "Elephant in the Valley." Accessed July 7, 2017. https://www .elephantinthevalley.com/.

Willis, Amanda M. 2009. "Mutiny in the Nursery: Sexual Harassment Liability for Young Children." Journal of Law and Education 38 (2): 245–76.

Yount, Kristen R. 2007. Understanding and Managing Organizational Behavior. 5th ed. Upper Saddle River, NJ: Prentice Hall.

Yount, Kristen R. 1991. "Ladies, Flirts, and Tomboys: Strategies for Managing Sexual Harassment in an Underground Coal Mine." Journal of Contemporary Ethnography 19 (4): 396–422. doi: 10.1177/089124191019004002.

Zimbroff, Jennifer. 2007. "Cultural Differences in Perceptions of and Responses to Sexual Harassment." Duke Journal of Gender Law & Policy 14 (2): 1311–42.

SEXUAL VICTIMIZATION OF MEN AND BOYS

The victimization of women and girls dominates most discussions on sexual violence; however, millions of male victims around the world experience this type of violence every year. Excluding men and boys from the conversation about sexual violence perpetuates the myths taught through the socialization of gender stereotypes: Society is led to believe that men are not susceptible to sexual violence, but the data from around the world prove otherwise. Men (and boys) experience many forms of sexual violence, including but not limited to rape, multiple perpetrator rape (gang rape), being made to penetrate an abuser, unwanted sexual contact, sexual exploitation, and sexual slavery. Yet, the language used to define *sexual violence* often excludes male experiences, as men experience sexual victimization differently than women. There is undeniable evidence to suggest that men are susceptible to many forms of sexual violence—in times of peace, and perhaps even more in times of war—and it is imperative that the violence perpetrated against men and boys be appropriately acknowledged so that male survivors do not need to continue to suffer in near silence.

Until relatively recently, definitions of *rape* and *sexual violence* excluded the notion that this type of victimization could be perpetrated against men and boys. Prior to 2012 in the United States, for example, the definition of *rape* according to the Federal Bureau of Investigation (FBI) was "the carnal knowledge of a female forcibly and against her will," which not only excluded males as victims but also perpetuated the myth that rape can only occur with force (Federal Bureau of Investigation 2014, 13). In 2013, the FBI changed the definition of rape to be gender-neutral, recognizing that women and men can be both victims and offenders of this crime. The new definition of rape in the United States, which is currently in use, is this: "The penetration, no matter how slight, of the vagina or anus with any body part or object, or oral penetration by a sex organ of another person, without the consent of the victim" (Federal Bureau of Investigation 2014, 13). Not only does this definition appropriately acknowledge that men and women can be both the victim and/or the perpetrator of rape; it also importantly negates the requirement of the act to be forced.

The definition of rape used by the U.S. Bureau of Justice Statistics (BJS) also acknowledges that males and females can be victims, and additionally it clarifies that force can be through both physical tactics and cohesive tactics:

> Forced sexual intercourse including both psychological coercion as well as physical force. Forced sexual intercourse means vaginal, anal or oral penetration by the offender(s). This category also includes incidents where the penetration is from a foreign object such as a bottle. Includes attempted rapes, male as well as female victims, and both heterosexual and same sex rape. Attempted rape includes verbal threats of rape. (Bureau of Justice Statistics 2014)

The World Health Organization (WHO) defines *rape* as "physically forced or otherwise-coerced penetration—even if slight—of the vulva or anus, using a penis, other body parts or an object" (Butchart, García-Moreno, and Mikton 2010, 11).

When discussing sexual victimization, however, it is incorrect to assume that rape is the only (or even the primary) method by which a victim is offended, and this is especially true for men and boys. For men and boys, sexual victimization includes rape, and it also includes (though is not limited to) equally serious offenses, such as being made to penetrate, attempted rape, unwanted sexual contact, sexual slavery/exploitation, sexual harassment, and nonconsensual oral sex. In a discussion of the sexual violence perpetrated against men and boys, it is imperative that the range of sexual offenses that men experience be considered.

Sexual violence is often described as *sexual abuse*, *sexual assault*, and/or *sexual victimization*, and these terms are often used interchangeably. The BJS defines *sexual assault* as follows:

> A wide range of victimizations, separate from rape or attempted rape. These crimes include attacks or attempted attacks generally involving unwanted sexual contact between victim and offender. Sexual assaults may or may not involve force and include such things as grabbing or fondling. Sexual assault also includes verbal threats. (Bureau of Justice Statistics 2014)

In the global context, the WHO defines *sexual violence* as

> any sexual act, attempt to obtain a sexual act, unwanted sexual comments or advances, or acts to traffic, or otherwise directed, against a person's sexuality using coercion, by any person regardless of their relationship to the victim, in any setting, including but not limited to home and work. (Butchart, García-Moreno, and Mikton, 2010, 11)

A sexual crime that disproportionately affects men is the act of being made to penetrate, which according to the Centers for Disease Control and Prevention (CDC) includes

> times when the victim was made to, or there was an attempt to make them, sexually penetrate someone without the victim's consent because the victim was physically forced (such as being pinned or held down, or by the use of violence) or threatened with physical harm, or when the victim was drunk, high, drugged, or passed out and unable to consent. . . . Among men, being made to penetrate someone else could have occurred in multiple ways: being made to penetrate a female's vagina or anus, or another man's anus, using one's own penis; being made to penetrate another man's anus, or a woman's vagina or anus, using one's own mouth; being made to penetrate a man's or woman's mouth using one's own penis. It also includes perpetrators attempting to make male victims penetrate them, though penetration did not happen. (Centers for Disease Control and Prevention 2014, 81)

It is important to consider all forms of sexual violence that men and boys experience and to not assume that there is a hierarchy of offenses or that sexual violence perpetrated against men is somehow a lesser offense than the sexual violence perpetrated against women. All types of sexual violence are serious offenses that have long-term psychological, emotional, and physical consequences for the victim.

The United States

Regardless of the victims' gender, obtaining accurate and reliable statistics on the prevalence of sexual victimization in the United States and globally is challenging. It is widely accepted that sexual violence against men and women is underreported, and due to gender stereotypes and expectations of masculinity the sexual victimization of men and boys is believed to be grossly underreported. However, despite the obstacles to reporting, there are a few population-based studies in the United States and throughout the world that demonstrate the extent to which men and boys are victims of sexual violence. The most reputable population-based study on the sexual victimization of men and boys in the United States is the CDC's National Intimate Partner and Sexual Violence Survey (NISVS). While admittedly imperfect, this study is one of a very small number of studies that attempt to better understand the experience of male victims of sexual violence in the United States.

The NISVS is a telephone survey of English- and Spanish-speaking persons over age 18 in the United States, intended to better understand issues of rape, sexual violence, stalking, and intimate partner violence of men and women. The survey was conducted in 2011, and the final report was produced in 2013. Of the 5,848 men who completed the survey, 1.7 percent reported being raped in their lifetime. The sample surveyed is intended to be representative, which therefore would infer that approximately 2 million, or 1 in 71, men in the United States have been raped in their lifetime. Of those who reported being victims of rape, nearly 45 percent were raped by an acquaintance, and an estimated 29 percent were raped by an intimate partner (Breiding et al. 2014).

The NISVS also collects data on other forms of sexual violence, such as sexual coercion, being made to penetrate, unwanted sexual contact, and non-contact unwanted sexual experiences. Nearly 1 in 4 men (23 percent) surveyed reported being victims of these other forms of sexual violence in their lifetime. Of those men who had experienced sexual violence, 9.5 percent indicated that the perpetrator of the violence was an intimate partner. When the types of sexual violence over a lifetime are reviewed separately, nearly 11 percent of men experienced unwanted sexual contact, 13 percent of men experienced non-contact unwanted sexual experiences, and an estimated 7 percent of men were made to penetrate in their lifetime. Being made to penetrate for a male victim could be compared to the experience of being raped for a female victim. When considering the severity of being made to penetrate, it is worth noting that 1

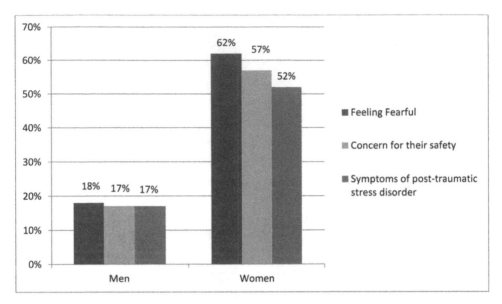

Figure 1. Negative Impacts Commonly Reported by Victims of Intimate Partner Violence*
*Among victims who experienced sexual violence, physical violence, and/or stalking by an intimate partner in their lifetime.
Source: The National Intimate Partner and Sexual Violence Survey (NISVS): 2010–2012 State Report. Atlanta, GA. National Center for Injury Prevention and Control, Centers for Disease Control and Prevention. https://www.cdc.gov/violenceprevention/pdf/NISVS-infographic-2016.pdf.

in 21 men (an estimate of more than than 7.6 million men) have been made to penetrate in their lifetime. Of those men, approximately 55 percent were made to penetrate an intimate partner and approximately 43 percent were made to penetrate an acquaintance.

The analysis of perpetrators of sexual violence against men varied among intimate partners, acquaintances, and strangers. Nearly 70 percent of men who experienced sexual coercion reported an intimate partner as a perpetrator, and about 52 percent of men who experienced unwanted sexual contact reported the perpetrator being an acquaintance. Of the men who experienced noncontact unwanted sexual violence, approximately 40 percent reported the perpetrator being an acquaintance, an estimated 31 percent reported the perpetrator being an intimate partner, and nearly 31 percent reported the perpetrator as being a stranger. Over the 12 months preceding the survey, 5 percent of men reported experiencing sexual violence (other than rape) in the previous year. Of those who experienced sexual violence in the 12 months preceding the survey, 1.7 percent reported being made to penetrate, 1.6 percent experienced unwanted sexual contact, and 2.5 percent reported noncontact unwanted sexual experiences.

Perhaps one of the most misunderstood aspects of sexual violence against men is the gender of the perpetrator. The sexual victimization paradigm places women as the victims of sexual violence and men as the perpetrators. Even in the case of male victimization, it has often been wrongly accepted that men are the likely suspects to perpetrate violence against other men. The NISVS data illustrates a very different image of the perpetrators of sexual violence against men: While the data indicate that male rape victims most often report that the perpetrators are men, the perpetrators of other forms of sexual violence— such as sexual coercion and being made to penetrate—are more often women. Approximately 79 percent of male victims of sexual violence report being victimized by a woman. Male victims of unwanted sexual contact and noncontact unwanted sexual experiences reported the perpetrators being men and women equally.

When considering race, multiracial men reported experiencing the highest prevalence of lifetime sexual violence (39.5 percent), followed by Hispanic men (26.6 percent), American Indian/Alaska Native men (24.5 percent), non-Hispanic black men (24.4 percent), non-Hispanic white men (22.2 percent), and Asian or Pacific Islander men (15.8 percent). Sexual identity also seemed to be a factor influencing prevalence of lifetime sexual violence: 40.2 percent of men who identified as being gay, 47.4 percent of men who identified as bisexual, and 20.8 percent of men who identified as heterosexual reported that they had experienced sexual violence other than rape during their lifetime.

The NISVS data also indicated a high prevalence of rape and sexual violence occurring at younger ages. Nearly 28 percent of men who reported that they experienced a completed rape were first raped before age 10. Of male victims who were made to penetrate a perpetrator, approximately 71 percent were victimized before age 25, nearly 50 percent were victimized between ages 18 and 24, an estimated 21 percent were victimized before age 18, and about 19 percent were victimized between ages 11 and 17. The National Institute of Justice conducted a study on sexual violence among college aged students and found that 6.1 percent of men reported experiencing sexual assault since entering college, which included attempted and completed sexual assault. Of those who experienced sexual assault, 3.4 percent reported incapacitated sexual assault and 0.7 percent experienced physically forced sexual assault (Krebs et al. 2007).

Additional studies that have explored the prevalence of sexual abuse of children indicate results similar to those identified in the NISVS. The CDC found that approximately 3 percent of male high-school students had experienced forced sexual intercourse, and over 5 percent reported being forced to engage in sexual activities other than intercourse (Kann et al. 2015). A population study conducted by John Briere and Diana Elliot found that slightly over 14 percent of men reported childhood sexual abuse. This study also found that nearly 39 percent of men reported at least one female to be the perpetrator of childhood sexual abuse (Briere and Elliot 2003). A 2005 study found that 16 percent of men reported childhood sexual abuse, and 40 percent of those men reported childhood sexual abuse perpetrated by a female (Dube et al. 2005). According to the results of these studies, one in six men in the United States experience sexual victimization before age 18.

Very few cases of male sexual victimization gain national attention in the same way that cases of female sexual victimization do. However, the sexual victimization of boys (compared to the victimization of men) has a greater likelihood of gaining public attention, perhaps because as children, boys are seen as a population that needs protection, whereas men are considered to be capable of protecting themselves. In the past few decades, the sexual abuse of boys by Catholic priests has made international headlines. The first cases of sexual abuse within the Catholic Church became public knowledge in the 1970s and 1980s, but it has taken many years for cases to be tried in court. The sexual abuse perpetrated against children by Catholic priests has been predominately directed toward young boys, and it includes such acts as having genitals fondled, being coerced or forced into receiving and/or performing oral and anal sex, and being forced to participate in masturbation. The John Jay College of Criminal Justice conducted a descriptive study on the nature and scope of sexual abuse of minors by Catholic priests and deacons in the United States from 1950 to 2002 (John Jay College of Criminal Justice Staff 2004). The survey data collected on 10,667 incidents of alleged sexual abuse of children under age 18 found that approximately 81 percent of the victims were male (approximately 19 percent were female, and approximately 1 percent declined to state gender).

The high number of abuses that have been reported indicates that many Catholic priests were responsible for the abuse of hundreds of youth, and there is also evidence of a widespread cover-up within the Church by people in positions of authority who knew of the abuse and allowed it to occur. BishopAccountability.org (2004) estimates that between 5,000 and 10,000 Catholic priests have been accused of sexually abusing children, yet only a small fraction of the priests have been tried, convicted, or sentenced for their crimes.

In the United States alone, over 3,000 civil lawsuits have been filed against the Catholic Church (including 5,679 persons alleging abuse), and although some suits have ended in convictions, most have been settled with monetary payments to the victims. Prior to 2002, the Roman Catholic Church spent over $3 billion to settle sexual abuse cases, and that number continues to rise. Some noteworthy settlements include the Roman Catholic Archdiocese of Boston settling for $85 million with 552 victims in 2003; the Roman Catholic Archdiocese of Portland, Oregon, settling for $75 million with 177 victims in 2007; and the Roman Catholic Archdiocese of Los Angeles settling for $660 million with over 500 victims in 2007. Many of the cases of sexual assault have been tried by secular authorities, and some perpetrators have been convicted and sentenced to prison. Many of the accused priests have been forced to resign from their positions.

Another well-known case of sexual victimization of young boys is that of Penn State University's former football defensive coordinator, Gerald "Jerry" Sandusky, who was found guilty of sexually abusing 10 preteen boys who attended his Second Mile charity over a 15-year period. The first allegations of abuse were reported in 1998, but it wasn't until more recently that he was tried for his crimes, and in 2012 he was sentenced to 30–60 years in prison. Sandusky was convicted of endangering the welfare of children, unlawful contact with minors, involuntary deviate sexual intercourse, indecent assault, and criminal intent to commit indecent assault. Other Penn State administrators were fired or resigned following the allegation, and even those who claim to have reported the suspected abuse to authorities were fired.

Sexual Victimization of Men in the Military

While the above statistics help to illuminate the prevalence of sexual violence among men and boys in the United States, two important populations are often excluded from the population based surveys: men who are members of the military and men who are incarcerated. During the past decade, sexual victimization of both men and women in the United States military has gained the spotlight in contemporary media outlets. Although the media—as is customary when discussing sexual violence—often reports on the sexual victimization of female servicemembers, the U.S. Department of Defense (DoD) estimates that the majority of servicemembers who are sexually victimized are male. Female servicemembers are more likely than their male counterparts to report their assaults, and considering the lower numbers of women in the military, they do have a higher likelihood of experiencing sexual violence compared to men. But, due to there being a much higher number of men than women in the military service, men do, in fact, account for the majority of sexual assault victims.

In an effort to account for sexual violence within the military, the DoD conducts yearly reviews of Restricted and Unrestricted Reports of sexual assault:

- *Restricted reporting* provides the victim with confidential access to medical care and advocacy services, but it does not require official investigations into the allegations, and the victim's command is not notified of the allegation.
- *Unrestricted reporting* allows for victims to access medical care and advocacy services, the incident is referred to the Military Criminal Investigation Organization (MCIO) for full investigation, and the military command is also notified.

The DoD instituted these two forms of reporting with the expectation that doing so would increase the likelihood that victims of sexual violence will report their assault due to increased confidentiality. Additional department policies were instituted to provide more comprehensive support to survivors, improve education about reporting options, and reduce barriers to reporting. The DoD reports on sexual assault, which according to the Uniform Code of Military Justice (UCMJ) includes "rape, sexual assault, nonconsensual sodomy, aggravated sexual contact, abusive sexual contact, and attempts to commit these offenses" (U.S. Department of Defense 2013, 52).

In 2015, the rates of Restricted and Unrestricted Reports from men and women increased, though it is unclear whether the incidence of crime has increased or the crime is being reported at a higher rate now than it was in the past. Male servicemembers accounted for 19 percent of the reports of sexual assault. For the 2015 fiscal year, 1,120 military men submitted Restricted and Unrestricted Reports of sexual assault. The data indicate that men are more likely than women to report sexual assault by multiple perpetrators (49 percent to 35 percent, respectively), that the assault occurred while they were at work (64 percent men, 33 percent women), and that the incident did not involve alcohol (U.S. Department of Defense 2016). Three out of four male victims reported multiple experiences of sexual victimization within the past year, and one-third of male victims indicated experiencing penetrative sexual assault. When victimized by a penetrative sexual assault, men were more likely than women to also report physical injuries or threats of violence accompanying the sexual victimization.

An independent assessment of sexual assault, sexual harassment, and gender discrimination in the military, conducted by the RAND Corporation in 2014, found similar results. The RAND Military Workplace Study (RMWS) surveyed nearly 560,000 active and reserve-component servicemembers over a two-month period. In an effort to capture the prevalence of different forms of sexual assault, the study included three mutually exclusive categories: penetrative assault, nonpenetrative assault, and attempted penetrative assault. The RMWS found that approximately 10,600 men (1 percent) in the service experienced some form of sexual assault during the study period. As was identified in the DoD study, men were more likely than women to be assaulted by multiple perpetrators during a single incident and were more likely to report that the assaults occurred most often during duty hours. Slightly over one-third of men (35 percent) who reported sexual victimization indicated that they experienced penetrative assaults. The RMWS also found that men were more likely than women to experience multiple incidents in the previous year. Of those who were victimized in the past year, 24 percent reported only one sexual assault, 62 percent reported nonpenetrative sexual assault, and 33 percent reported penetrative sexual assault. Junior enlisted members (both male and female) experienced the highest rates of sexual assault. When compared to women,

men were more likely to describe the assault as having been done with the intent to abuse or humiliate, as opposed to the assault being of a sexual nature (Morral et al. 2014).

Sexual Victimization of Incarcerated Men

Including the prevalence of sexual victimization of men in the military is necessary to help illustrate the magnitude of this problem, but the story of men's experiences of sexual violence is not complete without a discussion of the rates of sexual victimization of incarcerated males. Some of the literature suggests that when institutionalized populations are taken into account, males are more likely than women to be victims of sexual violence. However, no peer-reviewed studies or large-scale government studies were found that could concretely prove this statement.

In 2001, Human Rights Watch (HRW) produced a report entitled *No Escape: Male Rape in U.S. Prisons* to document prisoner-on-prisoner sexual assault in U.S. prisons. The lengthy report highlights brutal and widespread sexual victimization among male prisoners. As a purely qualitative study, the HRW report uses personal testimonies to illustrate the sexual assault experiences of male prison inmates. Prisoners discussed a range of abuses, including violent anal rape, gang rape, forced oral sex, and sexual slavery. Mentioned most often was the experience of being forced to perform sexual acts with another prisoner in exchange for protection, food, drugs, or other monetary items—which many referred to as "survival sex." Though most prisoners expressed feelings of guilt, shame, and anger over their engagement in sexual acts, many of the victims explained that they felt they had no other options if they were to survive in prison. To an outsider, such as a guard or a layperson, it may appear that the

---

Survival Sex

"Survival sex" is a term used to describe coerced sexual activity engaged in to gain protection (often from further abuse), food and water, drugs, monetary items, or other basic needs. It can be the means of survival for both men and women when they are homeless or are living in extreme poverty, in prisons, in refugee camps, or in conflict regions. Researchers have also noted that homeless youths, particularly LGBT youth, are especially likely to engage in survival sex. The longer they are homeless, the more likely it is that survival sex will occur, putting them at risk of exposure to sexually transmitted diseases or unplanned pregnancies, as well as increased risk of depression and physical and emotional trauma. As a result of engaging in survival sex, they may also become involved in criminal activity or become addicted to drugs.

sexual acts performed by these prisoners were consensual homosexual acts, but prisoner testimony in the HRW study illustrated that the sexual acts were performed under coercion, force, or the threat of force, and very few victims identified as being homosexual.

The National Inmate Survey (NIS) collects data on the prevalence and incidence of sexual assault in adult prisons and local jail facilities, as reported by inmates. The first NIS (referred to as NIS-1) was conducted in 2007, the second (NIS-2) in 2008–2009, and the third (NIS-3) in 2011–2012. Several reports were prepared based on the data collected by NIS-3, though no newer surveys have been conducted. Unfortunately, very little of the data collected by NIS-3 is reported by gender, so it is difficult to ascertain certain characteristics about the inmates who are victims of sexual violence. The results of the study are separated by sexual identity, mental illness, racial/ethnic demographics, and variations of sexual victimization, though because the results are not separated by gender, only general information about the prevalence of sexual violence perpetrated against incarcerated men can be reported.

The results of NIS-3 indicate that 1.7 percent of male prison inmates and 1.4 percent of male jail inmates experienced inmate-on-inmate sexual victimization. Sexual activity between an inmate and a facility staff member is referred to as "staff sexual misconduct," because in some cases prisoners report that the sexual experience was consensual. Staff sexual misconduct was higher than inmate-on-inmate sexual victimization in both prisons and jails: 2.4 percent of male prison inmates and 1.9 percent of male jail inmates reported having a sexual experience with a staff member. While inmates may report that some sexual activity with a staff member was consensual, it is important to recognize the power difference between an inmate and a facility staff member, which does influence an inmate's ability to fully consent to any sexual activity. While an inmate may report that the sexual activity was consensual, the acts are considered to be victimization due to the power differential between staff and inmate. As a population sample, the results of the NIS-3 suggest that 1,345,200 male prison inmates and 628,600 male jail inmates experienced sexual victimization (either inmate-on-inmate or staff misconduct) during incarceration in the year preceding the study (Beck et al. 2013a).

The NIS-2 (2008–2009) study found slightly higher rates of staff misconduct: 2.9 percent of male prison inmates and 2.1 percent of jail inmates reported engaging in sexual activity with facility staff members. The majority of staff sexual misconduct was perpetrated by female staff members: 69 percent of male prison inmates and 64 percent of male jail inmates who reported staff sexual misconduct indicated the sexual activity to be with female staff. Of those who reported staff sexual misconduct, 16 percent of male prison inmates and 30 percent of male jail inmates reported that the victimization occurred within the first 24 hours after their being admitted to the facility. Of the male inmates who reported inmate-on-inmate sexual victimization, 13 percent of prison inmates and 19 percent of jail inmates reported that the victimization took place within the first 24 hours after their being admitted into the facility (Beck et al. 2010).

The first National Former Prisoner Survey was conducted in 2008. The participants were former state prisoners under active supervision, which provides an important perspective from men who are no longer incarcerated. Of those former male prisoners who participated in the study, 4.2 percent reported inmate-on-inmate sexual victimization, and 5.4 percent reported engaging in sexual acts with a staff member. Just under 5 percent of the men reported having consensual sexual activity with staff, and slightly more than 1 percent reported having nonconsensual sexual activity with staff. The majority of victims (86 percent) who reported staff sexual misconduct reported that they experienced more than one incident, and nearly half (47 percent) reported more than one perpetrator. The majority (79 percent) of former inmates who reported staff sexual misconduct indicated that they engaged in sexual activity only with a female staff member. Of those who engaged in sexual activity only with female staff, approximately 86 percent indicated that at least one incident of sexual activity was consensual, and 42 percent said that at least one incident was nonconsensual. The rates were somewhat reversed for former inmates who reported staff sexual misconduct only with male staff. Approximately 5 percent of the men who reported staff sexual misconduct stated that they engaged in sexual activity only with a male staff member, and of those, 23 percent reported that the sexual activity was nonconsensual, and only 4 percent reported the sexual activity as being consensual. About 7 percent of former inmates reported engaging in sexual activity with both male and female staff members; of those, 3 percent indicated that the sexual activity was consensual and 11 percent said that it was nonconsensual. In this study, men who identified as homosexual (39 percent) or bisexual (34 percent) had higher rates of inmate-on-inmate victimization compared to men who identified as heterosexual (3.5 percent) (Beck and Johnson 2012).

In regard to the sexual victimization of incarcerated youth, the National Survey of Youth in Custody (NSYC-2) was conducted in 2012 and reported in *Sexual Victimization in Juvenile Facilities Reported by Youth, 2012* (Beck et al. 2013b). This study gathered information from state-owned, state-operated, local, and private juvenile facilities in every state in the United States and in the District of Columbia. Of those who participated in the survey, 8.2 percent of male youth in juvenile correctional facilities reported one or more incidents of sexual activity, and 2.2 percent of male youth reported forced sexual activity with another youth. Of the 1,390 (male and female) youth who reported being sexually victimized by a staff member, 89.1 percent were males who reported sexual activity exclusively with female staff, 5.2 percent were males who reported sexual activity with male staff, and 3 percent were males who reported being victimized by both male and female staff. While not separated by gender, black youth reported higher rates of sexual victimization by facility staff (9.6 percent), followed by white youth (6.4 percent) and then Hispanic youth (6.4 percent). Youth who identified as gay, bisexual, lesbian, or other experienced higher rates of youth-on-youth victimization (10.3 percent) compared to heterosexual youth (1.5 percent).

Major Laws

There are no laws in the United States that focus specifically on the rape or sexual victimization of men and boys; however, most state laws pertaining to rape and sexual violence are (at least in theory) gender-neutral, therefore applying to both men and women. Specific laws regarding the sexual victimization of children also apply to both boys and girls. With that said, the application of these laws most often protects women and children, as men are frequently wrongfully viewed as the perpetrators of abuse and are rarely acknowledged as the victims.

In the United States, the federal government does not regulate state laws prohibiting sexual violence; rather, each of the 50 states controls its own policies and sets standards for defining sexual violence and the punishments that follow convictions of sexual violence. Most states include laws defining rape and sexual assault, sexual abuse, sexual battery, or criminal sexual conduct. Consent is a primary issue taken into consideration when rape or any other forms of sexual victimization are being reviewed. Some state legislation does not define *consent* explicitly, but instead indicates that the use of force, or proof that the act was committed "against the will of the other person," is a necessary component for the sexual act to be considered a crime.

While the majority of state laws pertaining to sexual crimes are written so that they are gender-neutral, some continue to use language that supports the sexual violence paradigm that assumes women as victims and men as perpetrators. This creates serious problems for males seeking legal redress for such crimes being committed against them. As is often found around the world, rape is considered to be the most serious form of sexual violence that is punishable by law. Thus, even if the rape laws within a particular state are written using gender-neutral language, rape is not the victimizing experience most widely reported by men—so the men's experience of sexual violence (other than rape) is automatically assumed to be of lesser significance.

Many states do have laws against sexual violence, but none include the act of "being made to penetrate" in their definitions, which again excludes the crime most often experienced by men. Being made to penetrate is experienced by 1 in 21 men, and yet this is not explicitly cited as a sexual crime in any state legislation. Excluding "being made to penetrate" from legal definitions of *sexual violence* could make men feel less comfortable reporting the crime and could potentially make it harder to convict perpetrators of this form of sexual violence.

Perhaps in direct response to reports of high rates of sexual assault within incarcerated populations, in 2003 the U.S. government enacted the Prison Rape Elimination Act (PREA). This was the first law intended to protect prisoners from sexual violence and eliminate sexual violence in prisons. The law asserts that federal, state, and local correctional facilities are to enforce a zero-tolerance policy toward sexual violence in their facilities, which includes inmate-on-inmate and staff-on-inmate misconduct.

U.S. laws are somewhat more inclusive of males when it comes to the sexual abuse of children. Originally passed in 1974, and reauthorized in 2010, the Child Abuse Prevention and Treatment Act (CAPTA, Pub.L. 93-247) is the most comprehensive body of legislation in regards to protecting children. The act is intended to protect children from all forms of abuse, which include physical, psychological, emotional, and sexual harm. As with sexual violence perpetrated against adults, specific laws pertaining to the sexual abuse of children are typically handled by state legislation, though the federal government can oversee child abuse cases if the abuse occurs in more than one state (which applies most often in sexual exploitation or human trafficking). While statutory rape laws also vary by state, for adults to engage in sexual intercourse with persons between the ages of 14 and 18 (whether consensual or nonconsensual) is considered to be statutory rape in most states and is punishable by law. The age at which a person can consent to sexual intercourse does depend on individual state laws, but it is usually between 16 and 18 years of age. Some states also implement a close-in-age exception for those situations where the two people consenting to sexual activity are both within a specified age range; in those states, close-in-age sexual activity would therefore not be considered statutory rape.

Worldwide

In the global context, just as in the United States, the sexual victimization of men and boys is not often spoken about. The World Health Organization (WHO) regularly produces several reports dedicated to violence against women, but violence against men (and in particular, sexual violence against men) seems to be an afterthought. The WHO found that only about 54 percent of the 133 countries it sampled had conducted national prevalence surveys on sexual violence. Of those, it is fair to assume that many focused exclusively on sexual violence against women. Few countries consider male sexual victimization to be a significant issue worthy of expanded research and understanding.

As is to be expected, the prevalence of male sexual violence varies significantly worldwide. The WHO's 2002 World Report on Violence and Health reported on the prevalence of sexual violence in several countries and obtained these results: The prevalence of reported male lifetime sexual violence was 3.6 percent in Namibia, 13.4 percent in Tanzania, 18 percent in Kenya, 9 percent in Zimbabwe, and 20 percent in Peru. In addition, nearly 32 percent of men in the Caribbean (including nine countries), approximately 30 percent in Cameroon, 11 percent in Peru, and 0.2 percent in New Zealand reported their first sexual intercourse as being forced (Jerkes, Purna, and García-Moreno, 2002).

The Centers for Disease Control and Prevention (CDC), reporting on the prevalence of childhood sexual abuse in seven countries between 2007 and 2013, found a relatively high prevalence of sexual violence perpetrated against boys under age 18, though there was a rather wide range: 26 percent of men in Haiti, 17 percent of men in Kenya, 15 percent of men in Malawi, and 10 percent of men in Tanzania and Zimbabwe were victims of sexual violence before age 18 (Sumner et al. 2015).

A report entitled *What About the Boys?*—compiled in 2000 for the WHO—highlights research that has been done on the prevalence of violence against adolescent boys. The literature reviewed indicates a relatively high number of boys exposed to sexual violence. In Canada, one-third of men surveyed reported experiencing lifetime sexual abuse and nearly one in five men reported experiencing sexual violence in childhood or adolescence. Slightly over 7 percent of men surveyed in Sri Lanka reported that an older male coerced them into sex when they were younger, and 7 percent of boys age 16–18 in the Caribbean reported being sexually abused. In Zimbabwe, 30 percent of secondary-school students indicated that they had experienced sexual abuse, and half of those boys said that the perpetrator of their abuse was female. Approximately 31 percent of boys in Kenya reported being pressured into having sexual intercourse (Barker 2000).

In the CDC study mentioned above, Cambodia had the lowest rates of childhood sexual abuse for girls and boys (compared with the other six countries), though nearly 6 percent of boys reported experiencing sexual abuse before age 18. A comprehensive qualitative research project in Cambodia identified a high number of boys who were coerced into sexual activities—most often with male foreigners—in exchange for food, drink, clothing, accommodations, cash, or other bribes. The research used in-person interviews with boys, young men, and staff members at agencies providing services to boys who experienced sexual violence, and the study found that the young boys had experienced what is referred to as "sex tourism" throughout the country. In most accounts, young boys (preteen and teen) were coerced into returning to the home, guesthouse, or hotel of a tourist without prior knowledge of what was to be expected of them. Once at the residence, the boys were often asked to shower and then were persuaded to participate in sexual acts, such as oral sex (receiving and giving), anal sex, and anal penetration with a foreign object. The boys were encouraged to recruit other boys to return to the perpetrator's residence, and sometimes the sexual acts included four to five boys with one abuser. The boys reported feeling pain, embarrassment, guilt, fear, and shame after engaging in these sexual behaviors, but many said that they needed the money or other support (clothing, food, etc.) in order to survive (Hilton 2008). Survival sex is not uncommon for boys who experience poverty or who live on the streets.

Sexual Victimization of Men and Boys in Conflict

While the sexual victimization of men and boys in peacetime has yet to gain widespread international attention, the sexual victimization of men and boys in war and violent conflicts has received greater acknowledgment, especially over the past decade. Sexual violence in conflict, most notably for the intent of instilling fear and control over a population, takes on many forms, including rape (vaginal, anal, and oral), gang rape, sexual torture, mutilation of the genitals, castration, forced sterilization, sexual slavery, forced incest, sexual humiliation, and being forced to rape or sexually victimize others. Sexual violence in conflict is not limited to civilians; it includes violence perpetrated against detainees, prisoners of war, members of armed forced or armed groups, and child soldiers.

Most research on sexual violence in war and violent conflict focuses on the victimization of women and children. The first international case to identify wartime sexual violence of men as a crime was in the International Criminal Tribunal for the former Yugoslavia (ICTY). The ICTY played a historic role in the prosecution of sexual violence in war. As the ICTY transcripts illustrate, men were subjected to horrific forms of sexual violence during the war in the former Yugoslavia. While in detention, some men were forced to perform sexual acts, including oral sex, with other male detainees, often in front of an audience of soldiers, police, or bystanders. Some male detainees were severely sexually assaulted, such as being violently raped with a foreign object or having their genitals mutilated by their captors. The sexual assaults were orchestrated as a form of interrogation (as has been documented as a widely used interrogation technique in other violent conflicts).

The ICTY has completed 75 cases, and of those, nearly one-third have involved sexual violence against civilians (though most were against female civilians). The ICTY was the first international criminal tribunal to prosecute wartime sexual violence. The significance of the ICTY was not only that sexual violence perpetrated against men was acknowledged, but also that the perpetrators of the violence were held accountable. Perhaps even more noteworthy is that the ICTY was the first international body to acknowledge that rape could be prosecuted as a form of torture and that sexual enslavement could be prosecuted as a crime against humanity.

The first international trial to ever convict a person who perpetrated sexual violence against a man was the case against Duško Tadić, a member of the Serbian Democratic Party, who was found guilty in 1997. Among Tadić's crimes was that he, along with other uniformed men, confined thousands of Muslims and Croats in detention camps—and on one occasion forced a male detainee to bite off the testicles of another detainee. For his role in this and other atrocious acts, Tadić was found guilty of inhumane acts (crimes against humanity) and cruel treatment and was sentenced to 20 years in prison. The ICTY prosecuted several other men for the sexual victimization of men during the war in the former Yugoslavia. This historic tribunal set an international example that ending impunity for sexual violence perpetrated during war and conflict was possible, and that those responsible for such crimes could be punished.

Another stark example of the brutal sexual victimization of male detainees during war came in 2004 and 2006 when U.S. soldiers were found to have been using sexual violence against detainees as an interrogation tactic in the Abu Ghraib detention center in Iraq. Photographs and videos of U.S. soldiers sexually abusing detainees were publicized widely throughout the world, which is a painful reminder that these torture and humiliation techniques are being used in modern war. In an effort to obtain information, U.S. soldiers used sexual violence to humiliate and intimidate detainees and cause them severe pain. As Human Rights Watch reported, the classified investigation into the treatment of detainees found several acts of sexual violence perpetrated against the male prisoners, including forcibly arranging detainees in various sexually explicit positions for photographing; forcing groups of male detainees to masturbate while being photographed and videotaped; arranging naked detainees in a pile and then jumping on them; writing "I am a Rapist" [sic] on the leg of a detainee alleged to have forcibly raped a 15-year-old fellow detainee, and then photographing him naked; threatening male detainees with rape; and sodomizing a detainee with a chemical light and perhaps a broom stick (Human Rights Watch 2004, 26). These so-called interrogation techniques—in violation of international and humanitarian law—were apparently widespread in Iraq and quite possibly in Afghanistan and at the detention center at Guantánamo Bay, Cuba.

Sexual violence against men and boys has been reported in several conflicts around the world—the Democratic Republic of the Congo (DRC), Cambodia,

El Salvador, Northern Ireland, South Africa, and Sri Lanka, to name just a few. Over a 10-year period (between 1998 and 2008), sexual violence against men was reported in 25 different conflict-affected countries (Cohen and Nordås, 2014). Examples of the wartime sexual violence perpetrated against men can be found in studies conducted with men from the DRC and Liberia.

The Johns Hopkins–Refugee Law Project conducted a study of 447 male refugees living in a refugee settlement camp in western Uganda, where nearly all the participants were from the DRC (1 percent of participants were from a country other than the DRC). Of the men surveyed, over one in three men (approximately 39 percent) had experienced sexual violence in their lifetime, and approximately 13 percent reported experiencing sexual violence in the 12 months preceding the study (Glass et al. 2013). Another study found that during the civil war in Liberia (1989–2003), approximately 32 percent of male combatants experienced sexual violence and 16 percent were forced to be sexual servants (Johnson et al. 2008). Liberia's civil war was infamously known for its high number of child soldiers—with boys recruited not only as combatants, but also as sexual slaves and prostitutes. The Truth and Reconciliation Commission (2009) reported that boys were raped and were forced to rape others, including members of their own families.

In 2013, a United Nations (UN) Report of the Secretary-General focused on sexual violence in conflict and highlighted the experience of male victims in Afghanistan, Democratic Republic of the Congo, Libya, Mali, Somalia, Sudan, and the Syrian Arab Republic. In Afghanistan, men and boys were reportedly sexually abused by members of the Afghan National Police and the National Directorate of Security while in detention. In this context, sexual abuse was allegedly committed as a means to obtain information during interrogations. In Syria, it was reported that after government soldiers and government-controlled militia members forcefully entered homes and raped women and girls in front of their male family members, they then forced the men to rape their daughters and wives. There were also reports of sexual violence, including rape, against men and boys in Syrian detention centers (United Nations General Assembly Security Council 2013).

Major Laws

The 1998 Rome Statute of the International Criminal Court (ICC) was the first international document to identify rape as a crime against humanity, a war crime, and a potential act of genocide. The ICC uses gender-neutral language to define *rape* and *sexual violence*. Thus, the crime against humanity and war crime of *rape* is defined as follows:

> The perpetrator invaded the body of a person by conduct resulting in penetration, however slight, of any part of the body of the victim or of the perpetrator

with a sexual organ, or of the anal or genital opening of the victim with any object or any other part of the body.

The invasion was committed by force, or by threat of force or coercion, such as that caused by fear of violence, duress, detention, psychological oppression or abuse of power, against such person or another person, or by taking advantage of a coercive environment, or the invasion was committed against a person incapable of giving genuine consent. (International Criminal Court 2010, 5)

The crime against humanity and war crime of *sexual violence* is defined as this:

The perpetrator committed an act of a sexual nature against one or more persons or caused such person or persons to engage in an act of a sexual nature by force, or by threat of force or coercion, such as that caused by fear of violence, duress, detention, psychological oppression or abuse of power, against such person or persons or another person, or by taking advantage of a coercive environment or such person's or persons' incapacity to give genuine consent. (International Criminal Court 2010, 7)

The ICC definitions of *rape* and *sexual violence* are important because they use gender-neutral language that includes men and boys in the discussion about rape and sexual violence. Equally important is that the definitions of *sexual violence* and *rape* also include coercion "against a person incapable of giving genuine consent." The Rome Statute's recognition that rape and sexual violence in conflict can be war crimes and crimes against humanity forces the international community to acknowledge the significance of such crimes, even when they are perpetrated against men and boys. The Rome Statute is considered to lead the international community in understanding how to conceptualize wartime rape and sexual violence.

The UN as well has acknowledged the significance of sexual violence being used as a weapon in war and violent conflicts. In 2000, the UN Security Council adopted Resolution 1325 (UNSCR 1325) on Women, Peace and Security, which was the first UN resolution that, among other issues, specifically highlighted the use of sexual violence as a tactic to intimidate, instill fear, and control populations. However, regarding sexual violence, the resolution focused exclusively on the sexual violence perpetrated against women in war and violent conflicts. The UN has passed subsequent resolutions on women, peace, and security, including Resolution 1820 (passed in 2008), Resolution 1888 (passed in 2009), Resolution 1889 (passed in 2009), and Resolution 1960 (passed in 2010), all of which emphasized the need to prevent conflict-related sexual violence.

The language throughout most of the UN resolutions is predominantly gender-neutral, though the emphasis is often placed on protecting "women and children" from sexual violence. For example, Resolution 1820 reads, "Recalling its condemnation in the strongest terms of all sexual and other forms of violence committed against civilians in armed conflict, in particular women and children" (United Nations Security Council 2008, 2). Men and boys were not specifically identified as a population affected by sexual violence until the passing of Resolution 2106 in 2013. Resolution 2106 states the following:

> Noting with concern that sexual violence in armed conflict and post-conflict situations disproportionately affects women and girls, as well as groups that are particularly vulnerable or may be specifically targeted, while also affecting men and boys and those secondarily traumatized as forced witnesses of sexual violence against family members. (United Nations Security Council 2013, 2)

Subsequent resolutions, however, such as 2122 (passed in 2013) and 2242 (passed in 2015), fail to place any greater emphasis on the need to protect men and boys from wartime sexual violence.

For the most part, international humanitarian and criminal law has adopted gender-neutral language in reference to rape and sexual violence, and the International Criminal Tribunal of the former Yugoslavia demonstrated that sexual violence against men in wartime can be successfully prosecuted. It should be noted that during times of peace, international criminal law does not hold precedence in individual countries. Every country sets its own legislation for sexual violence, and as was found in the United States, many laws regarding sexual violence are implemented most often for the protection of women and children.

The WHO's report entitled "Global Status Report on Violence Prevention 2014" found that of the 133 countries that reported for the study, the majority had laws prohibiting sexual violence, though many countries admit that they are unable to fully implement the laws. For example, of the reporting countries, 99 percent had laws against statutory rape and 98 percent had laws against rape (forced sexual intercourse), but only 64 percent expressed that the laws for either statutory rape or rape were being fully enforced. Similarly, 94 percent of the reporting countries had laws against sexual violence without rape, but only 57 percent reported that the laws were being fully enforced. Further, 88 percent of the reporting countries had laws against noncontact sexual violence, but only 51 percent reported that the laws were being fully enforced (Butchart and Mikton 2014). Although these statistics illustrate that laws against rape and sexual violence do exist in most countries, there is a failure to fully implement the policies. Evidence from around the world also suggests that most domestic laws do not account for the sexual victimization of men.

Every country views rape and sexual violence differently, and few acknowledge male victims explicitly. Rape laws in many countries include only women as potential rape victims, whereas others acknowledge that men can be raped but suggest that only men can be the perpetrators of rape. There are very few instances where rape laws include men and women as both victims and perpetrators. For example, China's criminal law explicitly states that women can be the only victims of rape (which is punishable by death), though in 2015 an amendment was passed for the lesser crime of forcible indecency (punishable by up to five years in jail) to apply to both men and women as victims. In the United Kingdom, the Sexual Offenses Act 2003 acknowledged that men can be victims of rape, though it recognized only men as the perpetrators of rape. The crime of Assault by Penetration, however, applies to both men and women as victims and perpetrators. South Africa's laws prior to 2007 specified that only men could be charged with rape, and only women could be the victims of rape, but the Criminal Law (Sexual Offenses and Related Matters) Amendment Act, passed in 2007, expanded the definition of *rape* to include anal sex, oral sex, and sexual penetration with an inanimate object, and the law recognized men and women to be potential perpetrators and victims of rape.

The age of consent to sexual intercourse also varies by country. Nigeria has the lowest age of consent at 11 years old, and Bahrain and South Korea have the oldest age of consent at 21 years and 20 years, respectively. Most countries have an age of consent between 16 and 18 years, though many countries have what is referred to as a "close-in-age" exception (meaning that if the two individuals participating in sexual intercourse are within a certain age range, their act cannot be punished as statutory rape). In some countries, such as Libya, Pakistan, Sudan, Qatar, and Afghanistan, there is not a specified age of consent, but one must be married to engage in sexual intercourse. Age of legal consent to engage in sexual intercourse allows countries to punish perpetrators of sexual abuse against minors; however, the evidence suggests that the implementation of such laws most often applies to sexual intercourse with under-age females. With that said, most jurisdictions tend to protect the rights of male and female children equally because of their status as minors, though there is not the equal protection of adult male and female victims.

Regarding international laws, it is also important to note that there are currently 72 countries—Ghana, India, Yemen, and Jamaica are just a few—that continue to have laws prohibiting homosexuality. This is important because if the victim and the perpetrator of sexual violence were both male in any of these countries, the sexual violence would not be a crime of violence, but rather a crime of breaking laws prohibiting any homosexual activity. In such countries, both the victim and the perpetrator of sexual violence could be prosecuted, which inevitably would prevent the victim from reporting the crime to police. Europe seems to be the only region where there are no criminal laws prohibiting homosexual activity (although many European countries do have antigay policies that may make it more challenging for male victims to report such crimes).

Obstacles

There are multiple obstacles to reducing the prevalence of the rape and sexual victimization of men and boys in the United States and around the world.

The primary challenges have to do with cultural expectations of men and the masculine identity, a sexual victimization paradigm that assumes women are the only victims, and the exclusion of male experiences in the common terminology used to discuss and define sexual violence.

It is well established that reports of sexual violence and rape are underreported among all groups of people: women, men, boys, and girls. It is also generally acknowledged that men are even less likely than women to report sexual violence and rape, due in part to preconceived ideas about masculinity and what it means to be a man. Throughout the world, there are perceived notions of masculinity that result in unrealistic and unfair expectations of men. Preconceived gender norms and stereotypes are a disservice both to men and to women: Men are considered to be strong, in control of their bodies, dominant, sexually assertive, and even sexually predatory; women are considered to be weak, not in control of their bodies, prudish in their sexual behaviors, and in need of protection (from men and from society). For men to admit that they, too, can be vulnerable is to defy the gender stereotype, and for many male victims this results in feelings of shame, inadequacy, and guilt. With a lack of social service resources and legal frameworks to validate and support a male's experience of sexual violence, men will likely continue to feel like they have nowhere to turn for help when they experience sexual victimization.

The gender norms and stereotypes of masculinity and femininity drive a sexual victimization paradigm that assumes women are the victims and men are the perpetrators. The data clearly demonstrate that men are at risk of being sexually victimized by women, and until this fact is given as much attention as women being victimized by men, males' experiences of rape and sexual violence will continue to be a small addition to the conversation about sexual violence, rather than a central focus to the conversation.

As is illustrated by rape laws around the world, the act of rape is considered to be the harshest of sexual crimes, but rape is not the sexual experience that male victims most often report. Men experience nonconsensual sexual acts differently than women, but the commonly used definitions of *sexual victimization* exclude men's unique experiences. The most notable example is the exclusion of "being made to penetrate" from most definitions of *sexual violence*. To exclude the category of "being made to penetrate" from the conversation about sexual violence results in vast underreporting of the men who are victims of this type of sexually violent crime. The current definition of *rape* (victim penetration) disproportionately affects women, which results in the conversation focusing almost entirely on women's experiences as victims. Yet, the research indicates that men experience being made to penetrate nearly as often as women experience rape. Language can influence one's understanding of an experience, and if boys and men are overwhelmed with information in the media and within common culture about a crime that they have not experienced, they may tend to assume that the victimization they did experience (such as being made to penetrate) is not worthy of being reported as a crime—or even worse, they may assume that it is not considered to be a crime.

Some studies in the United States and elsewhere are beginning to include the act of "being made to penetrate" in the research on sexual violence, so that the experiences of male victims can be properly accounted for. However, being made to penetrate (which disproportionately affects men, though a woman can be forced to penetrate another woman or a man with her fingers, hands, or objects) is most often referred to as "other types of sexual violence," rather than as a stand-alone category like rape. Referring to "being made to penetrate" within the other category insinuates that it is a less serious crime and therefore has less serious consequences. If the definition of *rape* were to include both victim penetration and being made to penetrate, the rape of men would warrant as much attention as the rape of women. For men and boys who experience being made to penetrate, the inclusion of that terminology in population-based surveys will not only validate their experience as victims, but also likely encourage them to report such crimes. Excluding this category results in underreporting and in an under-representation of men's experiences, which directly relates to the supportive and protective services available to men and boys.

When asked in the National Intimate Partner and Sexual Violence Survey (NISVS) about whether they had experienced any form of sexual victimization in the preceding 12 months, 5.5 percent of women and 5.1 percent of men responded affirmatively (Breiding et al. 2014). This is a clear indication that when the proper terminology is used, both men and women are experiencing rather high rates of sexual violence. Yet, throughout the world, there is a gender bias in policing and prosecuting sexually violent crimes. The notion that men are perpetrators and women are victims influences the way police and the courts view sexual violence, and male experiences are not given the attention they deserve. Many countries use gender-neutral language when describing sexual violence, but many still do not. Even in countries where the laws are gender-neutral, there are a multitude of problems in the way the laws are implemented—ways that specifically affect male victims. Reducing the prevalence of rape and sexual victimization of men and boys requires a reframing of the conversation about sexual violence, so that the experiences of men and boys are appropriately included. Once the terminology being used to depict sexual violence includes male experiences, the laws and policies will need to be improved to accurately account for male sexual victimization.

The visibility of male victims of sexual violence has increased over the past decade—particularly in research on wartime sexual violence—but considerable progress is needed to fully represent the male experience. Efforts to better understand and account for male experiences of sexual victimization include using male-inclusive terminology in definitions and descriptions of sexual violence; creating and implementing policies and laws that account for male survivors' experiences; and developing gender-inclusive approaches to prevent and respond to sexual violence so that the vulnerability of both men and women are adequately represented.

Gianina Pellegrini

Further Reading

Barker, Gary. 2000. "What About the Boys? A Literature Review on the Health and Development of Adolescent Boys." World Health Organization. Accessed July 12, 2016. http://apps.who.int/iris/bitstream/10665/66487/1/WHO_FCH_CAH_00.7.pdf.

Beck, Allen J., Marcus Berzofsky, Rachel Caspar, and Christopher Krebs. 2013a. "Sexual Victimization in Prisons and Jails Reported by Inmates, 2011–2012." Washington, DC: Bureau of Justice Statistics, U.S. Department of Justice. Accessed July 23, 2016. https://www.bjs.gov/content/pub/pdf/svpjri1112.pdf.

Beck, Allen J., David Cantor, John Hartge, and Tim Smith. 2013b. "Sexual Victimization in Juvenile Facilities Reported by Youth, 2012." Washington, DC: Bureau of Justice Statistics, U.S. Department of Justice. Accessed July 24, 2016: http://www.bjs.gov/index.cfm?ty=pbdetail&iid=4656.

Beck, Allen J., Paige M. Harrison, Marcus Berzofsky, Rachel Caspar, and Christopher Krebs. 2010. "Sexual Victimization in Prisons and Jails Reported by Inmates, 2008–09." National PREA Resource Center. Accessed July 23, 2016. https://www.prearesourcecenter.org/file/154/sexual-victimization-prisons-and-jails-reported-inmates-2008-09.

Beck, Allen J., and Candace Johnson. 2012. "Sexual Victimization Reported by Former State Prisoners, 2008." National PREA Resource Center. Accessed July 23, 2016. https://www.prearesourcecenter.org/library/research/staff-and-inmate-relations.

BishopAccountability.org. 2004. "Sexual Abuse by U.S. Catholic Clergy: Settlements and Monetary Awards in Civil Suits." Accessed August 1, 2016: http://www.bishop-accountability.org/settlements/.

Breiding, Matthew J., Sharon G. Smith, Kathleen C. Basile, Mikel L. Walters, Jieru Chen, and Melissa T. Merrick 2014. "Prevalence and Characteristics of Sexual Violence, Stalking, and Intimate Partner Violence Victimization: National Intimate Partner and Sexual Violence Survey, United States, 2011." *Morbidity and Mortality Weekly Report* 63 (SS08): 1–18. Atlanta, GA: Centers for Disease Control and Prevention. Accessed July 15, 2016. https://www.cdc.gov/mmwr/preview/mmwrhtml/ss6308a1.htm.

Briere, John, and Diana M. Elliot. 2003. "Prevalence and Psychological Sequelae of Self-Reported Childhood Physical and Sexual Abuse in a General Population Sample of Men and Women." *Child Abuse & Neglect* 27 (10):1205–22. doi:10.1016/j.chiabu.2003.09.008.

Bureau of Justice Statistics. 2014. "Terms and Definitions: Violent Crime." Washington, DC: Office of Justice Programs, U.S. Department of Justice. Accessed July 15, 2016. http://www.bjs.gov/index.cfm?ty=tdtp&tid=31.

Butchart, Alexander, Claudia García-Moreno, and Christopher Mikton. 2010. "Preventing Intimate Partner and Sexual Violence Against Women: Taking Action and Generating Evidence." Violence and Injury Prevention. World Health Organization. Accessed July 18, 2016. http://www.who.int/violence_injury_prevention/violence /activities/intimate/en/index.html.

Butchart, Alexander, and Christopher Mikton. 2014. "Global Status Report on Violence Prevention 2014." Violence and Injury Prevention. World Health Organization. Accessed July 18, 2016. http://www.who.int/violence_injury_prevention /violence/status_report/2014/report/report/en/.

Cohen, Dara Kay, and Ragnhild Nordås. 2014. "Sexual Violence in Armed Conflict: Introducing the SVAC Dataset, 1989–2009." Journal of Peace Research 51(3): 418–428. doi: 10.1177/0022343314523028

Dolan, Chris. 2014. "Into the Mainstream: Addressing Sexual Violence Against Men and Boys in Conflict." Briefing paper prepared for workshop at Overseas Development Institute, London. Accessed August 1, 2016. http://www.refugeelawproject.org /files/briefing_papers/Into_The_Mainstream-Addressing_Sexual_Violence_against _Men_and_Boys_in_Conflict.pdf.

Dube, Shanta R., Robert F. Anda, Charles L. Whitfield, David W. Brown, Vincent J. Felitti, . . . Wayne H. Giles. 2005. "Long-Term Consequences of Childhood Sexual Abuse by Gender of Victim." American Journal of Preventive Medicine 28 (5): 430–38. doi:10.1016/j.amepre.2005.01.015.

Federal Bureau of Investigation. 2014. "Reporting Rape in 2013: Summary Reporting System (SRS) User Manual and Technical Specification." Criminal Justice Information Services (CJIS) Division. Uniform Crime Reporting (UCR) Program. Accessed July 17, 2016: https://ucr.fbi.gov/recent-program-updates/reporting-rape-in-2013 -revised.

Glass, Nancy, Chris Dolan, Andrea Wirtz, Onen Ongwech, Gerald Siranda, Kiemanh Pham, . . . Alexander Vu. 2013. "Identifying Sexual Violence and Access to HIV Service among Male Refugees in Uganda." Refugee Law Project. Accessed August 1, 2016. http://refugeelawproject.org/resources/briefing-notes-and-special-reports /11-sprpts-gender/326-identifying-sexual-violence-and-access-to-hiv-service -among-male-refugees-in-uganda.

Gorris, Ellen, and Anna Philo. 2015. "Invisible Victims? Where Are Male Victims of Conflict-Related Sexual Violence in International Law and Policy?" European Journal of Women's Studies November 22 (4): 412–27. doi:10.1177/1350506815605345.

Graham, Ruth. 2006. "Male Rape and the Careful Construction of the Male Victim." Social and Legal Studies 15 (2): 187–208. doi:10.1177/0964663906063571.

Hilton, Alastair. 2008. "'I Thought It Could Never Happen to Boys.' Sexual Abuse and Exploitation of Boys in Cambodia: An Exploratory Study." Accessed August 5, 2016. http://www.first-step-cambodia.org/fileadmin/user_upload/SPEAKING _TRUTH_edited_final_20-3-08.pdf.

Human Rights Watch. 2001. "No Escape: Male Rape in U.S. Prisons." Accessed July 27, 2016. https://www.hrw.org/reports/2001/prison/report.html.

Human Rights Watch. 2004. "The Road to Abu Ghraib." Accessed August 9, 2016. https://www.hrw.org/report/2004/06/08/road-abu-ghraib.

International Criminal Court. 2002. "Rome Statute of the International Criminal Court." Accessed July 18, 2016. https://www.icc-cpi.int/resource-library/Documents/RS -Eng.pdf.

International Criminal Court. 2010. "Elements of Crime." Accessed July 18, 2016. https://www.icc-cpi.int/resource-library/Documents/ElementsOfCrimesEng.pdf.

Jewkes, Rachel, Sen Purna, and Claudia García-Moreno. 2002. "Sexual Violence." In *World Report on Violence and Health*, edited by E. Krug et al., 147–81. The World Health Organization. Accessed July 10, 2016. http://www.who.int/violence_injury _prevention/violence/world_report/en/.

John Jay College of Criminal Justice Staff. 2004. "The Nature and Scope of Sexual Abuse of Minors by Catholic Priests and Deacons in the United States 1950–2002." Accessed February 20, 2017. http://www.usccb.org/issues-and-action/child-and -youth-protection/upload/The-Nature-and-Scope-of-Sexual-Abuse-of-Minors-by -Catholic-Priests-and-Deacons-in-the-United-States-1950-2002.pdf.

Johnson, Kirsten, Jana Asher, Stephanie Kayden, Amisha Raja, Rajesh Panjabi, Charles Beadling, and Lynn Lawry. 2008. "Association of Combatant Status and Sexual Violence with Health and Mental Health Outcomes in Postconflict Liberia." *Journal of the American Medical Association* 300 (6): 676–90.

Kann, Laura, Tim McManus, William A. Harris, Shari L. Shanklin, Katherine H. Flint, Joseph Hawkins, . . . Stephanie Zaza. 2015. "Youth Risk Behavior Surveillance: United States." *Morbidity and Mortality Weekly Review* 65 (6): 1–174. Atlanta, GA: Centers for Disease Control and Prevention. Accessed August 3, 2016. https:// www.cdc.gov/mmwr/volumes/65/ss/ss6506a1.htm.

Krebs, Christopher P., Christine H. Lindquist, Tara D. Warner, Bonnie S. Fisher, and Sandra L. Martin. 2007. "The Campus Sexual Assault (CSA) Study: Final Report." Washington, DC: National Criminal Justice Reference Service. Accessed August 21, 2016. http://www.ncjrs.gov/pdffiles1/nij/grants/221153.pdf.

Morral, Andrew, R., Kristie L. Gore, Terry L. Schell, Barbara Bicksler, Coreen Farris, Bonnie Ghosh-Dastidar, . . . Kayla M. Williams. 2014. "Sexual Assault and Sexual Harassment in the U.S. Military: Highlights from the 2014 RAND Military Work-place Study." Santa Monica, CA: RAND Corporation. Accessed August 9, 2016. http://www.rand.org/pubs/research_briefs/RB9841.html.

Rape, Abuse & Incest National Network. n.d. "Scope of the Problem: Statistics." Accessed August 14, 2016. https://www.rainn.org/statistics/scope-problem.

Sivakumaran, Sandesh. 2007. "Sexual Violence Against Men in Armed Conflict." *The European Journal of International Law* 18 (2): 253–76. doi:10.1093/ejil/chm013.

Sivakumaran, Sandesh. 2010. "Lost in Translation: UN Responses to Sexual Violence Against Men and Boys in Situations of Armed Conflict." *International Review of the Red Cross* 92 (877): 259–77. doi:10.1017/S1816383110000020.

Stemple, Lara. 2009. "Male Rape and Human Rights." *Hastings Law Journal* 60: 605–47. Accessed July 18, 2016. http://scienceblogs.de/geograffitico/wp-content/blogs.dir/70 /files/2012/07/i-e76e350f9e3d50b6ce07403e0a3d35fe-Stemple_60-HLJ-605.pdf.

Stemple, Lara, and Ilan H. Meyer. 2014. "The Sexual Victimization of Men in America: New Data Challenge Old Assumptions." *American Journal of Public Health* 104 (6): e19–e26. doi: 10.2105/AJPH.2014.301946.

Sumner, Steven A., et al. 2015. "Prevalence of Sexual Violence Against Children and Use of Social Services: Seven Countries, 2007–2013." *Morbidity and Mortality Weekly Report* 64 (21): 565–69. Atlanta, GA: Centers for Disease Control and Prevention. Accessed August 14, 2016. http://www.cdc.gov/mmwr/preview/mmwrhtml/mm6421a1.htm.

Townsend, Catherine, and Alyssa A Rheingold. 2013. "Estimating a Child Sexual Abuse Prevalence Rate for Practitioners: A Review of Child Sexual Abuse Prevalence Studies." Charleston, SC: Darkness to Light. Accessed July 13, 2016. https://www.d2l.org/wp-content/uploads/2017/02/PREVALENCE-RATE-WHITE-PAPER-D2L.pdf.

Truth and Reconciliation Commission. 2009. "Republic of Liberia Truth and Reconciliation Commission. Vol. II: Consolidated Final Report." Accessed August 4, 2016. http://www.pul.org.lr/doc/trc-of-liberia-final-report-volume-ii.pdf.

Turchik, Jessica A., Claire L. Hebenstreit, and Stephanie S. Judson. 2016. "An Examination of the Gender Inclusiveness of Current Theories of Sexual Violence in Adulthood: Recognizing Male Victims, Female Perpetrators, and Same-Sex Violence." *Trauma, Violence, & Abuse* 17 (2): 133–48. doi:10.1177/1524838014566721.

United Nations Department of Peacekeeping Operations. 2009. "Review of the Sexual Violence Elements of The Judgments of the International Criminal Tribunal for the Former Yugoslavia, the International Criminal Tribunal for Rwanda, and the Special Court for Sierra Leone in the Light of Security Council Resolution 1820." Accessed August 3, 2016. http://www.icty.org/x/file/Outreach/sv_files/DPKO_report_sexual_violence.pdf.

United Nations General Assembly Security Council. 2013. "Sexual Violence in Conflict: Report of the Secretary-General. A/67/792–S/2013/149 - 14 Mar 2013." Accessed August 10, 2016. http://www.un.org/sexualviolenceinconflict/key-documents/reports/.

United Nations International Criminal Tribunal for the former Yugoslavia. 2016. "Crimes of Sexual Violence." Accessed August 7, 2016. http://www.icty.org/en/in-focus/crimes-sexual-violence.

United Nations Security Council. 2000. "Resolution 1325." Accessed July 27, 2016. http://www.un.org/en/ga/search/view_doc.asp?symbol=S/RES/1325(2000).

United Nations Security Council. 2008. "Resolution 1820." Accessed July 27, 2016. http://www.un.org/en/peacekeeping/issues/women/wps.shtml.

United Nations Security Council. 2013. "Resolution 2106." Accessed July 27, 2016. http://womenpeacesecurity.org/media/pdf-scr2106.pdf.

U.S. Department of Defense. 2013. "Department of Defense Annual Report on Sexual Assault in the Military, Fiscal Year 2012." Sexual Assault Prevention and Response. Accessed August 8, 2016. http://www.sapr.mil/public/docs/reports/FY12_DoD_SAPRO_Annual_Report_on_Sexual_Assault-VOLUME_ONE.pdf.

U.S. Department of Defense. 2016. "Department of Defense Annual Report on Sexual Assault in the Military, Fiscal Year 2015." Accessed August 8, 2016. http://www.sapr.mil/public/docs/reports/FY15_Annual/FY15_Annual_Report_on_Sexual_Assault_in_the_Military.pdf.

STALKING

Stalking is "a pattern of repeated and unwanted attention, harassment, contact, or any other course of conduct directed at a specific person that would cause a reasonable person to feel fear." According to the Department of Justice, stalking can entail a vast array of behaviors, including

> repeated, unwanted, intrusive, and frightening communications from the perpetrator by phone, mail, and/or email; repeatedly leaving or sending victim unwanted items, presents, or flowers; following or laying [sic] in wait for the victim at places such as home, school, work, or recreation place; making direct or indirect threats to harm the victim, the victim's children, relatives, friends, or pets; damaging or threatening to damage the victim's property; harassing victim through the internet; posting information or spreading rumors about the victim on the internet, in a public place, or by word of mouth; obtaining personal information about the victim by accessing public records, using internet search services, hiring private investigators, going through the victim's garbage, following the victim, contacting the victim's friends, family, work, or neighbors, etc. (U.S. Department of Justice 2016)

Brian H. Spitzberg and William R. Cupach (2007) "identified eight groupings of stalking behaviors including: hyper-intimacy, mediated contacts, interactional contacts, surveillance, invasion, harassment and intimidation, coercion and threat, and aggression." Hyperintimacy behaviors include excessive courtship activities that "may include repeated, unsolicited efforts of communicating with the victim, sending numerous tokens of affection," and giving exaggerated messages of affection.

- Mediated contacts, also referred to as cyberstalking, are all forms of communication efforts using technologies, including Internet, cell phones, e-mail, and social media.
- Interactional contacts represent a range of activities the perpetrator might use to gain physical proximity to the victim. This may include sitting next to the person in public spaces; appearing at the victim's work, school, or community; intruding on the victim's personal space; and making indirect contact through third parties.
- Surveillance tactics are a systematic attempt to gain information about the victim or to determine the location of the victim without the victim's awareness or permission.
- Invasion tactics involve violating the victim's personal and legal boundaries; such activities may include obtaining information about the victim through physical means or electronic means or by breaking into and entering the victim's home, workplace, or car (Spitzberg and Cupach 2007, 70–72).

Harassment and intimidation include a wide variety of aggressive and/or threatening verbal or nonverbal actions designed to annoy, anger, or otherwise strain the victim. Harassing and intimidating behaviors include harming the person's reputation; spreading rumors; harassing the victim's friends, family, or colleagues; and engaging in persistent and unwanted efforts to contact the victim.

Coercion and threat behaviors include implicit or explicit suggestions of potential harm. Threats of violence may be made against the victim, the victim's friends and family, the victim's pet(s), and/or the victim's property. In some cases, the threat is against the stalker himself or herself in the form of threatening suicide. Physical aggression and violence involve the use of vandalism, weapons, physical assault, threat or attempt of sexual assault or rape, and threat or attempt of suicide or homicide.

The United States

According to a study from the Centers for Disease Control and Prevention (CDC), 6.6 million people are stalked every year in the United States (Black et al. 2011, 30). Women are targeted more than men, with 4.3 percent of women and 1.3 percent of men being victims of stalking every year. In addition, 1 in 6 women (16.2 percent) and 1 in 19 men (5.2 percent) experience stalking at some point in their lifetime. In terms of ethnicity, 1 in 5 black, non-Hispanic women experience stalking in their lifetime, and 1 in 6 white, non-Hispanic women, 1 in 7 Hispanic women, 1 in 3 multiracial non-Hispanic, and 1 in 4 American Indian/ Alaska Native women experience stalking in their lifetime. For men, the rates are 1 in 17 black, non-Hispanic men, 1 in 20 white, non-Hispanic men, and 1 in 20 Hispanic men experience stalking in their lifetime (Black et al. 2011, 29–34).

"For both female and male victims, stalking is most often committed by people they know or with whom they have a previous or current relationship. Two-in-three female victims of stalking (66.2 percent) report stalking by a current or former intimate partner and nearly one-in-four (24 percent) report stalking by an acquaintance"—whereas only 1 in 8 female victims (13.2 percent) report stalking by a stranger. Of male stalking victims, 4 in 10 (41.4 percent) report stalking by an intimate partner, and 40 percent report that they had been stalked by an acquaintance; only one-fifth (19 percent) report stalking by a stranger, and 5.3 percent report being stalked by a family member (Black et al. 2011, 32). The average duration of partner stalking is typically two years; most victims of partner stalking have noted that the stalking began while they were in a relationship with the stalker. When the couple separated, the stalking became more intense or frequent.

Research suggests that violence may occur in 27 percent to 48 percent of stalking cases (Meloy 2003, 660). There are a number of high-risk factors for stalking violence, including when a victim and stalker have been involved with each other in an intimate relationship, when there are or have been explicit threats of physical harm, when there is a history of using drugs and/or alcohol, and when a perpetrator does not suffer from psychosis. Younger victims of stalking, victims who have previously had an intimate relationship with their stalker, and victims whose stalker has a history of violent behavior are at a substantially higher risk of physical violence. One study reported that "the majority of men who killed or attempted to kill their expartners had stalked them prior to the violent act" (McFarlane et al. 1999, 311). The stalking behaviors that have the strongest association with intimate partner homicide are following the victim to work/school, destroying the victim's property, and leaving threatening messages.

Cyberstalking includes many types of behaviors, but it generally involves repeated threats and/or harassment through the use of electronics or other technology (phones, Internet, etc.). The behaviors occur more than once or are threatening enough that most people would be concerned or frightened. Common cyberstalking behaviors include monitoring the victim's e-mail, either directly on the victim's computer, or remotely; sending threatening e-mails to the victim and/or the victim's friends, family, or colleagues; using the Internet to access information on the victim through social media outlets or websites; breaking into the victim's social media, e-mail, online banking accounts, or other private Internet accounts; using the victim's e-mail or social media accounts to send false messages to other people or to purchase goods and services; and using car, computer, or phone tracking devices to locate and monitor the victim.

In a notable Supplemental Victimization Survey (SVS) to the National Crime Victimization Survey, 14 in every 1,000 persons in the United States over age 18 experienced stalking victimization. Of those individuals who reported being stalked, 26.1 percent also reported experiencing some form of cyberstalking during the course of the stalking (Baum et al. 2009, 1–5).

According to Leroy McFarlane and Paul Bocij, there are four distinct types of cyberstalkers: the vindictive cyberstalker, the composed cyberstalker, the intimate cyberstalker, and the collective cyberstalker:

- Vindictive cyberstalkers engage in higher rates of threatening and harassing behaviors than do other types of stalkers. They are adept enough with computers and electronics to harass their victims with constant and frequent e-mails and spam, and they may also resort to identity theft.
- Composed cyberstalkers want to annoy and irritate their victims. They want to cause distress, but they do not want to have a relationship with the victim.
- Intimate cyberstalkers aim to establish a relationship with the victim that is based on infatuation and obsessions. In some cases, the intimate cyberstalker is

or has been romantically involved with the victim; in other cases, the intimate cyberstalker is an acquaintance of or a stranger to the victim.

• Collective cyberstalkers engage in stalking activities with two or more victims (McFarlane and Bocij 2003).

Stalking is a significant public health issue. Victims of stalking have higher incidences of health and mental health disorders. Even when stalking experiences are compared to intimate partner violence experiences, stalking contributes uniquely to the development of public health issues. One study examined the severity of partner violence on safety and mental health outcomes among three groups of victims: women who reported moderate physical violence, women who experienced severe physical violence, and women who experienced both severe physical violence and stalking. The study concluded that stalking added to a victim's mental health issues and caused the victim to feel more threatened. More women who had experienced severe physical violence plus stalking met criteria for lifetime and current post-traumatic stress disorder and current anxiety than did women with moderate and/or severe physical violence without stalking experiences. In addition, more women in the severe physical violence plus stalking group reported current depression compared to the moderate physical violence group (Logan et al. 2006, 866–886).

A handful of research studies have examined and documented the protective and preventive coping behaviors that victims of stalking use. According to the Supplemental Victimization Survey (SVS) to the National Crime Victimization Survey, stalking victims report "changing their usual activities, receiving assistance from family, friends, and coworkers, and engaging in protective actions such as purchasing a caller identification system, carrying pepper spray, or changing their personal information" (Baum et al. 2009, 6). Some victims also took more formal actions, such as obtaining judicial restraining orders.

Safety planning is a process that involves, first, the ongoing assessment of risks, resources, and priorities, and then, the creation of strategies to maximize safety and to pursue short- and long-term goals. Establishing a stalking victim's safety requires safety planning that may vary based on the victim's individual needs and the type of stalking experienced. Ideally, professionals in the victim service, mental health, and criminal justice fields who are charged with assisting a stalking victim begin their supportive response with a stalking risk assessment. Risk assessment and safety planning for stalking victims are not one-time events; rather, they are ongoing processes that shift as new information becomes available and as risk and context change.

The Guidelines for Stalking Assessment and Management (SAM) uses three domains of assessment:

• The pattern of stalking behavior—such as communication about the victim, contact with the victim, and escalation of stalking behaviors;

- Risk factors related to the perpetrator—such as anger, obsessional feelings, problems with intimate relationships, and substance abuse; and
- Factors related to the victim's vulnerability—such as inconsistent attitude and behavior toward the perpetrator, inadequate resources, and relationship problems (Kropp et al. 2011, 305–6).

The Stalking Risk Profile (SRP), another approach to assessing stalking risk, includes five elements:

- The examination of the relationship between the victim and the stalker,
- The reasons for the stalker's behavior,
- The stalker's social and psychological realities,
- The victim's social and psychological vulnerabilities, and
- The mental health context and legal environment in which the stalking is occurring (Mullen et al. 2006, 445).

When drafting a safety plan for a stalking victim, safety planners need to consider the above risks and contexts carefully. For example, a person who is stalked by a former intimate partner may need to consider safety in the home. In contrast, a person being stalked by a colleague from work may require support from the shared employer regarding the unsafe working conditions. Furthermore, assessing the victim's potential risk of physical and sexual violence is a critical component of safety planning; it includes understanding the stalker's history of violence, use of weapons, stalking method(s), prior stalking behaviors toward the victim, and history of substance abuse. If a clinical assessment with the stalker is possible, clinicians are recommended to assess the stalker's attachment style, likelihood of ongoing stalking behaviors and plans, employment status, and social isolation, as these are all factors that contribute to an increased risk of physical violence toward the stalking victim (Mullen et al. 2006, 439–450).

According to Emily Spence-Diehl, safety planning with a victim of stalking should focus on the following domains: safety in the home, safety in the car, safety at work, safety in public, and safety on the Internet (Spence-Diehl 1999, 25–30). For example, victims may wish to conduct a safety assessment on their home to ensure that safety locks and other home security devices are in place and working. Safety at home could also include a safety escape plan, including a prepacked bag containing critical documents in case the stalking victim needs to flee the home. Stalking victims may want to check their car for any tampering each time they approach it, vary their driving routes, and drive with all the car doors locked.

To the extent feasible, victims ought to notify colleagues of the stalker's identity so that they may help protect the stalking victim in the workplace. Victims may want to develop a safety plan with personnel at their place of employment that would include not disclosing the victim's personal contact information to

How to Help Victims of Stalking

Because stalking is a crime that is often ongoing and that changes over time, many experts believe that an empowerment approach offers victims the greatest support. An empowerment approach keeps stalking victims' experience at the center of any decision-making. This requires social work practitioners, as well as family and friends, to do the following: (1) Listen carefully to the needs expressed by victims; (2) trust that victims are the most aware of their own needs and should be the lead decision-makers in any safety planning processes; and (3) help stalking victims restore a sense of control and equilibrium by setting appropriate personal boundaries, and by offering support that is consistent and reliable.

visitors and/or callers, relocating the victim's office, ensuring that the parking lot is secure, and providing an escort when the victim leaves the office.

Victims may wish to vary their travel routes, carry restraining order paperwork, and travel with others. Victims need to identify all virtual spaces that include their private information. Stalking victims may want to use Google searches and brainstorm a list of social media sources in order to identify areas where their private information may be available. Victims may want to temporarily shut down their social media accounts or adapt the privacy settings on those accounts. Furthermore, when necessary, victims may need to contact Internet sites to request the removal of their contact information.

Major Laws

The issue of stalking became a national concern in the United States following the murder of the former Beatles musician John Lennon on December 8, 1980. On that date, Mark David Chapman staked out the Manhattan apartment building where Lennon lived with his wife, Yoko Ono, and their son. As Lennon left his home, Chapman asked for and received a signed copy of Lennon's latest album. "Chapman waited until the couple returned to the apartment that night and shot Lennon in the back with a revolver" (Moshtaghian 2016).

In 1982, actress Theresa Saldana was attacked as she was leaving her home in West Hollywood. Saldana was stabbed 10 times with a hunting knife. "She survived only because a passing deliveryman stopped his truck, fought off the assailant and held him until the police arrived" (Grimes 2016). Saldana's attacker was a Scottish man who had entered the United States illegally and had used a private detective to find Saldana. After surviving the attack, Saldana formed Victims for Victims, an organization that assists victims of violent attacks and campaigns for antistalker laws.

In 1989, Robert John Bardo murdered 21-year-old actress Rebecca Schaeffer in her Los Angeles home. Bardo was a mentally unstable man who had been stalking Schaeffer. On the day she was murdered, Schaeffer reportedly agreed to give Bardo an autograph, as he had requested. Then she asked him to leave. Bardo returned later that day and shot and killed Schaeffer. He was arrested the next day. Marcia Clark, who later became famous as a prosecutor in the O. J. Simpson trial, was the Los Angeles County district attorney in charge of the case. The murder of Rebecca Schaeffer, along with the publicity of the John Lennon and Theresa Saldana cases, sparked the momentum to get the first antistalking law passed in California in 1990.

This legislative feat was achieved due to four main motivations: highly publicized cases of celebrity stalking and murder, cases in which an expartner stalked and committed violent acts despite existing restraining orders, exemplary media depictions of stalkers and violence, and the growing recognition that law enforcement and the criminal justice system were void of legislation to protect victims from ongoing stalking behaviors and threats. Over the course of a single year, there were five highly publicized stalking cases in Orange County, California. Four of those cases involved female victims who were stalked and murdered by former intimate partners. Three years later, stalking was criminalized in all states, either by modifications to existing harassment laws or through the creation of new stalking laws. Within the next 10 years, all U.S. states, the U.S. federal government, and the governments of numerous other countries around the world passed similar antistalking legislation.

Concerned that the quick passage of antistalking laws might have created statutes that were flawed in some way and were unenforceable, the U.S. Congress directed the Department of Justice's National Institute of Justice (NIJ) to create a model antistalking code. This effort produced a constitutional and enforceable law that could also be used as a model for states to use in developing and implementing antistalking legislature. The NIJ then commissioned the National Criminal Justice Association (NCJA) to implement the directive. In 1993, the NIJ released the Model Anti-Stalking Code, to be used as a guide for states writing antistalking laws. The model encouraged legislators to create laws that would make stalking a felony offense and also to establish penalties for stalking that would reflect the seriousness of the crime. In addition, antistalking legislation should include the means for criminal justice officials to take action, including legal tools allowing them to arrest, prosecute, and sentence offenders (National Institute of Justice 1996).

In 1994, "in recognition of the severity of crimes associated with domestic violence, dating violence, sexual assault, and stalking, Congress passed VAWA [Violence Against Women Act] as part of the Violence Crime Control and Law Enforcement Act" (Department of Justice 2009). Historically, laws, as well as social norms, have often justified violence against women. "Since the passage of VAWA, there has been a paradigm shift in how the issue of violence against women is addressed nationwide" (Department of Justice 2009). As part of VAWA, the Office on Violence Against Women (OVW) was created to administer financial and technical assistance so that communities could create programs and policies that will help end violence against women, including sexual assault, domestic violence, dating violence, and stalking.

According to the OVW, "VAWA was designed to improve the criminal justice responses" to violence against women and "to increase the availability of services to victims of these crimes." Furthermore, "VAWA requires a coordinated community response" to violence against women "to share information and to use their distinct roles to improve community responses" to domestic violence, dating violence, sexual assault, and stalking (Office on Violence Against Women 2017).

In 1994, VAWA created new procedures to combat stalking and added penalties for perpetrators of the crime. These included cases where an offender violated a protection order or a stalker crossed a state line to injure or harass the victim. To further strengthen protection for victims, the Driver's Privacy Protect Action (also referred to as the DPPA) was passed in 1994. Under the DPPA, which is a federal statute, personal information gathered by state Departments of Motor Vehicles cannot be disclosed without consent. This law was implemented five years after the murder of Rebecca Schaeffer—the murderer had located her address through the state's Department of Motor Vehicles records. In addition, the Interstate Stalking Law was passed to strengthen the 1994 VAWA by outlawing stalking in all federal jurisdictions, adding protections for victims who were being stalked by persons other than intimate partners or spouses. A law was also passed to deal with stalkers pursuing victims across state lines.

With funding from the OVW, the Stalking Resource Center (SRC) was established in July 2000 as part of the National Center for Victims of Crime, a not-for-profit organization. The aim of the SRC is "to raise national awareness of stalking and to encourage the development and implementation of multidisciplinary responses to stalking throughout the country" (Office on Violence Against Women 2010, 20). The SRC "has provided training to tens of thousands of victim service providers and criminal justice practitioners throughout the United States and has fostered innovations in programs for stalking victims and practitioners" (National Center for Victims of Crime 2007, 2). The National Crime Victim Helpline (1-800-FYI-CALL or 1-800-394-3255) is another service, operated by the not-for-profit organization National Victim Center, through which victims can receive "support to help them understand the impact of crime"; access victim compensation, if applicable; "learn about their legal rights and options"; and locate local service providers (National Center for Victims of Crime 2007, 16).

In 2005, Congress reauthorized the Violence Against Women Act (VAWA) through the Violence Against Women and Department of Justice Reauthorization Act (Pub.L. 109-162). The reauthorization enhanced penalties for repeat stalking offenses. The OVW stated this:

> First, Congress amended the interstate stalking provision to prohibit interstate travel with intent to kill, injure, harass or place under surveillance if the travel places such person in reasonable fear of death, serious bodily injury or causes substantial emotional distress. Second, VAWA 2005 increased federal sentencing provisions (1) by providing for a mandatory minimum term of imprisonment of one year for stalking in violation of a court order, and (2) by increasing the maximum term of imprisonment for a defendant who has previously been convicted of a prior stalking offense to twice the term otherwise provided. (Office on Violence Against Women 2007, 3)

In 2013, Congress again reauthorized the Violence Against Women Act (VAWA), updating the federal definition of *stalking* to address the issue of cyberstalking and recognize cyberstalking as a method of stalking that would be punishable by law. Under the VAWA reauthorization, stalking was also added as a category under the U-Visa petition process (see Section 101(a)(15)(U)(iii) of the Immigration and Nationality Act). Finally, the VAWA reauthorization acknowledged January as National Stalking Awareness Month.

Legal definitions of *stalking* vary state by state; typically, however, stalking involves intentional behaviors by an individual toward another person. The attention or actions are unwanted and make the recipient feel threatened or fearful. At the federal level, *stalking* is defined as conduct that includes "the intent to kill, injure, harass, intimidate, or place under surveillance with intent to kill, injure, harass, or intimidate another person" (Stalking Resource Center n.d.). In addition, the federal legislation specifies that the stalking behavior causes, or would be reasonably expected to cause, substantial emotional distress to the victim (U.S. Code, Title 18, Section 2261A). It is notable that the federal definition of *stalking* does not specify whether this conduct is a one-time event or a pattern of behavior over time. Thus, it is incumbent upon states to determine the scope of the behaviors that constitute stalking. To date, all 50 states and the District of Columbia have adopted criminal stalking statues.

At the state level, stalking laws typically include language on "course of conduct" (e.g., the type and number of inappropriate acts needed to establish that stalking is occurring) and language on "intent." In states in which "general intent" is the standard, the person committing the stalking behavior is accountable, even if the stalker did not intend to cause harm. Conversely, in states with "specific intent" stalking laws, the stalker must intend to cause harm or other malicious outcomes. State stalking laws also vary with regard to interpretations of fear, the level of perceived or actual threat, and whether or not the behavior is directed at the victim and/or at friends and colleagues of the victim.

Finally, states vary in the ways that they classify stalking as a crime. Many states consider stalking a felony crime when there is a second offense or an offense involving factors such as possession of a weapon. However, some states classify stalking as a felony on the first offense. Only one state, Maryland, classifies stalking solely as a misdemeanor, a lesser charge than a felony crime.

For many law enforcement agencies, cyberstalking is a particular challenge, especially if those agencies do not have the skills, expertise, or resources to investigate such crimes. As early as 1999, then vice president Al Gore commissioned the U.S. Department of Justice to examine the problem of cyberstalking and to provide recommendations about how to protect people from this crime. In 2002, in an attempt to respond to cyberstalking and other cybercrimes, the Federal Bureau of Investigation (FBI) created a Cyber Division. This includes a number of cyber squads composed of agents with special training in cybercrimes and technology. These agents investigate cyberstalking crimes and can provide support to local and state law enforcement agencies in tracking and prosecuting cases of cyberstalking.

In addition to the criminal justice process, victims in stalking cases may wish to pursue civil action. Unlike criminal law, civil law has a lower standard of burden of proof; liability is established through "preponderance of the evidence" rather than through the criminal standard of "beyond a reasonable doubt." Civil stalking statutes also allow for additional remedies, such as financial remuneration for losses sustained as a result of a stalker's behavior. To date, 13 states have instituted stalking statutes that allow stalking victims to pursue civil suits against stalkers.

Obstacles

Despite the prevalence and risk of harm of stalking, arrest rates, prosecutions, and convictions for stalking in the United States are low. The two largest obstacles to reducing stalking and prosecuting stalkers in the United States are lack of awareness and the role of technology in stalking crimes. Lack of awareness affects everyone: law enforcement, judges, prosecutors, and the public. Law enforcement, judges, and prosecutors are often not fully trained on the issues of stalking and the laws surrounding stalking. The public also faces a lack of awareness and understanding about what constitutes stalking and what laws exist to protect victims. There is an idea that stalkers are solely the crazed fans of celebrities, which can likely be attributed to the way in which stalking gained national attention. There are also dated ideas about sexual violence in the United States, along with an increase in the number of crime television shows that sensationalize such crimes as stalking, intimate partner violence, and rape. In addition to—or perhaps because of—misconceptions about who stalking happens to and when it happens, members of the public are largely unaware of the stalking laws that are in place to protect them. Furthermore, individuals may not seek protection because they are unaware of the services that are available to help them.

Another issue in the reduction of stalking is the rapid advancement of technologies. Cyberstalking is becoming increasingly common. While state laws contain provisions to protect individuals from cyberstalking, with new technologies being invented every day the prosecution of cyberstalking is often difficult. Unfortunately, many states' stalking laws have not kept pace with the use of technology to monitor and terrorize stalking victims; and without such legal support, it can be difficult to seek legal recourse for technology-based stalking.

Worldwide

The prevalence of stalking and the laws and policies aimed at criminalizing stalking differ from country to country. To date, many countries do not have national antistalking legislation. Of the countries that do have such legislation, some incorporate antistalking legislation into laws prohibiting domestic violence while others have extensive stand-alone antistalking legislation.

In 1999, Rosemary Purcell, Michele Pathé, and Paul E. Mullen conducted a stalking prevalence survey using a randomly selected sample of 3,700 adult men and women from the electoral roll in the Australian state of Victoria. The results showed that almost one in four respondents experienced stalking at some time in their life. One in "ten respondents reported a protracted course of stalking involving multiple intrusions that persisted for at least four weeks, with 2.9 percent exposed to this level of stalking in the previous 12 months." The majority of respondents who had reported stalking were female (75 percent), and 43 percent were between age 16 and age 30 when the stalking commenced. The vast majority (84 percent) of the perpetrators were male, and the majority of the victims were stalked by someone they knew (57 percent). For 29 percent of the victims, the stalking included explicit threats, and for 16 percent of victims the threats were made to harm such third parties as the victim's family or friends. Physical assaults were reported by 18 percent of the victims (Purcell, Pathé, and Mullen 2002, 114–120).

Major Laws

Antistalking legislation exists in every state and territory of Australia through the Crimes (Domestic and Personal Violence) Act of 2007 in New South Wales,

Section 21A of the Crimes Act of 1958 in Victoria, section 359 of the Criminal Code Act of 1899 in Queensland, section 19AA of the Criminal Law Consolidation Act of 1935 in South Australia, section 35 of the Crimes Act of 1900 in the Australian Capital Territory, section 338D of the Criminal Code Act Compilation Act of 1913 in Western Australia, section 192 of the Criminal Code Act of 1924 in Tasmania, and section 7 of the Domestic and Family Violence Act in the Northern Territory.

In Austria, the Anti-Stalking Act was enacted on July 1, 2006. The act made *beharrliche Verfolgung* ("persistent pursuit") a criminal offense that could be prosecuted under criminal law, and it made it possible for victims to apply for an interim injunction for protection against invasion of privacy. The introduction of section 107a StGB (Criminal Code), entitled "Persistent persecution," made stalkers liable for criminal charges if the stalking behavior interferes with the victim's life to an unacceptable degree. The act describes stalking behavioral patterns as trying to be close to the victim; contacting the victim by telecommunication, or other types of communications, such as e-mails, text messages, or letter; and attempting communication through third parties. According to the law, stalking also includes such actions by the perpetrator as ordering "goods or services for the victim by using the latter's personal data" or "inducing third parties to contact the victim by using the latter's personal data" (Council of Europe 2014, 17). The punishment for this offense can be imprisonment of up to one year.

In addition, "Persistent Persecution constitutes a criminal offense rendering the accused liable to public prosecution, which means that if the police learn about a stalking case then they are required to intervene." Finally, irrespective of the criminal complaint, stalking "victims can also apply for an interim injunction for the 'Protection against invasion of privacy.' In such cases, the court can impose the following prohibitions: prohibition of personal contact and persecution; of contacting via letters, phone calls or other means; to stay in precisely identified places; to disclose and/or circulate personal data and photographs of the endangered person; to order goods or services with third parties by using personal data of the endangered person; or to induce third parties to contact the endangered person." The protective injunctions "are issued for a maximum of one year but can be extended if the perpetrator fails to comply with the requirements" (Council of Europe 2014, 17–18).

The Bahamas passed the Domestic Violence (Protection Orders) Act 1997, which amended the Sexual Offenses and Domestic Violence Act to define, outlaw, and provide protection orders against stalking in the context of a domestic or dependent relationship. The law defines *stalking* as following a person persistently, watching a person at home or at work, and making continual unsolicited attempts to communicate with that individual or a member of that person's household. Under this act, orders of protection for stalking victims may include requirements that the respondent stay away from the victim's home, place of work, or other specified locality. The victim's children and/or other household members may also be named as protected parties under the order of protection.

Belgium included specific antistalking laws in Article 442bis of the Penal Code in 1998. The Belgian penal code made stalking illegal and called for a sentence of up to two years imprisonment and/or a fine in cases where the perpetrator should have known that his or her behavior would make the victim uncomfortable. In 2007, a cyberstalking provision was added to Article 145 §3bis of the Telecommunications Act of 2005; this provision extends the same punishments to cyberstalking as are mandated for non-cyberstalking.

Canada's criminal code (R.S.C., 1985, c. C-46, s. 264) prohibits criminal harassment. The criminal code defines *criminal harassment* as "repeatedly following the victim from place to place, repeatedly communicating with the victim, besetting or watching the place where the victim is located, or engaging in threatening conduct directed at the victim or to a member of the victim's family." A national victimization survey conducted in Canada in 2011 found that the five most common violence offenses committed against women were simple assault (49 percent), uttering threats (13 percent), serious assault (10 percent), sexual assault level I (7 percent), and criminal harassment/stalking (7 percent). Furthermore, women were three times more likely than men to be victims of criminal harassment (stalking). Among female youth, physical assault accounted for 47 percent of all violent crimes experienced, followed by sexual offenses (29 percent), uttering threats (11 percent), and criminal harassment/stalking (5 percent). Among female victims of criminal harassment/stalking, 85 percent of the perpetrators were men, and these men were most often (58 percent) current or former intimate partners of the female victims (Sinha 2013).

In the Czech Republic, stalking was enacted as a new criminal offense constituted in 2010 by Act No. 40/2009 Coll., Penal Code, provision §354th. The Czech criminal code defines *stalking* as long-term persecution characterized by threats of harm to the victim or a loved one, repeated unwanted attempts to contact the victim directly or via written or electronic forms of communication in ways that limit the victim's usual way of living. In addition, the code includes the misuse of a person's personal data in ways that cause that person to fear for personal safety.

In 2013, the European Parliament approved a bill allowing stalking victims, as well as victims of other types of sexual violence, to receive the same protections if they move to another EU country. This bill made it easier for victims to move freely throughout the European Union without fear of losing services and protections.

Denmark has laws against *forfølgelse* (pursuit), or stalking, in Section 265 of its criminal code. Section 265 punishes stalking with a fine or imprisonment for up to two years. In addition, the police have discretionary power to give a warning or a restraining order to an individual engaging in stalking behaviors. The law against stalking has been included in the criminal code since 1930 and was amended in 1965 and 2004.

In Germany, § 238 of the penal code defines *stalking* as trying to get close to another individual without the person's consent, including contacting the person via phone or other person; using that person's personal data; and threatening a person's safety. The penal code specifies that severe harassment can be punished with a prison sentence of up to three years and/or by a fine.

A large-scale victim survey among a representative German quota sample found that 15.2 percent of the respondents were victims of stalking, with nearly two-thirds of the victims being female respondents. However, unlike the prevalence surveys in the United States and England/Wales, the German survey found that respondents age 16 to 20 reported significantly lower victimization rates than did older respondents. The victim's offenders were most often expartners and former dates (39.6 percent), friends and neighbors (22.3 percent), and strangers (14.2 percent). On average, the stalking persisted for approximately four to six months (Hellmann and Kliem 2015, 700–718).

The Domestic Violence Act of 1996 in Guyana addresses harassment of women in the context of a domestic relationship. According to the act, harassment can include fear of physical or psychological violence, as well as threats of physical violence; damage to an individual's property that was done maliciously; persistent following of the person; hiding of property owned by the person; watching a person's location; making persistent, unwelcome attempts at communication; or using abusive language and/or behaviors that cause annoyance or result in ill-treatment of that person.

Stalking historically had been addressed under a range of different laws in India—until 2013, when the Indian Penal Code was amended specifically to outlaw stalking (S. 354D). The antistalking law was included under "Assault or Criminal Force to Woman with Intent to Outrage Her Modesty" and therefore applies only to men stalking women. The provision does include cyberstalking as a crime.

Ireland created antistalking legislation in 1997 under the Non-Fatal Offences Against Person Act. The act does not specifically refer to stalking, but it uses the term *harassment*, defined as "intentionally or recklessly, seriously interfering with the other's peace and privacy or causing alarm, distress, or harm to the other." The act states that "any person who without lawful authority . . . including by use of the telephone, harasses another by persistently following, watching, pestering, besetting or communicating with him or her shall be guilty of the offence" (Office of the Attorney General 1997). For prosecution, however, there must be two or more acts of the harassing behavior. The law allows a judge to make an order prohibiting the offender from contacting the victim.

The Harassment, Harmful Communications and Related Offences Bill 2017 criminalizes online stalking and harassment, including "revenge porn." Revenge porn is better described as the nonconsensual distribution of sexually explicit photos or videos. Victims of this offense have not given their consent to have such materials distributed, and it is often done without their knowledge. Offenders convicted under this act may receive sentences of up to seven years (D'Arcy 2017).

In 2001, Israel enacted the Law for the Prevention of Stalking (5762-2001). The law allows courts to issue protective orders against stalkers. Though the orders are issued for a maximum of only six months, they can be extended for another six months, and even longer, in special circumstances. The antistalking law is intended to protect individuals from threats and bodily harm.

Article 612 of the Italian Penal Code identifies stalking as a punishable offense. In cases where the victim is a pregnant woman, an expartner of the stalker, or a minor, the perpetrator can receive a prison sentence of up to six years. In other instances, the sentence is six months to four years in prison. According to the penal code, the offense has to occur persistently, and the victim must be in fear for herself or himself or others. The law explains that stalking includes an individual repeatedly harassing or threatening a person in order to cause a persistent state of anxiety or fear or to produce a justified fear for personal safety to the victim. Prosecution can take place after a victim complains; however, if the perpetrator has been previously warned by a law enforcement office, then prosecution begins under the authority of the law.

Rates of stalking have been growing faster in Japan than in any other country in the world. Stalking first received national attention in Japan in 1999 after a 21-year-old female student complained to the police that her former boyfriend was slandering and harassing her and threatening violence. The woman was later stabbed to death, and the public outcry led the Japanese government to enact antistalking laws, which prohibited stalking in the context of an intimate relationship. In 2011, a high-profile stalking case spread throughout Japan after Gota Tsutsui assaulted his former girlfriend, broke into her family's home, and stabbed her mother and grandmother to death. The investigation into the murder revealed that the father of the young woman had talked with the police on several occasions, but he was told that the police could not arrest the man. The woman first reported to the police that she had been injured four days prior to the murder, and the police issued three warnings to Tsutsui.

In 2013, Japan revised the country's antistalking laws to include e-mails and to allow the local public safety commission in the offender's residential area to warn offenders. Previously, Japan's antistalking laws banned repeated phone calls and faxing, but not e-mailing. "The revision obligates the local police to give notice to the requestor of the reasons for any denial of a request for a warning to an aggressor." The revision of the antistalking law went into effect on October 3, 2013 (Umeda 2013).

Malta addresses harassment in Article 251A of its Criminal Code, which states that "a person who pursues a course of conduct which amounts to harassment of another person, and which he knows or ought to know amounts to harassment of such other person, shall be guilty of an offence under this article." Malta also allows judges to create protection orders through both the civil and criminal laws. The law states that when a person is charged with a harassment offense the court may, in order to provide safety to the victim, issue a protection order against the perpetrator. This protection order permits the court to impose any restrictions on the accused that it deems necessary. The order can remain active for up to three years, depending upon the court's decision. If a protection of order is breached, a fine and/or a maximum imprisonment of six months can be given.

The Dutch Anti-Stalking Law, included in Article 258b of the Code of Criminal Law, states that "an individual who unlawfully, repeatedly, and willfully intrudes upon a person's privacy with the intent to force that person to do something, to refrain from doing something, or to instigate fear in that person will be punished as guilty of *belaging*. An individual found guilty is subject to a prison term with a maximum of three years or a fine of the fourth category. Prosecution can only occur at the request of the person against whom the crime was committed." *Belaging* is the name given to stalking in the Dutch law, which was enacted in 2000. A restraining order can be imposed and the court can mandate that the offender pay damage compensation or be taken into custody if the restraining order is violated, however, it is the victim's responsibility to go to civil court in order to institute these measures.

A study conducted in July 2007, of 1,027 persons of Dutch nationality, found that 16.5 percent of the respondents "reported a lifetime rate of stalking victimization and 3.9 percent reported experiencing stalking within the past 12 months. More than one in five women and almost one in seven men reported having been" stalked in their lifetime (Van Der Aa and Kunst 2009, 43).

The New Zealand Harassment Act 1997 defines *harassment* as one person engaging in a pattern of behavior that includes at least two separate occasions within a 12-month period. The harassing behaviors can include watching a person's place of residence or employment and following a person, whether there is physical contact or not. Stalking can also include going to the victim's home or interfering with their property, as well as sending or giving offensive material to the victim, and making him or her feel threatened.

The law clarifies that a person commits criminal harassment against another person in any case in which the offender intends to cause the victim to fear for his/her safety or the safety of his/her family and in which the offender knows that the harassment is likely to cause the victim to fear. An individual committing criminal harassment can face imprisonment for up to two years. The legislation also allows for any person who is being or has been harassed by another person to apply to the court for a restraining order.

In the Philippines, Penal Code Sec. 4 Articles 282-A–282-C is known as the Anti-Stalking Act of 2003. The act defines *unconsented contact* as "any contact with another individual that is initiated or continued in malicious and willful disregard of that individual's expressed desire that the conduct be avoided or discontinued." The act describes *stalking* as behavior that intentionally makes a person fear for his or her safety. Stalking behaviors include following the individual, approaching him or her in public or private place, watching the individual, sending him or her messages, and damaging the person's belongings or property. The act of stalking is punishable by imprisonment and/or a fine.

Poland introduced an antistalking law in 2001 in Penal Code Article 190a §§ 1, 2, 3 and 4. The code applies to anyone who threatens an individual or his or her family and makes that person fearful. The punishment for the offender is a fine and/or imprisonment of up to two years. The same punishment applies for an individual who pretends to be another person or uses the image of someone else or other personal data to cause harm, either physical or material.

In 2010, the Scottish Parliament added stalking to the Criminal Justice and Licensing (Scotland) Act. "The Scottish Crime and Justice Survey (SCJS) is a large-scale social survey which asks people about their experiences and perceptions of crime" (Murray 2016, 7). The results of the 2014–2015 survey found that 6.4 percent of respondents "experienced at least one type of stalking and harassment in the last 12 months." Among the respondents who had experienced stalking and harassment, "45.0% had received unwanted emails and texts, 32.7 % received silent, threatening or unwanted phone calls, and 21.9% were subject to obscene or threatening online contact." There was no statistically significant difference between the stalking experiences of males and those of females; they experienced stalking at rates of 6.0 percent and 6.8 percent, respectively. More than half (54.9 percent) of those who experienced stalking "in the last 12 months knew the offender in some way," with 15 percent reporting that the offender was their partner. Just under a third (30.8 percent) described the offender as a stranger (Murray 2016, 5).

The SCJS also included two items about cyberstalking and cyber harassment. Unwanted texts and e-mails were the most common form of cyberstalking reported in the survey; of the respondents who experienced stalking, 51 percent reported texts and e-mails. Just under a quarter (21.9 percent) of respondents said they received unwanted contact via social network sites.

Singapore passed the Protection from Harassment Act in 2014. The act creates numerous offenses. For the first offense—intentionally causing harassment, alarm, or distress—the act states that perpetrators are liable for a fine and/or for imprisonment for a term not to exceed six months. For the second offense, the act creates a crime focused on fear or provocation of violence. This statute outlaws the use of threatening, abusive, or insulting words or behavior, as well as other threatening, abusive, or insulting communication. Any person found guilty of this crime shall face a fine and/or imprisonment not to exceed 12 months.

Finally, the act creates a third crime: unlawful stalking. *Unlawful stalking* occurs when a person engages in a course of conduct that involves acts that cause harassment, alarm, or distress to the individual and for which the accused person *intends* to cause harassment, alarm, or distress to the victim. According to the act, *stalking acts* are defined as following the victim, making communications to the victim, entering or loitering outside or near the victim's home or business or a place the victim frequents, interfering with the property of the victim, giving or sending material to the victim, and keeping the victim under surveillance. An individual found guilty of stalking shall face a punishment of a fine and/or imprisonment not exceeding 12 months. The act also allows the victim to apply to the District Court for a protection order.

The South African Legislative Assembly passed the Protection from Harassment Act in 2011, written to come into effect in 2013. The act includes both direct and indirect conduct that causes an individual to feel threatened. The act defines *stalking behaviors* as following, watching, pursuing, or accosting the individual, loitering outside of or near the location of the victim, engaging in communication with the victim, and sending or delivering packages to the victim. The act allows the complainant to apply to the court for a protection order against the harassment, which prohibits the stalker from harassing the protected individual or from getting help from others in order to harass the individual.

Sweden introduced the crime of stalking into the country's Penal Code in 2011, although repeated harassment that meets the requirements for gross violation of integrity was criminalized prior to 2011. A national stalking prevalence study in Sweden found that 9 percent of respondents reported experiencing repeated harassment/stalking in their lifetime, and 2.9 percent had been harassed or stalked in the year preceding the study. The median number of incidents experienced by women victims of stalking was 30 incidents, while the median period over which these incidents occurred was six months. The corresponding rates for men victims of stalking were 20 incidents and 5.5 months. In most cases, the victim was stalked by someone he or she knew. In a quarter of cases, the perpetrator was a partner or expartner. In another quarter of cases, the perpetrator and the victim had a private (but nonpartner) relationship. In one-tenth of the cases, the perpetrator was a work colleague or student, and in six percent of cases the perpetrator was someone the victim came into contact with through work. Approximately one-third of respondents reported being stalked by a stranger (Dovelius, Öberg, and Holmberg 2006, 8–11).

The national survey also reported that victims who had a previous close relationship with the perpetrator were most subjected to stalking that included physical persecution, threats, and violence. Two-thirds of respondents with a close relationship to the perpetrator had been threatened, and over half had been subjected to violence. The study reported that for almost 30 percent of women victims, the harassment/stalking included elements of violence, while the corresponding percentage among men victims was just over 10 percent (Dovelius, Öberg, and Holmberg 2006, 12).

Uganda does not have antistalking legislation. However, Uganda passed the Domestic Violence Act 2010, which prohibits individuals from harassing a former or current domestic partner. The act defines *harassment* as a pattern of conduct that induces fear of harm, annoyance, and aggregation with the intent of inducing fear in the person. The act defines *stalking behavior* as repeatedly watching or loitering outside the victim's location, repeatedly making telephone calls to the victim, repeatedly sending or delivery communications to the individual, or repeatedly following, pursuing, or accosting the victim with the intent to induce fear, harm, annoyance, or aggravation in the victim. If the court believes that domestic violence has been or may be committed, the act allows the court to issue a protection order against the perpetrator.

Stalking has been prosecuted in the United Kingdom since 1997 through the Protection from Harassment Act. In England and Wales, the legal definition of *harassment* requires that it occur on a minimum of two occasions—except in exceptional circumstances. The offense is seen to have two levels. The first level refers to harassment that alarms the person or causes the person distress. The second (higher) level occurs when the offender causes another person to fear, on at least two occasions, that the offender will use violence against that other person. For the first-level offense, the penalty can include a fine and/or up to six months of imprisonment. A restraining order can be issued; and if the order is broken, a fine and/or six months of imprisonment can be ordered. For the higher-level offense, penalties can include a fine and/or up to five years of imprisonment. A restraining order can be issued: and if the order is broken, a fine and/or five years of imprisonment can be ordered.

In 2009, stalking victim Ann Moulds began a campaign in Scotland to enact a stalking law. Alex Reid, the man who stalked Moulds for two years, was convicted under a breach of the peace charge because there was no antistalking law in Scotland then. He was put on probation, and sentenced to 260 hours of community service. In addition, he was put on the sex offenders register for three years. Moulds had been forced to leave her home and business because of the stalking (Khaleeli 2010). Her campaign was a success, and a new law was passed in 2010.

This law, the Criminal Justice and Licencing (Scotland) Bill (2010), added two amendments to existing Scottish law to specifically address stalking. According to Paladin National Stalking Advocacy Service:

- The first, Clause 38, created an offence of putting someone in fear, alarm or distress, to catch all public and private behaviour. The clause requires a lower test of evidence and is essentially a catch all.

- The second, Clause 39, creates the specific offence of stalking, which is more serious. If the evidence is not considered strong enough then the police must consider the lower test, the safety net of Clause 38. Under the terms of this clause a person commits an offence, which will be known as stalking, where he or she stalks another person. The stalking occurs where the perpetrator engages in a course of conduct AND that conduct causes the victim to suffer fear or alarm. The clause applies where the perpetrator knows, or ought to know, in all circumstances that engaging in the course of conduct would be likely to cause the victim to suffer fear or alarm. ("Scottish Stalking Legislation" 2013).

Under the law, "conduct" includes the following action and behaviors:

- Where the perpetrator follows the victim or he/she contacts or attempts to contact the victim by any other person and through any other means;
- Where the perpetrator publishes any statement or other material relating to the victim;
- Where the perpetrator monitors the victim through the internet, email or any other form of electronic communications;
- Where the perpetrator enters the premises of the victim, loiters in any place private or public, interferes with any property and possession of the victim or any other person;
- Where the perpetrator gives anything to the victim or any other person or leaves an item that may be found by the victim; or
- Where the perpetrator watches or spies on the victim; and
- Acts in any other way that a reasonable person would expect a victim to suffer fear or alarm ("Scottish Stalking Legislation" 2013).

Following Scotland's widely publicized and praised legislation, England and Wales passed the Protection of Freedoms Act 2012. This bill amended the 1997 law. The new law includes two stalking offences. Stalking (section 2A) defines a person guilty of stalking if that person "pursues a course of conduct" involving stalking or harassment. Stalking (section 4A) concerns "fear of violence or serious alarm or distress" from a stalker. The incidents must take place at least two times and involve violence or "serious alarm or distress." A person convicted under this law may receive up to five years of imprisonment and/or a fine (Action Against Stalking n.d.).

In Northern Ireland, the law is a hybrid of the laws from England and Wales and Scotland. In Northern Ireland, the law requires at least two acts of harassment. The law distinguishes between acts of harassment (a more serious offense) and actions that may make individuals fear that violence will occur. To be convicted of the lower offense results in a fine and/or up to six months of imprisonment; the penalty for the higher offense is a fine and/or up to five years of imprisonment. As in England and Wales and Scotland, a judge in Northern Ireland can issue a restraining order, with the same penalties for breaking the restraining order. However, in Northern Ireland the law also allows for a civil

> ## Resources for Stalking Victims and Their Loved Ones
>
> Stalking can be a prolonged form of harassment. Getting nonjudgmental, trauma-informed support from helping professionals may be a critical component of coping and recovery. The Stalking Resource Center—a program of The National Center for Victims of Crime (https://victimsofcrime.org)—is available for victims of stalking and for loved ones who wish to support those victims. The center's Web site provides links to a variety of support resources, including a safety planning guide, information about address-confidentiality programs, and information about the use of technology in stalking victimization. In addition, the center has a helpline that can be reached at 855-4-VICTIM (855-484-2846).

remedy: The victim can be awarded damages for anxiety due to harassment, along with any financial losses that resulted from the harassment.

The 2013/14 Crime Survey for England and Wales (CSEW) examined intimate violence among adults age 16 to 59. The survey found that the types of intimate violence most commonly experienced among women since age 16 was nonsexual partner abuse (22.0 percent) and stalking (21.5 percent). Similarly, but at lower rates, the most commonly experienced types of intimate violence for men since age 16 were stalking (9.8 percent) and nonsexual partner abuse (9.6 percent). Further, the study found that young women between 16 and 19 and between 20 and 24 were more likely to be victims of stalking (7.5 percent and 7.8 percent, respectively) compared to all other age groups. In 2016, the survey revealed that 20.9 percent of women had experienced stalking since the age of 16. For men, the figures were similar to earlier surveys, with stalking being the most commonly experienced form of intimate violence (9.9 percent). Police recorded crime for 2016 revealed 2,252 cases of "domestic abuse related stalking," or 54 percent of violence against person offenses (CSEW 2016).

Amanda M. Stylianou
Sheila M. McMahon

Further Reading

Action Against Stalking. n.d. "Laws and Legislation." Accessed December 17, 2017. http://www.actionagainststalking.org/stalking-laws-and-legislation.html.

Baum, Katrina, Shannon Catalano, and Michael Rand. 2009. "Special Report: Stalking Victimization in the United States." NCJ 224527. Washington, DC: Bureau of Justice Statistics, U.S. Department of Justice. Accessed December 17, 2017. https://www.justice.gov/sites/default/files/ovw/legacy/2012/08/15/bjs-stalking-rpt.pdf

Belknap, Joanne Hillary Potter. 2005. "The Trials of Measuring the "Success" of Domestic Violence Policies. *Criminology and Public Policy* 4 (3): 559–56.

Bennett Cattaneo, Lauren, and Lisa A. Goodman. 2007. "New Directions in IPV Risk Assessment: An Empowerment Approach to Risk Management." In *Intimate Partner Violence*, edited by Kathleen A. Kendall-Tackett and Sarah M. Giacomoni, 1–17. Kingston, NJ: Civic Research Institute.

Black, Michelle C., Kathleen C. Basile, Matthew J. Breiding, Sharon G. Smith, Mikel L. Walters, Melissa T. Merrick, . . . Mark R. Stevens. 2011. "National Intimate Partner and Sexual Violence Survey (NISVS) 2010: Summary Report." Atlanta, GA: National Center for Injury Prevention and Control, Centers for Disease Control and Prevention. Accessed December 17, 2017. https://www.cdc.gov/violencepre vention/pdf/nisvs_report2010-a.pdf.

Breiding, Matthew J., Sharon G. Smith, Kathleen C. Basile, Mikel L. Walters, Jieru Chen, and Melissa Merrick. 2014. "Prevalence and Characteristics of Sexual Violence, Stalking, and Intimate Partner Violence Victimization—National Intimate Partner and Sexual Violence Survey, United States, 2011." *Morbidity and Mortality Weekly Report* 63 (SS08): 1–18. Atlanta, GA: Centers for Disease Control and Prevention. Accessed December 17, 2017. https://www.cdc.gov/mmwr/preview /mmwrhtml/ss6308a1.htm.

Council of Europe. 2014. "Compilation of Contributions from Member States on Key Challenges and Good Practices on Access to Justice for Women Victims of Violence at National Level." Accessed August 5, 2017. https://rm.coe.int/1680597b15.

Crime Survey for England and Wales (CSEW). 2016. "Domestic Abuse, Sexual Assault and Stalking." Office for National Statistics. Accessed December 17, 2017. https:// www.ons.gov.uk/peoplepopulationandcommunity/crimeandjustice/compendium /focusonviolentcrimeandsexualoffences/yearendingmarch2016/domesticabuse sexualassaultandstalking#what-is-happening-to-trends-in-intimate-violence.

D'Arcy, Ciarán. 2017. "Labour Publishes Bill to Criminalise 'Revenge Porn.'" *The Irish Times*. April 4. Accessed December 17, 2017. https://www.irishtimes.com/news /politics/oireachtas/labour-publishes-bill-to-criminalise-revenge-porn-1.3036410.

Dovelius, Anna Mia, Jonas Öberg, and Stina Holmberg. 2006. "Stalking in Sweden: Prevalence and Prevention." Brottsförebyggande rådet (BRÅ). Stockholm, Sweden: Swedish National Council for Crime Prevention. Accessed December 17, 2017. https:// www.bra.se/download/18.cba82f7130f475a2f1800024961/1371914734163 /2006_stalking_in_sweden.pdf.

Grimes, William. 2016. "Theresa Saldana, Actress and Attack Survivor, Dies at 61." *New York Times*, June 8. Accessed August 4, 2017. https://www.nytimes.com/2016/06/09 /arts/television/theresa-saldana-actress-and-attack-survivor-dies-at-61.html?_r=0.

Hellmann, Deborah F., and Sören Kliem. 2015. "The Prevalence of Stalking: Current Data from a German Victim Survey." *European Journal of Criminology* 12 (6): 700–18.

Khaleeli, Homa. 2010. "Stalkers Are Criminals—not 'Incompetent Suitors.'" *The Guardian*. January 28, 2010. Accessed December 17, 2017. https://www.theguardian .com/lifeandstyle/2010/jan/29/stalkers-are-criminals

Kropp, P. Randall, Stephen D. Hart, David R. Lyon, and Jennifer E. Storey. 2011. "The Development and Validation of the Guidelines for Stalking Assessment and Management." *Behavioral Sciences and the Law* 29 (2): 302–16.

Logan, T. K., Lisa Shannon, Jennifer Cole, and Robert Walker. 2006. "The Impact of Differential Patterns of Physical Violence and Stalking on Mental Health and Help-Seeking among Women with Protective Orders." *Violence Against Women* 12 (9): 866–86.

McFarlane, Judith M., Jacquelyn C. Campbell, Susan Wilt, Carolyn J. Sachs, Y. Ulrich, and Xiao Xu. 1999. "Stalking and Intimate Partner Femicide." *Homicide Studies* 3 (4): 300–16.

McFarlane, Leroy, and Paul Bocij. 2003. "An Exploration of Predatory Behaviour in Cyberspace: Towards a Typology of Cyberstalkers." *First Monday* 8 (9). Accessed December 17, 2017. http://ojphi.org/ojs/index.php/fm/article/view/1076/996.

Meloy, J. Reid. 2003. "When Stalkers Become Violent: The Threat to Public Figures and Private Lives." *Psychiatric Annals* 33 (10): 658–65.

Moshtaghian, Artemis. 2016. "Mark David Chapman, John Lennon's Killer, Denied Parole Again." *CNN*, August 29. Accessed August 4, 2017. http://www.cnn.com/2016/08/29/us/john-lennon-mark-david-chapman-denied-parole-ninth-time/index.html.

Mullen, Paul E., Rachel Mackenzie, James R. Ogloff, Michele Pathé, Troy McEwan, and Rosemary Purcell. 2006. "Assessing and Managing the Risks in the Stalking Situation." *Journal of the American Academy of Psychiatry and the Law Online* 34 (4): 439–50.

Murray, Kath. 2016. "2014/15 Scottish Crime and Justice Survey: Sexual Victimisation and Stalking." National Statistics. The Scottish Government. Accessed August 5, 2017. http://www.gov.scot/Resource/0050/00500370.pdf.

National Center for Victims of Crime. 2007. "The Model Stalking Code Revisited: Responding to the New Realities of Stalking." Accessed August 5, 2017. http://victimsofcrime.org/docs/default-source/src/model-stalking-code.pdf?sfvrsn=12.

National Institute of Justice. 1996. "Appendix B: A Model Antistalking Code for the States." In *Domestic Violence, Stalking, and Antistalking Legislation: An Annual Report to Congress under the Violence Against Women Act*, B-1. NCJ 160943. Rockville, MD: National Criminal Justice Reference Service. Accessed December 17, 2017. https://www.ncjrs.gov/pdffiles/stlkbook.pdf

Office of the Attorney General. 1997. "Non-Fatal Offences Against the Person Act, 1997." *Irish Statute Book*. Government of Ireland. Accessed August 5, 2017. http://www.irishstatutebook.ie/eli/1997/act/26/section/10/enacted/en/html.

Office on Violence Against Women. 2007. "Report to Congress on Stalking and Domestic Violence, 2005 through 2006." Washington, DC: U.S. Department of Justice. Accessed August 5, 2017. http://www.ncdsv.org/images/OVW_ReportToCongress StalkingAndDV_2005-2006.pdf.

Office on Violence Against Women. 2010. "The Office on Violence Against Women's Grant Funds Used to Address Stalking. Report to Congress." Washington, DC: U.S. Department of Justice. Accessed August 4, 2017. https://www.justice.gov/sites/default/files/ovw/legacy/2012/09/18/2010-stalking-rpt.pdf.

Office on Violence Against Women. 2016. "Stalking." Washington, DC: U.S. Department of Justice. Accessed August 4, 2017. https://www.justice.gov/ovw/stalking.

Office on Violence Against Women. 2017. "FY 2017 Budget Request." Washington, DC: U.S. Department of Justice. Accessed August 4, 2017. https://www.justice.gov/jmd/file/822296/download.

Purcell, Rosemary, Michele Pathé, and Paul E. Mullen. 2002. "The Prevalence and Nature of Stalking in the Australian Community." *Australian and New Zealand Journal of Psychiatry* 36 (1): 114–20.

"Scotland: Stalking Legislation." 2013. Paladin National Stalking Advocacy Service. Accessed December 17, 2017. https://paladinservice.co.uk/wp-content/uploads/2013/07/Scotland-Stalking-Legislation.pdf.

Sinha, Maire. 2013. "Measuring Violence Against Women: Statistical Trends." *Juristat: Canadian Centre for Justice Statistics* 1:3–120.

Spence-Diehl, Emily. 1999. *Stalking: A Handbook for Victims.* Holmes Beach, FL: Learning Publications.

Spitzberg, Brian H., and William R. Cupach. 2007. "The State of the Art of Stalking: Taking Stock of the Emerging Literature." *Aggression and Violent Behavior* 12 (1): 64–86.

Stalking Resource Center. n.d. "Federal Stalking Laws." Accessed August 5, 2017. http://victimsofcrime.org/our-programs/stalking-resource-center/stalking-laws/federal-stalking-laws#61a.

Umeda, Sayuri. 2013. "Japan: Two Laws Amended to Better Protect Women." Global Legal Monitor. Washington, DC: Library of Congress. Accessed August 5, 2017. http://www.loc.gov/law/foreign-news/article/japan-two-laws-amended-to-better-protect-women/.

U.S. Department of Justice. 2009. "Justice Department Commemorates Fifteen Years of the Violence Against Women Act," September 14. Accessed August 4, 2017. https://www.justice.gov/opa/pr/justice-department-commemorates-fifteen-years-violence-against-women-act.

Van Der Aa, Suzan, and Maarten Kunst. 2009. "The Prevalence of Stalking in the Netherlands." *International Review of Victimology* 16 (1): 35–50.

STATUTORY RAPE

Statutory rape is a criminal offense generally described as illicit or unlawful sexual intercourse with a person who has not yet reached the age of consent. Statutory rape is deemed a criminal offense, regardless of whether the act occurs with the minor's consent or not, as stated in *Michael M. v. Superior Court of Sonoma County*, 450 U.S. 464 (1981). The fact that a minor may not legally consent is enough to make any sexual contact between an adult and a minor unlawful. The crime does not have to involve the use of force. Even if the minor was willing, the offender is held accountable for the actions. However, if the couple is legally married, sexual activity between them is typically considered lawful, even if one of them has not reached the age of consent. Statutory rape laws were reformed in British codes as well as in the United States, as a response to growing middle-class concerns about the abuse of young girls, the morals of vulnerable working girls, and the spread of disease. In the 1970s, the case known as *Michael M. v. Superior Court of Sonoma County* brought wider changes in statutory rape legislation in the United States, in order to address increased concern about out-of-wedlock pregnancy among adolescents.

Since ancient times, sexual activity with a minor has always been criminalized one way or another. Documentation in legal codes exists for the criminalization of statutory crime as far back as the Babylonian and Roman empires, even if the crime was known under other names. From its inception, the intent was to protect the purity of female youth who were, at the time, considered property. In fact, often officials did not consider the violation of a young woman a criminal act, if she was deemed unchaste.

Rape, defined as sexual intercourse against the victim's will and usually by force, became established as a crime in Western society at the beginning of the early modern era. Under these laws, rape was solely a crime perpetrated against women. This is notable in the influential Chapter 34 of the Statute of Westminster II, enacted by Parliament under the reign of Edward I, in which women specifically are provided the right to bring a man to trial for rape. Here, rape is specified as the coerced sexual act of a male against a female. The crucial factor in identifying rape as a crime was the element of consent or willingness; that is, it had to be an action exerted against the victim in relation to the victim's lack of consent or with the victim being unwilling. In order to convict a rapist, court authorities required evidence that aligned with a set of "objective criteria" that was, in effect, very difficult to prove: that the victim had resisted the offender to the maximum of her possibilities, that she had cried out during the offense, that she had filed a complaint immediately, and finally, that her testimony was corroborated. Given these requirements, most rapes were not reported to the authorities—and rape continues to be a greatly underreported crime. Moreover, because the odds have traditionally been stacked against the victim during an inquest and trial, few reported rapes, according to experts, end with a conviction of the offender. Thus, misconceptions and stereotypes pertaining to women and rape led to the development of laws that were supposed to prevent violence against women, but which failed to prevent violence against women and failed to ensure justice for victims.

Consent, then, according to law historians, has been crucial to understanding rape as a crime. Rather than being viewed as a crime of violence, rape in past eras has been seen as similar to a consensual act of sexual intercourse, but one to which a woman did not agree. Moreover, women's testimony was viewed as unreliable and untrustworthy—thus, the requirement for a "corroboration" by somebody else. Decades of research and legislation reform have led to changes in the judicial definition and treatment of rape. It has also had an impact on sentencing rates, even though the element of consent continues to be an important factor in rape legislation.

The term *statutory rape* refers to the crime committed when a minor is sexually abused, with or without the minor's explicit consent. The crime of statutory rape is based upon the notion that an adult uses an inherent imbalance of power and often exploits the trust that the minor has placed in the adult. This may occur by way of deceitful or manipulative actions meant to "seduce" the minor into a sexual relationship. It also includes most cases of incest. The age of consent varies worldwide; nevertheless, in most parts of the world in which statutory rape laws exist, the crime involves an adult individual engaging in sexual intercourse with a minor on average between the ages of 12 and 18.

Statutory rape has always been a highly contentious issue. Supporters of statutory rape laws argue that criminalizing the sexual activity of adolescents serves to protect them, particularly from predatory actions by adults. They argue that, as proven by numerous studies, individuals younger than a certain age are not yet physically and emotionally mature enough to cope with sexual activity and its consequences (such as pregnancy and sexually transmitted diseases) and that, in general, adolescent are more vulnerable to bad decision-making. Finally, supporters of statutory rape laws believe that making statutory rape illegal will serve as a deterrent to it.

The United States

Consent is an important factor in statutory rape laws. *Statutory rape* is defined as sexual intercourse with a minor younger than a particular—and legally codified—age of consent. When an individual has sexual relations with a person younger than that specific age of consent, it is automatically implied that valid consent cannot be obtained. Therefore, the person has committed rape—that is, has engaged in sexual relations without the consent of the minor. As stated before, the age of consent varies across countries; even within some countries, such as the United States, it varies across jurisdictions. Nevertheless, by 1997, the age of consent in 28 U.S. states was 16 years; in most other U.S. states, it was 17 or 18 years.

In fact, according to historians, rape and statutory rape laws have undergone many changes over the last decades, especially throughout the late 19th century and the 20th century. These changes reflect how ideology and societal mores regarding adolescent sexuality have influenced statutory rape policies and laws. To begin with, laws are created to serve multiple functions, including educating the people, as well as regulating their behavior and punishing their infractions. As an educational instrument, for example, laws regulating sexuality provide guidance to adults about boundaries and what is allowed, so that they can abide by these boundaries and control their behavior as regards to sexual relationships with others—in particular, underage minors.

Beliefs about morality serve to buttress laws regulating sexual behavior. Many believe it is morally incorrect for adolescents to be sexually active—or at least, sexually active outside the bounds of matrimony. Criminalizing sexual activity with minors, then, serves to deter adults from enticing underage people into sexual behavior. In order to support new legislation, advocates of statutory rape laws have often expressed alarm about rising rates of sexual activity among teenagers. However, other experts argue that adolescent sexual activity has historically been the norm, and that the rates of sexually transmitted diseases and pregnancy among adolescents are far from being new phenomena.

Among the most recent legislative actions pertaining to statutory rape is the 1981 case *Michael M. v. Superior Court of Sonoma County*, in which the U.S. Supreme Court established, as one of the most important purposes of statutory rape laws, the need to decrease the number of teenage pregnancies. Among the reasons for concern enumerated in the ruling are the harmful consequences of teenage pregnancy for mothers and children, and the need among the states to decrease the medical and economic costs of pregnancy, as well as abortion rates among adolescents.

In the 1990s, the American Bar Association conducted a survey of over 20 states that were considering statutory rape legislation. Among the survey questions were the states' motivations for proposed legislative action. The main reasons provided by legislators across the states included the following: (1) the desire to protect minors from sexual intercourse; (2) the desire to protect minors from exploitative or predatory sexual relationships, particularly with older partners; (3) the desire to reduce and prevent teenage pregnancy; and (4) the desire to reduce the number of adolescent mothers receiving welfare benefits (Miller et al. 1998, 180).

Many scholars believe it is important to note that contemporary statutory rape legislation usually bars sexual activity with an unmarried person under

---

Michael M. v. Sonoma County Superior Court (1981)

The male petitioner in *Michael M. v. Superior Court of Sonoma County* was 17 when he was charged under California's statutory rape law. He argued that the law was unconstitutional because it discriminated on the basis of gender, as it made only men criminally liable for acts of sexual intercourse with women who were not their wives and were under age 18. The California Supreme Court declared the law unconstitutional, but in a ruling in 1981, the U.S. Supreme Court reversed the decision and stated that the law was constitutional. In the majority opinion, the justices argued that a primary purpose of the law was to prevent illegitimate teenage pregnancies; in this case, punishing men did not violate the equal protection clause of the Fourteenth Amendment and, therefore, was not unconstitutional.

the age of consent. In other words, the minor is considered a victim as long as the minor not married to the offender. According to law, minors are inherently incapable of giving valid consent to a sexual activity outside of the boundaries of marriage, yet different laws apply within the boundaries of legal matrimony. Most states allow minors to consent to marriage as long as they have parental or judicial permission. In short, sexual activity between a minor and an adult cannot be prosecuted as long as the two parties are married. Some critics argue, then, that the laws seem to proscribe sexual relations outside of marriage, rather than proscribing relations between partners with a specific age difference. In addition, these laws do not address situations in which a minor may have been coerced into marriage with an older adult.

An important change in statutory rape legislation has been the fact that the laws have evolved from being gender-specific to being gender-neutral. Statutory rape laws were first established to penalize males for having sexual relations with females under the age of consent to whom they were not married. Today, at least in the United States, the laws include both genders, male and female, for victims as well as for perpetrators. The laws also cover same-sex relationships. In some situations, the offender may be the same age as the victim. In most states, however, the law stipulates that the offender must be a specific number of years older than the victim in order to be charged with a felony. Regardless of age and circumstance, such offenders are in all likelihood required to register as sex offenders and have their names entered in a sex offender database.

Exact statistics for statutory rape are hard to come by, because many cases go unreported, a common phenomenon with rape in general. Of cases that are reported, the most common involve an adolescent female and an adult male. These cases tend to be more frequently reported due to mandatory child abuse laws, which compel medical authorities to report incidents to authorities. When a minor becomes pregnant and seeks medical treatment, as well as when a minor is treated for a sexually transmitted disease, if it is discovered that the minor is in a sexual relationship with an adult, the medical personnel are legally compelled to report the incident.

Statutory rape laws have been historically, and continue to be, a highly contentious issue. In order to fully comprehend the basis for conflict and debate in several arenas, political as well as cultural, it is important to understand the social and historic context.

Major Laws

Historians such as Christina M. Tchen (1983) and Carolyn E. Cocca (2004) have mapped the statutory rape laws in the United States all the way back to medieval English common law. Laws and statutes pertaining to rape can be found among the oldest codified laws in documented history. In the earliest definitions of *rape*, the main factor was the marital and physical state of the women. For instance, the gravest instances included forcible rape against a virgin betrothed to another man, a situation that was considered akin to destroying that individual's property. Rape of an unattached unmarried woman, on the other hand, was a misdemeanor. Punishment for the perpetrator typically involved paying a fine to the father of the victim. Often the victim was married off—sometimes to the perpetrator—to repair the damage.

Under English common law, consent became more important. A male could no longer be convicted of rape if the woman had consented to sexual intercourse. In 1275, however, age became an issue as statutory rape became written into law, forbidding sexual intercourse with a woman younger than 12 years of age. The age of consent was reduced to age 10 in the 1500s. In the North American colonies, the age of consent varied between 10 and 12. The laws, however, did not cover African American women. Such laws are seen by many historians as meant to protect single white women's purity, essential to their marketability as future wives. Most African American women were enslaved, and as such, considered property. In practice, then, they were denied the protection, such as it was, of statutory rape laws.

Statutory rape laws were harsher than those established for regular unmarried sexual activity—fornication—but they also allowed several lines of defense, including that the perpetrator was in error as to the age of the victim. The other defense was claiming that the victim was not a virgin—that is, that she was already sexually experienced. In other words, statutory rape laws covered unmarried women considered as previously chaste. Both defenses highlight the fact that the concern was less about the vulnerability of the victim than about her virtue or marital status. Both lines of defense remained in some form, considered to be valid in many states until the mid-1950s, while the "character" of the minor was considered a valid line of defense into the 1990s. No state retained the plausibility of such line of defense after 1998.

The dovetailing of a number of important social events, such as industrialization and urbanization, fueled monumental changes in the status of women and the working class, and, it follows, in legislation and policies pertaining to women and workers. Statutory rape laws changed across the United States in the late 1800s, when an alliance of religious conservatives, feminist activists, and workmen's organizations sought to pass several laws to deter men from preying on young working-class women—including raising the age of consent. Among the reasons why women's organizations and workmen's groups were concerned about the age of consent was that industrialization attracted tens of thousands of young women to work in city factories, which opened the door for greater personal autonomy and financial independence. Among the activities that these young women engaged in were myriad leisure events, in which they mixed freely with men while lacking traditional chaperones. These activities caused grave concern among the middle class for the morals of working class girls, in particular as to their status in the marriage market. Among many reformers, marriage was the ultimate goal to which working-class girls should aspire in order to, ideally, join the ranks of the middle class and adhere to its values and lifestyle. In other words, statutory rape laws were seen as a way to curb the sexuality of these young women and to deter men from access to them. This is not to say that activists for legislative reform were not also concerned about young women being abused or exploited by predatory males.

During this period of rapid industrialization in England, activists managed to pressure Parliament into raising the age of consent to 16 through the Criminal Law Amendment Act of 1885. This also exerted pressure in the United States, so that most states raised the age of consent to 16 or 18. There was much concern, however, that in an age in which young people commonly married in their adolescence, young men would not have access to young marriageable women, or else they would be penalized for giving free rein to their "natural" sexual desires. In consequence, many states decreased the level of penalty for minor males who engaged in sexual relations with a minor female. At the same time, the law also codified the requirement that females be of virtuous character previous to the relationship.

Historians explain that the new statutory rape laws were very similar to the traditional "seduction" laws, which punished males for "deceiving" a previously chaste woman into a sexual relationship with the promise of marriage. In other words, the victim was seen as being tricked into giving her consent. The new laws changed the essence of the deceit, into one in which women were incapable of consent. Underage women were, however, considered capable of giving their consent to marriage—and, it follows, to engaging in sexual intercourse within the bounds of marriage. It is important to note that in the late 1800s and early 1900s, while the average age of first marriage for women, according to the U.S. Census, was 22, it was not uncommon within some socioeconomic groups for women to be already married and mothers before they reached the age of consent.

In the 1970s, feminist activists achieved the passage of changes to statutory rape laws, related to "age span" and to gender. In most states, the adult had to be a specific number of years older than the minor in order to be prosecuted for a felony, and laws became gender-neutral in most states. In fact, statutory rape reform was part of a larger project of forcible rape reform, which started in 1973. At the time, reformers considered that statutory rape laws as they stood were less protective and more infantilizing than they should be. The reformers believed statutory rape laws should not see young women as passive individuals lacking agency, yet they also wanted to protect young women from coercive or predatory relationships. They also wanted to protect young males from similar situations (Cocca 2004). Among the reforms they managed to achieve, besides the gender-neutral language and age-span considerations, were the following:

1. Defining the offense as "sexual assault" or "sexual battery" to emphasize the violence implicit in the act
2. Grading the offense based on victim's age
3. Including touching and other nonpenetrative sexual activity
4. Eliminating the "promiscuity" clause that required young women to be virgins
5. Eliminating the "mistake-of-age" defense

Not everyone agreed with the redefinitions and reforms that were enacted in the new statutory rape laws. For instance, some argued that while young men and women may both be adversely impacted by early sexual activity, the harm they suffer is different. Numerous studies were cited that suggest that adolescent women tend to suffer low self-esteem; are not comfortable speaking their minds; are socialized to please; and are at risk for pregnancy, shame, and other adverse consequences that could result from their engaging in sexual relations before they are mature enough to do so. Moreover, girls are socialized to romanticize love and sex, so that they are more at risk for coercion and manipulation. Opponents of the new laws were also concerned that age-span provisions can obscure the possibility that young women may be coerced into sexual relationships by slightly older adults. Other critics argue that the marital exemption allowed in statutory rape laws obviates age and seems to privilege marital status, a factor that serves to perpetuate the stigmatization of young women.

It is important to note that both male and female adolescents can be victims of coercive and exploitative sexual relations. Male and female adults can also be charged as offenders. Nevertheless, a U.S. Department of Justice study published in 2005 showed that male adolescents are victims in about 5 percent of cases reported to law enforcement (Troup-Leasure and Snyder 2005, 1). Scant research has been done to shed light on how much more or less likely male adolescents are to date older partners, male or female. It is possible that cases of statutory rape in which the victim is male are largely underreported, because of prevalent gender stereotypes in which males will be seen as exploring their sexuality and engaging in sexual initiation, as opposed to being victimized sexually. However, as experts have amply demonstrated, male adolescents may also suffer lifelong psychological and emotional repercussions from sexually exploitative relationships.

Adult women accused of statutory rape often receive a higher level of media attention. Female felons must also register as sex offenders when sentenced for statutory rape. Nevertheless, a sexual relationship between adult women and minor males is believed by many to be one of the most underreported instances of statutory rape—possibly because despite the widespread media coverage most of these cases still receive, it is not publicly perceived as a crime in which the minor's innocence or virginity has been seriously "damaged," as was often the case with female victims of statutory rape.

Supporters of age gradation wanted to move away from perceptions of lost innocence. They argued, instead, that rather than protecting a minor's virginity, the new laws actually served to prevent sexual abuse. Nevertheless, statutory rape laws often make no differentiation, for example, between an adult molesting a child younger than age 10 and a 15-year-old who is in a caring relationship with an 18-year-old. Because no provision was made for the issue of consent upon sentencing, both types of perpetuators must register as sex offenders as perpetuators of statutory rape. Nevertheless, by the late 1990s most states had adopted age-span provisions, even if significant variations in the age span exist across the nation.

One of the main drivers of amendments and greater implementation of statutory rape laws in the 1990s was the conservative drive to reduce the numbers of out-of-wedlock births and young women dependent upon public assistance, most of whom were portrayed in the media and by many politicians as unmarried, poor, and minority women. In 1981, in the case of *Michael M. v. Superior Court of Sonoma County*, the U.S. Supreme Court ruled that statutory rape laws, which identified offenders as male, were constitutional under the equal protections granted in the Fourteenth Amendment of the U.S. Constitution. The language of the laws helped stem the prevalence of teenage pregnancy by deterring men from seeking to engage in sexual relationships with adolescent women. Not surprisingly, the ruling was then subject to much debate and criticism.

Adding to the controversy was the 1995 study on adolescent pregnancy published by the Alan Guttmacher Institute. The study found that 65 percent of adolescent mothers had children with partners 20 years of age or older. Subsequent studies showed that two-thirds of adolescent mothers were age 18 or 19 with partners age 20 and 21, and that about 25 percent of mothers age 15–17 had a partner their same age (Cocca 2004, 96). Moreover, the Guttmacher Institute found that rates of adolescent pregnancy had declined significantly since the 1980s, giving much credit for this event to the adolescents themselves, suggesting that more effective contraceptive methods were among the reasons for the decline (Darroch and Singh 1999).

The results of the Guttmacher Institute studies, however, fueled more support for harsher penalties for statutory rape. Much of the language, according to experts, mirrors the discourse used in the 19th century regarding the chastity of women, by linking the rise in children on public assistance to the rise in young women having children. In particular, the Personal Responsibility and Work Opportunity Reconciliation Act of 1996, or "welfare reform act," linked the rising number of children on welfare to the increase in out-of-wedlock births. In short, it blamed the rise in poverty rates on unwed young women. The welfare reform act had a section in which statutory rape is directly linked to adolescent pregnancy and its economic costs on the state, requiring that states draft programs to reduce pregnancies among unmarried women and expand awareness about statutory rape.

In the wake of the 1996 act and the surge in punitive statutory rape laws, many experts became concerned about the ramifications of criminally prosecuting teen pregnancy. Proposals began to appear that spanned from potential improvements to the elimination of many statutory rape laws. Among these were that the prohibition of sexual relations between minors and adults be limited to a differential span of a certain number of years, such as a decade, and that adolescents older than age 13 be included (Oliveri 2000). To date, legislation related to statutory rape covers a wide spectrum of offenses, from a misdemeanor to a severe felony, and includes such sentencing considerations as the ages of the victim and the perpetrator at the time of the relation, the age difference between the two, and whether intoxicants were involved. For instance, a different consideration might be given, depending on the state in which the offense occurs, if the victim and the perpetrator were both adolescent and close in age, known as the "Romeo and Juliet Law." Depending upon the circumstances, then, statutory rape is usually a state crime that can be charged as a misdemeanor or a felony; further, it is punishable with incarceration, probation, registration as a sex offender, and other types of sentencing— depending upon the state.

Obstacles

Critics have long pointed out that the language of the ruling and subsequent legislation obviated more important structural and economic problems as the root cause of poverty and the rise in teenage pregnancies. Critics also point out the institutional and prevalent racism of the policies, which blamed poor, young people of color for events that were rooted in larger and more complex social issues, such as poverty, lack of access to health care and education, and gender and economic inequality.

Many experts have researched and documented societal issues related to adolescent births and have concluded that the focus on statutory rape reflected the exasperation felt by policy-makers, legislators, and other decision-makers because of the difficulties they faced in solving complex social problems that were resulting in adolescent pregnancy and their desire to find simple solutions. In consequence, they privileged a view that saw the roots of the problem as issues of personal accountability and individual behavior, rather than the result of poverty, racism, and other societal factors. Experts argued, for instance, that young people in low-income communities face poor prospects for jobs, lack access to good education, lack marriage prospects due to poverty, and as a result, feel no incentive to postpone pregnancy and parenthood. Moreover, adolescents often have very little comprehension of the trials and difficulties involved in raising children, and they lack access to family-planning resources.

In fact, when adolescents enter into sexual relationships with older partners, they may be engaging in a type of rational behavior. Studies have found that some of the reasons young women have expressed for entering into relationships with older males are emotional stability, financial security, and material possessions, as well as such status-related reasons as prestige among their peers. A judicial recommendation report found that 20 percent of statutory rape offenders were in a romantic relationship with the victim, and that an arrest occurs in less than half of statutory rape cases (Simpson 2009).

On the other hand, concerns about statutory rape victims are very grave in relation to younger adolescents. Relatively small numbers of 13- and 14-year-old children are sexually active, according to experts, but those who are, are also at risk of having experienced a coercive sexual relation. Of women who had sexual intercourse when they were younger than age 14 and 60 percent of those who experienced sexual relations before age 15, 74 percent reported a coerced sexual relation. Aware of study results such as these, policy-makers and statutory rape law advocates are rightly concerned with wanting to protect young children from exploitative and coerced sexual relationships (Donovan 1997).

Regarding pregnancy among adolescents, however, most social scientists doubt that statutory rape laws can impact its prevalence. While acknowledging that statutory rape laws are necessary to protect minors who are vulnerable to coercive relations and predatory adults, the connection between statutory rape and adolescent pregnancy rates does not correlate with factors that impact teenage pregnancy rates. The problems of adolescent pregnancy avoid the fact that many young women choose to get pregnant and that the problems are far more complex than adult males preying on minor females. The limited opportunities and the societal and personal problems typical of entrenched poverty are more prevalent causes of adolescent pregnancy, and these are not addressed by statutory rape laws.

The debate in the media as well as in legislative circles was framed over the use of statutory rape laws as an instrument to deter predatory behavior of adult men in relation to adolescent women and to prevent adolescent pregnancies. The numbers, however, showed that only a small number of adolescent pregnancies resulted from relationships between an adult and a very young adolescent. For instance, in California, less than 3 percent of children born to adolescents in the late 1990s were to women age 15 or younger. Among the births for adolescents whose median age was 14.5, the fathers were men age 19 or younger. Of other adolescent births for the same study, the young mothers' median age was 17, and their partner was 21 (Donovan 1997). However, as found by the Guttmacher study (Darroch and Singh 1999), a significant decline in adolescent pregnancy rates occurred in the last decades of the 20th century, reportedly linked to several causes that had little relation to the application of statutory rape laws.

By 2015, the legislative flow veered toward softening laws related to adolescent sexual activity—perhaps due, in some measure, to the difficulties in prosecuting and enforcing statutory rape laws indiscriminately. Many states modified their laws by requiring a specific age-span difference between victim and offender. However, there are still laws that attempt to curb or deter sexual intercourse among same-age peers, and in some states, statutory rape cases are punished as harshly as instances of forcible rape.

Another obstacle to reducing statutory rape cases is enforcement. The only U.S. Supreme Court case related to statutory rape laws has been *Michael M. v. Superior Court of Sonoma County*, in 1981. Relatively few cases of statutory rape are reported, and even fewer are prosecuted. Among the problems faced usually is victims' unwillingness to appear in court and/or to accuse a romantic partner or the father of a child.

Another problem that authorities face is lack of knowledge. Surveys have shown that men involved with younger partners often ignore that a relationship with a minor is illegal, especially if the difference in age between the two parties is just a few years or if both are adolescents. In fact, although it is common knowledge that sexual relationships with minors are illicit, very few participants know specific rules or understand the definitions of such concepts as "rape" and "statutory rape." Complicating the issue even further, then, is the fact that different perceptions of the issue exist among lawmakers, authorities, alleged perpetrators, parents, and the public at large. Experts working with teenagers corroborate that young women seldom want to endanger a man with whom they are involved. They may also fear parental or relationship repercussions, such as domestic violence. Even in abusive relationships, partners are often perceived as a source of emotional support and other types of support. In fact, domestic violence victims may not see the relationship in terms of rape or abuse.

Furthermore, modern society is more diverse, and in some cultures relationships between young women and older men—sometimes much older men— are accepted and supported. In many traditional groups, older men are viewed as likelier to be better providers and caretakers for young women and their children. In other words, a teenager may have been socialized into cultural mores that place her at risk for statutory rape. According to experts, jailing a perpetrator who is liked and approved by the family and the immediate community is unlikely to change cultural mores and beliefs, especially when people are unaware of statutory rape laws.

While aware of and sensitive to cultural differences, authorities posit that they cannot overlook the best interests of the minors involved and of their children, and that they must also be mindful of the burden that addressing those interests places on social services for the state. Because no state routinely gathers information on the sexual partners of adolescents who use social services, unless the state has reason to suspect abuse, statistical information is unreliable. Moreover, trust is an important issue in health services settings, and medical staff members are mandated to report cases in which an adolescent communicates information that leads them to believe it is a case of statutory rape. Therefore, it is possible that medical service providers try to avoid being placed in a difficult position. In other words, public service providers are mindful of complying with the law, yet there is little incentive for them to aggressively seek information regarding their adolescent patients' sexual partners. Reporting them to authorities could cause adolescents to mistrust the organization and stop attending. On the other hand, health services staff may want to avoid liability for failure to report a case of abuse. In order to address such concerns, some states have moved to exempt some providers from some reporting requirements in cases of adolescent pregnancy.

Other social organizations are concerned that statutory rape laws might discourage fathers from becoming involved, financially and emotionally, with their children. Particularly with regard to children born to underage mothers, organizations that seek to encourage more parental involvement are concerned that statutory rape laws do not take the complexity of these cases into consideration. Statutory rape laws, according to many health or social services providers, may sometimes seem at odds with programs that promote treatment for pregnancy and sexually transmitted diseases and that provide family planning and contraceptives for sexually active adolescents. For instance, some states have proposed that an investigation be launched when an adolescent seeks treatment for a sexually transmitted disease at a clinic. "In Georgia, for example, where the legislature recently raised the age of consent to for sexual intercourse to 16, state law authorizes minors to consent to STD testing and treatment, but some health officials have suggested that a statutory rape investigation be initiated whenever an underage female seeks STD services" (Donovan 1996, 33).

Of special concern for public service providers and the legal system is the balance of power in a relationship involving adolescents. For instance, in a relationship in which the adult partner is much older than the adolescent, the risk is higher for manipulation and coercion, given the different levels of life experience and possibly status. In the United States, then, most state laws contemplate the age-span differential between sex partners in a statutory rape case. Due to legal standards and prosecutorial discretion, is unlikely that prosecutions occur for cases in which the age difference is of 2 to 4 years. According to one U.S. study, if the adolescent is between 15 and 17 years old and the sexual partner is 6 or more years older, then prosecutors may seek to proceed (Koon-Magnin and Ruback 2013, 1919). These are also some of the considerations that came into play for some advocates when, in 1996, the U.S. Congress recommended states exert more pressure on enforcing of statutory rape laws (Koon-Magnin and Ruback 2013; Miller et al. 1998).

However, some indicators appeared to show that experts and the public were not entirely on board. In fact, there was much debate on the topic, with some experts supporting selective enforcement, and others concerned about issues such as institutional racism bearing down on enforcement. They questioned whether statutory rape laws could actually reduce pregnancy rates, and many studies cast doubt on the reach expected from federal and state policies. They argued that any reduction in pregnancy rates would be minimal, but that incarcerating men for statutory rape would worsen the rates of incarcerated minorities. Furthermore, enforcing statutory rape laws indiscriminately did not take into account the needs of some adolescent mothers and their children, thus potentially creating a negative impact upon the vulnerable population the law was meant to serve. For instance, statutory rape offenders often must register as sex offenders. Stigmatizing men as sex offenders, particularly if they were in a relationship with an older teenager, would damage their future employment opportunities and the possibility of their contributing to the financial support of their children. Moreover, according to available statistics, males who are 5 or 6 years older than mothers who are 15 to 17 years old accounted for only about 20 percent of births to single adolescent females age 15 to 17. Nevertheless, in many places these relationships would be legally considered as statutory rape (Miller et al. 1998, 177).

In an important 1996 survey, close to 75 percent of Kansas district attorneys agreed that statutory rape should be aggressively enforced, but only 24 percent believed that enforcing statutory rape laws would actually decrease pregnancy rates. The attorneys' concern was focused on protecting young adolescents from becoming involved in abusive relationships and from engaging in behaviors for which they were not ready. Some respondents, however, believed that prosecution should depend upon the circumstances, and others worried about unintended effects—for example, that adolescents would be discouraged from seeking health care out of fear that their adult partners might be legally prosecuted. Opinions about legal penalties being an effective way to prevent statutory rape were also split, with 38 percent agreeing and 35 percent disagreeing (Miller et al. 1998).

Surveyed attorneys also disagreed about their perception of public support for aggressive enforcement of statutory rape laws, with 37 percent agreeing that it would count with public support and 26 percent in disagreement. Most believed that public support could be obtained but that gaining it would require such measures as public relations and education, and further, it could be gained only if the public perceived that prosecution would be impartial. Moreover, most believed that the public would support a case in which the offender is an adult and the victim is a child, but that the public probably would not support a case in which the couple was in a caring relationship and the partners had an age-span difference of 3 to 5 years. Over 50 percent of attorneys surveyed supported setting the age of consent at 15, while less than 20 percent believed the age should be 18 (Miller et al. 1998).

Finally, surveyed district attorneys agreed that age-span differences were an important consideration in the decision to prosecute. Prosecutors said they were less likely to proceed in a case in which the partners were close in age and the minor was around 16 years old. They were also less likely to proceed if both were involved in a relationship with parental approval. On the other hand, age difference was less important in cases in which coercion existed or the minor was developmentally disabled, and the surveyed attorneys were likelier to prosecute if a larger age-span difference existed—for example, if one party was 19 years old and the other was 13 to 15 years old. Prosecution was also more likely to occur if there was no prior relationship between the partners.

All surveyed attorneys said, however, that if they were given solid evidence they would prosecute a case of statutory rape aggressively. Lack of consent remains an important factor in statutory cases; that is, it is not, technically speaking, relevant. Evidence that serves to support a statutory case includes proof of a sexual relationship (such as a pregnancy that establishes paternity), credible witnesses, acknowledgment from the parties, evidence of psychological damage, and sexually transmitted disease. There are also important barriers to prosecuting a statutory rape case. In some states, claim to common-law marriage can serve as a defense to statutory rape prosecution.

In fact, recent studies show that, from 2000 to 2010, close to 250,000 individuals age 17 and under were married in the United States, including cases of 12-year-old girls in Alaska, Louisiana, and South Carolina. Of these, 167,000 occurred in 38 states, some of which do not have a minimum age of marriage. Other states categorized marriage of minors as "14 and younger," and a 2017 *New York Times* investigation uncovered the case of an 11-year-old being married to a 20-year-old who had impregnated her, in order to stop an investigation by child welfare authorities. A majority of child marriages occur between minor females and adult men, and they often serve to legalize a relationship that would otherwise violate statutory rape laws. Although numbers are not available for all states, the highest rates of child marriages are reported in Arkansas, Florida, Idaho, Kentucky, and Texas (Kristof 2017).

Child marriage places children at risk. A 2012 study shows that over 65 percent of marriages of underage people do not last. Moreover, underage marriages tend to force married minors to interrupt their schooling, endanger the health of child brides with early pregnancies, and anchor these brides and their children in poverty. Even though the number of child marriages is declining, children 16 and younger continue to be married in the United States (Hamilton 2012). On the other hand, a growing number of activists and organizations are increasingly advocating for all states to set a minimum marriage age or to ban child marriage altogether.

As important as it is to protect young people from exploitative relationships and from the consequence of their own decision-making, the results from these surveys serve to highlight an important factor: The goals of statutory laws are shaped by many purposes and interests—political and economic as well as social.

Kansas's district attorneys are not the only ones who question that aggressive enforcement of statutory rape laws would significantly impact adolescent pregnancy rates. Other studies support the findings. For instance, an American Bar Association study (Elstein and Davis 1997) surveyed prosecutors from 48 of the largest U.S. cities. About 75 percent of attorneys surveyed believed that enforcement authorities needed training in statutory rape, and they did not perceive reduction of adolescent pregnancy as a viable objective for statutory rape legislation. Reasons to prosecute tended to focus on the availability of solid evidence for the crime. Because they tended to find that there was not much public support for prosecuting cases of statutory rape, prosecutor discretion was the norm, and they tended to support a case-by-case assessment before proceeding. Although attorneys doubted the impact that enforcement of statutory rape law has on teenage pregnancy numbers, they believed that protecting children from harm was an important goal.

Upon making prosecution decisions, district attorneys also take into account the impact of their decisions upon existing policies. The majority of district attorneys in the Kansas survey (Miller et al. 1998) believed that aggressively prosecuting statutory rape cases would not have a negative impact on other policies pertaining adolescents, such as controlling sexually transmitted diseases or access to reproductive health care. However, adolescent advocates have argued that district attorneys are less familiar with issues of reproductive health among adolescents and teenage sexuality, and are more focused on prosecuting crime.

Aggressive prosecution of statutory rape may negatively impact paternity acknowledgment, for instance. Paternity acknowledgment benefits the child and helps provide better access to social benefits, as well as encouraging a relationship between father and child. Children advocates, then, often worry about the impact that criminal proceedings could have on mother and children. Other negative effects of statutory rape prosecution, according to the Kansas study (Miller et al. 1998), are the invasion of the victim's privacy and the possibility that adults being treated for sexually transmitted diseases may omit tracing their adolescent partners for fear of prosecution. These are some of the many potential unintended results that many activists take into consideration and that they advocate for policy-makers to consider when making legislative decisions.

In short, statutory rape is an issue for which there are many overlapping and often conflicting interests—family court, criminal court, and health services are a few. Sentences handed down by criminal courts may conflict with provisions for visitation and paternity rights. Statutory rape laws often raise the question of how to cope with cases in which rape was not forcible, in which the adolescent mother does not want to press charges against her partner, and in which the interests of the child are best served by the father being involved in the child's life.

According to many experts, an important obstacle to using statutory rape legislation to change or control adolescent behavior is that the brains of adolescents are not developed enough for these young people to consider long-term views and consequences. Although there is no consensus on the age at which this development is complete, most experts believe it ranges from older adolescence to young adulthood. In fact, many developmental experts argue that children and adolescents tend to consider themselves to be invulnerable to danger, and thus they do not carefully consider the risks of behaviors that seem attractive to them. In the United States and many other countries, then, laws have been established to impose legal limitations on various activities according to age—marrying, obtaining a driver's license, voting, and others. With the intent to protect sexually active adolescents from the negative consequences of poorly made choices, states require that adolescents reach a specific age of maturity before their consent is considered legally valid. Moreover, controlling the behavior of adolescents is problematic because, as most experts explain, teenagers usually strive for independence yet are not ready for complete independence. Adolescents lack the life experience and emotional and mental abilities necessary for informed and mature decision-making. Moreover, one adolescent may mature at a different pace than another adolescent.

Adolescents typically undertake riskier behaviors than adults, such as engaging in unprotected sexual relations, drug experimentation, and physical behaviors like reckless driving. Despite these factors, experts and legislators generally understand that adolescents must be gradually allowed autonomy in order to grow into young adulthood with the social and practical skills needed to survive on their own. Legislators, policy-makers, parents, health providers, other involved adults, and even the adolescents themselves often disagree about the degree of autonomy that an adolescent must be given, so that there are often contentious debates on a range of issues—from judging an adolescent as an adult in a court of law, to the legal age of consent for sexual activity.

There continues to be some level of disagreement among experts about the most appropriate age of consent, but in most states consensus has been reached to set it to between age 16 and 18, with a recent breakdown establishing it as follows: age 16 in 29 states; age 17 in 7 states, and age 18 in 14 states. Further, most states have now enacted legislation that decriminalizes sexual intercourse between partners within prescribed age spans, when at least one of the partners is under the legal age of consent.

Besides raising the age of consent and adding the age-span differential considerations, other changes have been enacted in recent decades. Over time, varied definitions of *consent* were developed in order to address different situations. Critics argued that in other instances of crime involving force, such as robbery, there was no standard seeking to identify the victim's consent, nor was the burden of proof placed on the victim to evidence lack of consent. Because of the problems inherent with the standard of consent, the issue of consent was eliminated from laws pertaining to forcible rape, so that it is usually not included in the description of the crime.

In relation to sexual crimes involving minors, most law codes establish that consent may not be used a defense. However, most studies involving adolescent sexuality support conserving the age of consent. A 2013 survey suggests that people are almost universally concerned with sexual crimes against younger adolescents—those between 12 and 15 years of age. As victims' age approaches 16 and older, however, concern and criticism among surveyed respondents decreased significantly, with condemnation rates being extremely low for adolescents 19 and above (Koon-Magnin and Ruback 2013, 1919).

Also of concern are situations that blur the line between what may be represented as consensual sex with very young adolescents, but on closer inspection may involve coercion. Studies consistently show that young girls tend to suffer from low self-esteem and eagerness to please, which makes them easy to coerce and manipulate into becoming sexually active. Lack of experience also comes into play when they agree to a sexual relation that may be exploitative. Even though a young adolescent may look and act older than her age, activists posit, she is not yet emotionally or legally competent to consent to sex. In fact, sexually active young adolescents—as young as 11 or 12 years old—are often involved with older males, and vulnerable to coercion and abuse.

Abundant cases show that young girls often agree to sexual relations without a full understanding of their sexuality and sexual relations, or agree out of coercion and misunderstanding as to what *consensual* really means. In fact, research indicates that sexual behavior of young girls has usually little to do with expressing autonomy and sexual desire, and more to do with the desire to please, to gain the attention of boys, and to receive affection. Therefore, according to children advocates, statutory rape laws may not serve to immediately impact the sexual behavior of more mature teenagers, but the laws do serve to protect vulnerable adolescents, and given this, they should continue to stand.

On the other hand, while acknowledging that statutory rape laws seek to protect vulnerable adolescents from disadvantageous relationships and such negative consequences as psychological and physical harm, sexually transmitted diseases, and early pregnancy, advocates for reforms of statutory rape law believe that the laws that sought to protect vulnerable adolescents were often framed in paternalistic ways that infantilize and restrict the choices made by adolescent minors. In fact, they point out that the laws often seem to reflect the age-old "seduction laws," in which women were seen as passive, lacking in will, and subject to deceit and at heightened risk of being taken advantage. The issue became prey to political concerns that sought to cut welfare and other benefits to low-income mothers—measures that increase inequality and discrimination and serve to criminalize and punish the behavior of already disadvantaged groups. This was particularly the case in the 1980s and 1990s, when the language that framed the statutory laws discourse tended to demonize minority and low-income groups.

The debate around statutory rape laws, in general, reflects that society feels responsible and entitled to regulate the sexuality of minors and their sexual objectification by others; it reflects the desire to help minors grow safely into adulthood. Social scientists often argue, however, that awareness and education may achieve greater results in decreasing adolescent pregnancy rates and early sexualization than statutory rape laws would, and these experts encourage authorities to consider pregnancy and sexualization on a case-by-case basis. Studies have shown, for instance, that awareness has been instrumental in reduction of such risky behaviors as smoking, over long periods of time, and that greater access to effective contraception has helped reduce the prevalence of unprotected sex among teenagers. In other words, while statutory rape laws may decrease in some ways—however minimal—pregnancy rates among adolescents, this decrease may be limited due to the fact that most teenage pregnancies result from relationships between partners close in age. Moreover, enforcement of statutory rape laws should be accompanied by reduction of the societal factors that fuel adolescent pregnancy; this includes providing greater access to health care, education, public services, and other actions that discourage the behaviors and risks that may lead adolescents to become pregnant.

The age span between victim and offender is one of the most important factors in how people perceive statutory rape. Studies on perception and attribution have shown that respondents are more supportive of younger victims and more willing to assign responsibility to older adolescents for their sexual behavior. Other studies also consistently show that statutory rape laws vary greatly across states, but that the laws do not impact patterns of teenage sexual behavior, which tend to be consistent across states. In other words, it is unlikely that statutory rape laws impact adolescent sexuality much. Surveys show that most in the public do not assign much weight to statutory rape legislation either, even though they are more concerned about sexual activity among younger adolescents than among older ones.

Also worth noting is a 2013 study that found the majority of statutory rape offenders to be under age 25. Most of the adolescents surveyed—close to 74 percent—perceived more culpability the larger the age span between the sexual partners, but they also demonstrated very scant knowledge about statutory rape laws. This supports the concern of many experts who argue that there is a great need to educate adolescents about statutory rape concepts and legislation (Oudekerk, Farr, and Reppucci 2013, 858).

Education and awareness are important across the board. Statutory rape is also an issue of familial relationships of power; for instance, it is often tied to incest, and it often occurs between an older male relative and a younger male or female child or adolescent. Such instances carry grave repercussions for victims, who often suffer the lifelong consequences of the abuse perpetuated against them. Prosecuting instances of incest is complex, due to the fact that victims seldom want to testify against the perpetrator.

In general, however, legislative efforts to regulate the sexual activity of teenagers have proven largely unsuccessful. A survey conducted by the U.S. Department of Health and Human Services shows that over 30 percent of female adolescents and 40 percent of male adolescents in the United States have had sexual relations before ninth grade. By the time they reach 11th and 12th grades, between 50 to 60 percent of adolescents in the United States have become sexually active (U.S. Department of Health and Human Services 2013, 33). The 1996 Welfare Reform Act, then, which aims to regulate the sexual behavior of adolescents by recommending the aggressive enforcement of statutory rape laws, does not correlate with the realities of adolescent sexual behavior.

Legislation pertaining to adolescent behavior and the desire to protect adolescents from predatory adults and bad decision-making, according to experts, needs to create a balance between the guidance and protection they require and the autonomy they need in order to become healthy adults. Experts also recommend that decisions regarding policy and legislation be based on empirical studies and data, and that these decisions take into account the complex needs and social context of adolescents. Most studies support the existence of age of consent laws and support statutory rape legislation that protects the young against coercive and exploitative relationships; but some forms and applications of laws may be more effective than others.

Worldwide

Laws regarding statutory rape vary across countries; yet in most societies, sexual intercourse with minors under the age of consent is considered a crime. How the crime is conceptualized and punished, and how the laws are enforced, however, also vary greatly, depending upon the cultural mores and legal system of each country.

An understanding of when adolescents are ready to engage in sexual relations varies across cultures. In some, adolescents are considered ready to become sexually active after they reach puberty. As in many states of the United States, in some countries statutory rape laws do not apply if the parties are legally married to each other. Gender further complicates the issue, as in some countries the age of consent differs for same-sex sexual intercourse and for heterosexual relations. The wording of statutory rape laws around the world also reflects cultural mores. In Mexico, for example, some statutory rape codes position as the victim a young woman between ages 12 and 18, and those codes conceive of her as "passive" and the male as "active," reflecting traditional patriarchal stereotypes of women and men. Such laws also take into account whether the victim was sexually experienced and whether she was deceived into the relationship. Whereas it used to be possible in some Latin American societies for the statutory rape offender to "repair the crime" by marrying the victim, today the more common result is a sentence that includes incarceration.

Finally, though estimates are hard to come by because statutory rape is an underreported crime, in recent decades the rise of globalization and ease of traveling have fueled a rise in sex tourism with children worldwide. This has led to high levels of trafficking, including the abduction of children for labor and sexual exploitation.

Major Laws

To curtail trafficking and sexual exploitation of minors, some countries—the United States among others—have age of consent laws that transcend borders. In this manner, U.S. citizens abroad are required to abide by age of consent laws in the United States. They risk running afoul of U.S. law if they engage in sexual activities with a minor abroad. Neither ignorance of the law nor mistaking the victim's age can be used as a defense.

Nevertheless, the age of consent in most economically developed nations has gradually shifted to 14 and 16 or older. For many societies, however, the age of consent may still be 13–14, or lower. The age of consent in Albania, Austria, Bosnia, China, Croatia, Estonia, Germany, Hungary, Italy, Macedonia, and Serbia is 14; in the United Kingdom and Canada, it is 16. In Argentina, Burkina Faso, Cypress, Nigeria, Spain, South Korea, Syria, and parts of Japan and India, the age of consent has been set at 13.

Activists are concerned because a very low age of consent places young people at grave risk of exploitation and is a contributing factor to the sex-slavery industry that prevails in Southeast Asia and other parts of the world. It has also, until recently, placed young girls at risk of child marriages at extremely early ages to much older men, as has occurred in India and in some Muslim societies. Differences are also often found across ethnic, religious, and geographic or regional lines within the same country. Child marriage is embedded in many cultures, for religious or economic reasons or both. Patriarchal cultures often see child marriage as a way to protect the purity and maximize the childbearing potential of young women. In other cultures, it is a mechanism of survival, and girls are married off to protect them from starvation or rape. Regardless of the motivations, international experts have long warned that child marriage hinders development and economic growth in communities, isolates girls, and places the girls at risk for exploitation and abuse, as well as health complications.

Estimates about the rates of child marriages may vary, because not all countries are able to maintain accurate records, but in general the highest prevalence rates are found in South Asia, Africa, and the Middle East. While some argue that the highest rates are found in India, others argue that the highest rates of child marriage take place in Saudi Arabia. Around the world, according to recent numbers provided by child advocate organizations, over 700 million girls today have been married before age 18. Of these, one-third were under 15 when they married (Lenhardt et al. 2016, vi)

Although child marriages have been banned in a few countries, such as in India and Guatemala, reports worldwide show that it is still a common practice in many countries. Guatemala, in Central America, established the minimum age of consent at 18 in 2015, after public outrage stemming from publicized accounts of girls being married as young as age 12. In 1929, India set the minimum age for consent for girls at 15 and for boys at 18. After several revisions in the ensuing decades, in 1978 the minimum age for marriage was set at 18 for women and 19 for men. Although the law has been challenged several times by different groups, child marriage has decreased over 45 percent since 2001, according to Indian government reports. In early 2016, an attempt to raise the age of consent from 16 to 18 in Pakistan failed. According to a 2014 UNICEF report, India is among the 10 countries in the world with the highest rates of child marriage. (The other countries are Nepal, Burkina Faso, Ethiopia, Guinea, Central African Republic, Mali, Chad, Bangladesh, and Niger.) In India, nearly 30 percent of women are married before age 13. They are also more likely to be poor and uneducated (UNICEF 2014).

In some countries, child marriage is legal and children may be married as young as toddlers. For instance, Saudi Arabia has no minimum age for marriage, and girls as young as age 8 or 9 may attract very high bride prices from wealthy grooms, enough to seem an attractive option to economically struggling families. In fact, estimates indicate that Saudi Arabia has the highest number of child marriages in the Middle East, a practice that has sparked international outrage for years. Activists point out, however, that the prevalence of child marriages in Saudi Arabia has been treated with indifference or scant forcefulness by such international bodies as the United Nations, and by such powerful countries as the United States.

Despite having failed to publicly denounce Saudi Arabia specifically, as critics argue, the United Nations has made several proclamations against child marriage in general, and several international conventions forbid child marriage, defining 18 as the age of consent or adulthood. These declarations stem from the argument that early marriages hinder emotional, physical, and economic development for girls and perpetuate inequality and poverty around the world. Although child marriage is somewhat more prevalent in less-developed countries, child marriage occurs in societies around the world. Some experts believe that despite rising consciousness-raising and international regulation, if current trends continue, by 2020 over 140 million girls will be married before reaching adulthood (Coleman et al. 2013).

Obstacles

Enforcement may vary across countries; in fact, it may be unevenly applied even within national boundaries. In some countries, for instance, legal procedures are enacted only when the age span between the parties is considered egregious—or when unacceptable ethical violations are involved, such as when the adult is in a position of power in relation to the minor. Cases that reflect ethical violations might include those in which the perpetrator was a teacher or a priest. These can be problematic, however. For instance, in traditional societies, in which respect for male authority is deeply entrenched, prosecution may be difficult; in such communities, societal mores often penalize the victim for speaking out, rather than condemning the perpetrator. Therefore, victims commonly fear reporting rape. In fact, in some extremely conservative societies, young victims of rape may be shunned—or even murdered in "honor killings," which are seen as necessary to salvage family honor. Prosecuting and proving statutory rape cases, then, may be extremely difficult when the victim perceives the consequences of speaking out as far worse than those of seeking justice.

Studies have found that children from rural areas are about twice as likely as those from urban areas to be married as children. A 1970s study in Spain found that in rural communities—as opposed to more sophisticated urban societies—instances of felony statutory rape and incest, often between an older male relative and a female minor, go largely unreported. Young girls are placed more at risk when they enter puberty, especially if the female head of the household becomes sick or dies and the family lives in isolated conditions. Among the most important causes for these events, according to researchers, is the entrenched patriarchal mores that are typical in such societies (Morillas Cueva 1976). Since that 1970s study, however, legal codes pertaining to statutory rape have been reformed in many regions worldwide, including Latin America and Europe.

Finally, the worldwide prevalence of sex tourism often makes it difficult to prosecute. Although prostitution involving minors is not precisely legal in some countries, the practice is lightly regulated and commonly involves the participation of corrupt government authorities. Child sex tourism has surged globally as a multibillion-dollar business, involving the commercialization and exploitation of children for sexual purposes. It is difficult to find accurate estimates of its prevalence, yet countries in poor regions of East Asia, among others, have raised international controversy for becoming noted destinations for sex tourism, often involving minors. In some countries, such as Thailand, it has been estimated that close to 40 percent of sex workers are children (Taran and Moreno-Fontes Chammartin 2003, 11). The United States and Britain, among others, have developed severe sanctions and legislation in order to curtail their citizens' participation in sex tourism with children abroad. Governments and international organizations have developed incentives, protocols, conventions, and other instruments in order to stop human trafficking and the sexual exploitation of children. Among the initiatives proposed, there is consensus that promoting education among girls is one of the most important factors, as girls with higher levels of education are less likely to marry before they reach the age of consent. At the international level, policies being promoted by the United Nations and other international organizations include raising diplomatic pressure, providing support in developing nations, strengthening pertinent legislation, and offering economic incentives—as well as promoting initiatives to expand education, raise awareness, fight child marriage and trafficking, and provide access to family, reproductive, and maternal health.

Trudy Mercadal

Further Reading

Brownmiller, Susan. 1993. *Against Our Will: Men, Women, and Rape*. Reprint ed. New York: Ballantine Books.

Cocca, Carolyn E. 2004. *Jailbait. The Politics of Statutory Rape Laws in the United States*. Albany: State University of New York Press.

Coleman, Isobel, Laura Laski, Gayle Lemmon, Nice N. Leng'ete, Donald Steinberg, and Rachel Vogelstein. 2013. "Child Marriage: Geography of a Problem." UN Council of Foreign Relations. Accessed March 30, 2016. http://www.cfr.org/peace-conflict-and-human-rights/child-marriage/p32096#!/?cid=otr_marketing_use-child_marriage_Infoguide#!%2F.

Darroch, Jacqueline E., and Susheela Singh. 1999. "Why Is Teenage Pregnancy Declining? The Roles of Abstinence, Sexual Activity and Contraceptive Use." Occasional Report No. 1. New York: The Alan Guttmacher Institute. Accessed January 16, 2015. http://citeseerx.ist.psu.edu/viewdoc/download?doi=10.1.1.295.2015&rep=rep1&type=pdf.

Donovan, Patricia. 1996. "Can Statutory Rape Laws Be Effective in Preventing Adolescent Pregnancy?" *Perspectives on Sexual and Reproductive Health* 29 (1): 30–36. The Alan Guttmacher Institute. Accessed December 10, 2017. https://www.guttmacher.org/sites/default/files/article_files/2903097.pdf.

Elstein, Sharon, and Noy Davis. 1997. *Sexual Relationships between Adult Males and Young Teen Girls: Exploring the Legal and Social Responses*. Washington, DC: American Bar Association Center on Children and the Law. Accessed December 13, 2017. https://www.americanbar.org/content/dam/aba/migrated/child/PublicDocuments/statutory_rape.authcheckdam.pdf.

Fischel, Joseph. 2016. *Sex and Harm in the Age of Consent*. Minneapolis: University of Minnesota Press.

Freedman, Estelle B. 2013. *Redefining Rape*. Cambridge, MA: Harvard University Press.

Hamilton, Vivian E. 2012. "The Age of Marital Capacity: Reconsidering Civil Recognition of Adolescent Marriage." *Faculty Publications*, Paper 1430. College of William and Mary Law School. Accessed April 15, 2017. http://scholarship.law.wm.edu/facpubs.

Koon-Magnin, Sarah, and R. Barry Ruback. 2013. "The Perceived Legitimacy of Statutory Rape Laws: The Effects of Victim Age, Perpetrator Age, and Age Span." *Journal of Applied Social Psychology* 43 (9): 1918–30.

Kristof, Nicholas. 2017. "11 Years Old, a Mom, and Pushed to Marry Her Rapist in Florida." *New York Times*, May 26. Accessed May 29, 2017. https://www.nytimes.com/2017/05/26/opinion/sunday/it-was-forced-on-me-child-marriage-in-the-us.html.

Lenhardt, Amanda, Lisa Wise, Georgiana Rosa, Hollie Warren, Frances Mason, and Rukayah Sarumi. 2016. "Every Last Girl." Every Last Child Series. London: Save the Children Fund.

Miller, Henry L., Corinne E. Miller, Linda Kenny, and James Clark. 1998. "Issues in Statutory Rape Law Enforcement: The Views of District Attorneys in Kansas." *Family Planning Perspectives* 30 (4): 177–82.

Morillas Cueva, Lorenzo. 1976. "El delito del estupro—Incesto." *Anuario de derecho penal y ciencias penales* 29 (2): 293–328.

Oliveri, Rigel C. 2000. "Statutory Rape Law and Enforcement in the Wake of Welfare Reform." *Stanford Law Review*, 52: 463–508.

Oudekerk, Barbara A., Rachel H. Farr, and Nicholas D. Reppucci. 2013. "Is It Love or Sexual Abuse? Young Adults' Perceptions of Statutory Rape." *Journal of Child Sexual Abuse* 22 (7): 858–77.

Sielke, Sabine. 2009. *Reading Rape: The Rhetoric of Sexual Violence in American Literature and Culture, 1790–1990.* Princeton, NJ: Princeton University Press.

Simpson, A. R. 2009. "Judicial Recommendations Against Removal: A Solution to the Problem of Deportation for Statutory Rape." *New England Journal on Criminal & Civil Confinement* 35 (2): 489–512.

Taran, Patrick A., and Gloria Moreno-Fontes Chammartin. 2003. "Getting at the Roots: Stopping Exploitation of Migrant Workers by Organized Crime." In *Perspectives on Labour Migration, No. 1.* Geneva: International Labour Office. http://www.ilo.org /wcmsp5/groups/public/---ed_protect/---protrav/---migrant/documents/publication /wcms_232364.pdf.

Tchen, Christina M. 1983. "Rape Reform and a Statutory Consent Defense." *Journal of Criminal Law and Criminology* 74 (4): 1518–55.

Troup-Leasure, Karyl, and Howard Snyder. 2005. "Statutory Rape Known to Law Enforcement." *Juvenile Justice Bulletin.* Washington, DC: Office of Juvenile Justice and Delinquency Prevention. Accessed April 15, 2017. https://www.ncjrs.gov/pdffiles1 /ojjdp/208803.pdf.

United Nations Children's Fund. 2014. *Ending Child Marriage: Progress and Prospects.* New York: UNICEF. Accessed December 13, 2017. https://www.unicef.org/media /files/Child_Marriage_Report_7_17_LR.pdf

U.S. Department of Health and Human Services. 2013. *Child Health USA 2012.* Health Resources and Services Administration, Maternal and Child Health Bureau. Rockville, MD: U.S. Department of Health and Human Services. Accessed April 15, 2017. https://mchb.hrsa.gov/chusa12/.

Waites, Matthew. 2005. *The Age of Consent: Young People, Sexuality, and Citizenship.* London: Palgrave McMillan.

Watkins, Christine. 2013. *Age of Consent (At Issue).* San Diego, CA: Greenhaven Press.

STRANGER RAPE

Stranger rape is rape or sexual assault committed by someone unknown to the victim. It can involve victims of any age or sex. Some U.K. police forces use a definition that classifies *stranger rape offenses* as cases "where victims have no previous knowledge of the offender, had not knowingly met them before and would, therefore, be unable to name them or provide information about their identity. They would also include cases in which there had been a brief, or single, encounter within a short period, but only to such an extent that a victim might be able to identify the offender but would not describe him as an acquaintance" (HMIC and HMCPSI 2012, 29).

Most statistics indicate that stranger rape is relatively uncommon. The Rape, Abuse & Incest National Network (RAINN) reports that in 7 out of 10 cases of sexual assault, the victim knew the perpetrator (Perpetrators of Sexual Violence n.d.). Stranger rape can happen in a variety of situations. Typically, it takes place in one of three ways:

- In a blitz sexual assault, the perpetrator "quickly and brutally assaults the victim with no prior contact." This often occurs in a public place at night.
- In contact sexual assault, the perpetrator tries to lure the victim, perhaps by flirting, to a place, such as a car, where the sexual assault will occur.
- Home invasion sexual assault takes place when the perpetrator breaks into the victim's house and then commits a sexual assault (Sexual Assault n.d.).

Stranger rape can also take place in conflict zones and in instances of ethnic or genocidal rape. In cases of multiple perpetrator rape, one or more of the perpetrators might be known to the victim, but not all of them. Stranger rapes may also take place after the perpetrator meets and targets a victim in a bar or club. If the victim was raped while drugged or unconscious, she or he may not know who committed the assault.

In 1987, Susan Estrich coined the term "real rape" in her book by the same name. Estrich had been raped by a stranger, and she wrote, "The law's abhorrence of the rapist in stranger cases like mine has been matched only by its distrust of the victim who claims to have been raped by a friend or neighbor or acquaintance" (Estrich 1987, 4). Estrich calls cases that do not involve strangers or use force "simple rape." She asserts in her book that "a 'simple rape'" is a 'real rape'" (Estrich 1987, 7).

In the United States, and in some other countries, stranger rape has often involved a racial component as well. From the 19th century on, black men have often been seen as highly sexualized. Black men who even looked at white women risked being lynched. For example, 14-year-old Emmett Till (1941–1955) was accused of whistling at or flirting with a white woman, Carolyn Bryant, in a small grocery store in Mississippi. A few nights later, Bryant's husband and some other men tortured and killed Till, then threw his body into the Tallahatchie River. The image of the "big black buck" continues in popular media depictions, where black men, along with other men of color, are overrepresented as perpetrators of sexual violence (Finley 2016, 55).

Studies, however, demonstrate that many people continue to believe that stranger rape is a more serious crime than sexual assaults in which the victim knows the perpetrator. According to one researcher, "victims of 'date rape' are typically viewed as less harmed than victims of 'stranger rape'; and 'date rapists' are typically viewed as less serious offenders, and frankly less culpable than stranger rapists. Date rape is often viewed more in traditionally civil than in traditionally criminal terms; that is, as an unfortunate encounter in which the two parties share culpability because of too much alcohol and too little clear communication." He also notes that jurors are less likely to find defendants guilty in such cases (Lisak 2011, 50).

In January 2017, a New York City police captain's remarks about stranger rape sparked public outrage. In discussing a rise in sexual violence in Brooklyn, Captain Peter Rose remarked, "It's not a trend that we're too worried about because out of 13 [sex attacks], only two were true stranger rapes." He went on to say, "If there's a true stranger rape, a random guy picks up a stranger off the street, those are the troubling ones" (Hogan 2017). Rose later apologized for his statements.

United States

Prevalence

Sexual assaults of all sorts are underreported. In 2014, according to the National Crime Victimization Survey, victims reported only 33.6 percent of rape and sexual assaults to police (Truman and Langton 2015, 7). In general, the statistics indicate that stranger rape occurs less frequently than sexual assaults committed by someone known to the victim. The National Crime Victimization Survey for 2010 reports that 25 percent of rape and sexual assaults against women were committed by strangers. The figures for men were based on 10 or fewer cases, but they also indicate that most assaults were committed by individuals known to the victims (Truman 2011, 9). In the majority of sexual assaults, the victim knew the perpetrator.

A report published in 2014 by the Centers for Disease Control and Prevention (CDC) used data from the 2011 National Intimate Partner and Sexual Violence Survey. In total, 14,155 interviews took place; 6,879 women and 5,848 men completed the telephone survey. Those being interviewed were asked about specific types of sexual violence, including "rape (completed or attempted forced penetration or alcohol- or drug-facilitated penetration) and sexual violence other than rape, including being made to penetrate a perpetrator, sexual coercion (non-physically pressured unwanted penetration), unwanted sexual contact (e.g., kissing or fondling), and noncontact unwanted sexual experiences (e.g., being flashed or forced to view sexually explicit media)" (Breiding et al. 2014).

Though most instances of rape and sexual coercion reported by the respondents indicated the assaults were committed by an intimate partner or an acquaintance, nearly half of the women (49.3 percent) reported "noncontact

Table 1. Violent Victimizations, by Type of Crime and Victim–Offender Relationship, 2010

RELATIONSHIP TO VICTIM	VIOLENT CRIME		RAPE/SEXUAL ASSAULT		ROBBERY		AGGRAVATED ASSAULT		SIMPLE ASSAULT	
	Number	Percent	Number	Percent	Number	Percent	Number	Percent	Number	Percent
Male Victims										
Total	1,956,320	100%	15,020!	100%!	302,400	100%	420,460	100%	1218,440	100%
Nonstranger	781,300	40%	11,730!	78%!	51,780	17%	208,020	49%	509,770	42%
Intimate[a]	101,530	5%	—	—	22,110!	7%!	29,290!	7%!	50,140	4%
Other relative	111,680	6%	—	—	1,900!	1%!	41,710	10%	68,070	6%
Friend/ acquaintance	568,090	29%	11,730!	78%!	27,780!	9%!	137,020	33%	391,560	32%
Stranger	934,520	48%	1,220!	8%!	216,330	72%	154,680	37%	562,290	46%
Unknown[b]	240,500	12%	2,070!	14%!	34,280!	11%!	57,760	14%	146,380	12%
Female Victims										
Total	1,854,980	100%	169,370	100%	176,270	100%	304,720	100%	1,204,620	100%
Nonstranger	1,182,330	64%	124,303	73%	76,140	43%	163,150	54%	819,010	68%
Intimate[a]	407,700	22%	29,010!	17%!	36,540	21%	71,640	24%	270,510	22%
Other relative	162,510	9%	12,920!	8%!	18,540!	11%!	14,510!	5%!	116,530	10%
Friend/ acquaintance	612,130	33%	82,100	48%	21,070!	12%!	76,990	25%	431,970	36%
Stranger	562,580	30%	41,950	25%	93,760	53%	114,460	38%	312,410	26%
Unknown[b]	110,070	6%	3,390!	2%!	6,360!	4%!	27,110!	9%!	73,210	6%

Note: Detail may not sum to total due to rounding.

! Interpret with caution; estimate based on 10 or fewer sample cases, or coefficient of variation is greater than 50%.

— Less than 0.5%.

[a] Defined as current or former spouses, boyfriends, or girlfriends.

[b] Includes relationship unknown and number of offenders unknown.

Source: Truman, Jennifer L. 2011. "Criminal Victimization, 2010." Table 5. NCJ 235508. Washington, DC: Bureau of Justice Statistics. Accessed December 20, 2017. https://www.bjs.gov/content/pub/pdf/cv10.pdf.

Table 2. Lifetime Reports of Sexual Violence among Victims, by Type of Perpetrator* and Sex of Victim, National Intimate Partner and Sexual Violence Survey, United States, 2011

	CURRENT/FORMER INTIMATE PARTNER			FAMILY MEMBER†			PERSON OF AUTHORITY§			ACQUAINTANCE¶			STRANGER		
	%**	(95% CI)	Estimated No. of Victims††	%**	(95% CI)	Estimated No. of Victims††	%**	(95% CI)	Estimated No. of Victims††	%**	(95% CI)	Estimated No. of Victims††	%**	(95% CI)	Estimated No. of Victims††
Women															
Rape	45.4	(41.3–49.5)	10,574,000	12.1	(9.4–15.4)	2,823,000	2.6	(1.5–4.6)	611,000	46.7	(42.5–51.0)	10,889,000	12.9	(10.7–15.6)	3,037,000
Completed or attempted forced penetration	43.1	(43.2–53.1)	8,264,000	14.9	(11.5–19.2)	2,566,000	—§§			38.8	(33.9–43.9)	6,660,000	11.0	(8.7–13.8)	1,894,000
Completed alcohol- or drug-facilitated penetration	43.4	(34.7–46.4)	4,558,000	—			—			58.4	(52.5–64.0)	6,582,000	12.4	(9.2–16.4)	1,395,000
Other sexual violence	36.0	(33.5–38.6)	19,082,000	16.7	(14.8–18.7)	8,845,000	7.6	(6.4–9.2)	4,043,000	43.4	(40.8–46.0)	22,963,000	43.0	(40.4–45.6)	22,794,000
Made to penetrate	53.2	(36.0–69.7)	374,000	—			—			—			—		
Sexual coercion	74.1	(69.5–78.3)	11,156,000	8.1	(5.1–12.4)	1,213,000	6.1	(4.1–9.2)	925,000	25.5	(21.1–30.5)	3,841,000	—		
Unwanted sexual contact	23.4	(20.6–26.4)	7,711,000	22.1	(19.4–25.0)	7,286,000	8.9	(7.1–11.0)	293,000	47.2	(43.9–50.6)	15,586,000	21.1	(18.5–23.9)	6,967,000
Noncontact unwanted sexual experiences	25.6	(23.8–29.5)	10,311,000	15.1	(13.0–17.5)	5,879,000	3.7	(2.7–5.1)	1,436,000	33.5	(30.6–36.7)	13,017,000	49.3	(46.1–52.4)	19,113,000
Men															
Rape	28.0	(18.4–42.6)	572,000	—			—			—			44.9	(32.2–58.3)	885,000	—

(Continued)

433

Table 2. (*Continued*)

	CURRENT/FORMER INTIMATE PARTNER			FAMILY MEMBER†			PERSON OF AUTHORITY§			ACQUAINTANCE¶			STRANGER		
	%**	(95% CI)	Estimated No. of Victims††	%**	(95% CI)	Estimated No. of Victims††	%**	(95% CI)	Estimated No. of Victims††	%**	(95% CI)	Estimated No. of Victims††	%**	(95% CI)	Estimated No. of Victims††
Completed alcohol- or drug-facilitated penetration	—	—	—	—	—	—	—	—	—	51.0	(34.1–67.7)	667,000	—	—	—
Other sexual violence	40.7	(36.8–44.7)	10,828,000	5.5	(4.0–7.6)	1,471,000	6.5	(4.8–8.7)	1,723,000	45.6	(41.7–49.6)	12,134,000	27.2	(23.8–30.8)	7,221,000
Made to penetrate	54.5	(46.8–62.1)	4,151,000	—	—	—	—	—	—	43.0	(35.5–50.8)	3,271,000	8.6	(5.4–13.2)	651,000
Sexual coercion	69.5	(61.6–76.3)	4,554,000	—	—	—	—	—	—	26.7	(20.4–34.0)	1,748,000	—	—	—
Unwanted sexual contact	22.6	(18.1–28.0)	2,771,000	6.1	(4.0–9.1)	741,000	6.7	(4.3–10.3)	820,000	51.8	(45.9–57.6)	6,339,000	23.7	(18.9–29.3)	2,903,000
Norcontact unwanted sexual experiences	30.9	(26.0–36.3)	4,686,000	7.2	(4.9–10.5)	1,088,000	7.0	(4.9–9.8)	1,056,000	39.2	(34.3–44.3)	5,939,000	30.9	(26.4–35.7)	4,674,000

Notes: Abbreviation: CI = Confidence interval

* Relationship is based on victims' reports of their relationship at the time the perpetrator first committed any violence against them. Because of the possibility of multiple perpetrators, combined row percentages might exceed 100%.

† Includes immediate and extended family members.

§ Includes, for example, boss, supervisor, superior in command, teacher, professor, coach, doctor, therapist, and caregiver.

¶ Includes friends, neighbors, family friends, first date, someone briefly known, and persons not known well.

** Percentages are weighted.

†† Rounded to the nearest thousand.

§§ Estimate is not reported; relative standard error > 30% or cell size ≤ 20.

Source: Breiding, Matthew J., Smith, Sharon G., Basile, Kathleen C., Walters, Mikel L., Chen, Jieru, and Merrick, Melissa T. 2014. "Prevalence and Characteristics of Sexual Violence, Stalking, and Intimate Partner Violence Victimization—National Intimate Partner and Sexual Violence Survey, United States, 2011." *Morbidity and Mortality Weekly Report* 63 (SS08): 1–18. Centers of Disease Control and Prevention. Accessed December 20, 2017. https://www.cdc.gov/mmwr/preview/mmwrhtml/ss6308a1.htm.

unwanted sexual experiences" with strangers. Men were the victims of such contact in 30.9 percent of cases. In victims of stalking, 16.2 percent of the women reported being stalked by strangers; 20 percent of the men said they had been stalked by strangers (Breiding et al. 2014).

In 2006, a report discussed findings from the National Violence Against Women Survey conducted in 1995 and 1996, which asked 8,000 women and 8,000 men about their experiences with sexual violence. The survey questioned individuals about assaults over the person's lifetime, as well as during the year preceding the survey. The survey screened men and women for experiences of rape and attempted rape, as events that took place or were attempted "without the victim's consent that involved the use or threat of force in vaginal, anal, or oral intercourse" (Tjaden and Thoennes 2006, 3). Combining rape and attempted rape figures, the report estimated that 17.6 percent of the women and 3 percent of the men who were surveyed had been sexually assaulted at some point in their lives. The authors of the report suspect that actual figures could be higher, however, since the survey excluded children and teens under age 18, as well as homeless and institutionalized individuals and those who did not live in households with telephones. Most of the victims surveyed had been raped by someone they knew. The statistics from female respondents indicated 16.7 percent were raped by strangers; for male respondents, the figure was 22.8 percent. However, the report also noted that "although male victims were more likely than female victims to be raped by an acquaintance or a stranger, it is noteworthy that women are at significantly greater risk than men of being raped by all types of offenders, including acquaintances and strangers (Tjaden and Thoennes 2006, 21). Most women (80.9 percent) did not report the rape to the police. Of that number, slightly more (20.9 percent) reported being raped by someone they were not intimate with. Of those who reported their rapes, 18 percent had been raped by an intimate partner (Tjaden and Thoennes 2006, 34).

Most states report similar figures on stranger rape. For example, a 2007 study in Utah reported that most sexual assaults were committed by "a family member (30.9%), intimate partner such as a spouse or boyfriend or girlfriend (20.8%), friend (14.3%), neighbor (9.9%), babysitter (2.2%), or coworker (1.8%)." Stranger rapes occurred in 13.3 percent of the reported cases (Utah Department of Health n.d.). Nevertheless, in a few places, reports of stranger rape are increasing. The New York City police department reported an increase of 49 stranger rape cases from 2014 to 2015. The New York Times noted that the trend was increasing, "with 68 occurring in the first half of 2015 and 99 in the second half" (Bellafante 2016).

Despite the statistical evidence indicating that most victims of sexual assaults know their assailants, the myth of the stranger in the dark street persists as the typical image of a rapist. Studies reveal that many victims do not report sexual assaults because they fear they will not be believed. This is particularly true when the victims know their attackers and/or have been drinking alcohol or using drugs. For example, one study of college women, published in 2011, noted that women were more likely to report rapes committed by a stranger. The study interviewed 2,000 college women about their experiences in 2006. The study examined only the most recent or only rape. For those who experienced rapes in that year, only 11.5 reported them, and only 2.7 percent of those who were assaulted while using drugs or alcohol reported the crime. The authors of the study note that those who do report rapes, however, are more likely to receive medical attention, as well as perhaps preventing a perpetrator from raping again (Wolitzky-Taylor et al. 2011).

The National Survey of Children's Exposure to Violence conducted telephone interviews with 4503 children (or their caregivers) in 2011. The children were aged one month to age 17. The caregivers of those under 10 years old were interviewed for the survey. Girls age 14 to 17 were most the most likely to be sexually assaulted. Almost 23 percent reported they had been sexually assaulted, and almost 11 percent had been victimized in the year of the survey. This included attempted or completed rape (8.1 percent), sexual harassment (13.6 percent), and "unwanted Internet sexual solicitation (12.9 percent). Sexual assault by an unknown adult occurred in 3.8 percent of the girls and 0.1 percent of the boys (Finkelhor, Turner, and Shattuck 2013).

In a study of incarcerated adolescents published in 2002, the authors noted that both male and female perpetrators were most likely to assault people they knew. The study used a written questionnaire and examined 805 youths: 707 boys, 91 girls, and 7 of undesignated gender. Of the respondents, 79 boys (11 percent), 9 girls (10 percent), and 5 of undesignated gender (71 percent) admitted to having coerced someone to have sex; 165 did not answer the question. The victims of both boys and girls were primarily people they knew; only two of the boys (4 percent) assaulted strangers, and only one girl (14 percent) did so (Morris, Anderson, and Knox 2002).

Major Laws

In general, rape laws cover rape and sexual assault committed by both strangers and those who are known to the victim. Within the United States, there are federal laws, but each state also has its own statutes. Scholars have noted the confusion that the differences cause, as what is rape in one state may not be rape in another. According to the authors of a 2012 paper, "sex crimes are named and defined differently and range from sexual penetration to acts of sexual violence that do not involve penetration, such as sexual contact and exposure. In some states, special terminology has been applied to refer to the sexual penetration of men and anal penetration of women, including sodomy and deviate sexual intercourse" (Tracy et al. 2012, 3). Moreover, the understanding of law enforcement agencies, researchers, support groups, and the general public may not match what is codified in law.

American rape law followed British common law, and many statutes have remained much the same since the 18th century. Under these older legal guidelines, rape occurred when a man penetrated a woman's vagina with his penis with force and against her will. To prove rape, a woman often had to prove that she had screamed and resisted and that the man had indeed used force. Women who were considered "unchaste" could not be raped, and a woman's prior sexual history could be entered into the court testimony. In addition, under the law, a man could not rape his wife, as it was assumed she gave the rights to her body to her husband upon marriage. Some states did not criminalize marital rape until the 1990s, though it has been illegal under federal law since the Sexual Abuse Act of 1986.

In 2012, the Federal Bureau of Investigation (FBI) changed the definition of *rape* used in its Uniform Crime Reporting (UCR) Program. The definition had been "The carnal knowledge of a female, forcibly and against her will." The new definition is "The penetration, no matter how slight, of the vagina or anus with any body part or object, or oral penetration by a sex organ of another person, without consent of the victim" (Federal Bureau of Investigation 2014). The U.S. Military Code also updated its definition of *rape* in 2007 from "vaginal penetration of a woman" to a broader definition of *sexual assault* that includes "nonconsensual sex acts committed against women and men."

Though many jurisdictions have passed new laws on sexual assault, some states still have rape and sexual assault laws that reflect traditional ideas about rape. For example, Mississippi (as of January 2017) defines *rape* as "Any person who assaults with intent to forcibly ravish any female of previous chaste character." In Mississippi, sexual battery can apply to women or men, but it includes only "sexual penetration," and statutory rape also includes only acts of sexual intercourse. The state still has a law against "Unnatural Intercourse," defined as "the detestable and abominable crime against nature committed with mankind or with a beast" (Rape, Abuse & Incest National Network 2016). There are no sexual assault laws against sexual touching and fondling, which means that such incidents have to be treated as simple misdemeanors.

Forensic evidence is important in the prosecution of crimes of sexual assault. Such evidence can be especially significant in cases where the victim does not know the perpetrator. Under the Survivors' Bill of Rights Act of 2016 (Pub.L. 114-236), survivors have "the right not to be prevented from, or charged for, receiving a medical forensic examination." The sexual assault evidence collection kit, commonly known as a "rape kit," must then be preserved without charge, and rape survivors have to be notified if there are plans to destroy any rape kit they submitted. Survivors must also be notified if significant results are obtained from the rape kit, including "a DNA profile match, toxicology report, or other information collected as part of a medical forensic examination" (Survivors' Bill of Rights Act 2016).

The Survivors' Bill of Rights Act came about after rape survivor Amanda Nguyen discovered that under Massachusetts law, she had to request—every six months—that her rape kit not be destroyed. Nguyen founded the nonprofit organization Rise primarily to change legislation. Working with House members and Senator Jeanne Shaheen, the bill passed in unanimous votes in both chambers of Congress.

Having a rape examination done and having a rape kit filed does not mean the kit will be processed in a timely manner. Authorities have reported on the enormous backlog of unprocessed rape kits, and many have commented on how serious this problem is. In 2014, experts suggested there were most likely well over 100,000 untested rape kits. In 2006, a Detroit crime lab discovered over 11,000 untested kits, some of them more than 10 years old. After 2,000 of them were tested, "more than 100 serial rapists were identified." As of June 2014, "8 men have been sent to prison, and charges have been lodged against 61 others" (*New York Times* Editorial Board 2014).

To assist in the processing of rape kits, in 2004 Congress passed the Debbie Smith Act (reauthorized in 2008 and 2014), which provides funding for testing in public crime laboratories. However, Congress did not appropriate sufficient funding for the process. The Sexual Assault Forensic Evidence Reporting Act (SAFER Act), passed in 2013 as part of the reauthorization of the Violence Against Women Act of 2013, increased the minimal level of funding; it also requires recipients of the funding to submit testing plans, and it allows for audits of sexual assault evidence backlogs. The SAFER Act requires the FBI to set standards and protocols for testing and provide training to state and local governments.

Obstacles

Depictions in the media—both in fictional stories and in news reports—tend to emphasize sexual assaults by strangers. One U.K. study that focused on news reporting there in 2006 "found that attacks by strangers accounted for over half of the press reports about rape, despite the fact that less than 17 percent of rapes in the UK are stranger rapes." The study also found that "over half of the reports" focused on rapes in public places, even though this fits only 13 percent of rapes (Kitzinger 2009, 86).

Yet studies also indicate that those whose assaults are similar to the stereotypical "stranger in a dark alley" scenario may also not be believed. A 2013 Human

Rights Watch report on the handling of sexual assaults in Washington, D.C., provides several examples of such incidents that either were not investigated or were mislabeled. Some cases were placed in an "Office Information" category, which means they were not assigned a case number and were "closed by definition" (Human Rights Watch 2013, 10). Among the 82 cases filed in Office Information between 2009 and 2011 were several in which the victim, after drinking in a bar, was attacked by a stranger. The investigating officers in these examples either did not assign case numbers or did not follow up with investigations. In one example, the police allegedly told the victim that "because she did not remember anything there was nothing to report" (Human Rights Watch 2013, 11). In another example, reported by a nurse, a woman was attacked by a stranger as she was opening the door to her apartment. After the woman "urinated on herself in fear" the perpetrator did not complete the assault, though he had torn off the woman's dress and leggings. Instead of attempted rape, the detective listed the case as simple assault and burglary. In another case, in which the victim was sexually assaulted after being handcuffed and driven to another location, the detective labeled the incident as a kidnapping—without mentioning the sexual assault (Human Rights Watch 2013, 12). The Human Rights Watch report also documents instances in which victims reported that law enforcement officers did not believe their stories, and sometimes even threatened the victims.

During the Human Rights Watch investigation, the Washington, D.C., police—the Metropolitan Police Department (MPD)—made some changes in how it handles sex crimes. Following the publication of the report, the Washington, D.C., city council hired an independent group of legal experts to review the report. The team concluded that the Human Rights Watch methodology was sometimes flawed, but that the police department's practices were "inadequate" (Walters 2013).

Experts note that many rape cases are never brought to trial and that they are often difficult to win when they are. If the accuser is inconsistent or his or her memory is faulty, the jury will often believe the alleged assault did not take place. The June 2017 trial of entertainer Bill Cosby, which ended in a mistrial, brought to light some issues concerning how often women are believed, as well as issues of due process. One criminology professor suggests that "when jurors are questioned during voir dire [the preliminary examination of jurors for a trial], and when judges give their instructions to the jury members before they deliberate, jurors could be educated about how rape and sexual assault victims often behave." They could be told that victims may suffer "vagaries of memory," and that a woman may continue to have "contact with someone who assaulted her, particularly when the man could influence her career" (Chira 2017).

Studies demonstrate that many people expect victims of rape to behave in a particular way. When victims do not conform to stereotypical behavior, their stories may not be believed, even in cases of stranger rape. Furthermore, unknown perpetrators are more difficult to apprehend. A 2015 article by T. Christian Miller of *ProPublica* and Ken Armstrong of The Marshall Project highlights both these points. The article documents the problems of finding a serial rapist and also covers the story of a victim who was not believed. A combination of skill, luck, and determination by a few police officers led to the discovery that the man they were looking for was a serial rapist. Marc O'Leary committed five attacks—four in Colorado and one in Washington state—after he attacked 18-year-old Marie [her middle name, used for the article] in Lynnwood, Washington. Police there did not believe her account of being attacked, and so Marie recanted, saying she had made up the story. She was later charged with making a false report, a gross misdemeanor. Meanwhile, O'Leary continued to "hunt" his "targets," typically women much older than Marie. He was careful to remove traces of his genetic material from crime scenes, but he said, "If Washington had just paid attention a little bit more, I probably would have been a person of interest earlier on." Marie's case, for example, was labeled "unfounded" by the Lynnwood police department. Lynnwood police sergeant Rodney Cohnheim noted that Marie "was victimized twice." As a result of the case, now "investigators must have 'definitive proof' of lying before doubting a rape report." O'Leary was sentenced to 327 and one-half years in prison for the attacks in Colorado. He pleaded guilty to 28 rape counts and additional felonies (Miller and Armstrong 2015).

The destruction of rape kits and the backlog of kits that remain untested are also obstacles to identifying and prosecuting rape cases. In 2015, journalists from *USA Today*, Gannett newspapers, and TEGNA television stations found "at least 70,000 untested rape kits at more than 1,000 police agencies." The article written about these findings emphasized that this is only a fraction of the number nationwide. This study, done before the passage of the Survivors' Bill of Rights Act, noted that in many jurisdictions there had been no inventory of rape kits, though the *USA Today* article spurred some agencies to begin keeping a count (Reilly 2015).

Differences in state and federal laws can obstruct the prosecution of sexual assault crimes. For example, in New York, despite passage of federal laws on rape kit backlogs and the Survivors' Bill of Rights, and the passage of a New York bill that provides assistance for the state's rape kit backlog problem, there remains a loophole in the law. Under the state's Public Health law (as of February 2017), hospitals can dispose of rape kits after 30 days unless law enforcement or the victim requests that a kit be kept. Though hospitals are supposed to notify the sexual assault victims before kits are destroyed, they do not always do so. In addition, under New York Public Health law, "no hospital or treating practitioner shall be liable in civil damages for failing to comply with the

Sexual Assault Forensic Exam (Rape Kit)

Sexual assault victims in the United States do not have to report the crime to police in order to have a forensic examination performed. Most such exams are performed at a hospital, but not all hospitals are equipped to do them. During a sexual assault forensic exam, trained professionals gather evidence, including possible traces of DNA that can be used to identify the perpetrator. Survivors of sexual assault are first given medical care. Then they are asked about the assault, as well as questioned about their health and their recent consensual sexual activity. Rape survivors are given a head-to-toe examination, which may include internal exams and the swabbing of mouth, vagina, and anus. Sometimes blood, urine, or hair samples are taken. Clothes and other evidence may also be collected. There is no cost for the exam under the Violence Against Women Act. However, recent reports indicate that hospitals and physicians often tack on additional costs for services provided to rape survivors despite the VAWA provisions. Nevertheless, professionals say rape victims should not let the fear of medical costs prevent them from seeking and obtaining an exam. Additional details and resources are available on the Rape, Abuse, & Incest National Network (RAINN) website; https://www.rainn.org/articles/rape-kit.

requirements." As a result, there are no fees or other consequences for hospitals that do not notify sexual victims or do not store rape kits properly (Li 2017).

Worldwide

Prevalence

While rape is an underreported crime throughout the world, statistics in official surveys, records, and studies do not always distinguish stranger rape from other types of rape. In addition, it is difficult to compare figures because definitions of *rape* differ from country to country, as do reporting processes. In the United Kingdom, a 2012 investigation by Her Majesty's Inspectorate of Constabulary (HMIC) and Her Majesty's Crown Prosecution Service Inspectorate (HMCPSI) indicated that rapes were sometimes reported and then reclassified as "no crime." The report notes, "There were wide variations across forces in the number of rapes that remained on the system (and so were investigated) compared to those that were 'no crimed' (i.e. removed from the crime recording system because the police decide that a crime has not been committed)" (HMIC and HMCPSI 2012, 6). In addition, throughout the world, statistics in official surveys, records, and studies do not always distinguish stranger rape from other types of rape, or the categories may include only partner and nonpartner rape. In many jurisdictions, the police do not distinguish stranger rapes from nonstranger rapes in the records. However, in the United Kingdom, in police cases "where the relationship between the offender and victim is unknown or 'stranger' **and** the offence is: murder with a sexual or unknown motive, all rapes and attempted rapes, all sexual assaults with aggravating factors, or abductions with a sexual element," the police force must report the case to the Serious Crime Analysis Section (SCAS) (HMIC and HMCPSI 2012, 30). The forces must also submit full case papers to SCAS for such cases.

The 2013/2014 Crime Survey for England and Wales (CSEW) indicated that most female victims were sexually assaulted by a partner or and expartner (47 percent) or by someone they knew (33 percent). Of the respondents, 16 percent reported that they did not know the offender (Office for National Statistics 2015, 19). For men, the number of victims was too small to break down into equivalent categories. "A higher percentage of victims were under the influence of alcohol when the offender was a stranger (38%) compared with when the offender was a partner/expartner (14%). The percentage of victims that didn't know whether or not they had been drugged was also higher when the offender was a stranger (13% compared with 2%)" (Office for National Statistics 2015, 21).

Individuals were also asked about their beliefs about victims of sexual violence: "the majority of people thought that victims were not responsible for someone sexually assaulting or raping them when they were drunk (66%), under the influence of drugs (60%) or if they had been flirting heavily beforehand (56%)" (Office for National Statistics 2015, 25). However, "women were more likely than men (59% and 53% respectively) to think the victim was not responsible for someone sexually assaulting or raping them if they had been flirting heavily beforehand" (Office for National Statistics 2015, 26).

The number of sexual assaults reported to police in the England and Wales doubled between 2011and 2016. There were 10,160 cases reported in 2011–2012, but 23,851 in 2015–2016. Some experts believe this is occurring because more people were willing to report sexual assaults after the Jimmy Savile sexual abuse scandal and public campaigns that have pushed the notion that victims will be believed. Jimmy Savile was a well-known radio and television personality who died in 2011. After his death, reports of his sexual assaults on children began to be investigated. An investigation called Operation Yewtree was launched by the Metropolitan Police Service to look into the allegations made against Savile, as well as other alleged perpetrators. Savile is believed to have abused hundreds of children, boys and girls, as well as some adults, often finding his victims at hospitals and schools (Halliday 2014).

A study by Hannah Bows and Nicole Westmarland published in 2017 challenged the existing views on sexual assault in the United Kingdom that involved victims 60 years old and above. The aim of the study was to challenge "real rape" stereotypes that most victims are young and are attacked by strangers.

Few studies have focused exclusively on older victims, because "generally, society does not identify older people as being at risk from sexual assault and thus family, friends and professionals may miss the signs" (Bows and Westmarland 2017, 4). Nevertheless, Bows and Westmarland assert there is also a "real-rape older victim stereotype," popularized in the media, in which the victim is fragile and vulnerable. For example, these were the victims of Delroy Grant, the "Night Stalker." A few studies have either found or focused on such rapes. One study done in 2005 found that two-thirds of the perpetrators of sexual assault on older women were strangers. Another study, which examined stranger rape cases of women age 60 and older, found "older women were more likely to be raped by a White, male stranger who had a significantly more previous convictions and assaults typically took place in the victim's home" (Bows and Westmarland 2017, 3).

Bows and Westmarland used freedom of information requests to police forces to obtain records in England, Wales, Northern Ireland, and Scotland. Out of 87,230 cases of rape examined in the study, there were 655 cases (0.75 percent) in which the victim was 60 years old or older. In these cases, the victim most often knew the perpetrator. Of those perpetrators who were known, 26 percent were acquaintances and 20 percent were husbands or partners; 20 percent were strangers. Most assaults took place within the home of the victim (Bows and Westmarland 2017, 9). Thus, Bows and Westmarland found that the rape of older women in these jurisdictions did not fit the real rape stereotype for older victims.

Delroy Grant, the Night Stalker

Delroy Grant, who became known as the Night Stalker, sexually assaulted elderly victims between 1992 and 2009 in south London, Kent, and Surrey. Investigators believe he may have attacked as many as 600 individuals, including some men, but he was convicted on 20 counts that included rape, attempted rape, indecent assault, and burglary. The police formed Operation Minstead to begin looking for him in 1998, after he was linked to two rapes. However, investigators made several mistakes during the course of the investigation, such as confusing his DNA with that of another suspect, which allowed him to remain free to commit more crimes. He typically sought out his victims in older suburban homes, well shaded by trees and with windows that were easy for him to break into. Once inside, he cut telephone lines and removed lightbulbs. The attacks on his elderly victims were brutal and often lasted for hours. Grant was finally arrested in 2009. In 2011, he received concurrent life sentences, and he must serve a minimum of 27 years in prison.

In 2013, the British Transport Police, Transport for London (TfL), the Metropolitan Police, and the City of London Police launched Project Guardian. The project's purpose was to eliminate unwanted sexual behavior in the transport system. The project was launched after a 2013 TfL survey revealed that an estimated 15 percent of people in London had experienced unwanted sexual behavior while using public transit. The project sent specially trained uniformed and plainclothes officers on patrol and dedicated a text number to enable victims and witnesses to report such crimes. The project ended in April 2015 when a new project, Report It to Stop It, was launched. Most of the sexual crimes in transit areas are committed by people unknown to the victims. Research indicated that many individuals did not report the crimes because they did not think police would try to catch the offenders. According to the British Transport Police, Report it to Stop It has attempted to "overcome this barrier" by demonstrating "that multiple reports about an offender can help police to build a picture so that we can catch them" (British Transport Police n.d.).

The Scottish Crime and Justice Survey (SCJS) involves face-to-face interviews of 12,045 individuals in private households. Those examined are at least 16 years old, and they also take a "self-completion" questionnaire. In the 2012–2013 survey, 3 percent of adults indicated that they had experienced at least one serious sexual assault since age 16. Of the women surveyed, 4 percent had experienced such assaults; of the men surveyed, only 1 percent said they had. Additional findings included the following: "83% of those who had experienced serious sexual assault since age 16 said that that they knew the offender in some way. 54% said that the perpetuator was their partner." Only 19 percent had reported the most recent (or only) sexual assault to the police. For stalking victims, 58 percent knew the perpetrator, and 29 percent did not know their stalker (Scottish Government 2014).

A study published in 2012 analyzed rape cases reported to the police in Gauteng province in South Africa in 2003. The study compared multiple perpetrator rape (gang rape) and single perpetrator rape in a sample of 1,886 (1,558 single perpetrator cases and 328 multiple perpetrator cases). The study found that "multiple perpetrator rapes were overwhelming perpetrated by men or boys known just by sight or by strangers." This occurred in 65.9 percent of cases, while 27.1 percent of multiple perpetrator victims were raped by people they knew. In single perpetrator rapes, the victims were raped by relatives (12 percent), by current or expartners (17.3), or by friends/acquaintance/neighbors (37.6 percent), while only 28.5 percent were raped by strangers or someone they only knew by sight (Jewkes et al. 2012, 14). These differ from the findings of some other studies done on male rapists in the Eastern Cape province of South Africa, which indicate that multiple perpetrator rape (MPR) is often perpetrated by boyfriends. The study's authors suggest that this may be because women are less likely to report the cases because they fear being stigmatized. The authors also found that MPR often took place outdoors, when the victim was alone or accompanied, and on weekends.

A 2015 factsheet published online by the NSW Rape Crisis Centre (in New South Wales, Australia) reports that one in five Australian women will be sexually assaulted in their lifetime, while seven percent of adult men will experience sexual assault. According to the factsheet, in 70 percent of sexual assault cases, the victim knows the offender. The percentage is higher when "known by the victim" includes family, friends, work and social colleagues, and dates. According to the factsheet (but based on statistics from 1996), "Sexual assault by a stranger accounts for less than 1% of sexual violence and an attack by a stranger in a dark place is even less common" (Rape and Domestic Violence Services Australia 2015).

In India, a woman died in 2012 after a brutal gang rape on a New Delhi bus. This case was highly publicized and launched public outcries and protests. Similarly, protests took place after the rape of a 74-year-old nun in West Bengal. A group of men burglarized the convent, stole some money, and raped the nun in 2015. Despite these high-profile cases, a study reports that nearly 90 percent of sexual assault cases in India were perpetrated by people the victims knew. In 2014, the National Crime Records Bureau (NCRB) reported 337,922 cases of violence against women, and 33,707 cases of rape. New Delhi was the city with the highest number of reported rapes (1,813). In discussing the number of rapes committed by people known to the victims, Ranjana Kumari, director of the Centre for Social Research in New Delhi, said, "Across the world, it's well known that stranger rape is not really the problem, and the majority of rapes are committed by people known to the victims" (Bhalla 2015).

Nevertheless, in London, Ontario, Canada, reports indicate a rise in stranger rape. In 2017, stranger rape cases surpassed the number of cases of acquaintance rape, according to London Abused Women's Centre. The organization reported that between January 2016 and January 2017, 93 women reported stranger rape, while 77 reported cases of "date rape." Many of the attacks by strangers occurred at parties. The women did not remember the assaults, and only realized that they had suffered a sexual assault because of missing undergarments or "excess fluids surrounding their bodies" (CBC News Staff 2017).

Major Laws

Every nation has its own laws on rape and sexual assault. In most instances, the laws do not distinguish between stranger rape and rape by someone known to the victim, except when the perpetrator and the victim are married or related to each other. Between 2014 and 2015, Equality Now surveyed sexual violence laws in 82 jurisdictions around the world. According to the report, marital rape is expressly legal in "Ghana, India, Indonesia, Jordan, Lesotho, Nigeria, Oman, Singapore, Sri Lanka and Tanzania. In four of these, marital rape is expressly legal even where the 'wife' being raped is a child 'bride' and the 'marriage' is in violation of minimum age of marriage laws." The study also found that "rape is treated as an issue of morality" rather than a crime of violence in "at least" fifteen countries, including "Afghanistan, Belgium, China, India, Indonesia, Jordan, Luxembourg, Netherlands, Nigeria, Pakistan, Palestine, Peru, Singapore, Taiwan and Yemen." Some countries permitted convicted rapists to escape punishment if they married the woman or girl they had raped, even if the victim was a child (Equality Now 2017, 4).

Many countries have updated their sexual assault laws to follow current definitions and beliefs about bodily autonomy. In the United Kingdom, rape and sexual assault are charged under the Sexual Offences Act 2003, which went into effect in 2004. The law broadened the definition of *rape* to include the penetration of mouth and anus, as well as the vagina, without consent; created a new offense, "assault by penetration," which includes the coercive insertion of any body part or object into the vagina or anus; and broadened sexual assault to include any type unwanted sexual touching. The law also broadened, clarified, and established laws concerning the rape of children and those who have mental disorders. In addition, the law created offenses that cover giving someone substances without his or her knowledge and consent with the intention of incapacitating that person for the purpose of having sexual activity (Sexual Offenses Act 2003 2009).

Because the law defines *consent* only as "a person consents if he agrees by choice, and has the freedom and capacity to make that choice" (Legislation.gov.uk 2003), each case must be considered individually. One 2015 case received a great deal of public attention after the trial judge, John Pini QC, ruled that there was "insufficient evidence from which the jury could determine lack of capacity" by the female victim, and stopped the trial. At issue was whether the woman had "consented to sex, but was too drunk to remember that she had done so." The Crown Prosecution Service won a repeal to restart the case and to admit a video that clearly showed the woman "inert and unresponsive" while one of a group of men raped her (Barrett 2015). In 2015, new regulations made it necessary for rape suspects to prove to police and prosecutors that the complainant consented "with full capacity and freedom to do so" (Rayner and Gardner 2015).

In 2016, Germany passed a "no means no" law. In part, the law was spurred by mob attacks that took place during New Year's celebrations in Cologne. Two men, who were seeking asylum from Algeria and Iraq, were released with suspended jail sentences, though they had been found guilty. Under the new law this will not be possible, because all cases in which the victim does not give consent for sexual contact have been made punishable crimes. Before the law was changed, the victim had to demonstrate that she had physically resisted the attack (Huggle 2016).

In India, the Justice Verma committee, headed by Justice J.S. Verma, was created in December 2012 to recommend changes to the criminal law on sexual assault. The committee issued its report on January 23, 2013. Many of the recommendations, though not all, were then incorporated into the Criminal Law (Amendment), Act 2013, which updated the Indian Penal Code. Before the changes, the law defined rape only as penile-vaginal penetration without the consent of the woman. It did not include penetration by fingers or other objects, nor did it include oral sex. The new law includes in its rape definition, oral sex, as well as the penetration of the mouth, urethra, vagina, and anus by penis or other objects. Non-penetrative sex is covered under "outraging the modesty of a woman." The act also repealed provisions in the earlier law that permitted the cross-examination of the victim to include her prior sexual history and eliminated the "two-finger test," a medical examination of rape complainants that was used to demonstrate if she had had intercourse. The new law removed the discretion that judges had over sentencing of rapists, and increased penalties for some crimes, including gang rape (Satish 2016).

Obstacles

Throughout the world, studies note that rape myths often prevent rape victims from reporting rapes and hinder the conviction of rapists when victims do report their assaults. In some nations, women who report sexual assaults may be arrested for adultery or fornication. In some countries, such as in an Ethiopian case highlighted by Equality Now, a woman may be pressured into marrying her rapist, or she may have to prove that she was a virgin (Equality Now 2017, 21). In Germany before the recent changes in the rape law, a woman had to prove she had physically resisted her rapist, which meant there were few rape convictions.

Beliefs that women are responsible for their rapes can be seen all over the world. For example, after the brutal gang rape of a 23-year-old woman on a bus in New Delhi in 2012, the bus driver told filmmaker Leslee Udwin, "A decent girl won't roam around at nine o'clock at night. A girl is far more responsible for rape than a boy." He also said that the woman should not have fought back. Udwin also interviewed a man who had raped a five-year-old girl. He told the interviewer that the girl's life had no value because "she was a beggar girl" (Udwin 2015).

A study published in 2015 examined rape cases reported to one U.K. police department over a period of two years to see how closely or how often they fit the myth of "real rape." Such cases involve attacks by strangers, use force, often with a weapon, and take place in a deserted outdoor space. In this mythical scenario, the victim physically resists and often has visible injuries. The researchers found that in her sample, "no cases involved every aspect of the 'real rape' myth" (Waterhouse et al. 2016, 7). In most cases, victims knew their attackers. In some cases classified as "stranger rape," the victim had spent some time with the perpetrator, for example, in a bar or club. Many of the stranger rapes took place after the attacker met the victim in such a place, and targeted the victim as someone who was vulnerable. Because the victim was already intoxicated or unconscious, the attacker did not have to use force, and the victim may not have resisted or sustained serious injuries. Nevertheless, the authors noted that there was a slightly higher conviction rate for cases of stranger rape, which fits with findings in other studies that suggest jurors are affected by rape myths (Waterhouse et al. 2016).

Some recent studies have demonstrated the need to look beyond the stereotypical rape victim being a young woman. For example, several studies have noted that male victims are more likely to be reluctant to report sexual assaults. Therefore, the sexual assaults of men are more underreported than sexual assaults of women (Lundrigan and Johnson 2013, 780). The 2017 study by Bows and Westmarland demonstrates the need to look at older victims of sexual violence.

A report on investigation into rape reporting and prosecution published by Her Majesty's Inspectorates of Constabulary (HMIC) and the Crown Prosecution Service (HMCPSI) in 2012 noted that when crimes of rape were incorrectly removed from records, victims did not receive services and offenders were able to commit more crimes. The report recommended "that forces should initially consider every 'stranger' rape to be part of a pattern of serial offending, so that investigation officers consider the wider links to other crimes" (HMIC and HMCPSI 2012, 6). One reason for using rape classifications is to recognize the "challenges" of investigating stranger rape and that such cases may require more intelligence gathering in order to solve them. However, the investigation found that many police forces did not classify their rape cases. In addition, the investigation found differences in how departments handled DNA and forensic evidence.

Globally, there are many obstacles to reporting rape cases and then taking them to court, including a lack of trained personnel who know how to collect DNA and facilities to process rape kits. Equality Now suggests that in some countries, such as Nigeria, poor families accept money from perpetrators because they cannot afford to take a case to trial. Equality Now also found that 43 jurisdictions required a medical examination be performed by "designated or accredited personnel." However, at least 16 of these places charged a fee for the service, which could prevent some victims going forward with a trial. In some places, medical tests are proof of penetration, rather than the collection of DNA. In a few countries, such as Yemen, medical evidence and a witness are necessary to prove rape took place. In Pakistan, the complainant's statement must "inspire confidence" as well as be supported by medical evidence (Equality Now 2017, 46).

Merril D. Smith

Further Reading

Barrett, David. 2015. "Rape Consent Trial led to Landmark Appeal." *The Telegraph,* February 12. Accessed June 24, 2017. http://www.telegraph.co.uk/news/uknews /crime/11409596/Rape-consent-trial-led-to-landmark-appeal.html.

Bellafante, Ginia. 2016. "Rape by Strangers." *New York Times,* January 22. Accessed July 18, 2017. https://www.nytimes.com/2016/01/24/nyregion/rape-by-strangers -new-york-city.html.

Bhalla, Nita. 2015. "Almost 90 Percent of India's Rapes Committed by People Known to Victim." *Reuters*, August 21. Accessed July 23, 2017. http://in.reuters.com/article /india-women-crime-rape-idINKCN0QQ0QS20150821.

Bows, Hannah, and Nicole Westmarland. 2017. "Rape of Older People in the United Kingdom: Challenging the 'Real-Rape' Stereotype." *British Journal of Criminology* 57 (1): 1–17.

Breiding, Matthew J., Sharon G. Smith, Kathleen C. Basile, Mikel L. Walters, Jieru Chen, and Melissa T. Merrick. 2014. "Prevalence and Characteristics of Sexual Violence, Stalking, and Intimate Partner Violence Victimization—National Intimate Partner and Sexual Violence Survey, United States, 2011." *Morbidity and Mortality Weekly Report* 63 (SS08): 1–18. Atlanta, GA: Centers of Disease Control and Prevention. Accessed July 19, 2017. https://www.cdc.gov/mmwr/preview/mmwrhtml /ss6308a1.htm.

British Transport Police. n.d. "Report It to Stop It." Accessed July 23, 2017. http:// www.btp.police.uk/advice_and_information/how_we_tackle_crime/report_it_to _stop_it.aspx.

CBC News Staff. 2017. "Rate of 'Stranger Rape' at an All Time High in London." *CBC News*, March 16. Accessed July 18, 2017. http://www.cbc.ca/news/canada/windsor /stranger-rape-london-1.4027424.

Chira, Susan. 2017. "A Post-Cosby-Trial Question: Is the System Stacked Against Women?" *New York Times*, June 20. Accessed July 22, 2017. https://www.nytimes .com/2017/06/20/arts/television/bill-cosby-mistrial-sexual-assault-andrea-con stand.html.

Equality Now. 2017. "The World's Shame: The Global Rape Epidemic. How Laws Around the World Are Failing to Protect Women and Girls from Sexual Violence." Accessed July 24, 2017. https://www.equalitynow.org/sites/default/files/Equality NowRapeLawReport2017_Spreads.pdf.

Estrich, Susan. 1987. *Real Rape: How the Legal System Victimizes Women Who Say No.* Cambridge, MA: Harvard University Press.

Federal Bureau of Investigation. 2014. "Frequently Asked Questions about the Change in the UCR Definition of Rape." Accessed July 20, 2017. https://ucr.fbi.gov/recent -program-updates/new-rape-definition-frequently-asked-questions.

Finkelhor, David, Heather A. Turner, and Anne Shattuck. 2013. "Violence, Crime, and Abuse Exposure in a National Sample of Children and Youth: An Update." *Journal of the American Medical Association (JAMA) Pediatrics* 167 (7): 614–21. Accessed July 19, 2017. http://jamanetwork.com/journals/jamapediatrics/fullarticle /1686983?resultClick=1.

Finley, Laura L. 2016. *Domestic Abuse and Sexual Assault in Popular Culture*. Santa Barbara, CA: Praeger.

Guardian Staff. 2009. "Sexual Offences Act 2003." *The Guardian*, June 15. Accessed July 23, 2017. https://www.theguardian.com/commentisfree/libertycentral/2009 /jun/01/sexual-offences-act-2003.

Halliday, Josh. 2014. "Jimmy Savile: Timeline of His Sexual Abuse and Its Uncovering." *The Guardian*, June 26. Accessed July 22, 2017. https://www.theguardian.com /media/2014/jun/26/jimmy-savile-sexual-abuse-timeline.

HMIC and HMCPSI. 2012. "Forging the Links: Rape Investigation and Prosecution." Accessed July 23, 2017. http://www.justiceinspectorates.gov.uk/hmicfrs/media /forging-the-links-rape-investigation-and-prosecution-20120228.pdf.

Hogan, Gwynne. 2017. "Sex Attacks Up 62 Percent in Greenpoint as Most Cases Remain Unsolved." *Dnainfo*, January 6. Accessed July 18, 2017. https://www.dnainfo.com /new-york/20170106/greenpoint/rapes-nypd-arrest.

Huggler, Justin. 2016. "Germany Passes 'No Means No' Rape Law. July 7. *The Telegraph*, July 7. Accessed June 24, 2017. http://www.telegraph.co.uk/news/2016/07/07/ger many-passes-no-means-no-rape-law/.

Human Rights Watch. 2013. "Capitol Offense: Police Mishandling of Sexual Assault Cases in the District of Columbia." Accessed July 23, 2017. https://www.hrw.org/sites /default/files/reports/us0113ForUpload_2.pdf.

Jewkes, Rachel, Lisa Vettern, Ruxana Jina, Nicola Christofides, Romi Sigsworth, and Lizle Loots. 2012. "What We Know—and What We Don't: Single and Multiple Perpetrator Rape in South Africa." *South Africa Crime Quarterly* 41: 11–19.

Kitzinger, Jenny. 2009. "Rape in the Media." In *Rape: Challenging Contemporary Thinking*, edited by Miranda A. H. Horvath and Jennifer M. Brown, 74–98. Cullompton, UK, and Portland, OR: Willan Publishing.

Legislation.gov.uk. 2003. "Sexual Offences Act 2003. Section 74." Accessed July 23, 2017. http://www.legislation.gov.uk/ukpga/2003/42/section/74.

Li, Jennifer. 2017. "Loophole Allows New York Rape Kits to Go into Trash After 30 Days." *Rise* (blog), February 11. Accessed July 22, 2017. http://www.risenow.us/blogs/2017 /2/11/loophole-allows-new-york-rape-kits-to-go-into-trash-after-30-days.

Lisak, David. 2011. "Understanding the Predatory Nature of Sexual Violence." *Sexual Assault Report* 14 (4): 49–64. Accessed July 19, 2017. http://www.davidlisak.com /wp-content/uploads/pdf/SARUnderstandingPredatoryNatureSexualViolence.pdf.

Lundrigan, Samantha, and Katrin Mueller-Johnson. 2013. "Male Stranger Rape: A Behavioral Model of Victim-Offender Interaction." *Criminal Justice and Behavior* 40 (7): 763–83.

Miller, T. Christian, and Ken Armstrong. 2015. "An Unbelievable Story of Rape." *Pro-Publica and The Marshall Project*, December 16. Accessed July 19, 2017. https://www.propublica.org/article/false-rape-accusations-an-unbelievable-story.

Morris, Robert E., Martin M. Anderson, and George W. Knox. 2002. "Incarcerated Adolescents' Experiences as Perpetrators of Sexual Assault." *Journal of the American Medical Association (JAMA) Pediatrics* 156 (8): 831–35. Accessed July 19, 2017. http://jamanetwork.com/journals/jamapediatrics/fullarticle/203680?resultClick=1.

New York Times Editorial Board. 2014. "Rape Evidence Backlog." *New York Times*, June 28. Accessed July 22, 2017. https://www.nytimes.com/2014/06/29/opinion/sunday/rape-evidence-backlog.html?_r=0.

Office for National Statistics. 2015. "Chapter 4: Violent Crime and Sexual Offences—Intimate Personal Violence and Serious Sexual Assault." *2013/14 Crime Survey for England and Wales (CSEW)*. Accessed July 23, 2017. http://webarchive.nationalarchives.gov.uk/20160106113348/http://www.ons.gov.uk/ons/dcp171776_394500.pdf.

"Perpetrators of Sexual Violence: Statistics." n.d. Rape, Abuse & Incest National Network (RAINN). Accessed July 18, 2017. https://www.rainn.org/statistics/perpetrators-sexual-violence.

Rape, Abuse & Incest National Network. 2016. "Rape and Sexual Assault Crime Definitions." Accessed July 19, 2017. https://apps.rainn.org/policy/compare/crimes.cfm.

Rape and Domestic Violence Services Australia. n.d. "Myths and Facts Factsheet." Accessed July 23, 2017. http://www.rape-dvservices.org.au/Portals/0/Users/003/03/3/Factsheets%20and%20Brochures/Factsheet%20-%20Myths%20of%20sexual%20assault%20-%20PDF%20-%20June%202015.pdf.

Rayner, Gordon, and Bill Gardner. 2015. "Men Must Prove a Woman Said 'Yes' under Tough New Rape Laws." *The Telegraph*, January 28. Accessed July 24, 2017. http://www.telegraph.co.uk/news/uknews/law-and-order/11375667/Men-must-prove-a-woman-said-Yes-under-tough-new-rape-rules.html.

Reilly, Steve. 2015. "70,000 Untested Rape Kits USA Today Found Is Fraction of Total." *USA Today*, July 16. Accessed July 22, 2017. https://www.usatoday.com/story/news/2015/07/16/untested-rape-kits-we-found--small-part---total/29902341/.

Satish, Mrinal. 2016. "Forget the Chatter to the Contrary, the 2013 Rape Law Amendments Are a Step Forward." *The Wire*, August 22. Accessed July 23, 2017. https://thewire.in/60808/rape-law-amendments-2013/.

Scottish Government. 2014. "Scottish Crime and Justice Survey 2012/13: Sexual Victimisation and Stalking." Accessed July 23, 2017. http://www.gov.scot/Publications/2014/06/3479.

Sexual Assault. n.d. Rape, Abuse & Incest National Network (RAINN). Accessed July 18, 2017. https://www.rainn.org/articles/sexual-assault.

Survivors' Bill of Rights Act. 2016. 114th Congress. Accessed July 22, 2017. https://www.congress.gov/bill/114th-congress/house-bill/5578/text.

Tjaden, Patricia, and Nancy Thoennes, 2006. "Extent, Nature, and Consequences of Rape Victimization: Findings from the National Violence Against Women Survey." Washington, DC: U.S. Department of Justice. Accessed July 17, 2017. https://www.ncjrs.gov/pdffiles1/nij/210346.pdf.

Tracy, Carol E., et al. 2012. "Rape and Sexual Assault in the Legal System." Paper presented to the National Research Council of the National Academies Panel on Measuring Rape and Sexual Assault in the Bureau of Justice Statistics Household Surveys Committee on National Statistics. Accessed May 29, 2017. http://www .womenslawproject.org/wp-content/uploads/2016/04/Rape-and-Sexual-Assault -in-the-Legal-System-FINAL.pdf.

Truman, Jennifer L. 2011. "National Crime Victimization Survey: Criminal Victim- ization, 2010." NCJ 235508. Washington, DC: Bureau of Justice Statistics, U.S. Department of Justice. Accessed July 18, 2017. https://www.bjs.gov/content/pub /pdf/cv10.pdf.

Truman, Jennifer L., and Lynn Langton. 2015. "National Crime Victimization Survey: Criminal Victimization, 2014." NCJ 248973. Washington, DC: Bureau of Justice Statistics, U.S. Department of Justice. Accessed July 19, 2017. https://www.doc umentcloud.org/documents/2645931-National-Crime-and-Victimization-Survey -2014.html.

Udwin, Leslee. 2015. "Delhi Rapist Says Victim Shouldn't Have Fought Back." *BBC News Magazine*, March 3. Accessed June 4, 2017. http://www.bbc.com/news/maga zine-31698154.

Utah Department of Health. n.d. "Rape and Sexual Assault." Violence & Injury Preven- tion Program. Accessed July 18, 2017. http://www.health.utah.gov/vipp/topics/rape -sexual-assault/.

Walters, Joanna. 2013. "Washington DC Police 'Need Better Training to Help Sex Assault Victims.'" *The Guardian*, June 27. Accessed July 23, 2017. https://www.theguard ian.com/world/2013/jun/27/washington-police-sex-assault-victims-report.

Waterhouse, Genevieve F., Ali Reynolds, and Vincent Egan. 2016. "Myths and Legends: The Reality of Rape Offences Reported to a UK Police Force." *The European Journal of Psychology Applied to Legal Context* 8 (1): 1–10. Accessed July 24, 2017. http:// ejpalc.elsevier.es/en/myths-legends-the-reality-rape/articulo/S18891861150002 44/#.WXebSNPyu8V.

Wolitzky-Taylor, Kate B., et al. 2011. "Reporting Rape in a National Sample of College Women." *Journal of American College Health* 59 (7): 582–87. Accessed July 18, 2017. http://pubmedcentralcanada.ca/pmcc/articles/PMC3211043/.

W

WARTIME RAPE

Wartime rape is any form of sexual violence that is perpetrated by military forces during an armed conflict. The armed conflict may be an internal (civil war) or an international one. In order for rape to be considered wartime rape in this environment, it should be perpetrated by combatants. When it is perpetrated by civilians, it is considered a common crime rather than wartime rape. Contemporary scholarship studies the topic of wartime rape under the more comprehensive heading of sexual and gender-based violence (SGBV).

Historical accounts of wartime rape go back to antiquity and ancient religious texts. Until modern times, wartime rape was considered to be an offense against the community of the victim, who is a female, or a property crime against her male relatives. As such, there have been communities and epochs that punished such offenses as criminal acts and others that considered them normal parts of war.

In different historical contexts, it is possible to find wartime rapes that have been perpetrated on women or men in the form of opportunistic rapes (when rape is considered to be a reward for fighting), rapes to demonstrate victory in war as a final seal of feminizing/humiliating the enemy, and systematic or genocidal rapes to deport people from an area or destroy them and their identities. Despite this diversity in the ways in which and purposes for which the rapes are perpetrated, rape in general and wartime rape in particular have long been associated with sex and men's "uncontrollable" sexual desires and lust, as an evolutionary instinct. Especially in the context of war—or so this mentality assumed—rape became inevitable as a result of the lack of the availability of sex for soldiers and the general environment of lawlessness that freed soldiers from legal and social restraints on their urges. While there have been wars where soldiers (especially mercenaries) were set free to rape and pillage as a reward/payment for their work, states have usually considered wartime rape undesirable because of its damaging effects on military objectives through the disturbance of discipline, the breeding of hostility among the local populations, and the spread of venereal diseases. Armies even tried to offer their soldiers brothel access and prostitutes in order to prevent rape, because providing release to soldiers' sexual drives, they thought, would make raping unnecessary. The French Army in Indochina, for instance, had a mobile field brothel.

The Japanese Army, in the 1930s and 1940s, kept women whom they forced into prostitution (so-called "comfort women") in military brothels. The American military also allowed brothels on army base camps in Vietnam. These policies did not stop wartime rape, but the idea underlying these policies—namely, the idea that rape occurs due to the sexual needs of soldiers—stopped states from effectively prosecuting and punishing offenders. Wartime rape, as a result, could not enter the list of crimes prohibited by the international community in modern international law. Women's movements, which regarded wartime rape as an important problem since the late 19th century and considered the impunity enjoyed by the perpetrators as the source of this widespread crime, have focused on international law as a remedy. Feminist critiques of wartime rape, the ideology surrounding it, the silence of international law on it, and the immunity granted to its perpetrators were eventually heard, and in the 1990s modern international law, after ignoring wartime rape for a long time, put forth a clear definition and prohibition of it in its various forms.

The official definition of wartime rape was established first by the ad hoc International Criminal Tribunal for Rwanda (ICTR) and International Criminal Tribunal for the former Yugoslavia (ICTY) and then by the Rome Statute of the International Criminal Court (ICC). In the case against Jean-Paul Akayesu in 1998 at the ICTR, the indictment said that "acts of sexual violence include forcible sexual penetration of the vagina, anus or oral cavity by a penis and/or of the vagina or anus by some other object, and sexual abuse, such as forced nudity." The court, then, delivered the legal definition of *rape* in its judgment: "a physical invasion of a sexual nature, committed on a person under circumstances which are coercive" (International Committee of the Red Cross 1998).

The permanent ICC's Rome Statute also gives an international legal definition of rape in its Elements of Crimes, defining rape both as a crime against humanity and as a war crime. As a crime against humanity (which may or may not be wartime rape), the elements of rape are these:

> The perpetrator invaded the body of a person by conduct resulting in penetration, however slight, of any part of the body of the victim or of the perpetrator with a sexual organ, or of the anal or genital opening of the victim with any object or any other part of the body. The invasion was committed by force, or by threat of force or coercion, such as that caused by fear of violence, duress, detention, psychological oppression or abuse of power, against such person or another person, or by taking advantage of a coercive environment, or the invasion was committed against a person incapable of giving genuine consent. (International Criminal Court 2011)

For these acts to qualify as a crime against humanity, the Statute requires that they be "part of a widespread or systematic attack directed against a civilian population."

As a war crime, the Rome Statute defines *rape* in the same way while requiring the invasion to take place "in the context of and was associated with an international armed conflict" where "the perpetrator was aware of the factual circumstances that established the existence of an armed conflict." Current international law, therefore, considers rape a war crime: a crime against humanity as well as a possible tool of genocide under certain circumstances.

Even after the international legal developments, the commonality of wartime rape did not decrease. This drew criticism from feminists, who argued that instead of legal remedies being offered for retribution, the underlying causes of wartime rape should be dealt with—such as nationalism, masculinities, militarization, gendered security agendas of states, hierarchies, and political economies of structural violence.

The United States

The U.S. Civil War (1861–1865) is a major historical event in the study of wartime rape, not necessarily because of the prevalence of rape during this war compared to its prevalence in other armed conflicts, but because it produced a key legal document (although a domestic one rather than international) that became a germ for the current international humanitarian law. The Lieber Code (General Order No. 100, the Instructions for the Government of Armies of the United States in the Field), which was prepared as an army manual for the Union Army by Francis Lieber, a legal scholar, became the guide for later European efforts to codify the laws of war. In Articles 44 and 47 of this manual, wartime rape was prohibited, clearly requiring "the penalty of death, or such other severe punishment as may seem adequate for the gravity of the offense" (Lieber 1863). The extent to which the Lieber Code's articles regarding wartime rape had to be sanctioned is open to debate. Some historians argue that rape was rare during the Civil War because of the nature of the war being a fight of brother against brother and because of the culture of restraint at the time as a defining characteristic of manliness. In the few cases that wartime rape occurred, the argument goes, the Lieber Code was enforced and perpetrators were executed. Other historians claim that rape was widespread, especially against black women, and the fact that prosecutions for rape were few (court-martial numbers are reported to be around 450, all against Union soldiers) is a result of the general impunity enjoyed by perpetrators of this crime throughout history. These historians consider the widespread nature of venereal disease among soldiers during the Civil War to be an indication of pervasive wartime rape.

Because the United States had not seen many wars on its territory, most wartime rapes perpetrated by American soldiers took place in other countries where the U.S. military was involved in an armed conflict. The Philippine–American War and the resulting American occupation (1899–1902), for instance, witnessed widespread rape. Although the stories are marginalized in official history, court-martial records reveal cases of wartime rape while the Lieber Code was still valid as the manual of the U.S. Army.

Wartime rape occurred in later conflicts in which the U.S. Army was involved. During these conflicts, new/updated versions of the Law of War manuals issued by the War Department (later the Department of Defense) were in effect (in 1914, 1917, 1934, 1940, 1956, 1976, and 2015), prohibiting wartime rape. The manual that was prepared in 1956, after the United States signed and ratified the Geneva Conventions of 1949 (which mentioned rape for the first time in international law), became the basis of the later amended versions of the current manual, which is called FM 27-10 (Field Manual 27-10). An updated edition of the Law of Land Warfare (FM 6-27) is also being prepared.

One of the wars in which the U.S. Army was involved and in which widespread wartime rape occurred was World War II (1939–1945). Deriving cases from the U.S. Military Archives and from trial records, historians have demonstrated that American soldiers along with Allied troops raped women in both Europe and Asia. As a result of hundreds of cases of wartime rape in England, France, and Germany, 70 soldiers from the U.S. Army were executed. In Asia, Okinawa Island in Japan became a stage for mass rapes starting during World War II and continuing during the occupation by U.S. troops after the war. Court-martials for these assaults, though, were rare (more common when the alleged perpetrator was black), exhibiting the general impunity for wartime rape.

The Vietnam War (1955–1975) also witnessed wartime rape, predominantly by the South Vietnamese and American troops. As events such as the "Incident on Hill 192" and the "Mai Lai Massacre" reveal, violence, including sexual violence, against civilians was common; despite the inability of most victims to report the assaults, as well as the U.S. military's resistance to prosecuting those responsible, there were over 80 court-martials for rape and related crimes during the Vietnam War.

The latest armed conflict in which the U.S. military was involved and news about wartime rape surfaced was the U.S. invasion of Iraq and the war that followed (2003–2011). Mahmudiyah rape and killings and Abu Ghraib prison abuses are the most publicized examples of such violence. Those responsible for the Mahmudiyah rapes and killings were later prosecuted and convicted by American courts. Some of the soldiers responsible for the Abu Ghraib abuses were court-martialed, but they either were cleared of the charges or received very light sentences.

Despite the fact that the U.S. Army prohibited rape in its own manuals long before international law handled the matter, wartime rape is commonly perpetrated by American soldiers. Scholars point out two interrelated reasons for this: First, although the Army codes prohibit rape (with the early versions even

Military Culture and Rape

Scholars point out two interrelated reasons for the ongoing perpetration of wartime rape by American soldiers. First, although rape is prohibited by law, in circumstances of war these laws are rarely acknowledged, leading to very few prosecutions and even fewer convictions, with light sentences. The second and related cause of the ongoing sexual violence is the fact that soldiering and fighting are closely connected to the idea of masculinity, which is associated with aggressive behavior. Military culture is based on a type of male bonding among soldiers, which is ensured through an emphasis on masculinity—where everything that is considered to be feminine (such as women and gays) is placed as the "other" against a "we," the masculine heroes of the nation. Many academic studies as well as reports by women's organizations suggest that the policies to reduce rape in war, therefore, should be geared toward a change of attitude among the higher command in terms of punishing perpetrators and a change of the existing military culture in which masculinity and violence are glorified.

carrying a death penalty), these articles are rarely sanctioned, leading to very few prosecutions and even fewer convictions with only light sentences. The ideology underlying soldiers being granted a "free pass" can be summarized by such statements as "Boys will be boys," "Boys need some fun ("boom boom," as it was called during the Vietnam War) after a hard day of fighting," and "Heroes who sacrifice themselves to defend freedom." It is almost impossible for the victims to report rape, it is very difficult for other soldiers to report crimes committed by their comrades, and the military is mostly unwilling to punish perpetrators. The second and related cause of the ongoing sexual violence is the fact that soldiering and fighting are closely connected to the idea of masculinity, which is associated with aggressive behavior. Military culture is based on a type of male bonding among soldiers, which is ensured through an emphasis on masculinity in which everything that is considered to be feminine (such as women and gay men) is viewed as the "other"—against a "we," the masculine heroes of the nation.

Therefore, the policies to reduce rape in war should be geared toward (1) a change of attitude by the higher command in terms of punishing perpetrators and (2) a change of the existing military culture in which masculinity and violence are glorified.

Worldwide

Wartime rape has been common in various (international and internal) conflicts around the world throughout history. Some armed conflicts witnessed opportunistic rapes—where soldiers, considering women to be part of the booty that they deserved, have taken the opportunity to "plunder the enemy's women." The extreme brutality of ancient and medieval wars included rape as just another violent act in the current conquest. The ancient stories, myths, art, literature, and religious texts also dealt with the subject of rape, such as in the cases of the rape of the Sabine women and the rape of Lucretia. Greeks and Romans raped enslaved adult males and boys, too, as symbols of victory and the enemy's defeat. Later, during the Hundred Years' War (1337–1453), English kings Richard II and Henry V prohibited rape for their own armies, but widespread assaults continued anyway. In 1474, the first international (among the kingdoms of Central Europe) conviction for wartime rape was handed down: Peter Von Hagenbach, a Burgundian governor, was tried, convicted, and executed for the atrocities that happened under his command in the territories of the Holy Roman Empire.

Modern wars in Europe also became stages for rape, despite the emergence of more disciplined regular armies whose conduct increasingly became ordered by army manuals as well as international norms and laws. Some of these incidents were opportunistic rapes resulting from the sexist beliefs that women are sexual objects or property of the enemy that can be "taken" as rewards after long and hard days of fighting and sexlessness. Victorious armies also considered rape as a tool to ultimately prove that the enemy had been defeated/feminized through their men's inability to protect their women or through being raped themselves. Despite the fact that rape was prohibited due to its potential negative impact on strategic goals and the fact that it was considered to be unacceptable by such European jurists as Hugo Grotius (known as the father of international law), many armies have overlooked rape cases, which has led to the impunity that encouraged more rapes. Some armies have also used rape as a weapon of war, to demoralize and annihilate enemy populations—that is, as a tool for ethnic cleansing or genocide.

Major Laws

Starting in the 19th century, international humanitarian law developed rapidly. Inspired by the ideas of the Enlightenment regarding civilization and civilized behavior—as well as by developments in military technology that were making warfare ever more destructive—European statesmen and legal scholars prepared international laws to civilize the conduct of warfare and make it more humane. Several attempts were made to codify the existing customs and new laws to that effect. One of the most important, albeit unsuccessful, attempts was the Brussels Conference of 1874. Delegates gathered to codify the laws of war on land for the first time, taking the Lieber Code as a model. Although the draft code (which was adopted as a declaration rather than a convention because of the disagreements among participating states) was largely copied from the Lieber Code, it omitted the parts prohibiting wartime rape. The resulting Brussels Declaration later served as a draft convention at the first Hague Peace Conference (1899), where participants gathered to codify—for the first time in history—laws of war on land. The Hague Conventions, therefore, despite having their roots in the Lieber Code, did not mention rape as a practice to be prohibited. The only relevant article is Article 46 of The Hague II (Laws and Customs of War on Land), which states, "Family honors and rights, individual lives and private property, as well as religious convictions and liberty, must be respected" (Hague Peace Conference 1899). The Hague Conventions of 1907 contained the exact same article.

At the Nuremberg and Tokyo criminal tribunals, established after World War II, the charters did not specify rape as one of the crimes under their jurisdiction. Later international legal documents handled wartime rape to different degrees. Article 27 of the Geneva Conventions (1949) relative to the Protection of Civilian Persons in Time of War (Convention IV) mentioned rape in an international treaty for the first time: "Women shall be especially protected against any attack on their honour, in particular against rape, enforced prostitution, or any form of indecent assault" (Geneva Conventions 1949). The Geneva Conventions, however, did not include rape among the grave breaches—which are regarded as the most serious crimes, requiring state parties to prosecute the perpetrators or surrender them to other states/courts for prosecution.

The Geneva Conventions were amended in 1977 by the Additional Protocols, one of which prohibited rape (Protocol II relating to the Protection of Victims of Non-International Armed Conflicts) openly with the language of "prohibition" for the first time: Article 4(2) of Protocol II states, "Without prejudice to the generality of the foregoing, the following acts against the persons referred to in paragraph I are and shall remain prohibited at any time and in any place whatsoever: (a) violence to the life, health and physical or mental well-being of persons, in particular murder as well as cruel treatment such as torture, mutilation or any form of corporal punishment; (b) collective punishments; (c) taking of hostages; (d) acts of terrorism; (e) outrages upon personal dignity, in particular humiliating and degrading treatment, rape, enforced prostitution and any form or indecent assault; (f) slavery and the slave trade in all their forms; (g) pillage; (h) threats to commit any or the foregoing acts" (Geneva Conventions 1977). The list of grave breaches in the Additional Protocols excluded rape as well.

International law dealt with rape more seriously after widespread sexual violence in the armed conflicts of 1990s was publicized. The statutes and convictions of the International Criminal Tribunal for Rwanda (ICTR) and the International Criminal Tribunal for the former Yugoslavia (ICTY) included wartime rape to differing degrees. The Statute of the ICTY (established in 1993, amended in 2003) included rape among its list of crimes against humanity in Article 5, and it was used to convict over 30 individuals for related crimes. Some of these judgments were particularly groundbreaking, because they were the first convictions for these crimes:

- For rape as torture, the *Čelebiči Judgment* (Mucić et al. [IT-96-21]), November 16, 1998;
- For a war crime, the *Furundžija Judgment* [IT-95-17/1], December 10, 1998; and
- For a crime against humanity, the *Foča Judgment* (Kunarac et al. [IT-96-23 & 23/1]), February 22, 2001.

The Statute of the ICTR (established in 1994) also included rape as a crime against humanity (Article 3) in addition to its list of war crimes (Article 4). With the *Akayesu Judgment* (on September 2, 1998), the tribunal issued the first conviction in history for rape as a means of genocide (International Committee of the Red Cross 1998).

Although the tribunals issued such historical judgments, they have also been criticized because of their shortcomings in addressing sexual violence, such as overlooking many cases and taking only symbolic decisions rather than providing justice for all survivors. Despite possible shortcomings, these verdicts set precedents, especially for the young permanent International Criminal Court (ICC), which was established on July 17, 1998, and started functioning on July 1, 2002. The Statute of the ICC—the Rome Statute—includes rape on its list of crimes against humanity (Article 7) and its list of war crimes (Article 8); and in Article 6(b) of its Elements of Crimes, it mentions rape as being among possible acts of genocide, putting wartime rape under the jurisdiction of the court (International Criminal Court 2011).

The United Nations (UN) Security Council also passed several resolutions to prevent rape in war. Resolution 1325 (October 31, 2000), which calls on states to include women and gender-perspective in issues related to international peace and security, also demands the protection of women from sexual violence in armed conflicts. Resolution 1820 (June 19, 2008) condemns wartime rape and affirms that "rape and other forms of sexual violence can constitute war crimes, crimes against humanity or a constitutive act with respect to genocide." Resolution 1888 (September 30, 2009) and Resolution 1889 (October 5, 2009) also condemn sexual violence in armed conflicts, calling for action. Resolution 1960 (December 16, 2010) and Resolution 2106 (June 24, 2013) call for the monitoring and prevention of sexual violence, and Resolution 2122 (October 18, 2013) supports, for survivors of rape, "access to the full range of sexual and reproductive health services, including regarding pregnancies resulting from rape, without discrimination" (United Nations Security Council 2016).

Historical Cases

Depending on the historical, political, social, economic, and cultural circumstances and structures, wartime rape happens for different reasons, serves
different purposes, and affects individuals and societies in different ways. The
conflicts that saw the highest number of (and most analyzed/most publicized)
sexual violence cases can be explored as examples of the abundance of this violence and its variety in modern times, as well as the failures of the international
community in terms of addressing them.

The Napoleonic Wars (1803–1815) witnessed widespread violence and
destruction, which included wartime rape by all sides of the conflict. Brutality
and plundering were everywhere committed by French armies, Portuguese and
British forces, and others. One well-known case during the wars that illustrates
the extent and character of the violence is the Siege of San Sebastián. When the
Allied forces under British command captured the Spanish city from the French,
the Allied troops—seeking to avenge their own losses—set about looting, burn-
ing, and raping to a degree that left the city of San Sebastián devastated.

The most famous incidence of wartime sexual violence during World War I
(1914–1918) is "the Rape of Belgium," which is a term used both figuratively
to describe the invasion of neutral Belgium by Germany and literally to refer
to the war crimes perpetrated during that period. While some historians maintain that these stories were fabricated by the British as part of war propaganda
efforts, others argue that rape and other forms of violence truly were committed
during the invasion, and on a mass scale. These outrages were part of the violence that accompanied the invasion rather than being part of any known plan
or strategy; German soldiers were invading the Belgian territory and everything
in it. After the war, a small number of cases were prosecuted in Germany for
alleged war crimes (the Leipzig War Crimes Trials), and one case was brought
to trial in Belgium. The indictments did not include rape.

The atrocities in World War II are numerous. Rape and sexual slavery were
also common aspects of these atrocities committed on all fronts by both sides
of the conflict for different reasons. One such massacre, the Rape of Nanking,
occurred during the Japanese invasion of China in 1937 preceding the war.
Tens of thousands of women, men, and children were raped, mutilated, and
tortured during the six-week-long invasion and occupation. The International
Military Tribunal for the Far East (often called the Tokyo Tribunal) prosecuted
several Japanese officials for the Nanking massacres, and a limited number
of the indictments and verdicts included rape (called "inhumane treatment,"
"ill-treatment," and "failure to respect family honor and rights," based on
related articles of The Hague Conventions of 1899 and 1907).

The Tokyo Tribunal failed, however, to address one of the worst and systematic cases of sexual abuse during World War II: "comfort women." The

Japanese Imperial Army forced tens of thousands of women (the number is estimated to be between 80,000 and 200,000) from Korea, China, Indochina, the Philippines, and other territories in the area into prostitution, supposedly to prevent wartime rape (hence the resulting problems of venereal disease and hostility among the populations in occupied territories) by providing soldiers with sexual outlets. These women were kidnapped or were tricked into sexual slavery (believing they were getting into other occupations) and then were kept in military brothels, where they were raped and tortured throughout the war. The Tokyo Tribunal did not prosecute anyone responsible for the crimes. The only prosecutions regarding this issue took place in 1948 at the Batavia Military Tribunal (a court-martial held by the Netherlands), where the Dutch women who were enslaved by the Japanese (kidnapped from the Dutch East Indies) brought their case. On numerous occasions, former comfort women have filed lawsuits against the Japanese government, demanding public apologies and acknowledgment of the crimes.

Wartime rape also occurred in other fronts in World War II. Europe witnessed rape by both sides during the war. Nazi atrocities, especially in Eastern and Southeastern Europe, included mass rapes perpetrated against Jewish, Russian, Polish, and other women in the occupied areas. The German Army also had a military brothel system (Wehrmacht brothel system), which kidnapped women to force them into prostitution. Although none of these crimes became subject to prosecution at Nuremberg, the Nuremberg Tribunal reported about them happening in places such as Smolensk, in the former Soviet Union.

The Allies committed mass rapes, too. For instance, goumiers (Moroccan troops) within the French Army, as well as British troops, committed mass rapes during the Allied invasion of Italy and Germany. British troops (made up of Australian, New Zealand, British, and Indian soldiers) also committed rapes during the occupation of Japan; these rapes resulted in several court-martials.

The most widespread and publicized of wartime rape during World War II, however, is the rape of German women by Soviet soldiers during in the occupation of Berlin in 1945. While Soviet troops committed rapes in Romania, Yugoslavia, Austria, and Hungary (while mostly refraining from it in Bulgaria), what happened in Berlin drew the most attention. It is estimated that 100,000 to 2 million German women survived sexual violence between 1945 and 1948. The events are usually interpreted as revenge for Nazi crimes or the behavior of binge-drinking soldiers who felt entitled to the "booty" after long and arduous fighting. The authorities did not do much to stop the attacks—Stalin was even reported to call for understanding for the exhausted soldiers (Dijlas 1962)—and prosecutions were rare. The issue was never brought up at the Nuremberg trials, which led to claims about the trials being "victor's justice."

In 1971, during Bangladesh's war for independence from Pakistan, it is estimated that mass rapes occurred, leaving 200,000–400,000 women as *birangonas* (survivors of wartime rape). The assaults are often interpreted as part of a genocidal campaign by the Pakistani Army against the Bengalis (Muslims and Hindus)—particularly because of the devastating effects of sexual violence on the community: Survivors were stigmatized and ostracized, leading them to flee the country or commit suicide.

In 2009, the International Crimes Tribunal was established in Bangladesh, for prosecuting those responsible for the atrocities in 1971. The Pakistani perpetrators could not be caught and prosecuted; however, several perpetrators who are in Bangladesh were tried and sentenced for various crimes, including rapes during the war.

In the former Yugoslavia, the civil war that lasted from 1991 to 2001 became a stage for mass rapes. The Bosnian War (1992–1995), in particular, saw widespread and planned genocidal rape as part of an ethnic cleansing campaign against Bosnian Muslims; this drew the interest of the world public to the phenomenon of wartime rape. The terminology of "rape camps" was introduced for the first time, as 20,000 to 50,000 Muslim and Croatian women were held in camps (such as Omarska, Foča, Trnopolje, Keraterm, Uzamnica, Vilina Vlas, and Manjača) run by Serbian forces and were systematically raped.

Rape was committed by all sides during the conflict, but strategic sexual violence planned by the high command and practiced by the officers was a tool that the Serbians used particularly to clear Bosnian Muslims from the area. The government in Belgrade (using the Ram Plan and the Brana Plan, which were military plans developed in 1990 and 1991 for ethnic cleansing) is reported to have deliberately targeted Muslim women to cause fear and panic and to encourage the Muslim communities to leave and never come back (Bergoffen 2005, 73; Card 2010, 269). Forced pregnancies in the rape camps—women were raped until they got pregnant with "Serbian" babies and kept in the camps until time for safe abortions passed—were also part of the ethnic cleansing campaign, which some scholars interpret as a form of biological warfare and genocide (Allen 1996; MacKinnon 1993). The effects of these forced pregnancies on the community—preventing reproduction, stigmatizing women, and producing stigmatized war babies—are considered to be genocidal, aimed at destroying the community through biological and social trauma.

The conflict in Bosnia ended in 1995, but war and wartime rape did not leave former Yugoslavia. The conflict that started in Kosovo in 1998 witnessed another campaign of sexual violence, as the Serbian forces attempted to expel Kosovar Albanians from parts of Kosovo to establish control over the region.

On May 25, 1993, the UN Security Council passed Resolution 827, establishing the first international criminal tribunal since Nuremberg and Tokyo to prosecute individuals responsible for the atrocities in the former Yugoslavia. The International Criminal Tribunal for the former Yugoslavia (ICTY) prosecuted and convicted some of the perpetrators as well as commanders and political officials; this put responsibility for wartime rape, in addition to other war crimes, at the command level.

The civil war that had been going on in Colombia since the 1960s saw widespread violence, including sexual violence against women, perpetrated by the government forces, paramilitaries, and guerrillas. (On June 23, 2016, both sides signed a cease-fire, but the public rejected the deal via referendum; a revised agreement was signed in November 2016.) One of the most important reasons for the rapes committed during the Colombian conflict was to terrorize the communities in order to displace them and acquire their lands. Women who were suspected of being political activists were also systematically assaulted in detention. Since the government is a major participant in the violence, prosecutions have not been pursued. The ICC put Colombia under preliminary examination, but no cases were opened.

During the three-month-long genocide in 1994, Rwanda saw the slaughter of approximately 800,000 of its people. The atrocities included widespread rape as well (250,000–500,000 women are estimated to have been victims). Under the Hutu-dominated government's instructions and propaganda, the *Interahamwe* (the Hutu paramilitaries) together with government forces perpetrated most of the rapes against Tutsi women, with the intention of destroying the Tutsi minority by destroying reproductive potential (mutilation, deliberate HIV infection by "rape squads," and murder often followed rapes), as well as through the inception of physical, psychological, and social trauma. Women who survived after being raped suffered from HIV, pregnancy (an estimated 2,000–5,000 war babies were born), stigmatization, and ostracism.

On November 8, 1994, by Resolution 955, the UN Security Council established the International Criminal Tribunal for Rwanda (ICTR) to prosecute the perpetrators of the genocide. While the ICTR issued the first judgment for rape as an act of genocide in the Akayesu Judgment, the tribunal has been criticized for failing to investigate and bring rape charges in most cases.

During the 11-year civil war (1991–2002) between the Sierra Leone government and the Revolutionary United Front (RUF) militia, mass rapes, sexual mutilation, sexual slavery, and forced marriages were perpetrated by the militia against the civilian population. The militia's main objective was to displace the population from certain areas by terrorizing them—so that the militia could extract resources (such as diamonds) from these areas in order to finance the ongoing war. Rapes, especially gang rapes, and forced marriages ("bush wives," as the women are called) also served the purpose of creating bonding among the militia.

In January 2002, in collaboration with the UN, Sierra Leone established the Special Court for Sierra Leone in order to prosecute those responsible for atrocities committed during the civil war. The court convicted individuals of war crimes and crimes against humanity, including rape, through such ground-breaking judgments as *The Prosecutor v. Issa Hassan Sesay, Morris Kallon and Augustine Gbao* in 2009; this was the first international conviction for sexual slavery and forced marriage as a crime against humanity (Special Court for Sierra Leone 2009).

The civil war that has been going on in the Democratic Republic of the Congo (DRC) since the 1990s turned the DRC into "the rape capital of the world," exposing women, men, and children to rape by the militia groups, as well as by government officials and civilians who took advantage of the lawless environment (Kristof and WuDunn 2009). Initially, widespread rape started in the DRC as part of the armed conflicts of 1990s; it continued as various militia groups that were fighting over the control of valuable minerals started to use rape as part of a strategy of attacking the social fabric. The violence increased as civilians and others started to perpetrate rapes, seeing the weakness of the security forces, the government, and the justice system—and the resulting impunity—as an opportunity. It has been argued, furthermore, that the inter-national attention being paid to wartime rape in the DRC encouraged more mass rapes, as certain militia groups wanted to use rape to gain prominence so that the government would negotiate with them. The UN peacekeeping forces in the country have also been unable to prevent sexual violence, as was demon-strated by the Luvungi mass rape incident in 2010 when the Mai Mai Sheka militia raped 387 civilians.

In 2004, the ICC started an investigation of the war crimes and crimes against humanity, including wartime rapes committed during the armed con-flicts in the DRC. Although no rape convictions in the cases in the DRC have occurred yet, another case at the ICC—involving a former vice president of the DRC—resulted in the first conviction for rape as a war crime and a crime against humanity. In March 2016, Jean-Pierre Bemba was convicted as the com-mander of forces who committed murder, rape, and pillage in the Central Afri-can Republic in 2002–2003 (International Criminal Court 2016).

During the civil war and the resulting humanitarian crisis in Sudan—which started in 2003, between the government (with the government-backed militia Janjaweed) and rebel groups—mass rapes have been perpetrated against the non-Arab population of Darfur with the intention of eradicating them from the region. Hence, the systematic campaign perpetrated by the government and Janjaweed has been interpreted as genocidal rape.

In June 2005, the ICC opened an investigation into the atrocities in Darfur. Several government officials, including the head of state Omar al-Bashir and the leader of Janjaweed Ali Kushayb, were indicted on charges including rape as a war crime and crime against humanity.

Other ongoing conflicts in the Middle East and Africa are also packed with various forms of violence, including rape. The Syrian civil war, for instance, which has been going on since 2011, has led to the rape of thousands of women, men, and children by various fighting groups (such as the Islamic State of Iraq and Syria, or ISIS) and government forces in their attempt to intimidate the population and ensure obedience and social control. Some of the groups, such as ISIS, have adopted rape as a central policy, declaring the rape of non-Muslims (or non-Sunnis) to be acceptable through fatwas and bragging about the crimes the groups have committed, such as the sexual enslavement of women captured as booty.

The kidnapping and sexual enslavement of women by the extremist group Boko Haram, in Nigeria, is another example of systematic attacks on women during armed conflicts. As part of its military strategy to dominate the rural areas, intimidate local populations, and recruit new members around its ideology, this militant Islamist group has kidnapped, hoarded, forcefully "married," and raped hundreds of women and girls. One such incident, the kidnapping of nearly 300 schoolgirls from Chibok, Nigeria, in April 2014, was highly publicized. While some of the girls later managed to escape after being sexually abused, many have gone missing. Boko Haram announced that they have been made into "wives" of the fighters or sold into slavery.

Engaging in sexual violence as a strategy has been interpreted not only as a way for these nonstate actors to control the populations through fear and through the establishment of ethnic, religious, ideological, or sectarian hierarchies (which in turn helps bonding within the group). It is also a way for the fighters to assert their hypermasculinity against their internal and external enemies.

There have also been reports of sexual abuse by the UN peacekeepers who are deployed in conflict areas to prevent such abuses. Such abuses have been in the form both of rape and of the sexual exploitation of these vulnerable people in exchange for food and money for sex ("survival sex"). These reports (such as those that came from Bosnia, the DRC, and Haiti) have triggered the UN to investigate its own personnel. However, the prosecutions of peacekeepers are left to the peacekeepers' home countries; this and other flaws in the workings of the UN have led to a lack of justice and a lack of prevention.

Tuba Inal

Further Reading

Ahram, Ariel. I 2015. "Sexual Violence and the Making of ISIS." *Survival* 57 (3): 57–78.

Allen, Beverly. 1996. *Rape Warfare: The Hidden Genocide in Bosnia-Herzegovina and Croatia.* Minneapolis and London: University of Minnesota Press.

Anderson, Letitia. 2010. "Politics by Other Means: When Does Sexual Violence Threaten International Peace and Security?" *International Peacekeeping* 17 (2): 244–60.

Anonymous. 2005. *A Woman in Berlin: Eight Weeks in the Conquered City: A Diary*. New York: Metropolitan Books.

Askin, Kelly D. 1997. *War Crimes Against Women: Prosecution in International War Crimes Tribunals*. The Hague, Netherlands: Martinus Nijhoff Publishers.

Autesserre, Severine. 2012. "Dangerous Tales: Dominant Narratives on the Congo and Their Unintended Consequences." *African Affairs* 111 (443): 202–22.

Baaz, Maria Eriksson, and Maria Stern. 2013. *Sexual Violence as a Weapon of War: Perceptions, Prescriptions, Problems in the Congo and Beyond*. London and New York: Zed Books.

Bahun, Sanja, and Julie VG Rajan, eds. 2015. *Violence and Gender in the Globalized World: The Intimate and the Extimate*. 2nd ed. Surrey and Burlington, UK: Ashgate.

Barnett, Louise. 2010. *Atrocity and American Military Justice in Southeast Asia: Trial by Army*. London and New York: Routledge.

Bassiouni, M Cherif. 2010. "Perspectives on International Criminal Justice." *Virginia Journal of International Law* 50 (2): 269–323.

Beevor, Antony. 2007. *Berlin: The Downfall 1945*. London: Penguin.

Bergoffen, Debra B. 2005. "How Rape Became a Crime against Humanity: History of an Error." In *Modernity and the Problem of Evil*, edited by Alan D. Schrift, 66–80. Bloomington and Indianapolis: Indiana University Press.

Bergsmo, Morten, Alf Butenschon Skre, and Elisabeth J. Wood, eds. 2012. *Understanding and Proving International Sex Crimes*. Oslo, Norway: Torkel Opsahl Academic.

Booth, Ken, ed. 2001. *The Kosovo Tragedy: The Human Rights Dimensions*. London and Portland, OR: Frank Cass.

Brook, Timothy, ed. 1999. *Documents on the Rape of Nanking*. Ann Arbor: University of Michigan Press.

Brownmiller, Susan. 1993. *Against Our Will: Men, Women and Rape*. Reprint ed. New York: Ballantine Books.

Card, Claudia. 2010. *Confronting Evils: Terrorism, Torture, Genocide*. New York: Cambridge University Press.

Carpenter, R. Charli. 2010. *Forgetting Children Born of War: Setting the Human Rights Agenda in Bosnia and Beyond*. New York: Columbia University Press.

Chang, Iris. 1997. *The Rape of Nanking: The Forgotten Holocaust of World War II*. New York: Penguin.

Cohen, Dara Kay. 2016. *Rape during Civil War*. Ithaca, NY: Cornell University Press.

Dawes, James. 2013. *Evil Men*. Boston, MA: Harvard University Press.

D'Costa, Bina. 2011. *Nationbuilding, Gender and War Crimes in South Asia*. New York: Routledge.

De Brouwer, Anne-Marie. 2005. *Supranational Criminal Prosecution of Sexual Violence: The ICC and the Practice of the ICTY and the ICTR*. Antwerp, Belgium, and Oxford, UK: Intersentia.

Dijlas, Milovan. 1962. *Conversations with Stalin*. New York: Harcourt Brace.

Doubt, Keith. 2006. *Understanding Evil: Lessons from Bosnia*. New York: Fordham University Press.

Eisenstein, Zillah. 1996. *Hatreds: Racialized and Sexualized Conflicts in the 21st Century*. New York and London: Routledge.

Enloe, Cynthia H. 2000. *Maneuvers: The International Politics of Militarizing Women's Lives*. Berkeley: University of California Press.

Eriksson, Maria. 2011. *Defining Rape: Emerging Obligations for States under International Law?* Leiden, Netherlands: Martinus Nijhoff.

Fletcher, Ian. 1995. *In Hell Before Daylight: The Siege and Storming of the Fortress of Badajoz, 1812*. 2nd ed. Staplehurst, UK: Spellmount.

Fremont-Barnes, Gregory. 2002. *The Napoleonic Wars: The Peninsular War 1807–1814*. Oxford, UK: Osprey Publishing.

Geneva Conventions. 1949. "Convention (IV) Relative to the Protection of Civilian Persons in Time of War, 12 August 1949." Geneva: International Committee of the Red Cross. Accessed February 19, 2017. https://ihl-databases.icrc.org/applic/ihl/ihl.nsf/INTRO/380?OpenDocument.

Geneva Conventions. 1977. "Protocol Additional to the Geneva Conventions of 12 August 1949, and Relating to the Protection of Victims of Non-International Armed Conflicts (Protocol II), 8 June 1977." Accessed February 19, 2017. https://ihl-databases.icrc.org/applic/ihl/ihl.nsf/INTRO/475?OpenDocument.

Gerster, Robin. 2008. *Travels in Atomic Sunshine: Australia and the Occupation of Japan*. Carlton North, Australia: Scribe Publications.

Hagemann, Karen, and Stefanie Schuler-Springorum, eds. 2002. *Home/Front: The Military, War and Gender in Twentieth-Century Germany*. Oxford, UK: Berg.

Hague Peace Conference. 1899. "Convention with Respect to the Laws and Customs of War on Land." Treaty Series 403. Accessed February 20, 2017. http://avalon.law.yale.edu/19th_century/hague02.asp.

Halfond, Gregory I., ed. 2015. *The Medieval Way of War*. Surrey and Burlington, UK: Ashgate.

Hansen, Lene. 2001. "Gender, Nation, Rape: Bosnia and the Construction of Security." *International Feminist Journal of Politics* 3 (1): 55–75.

Hedgepeth, Sonja M., and Rochelle G. Saidel, eds. 2010. *Sexual Violence Against Jewish Women During the Holocaust*. Waltham, MA: Brandeis University Press.

Heineman, Elizabeth D., ed. 2011. *Sexual Violence in Conflict Zones: From the Ancient World to the Era of Human Rights*. Philadelphia: University of Pennsylvania Press.

Inal, Tuba. 2013. *Looting and Rape in Wartime: Law and Change in International Relations*. Philadelphia: University of Pennsylvania Press.

International Committee of the Red Cross. 1998. "ICTR, The Prosecutor v. Jean-Paul Akayesu." ICTR-96-4-T. *How Does Law Protect in War?* Accessed February 19, 2017. https://casebook.icrc.org/case-study/ictr-prosecutor-v-jean-paul-akayesu.

International Criminal Court. 2011. "Elements of Crimes." The Hague, Netherlands: International Criminal Court. Accessed February 19, 2017. https://www.icc-cpi.int/NR/rdonlyres/336923D8-A6AD-40EC-AD7B-45BF9DE73D56/0/ElementsOfCrimesEng.pdf.

International Criminal Court. 2016. *The Prosecutor v. Jean-Pierre Bemba Gombo*. ICC-01/05-01/08. Case Information Sheet. Accessed February 19, 2017. https://www.icc-cpi.int/car/bemba/Documents/BembaEng.pdf.

Kirby, Paul. 2012. "How Is Rape a Weapon of War? Feminist International Relations, Modes of Critical Explanation and the Study of Wartime Sexual Violence." *European Journal of International Relations* 19 (4): 797–821.

Kristof, Nicholas D., and Sheryl WuDunn. 2009. *Half the Sky: Turning Oppression into Opportunity for Women Worldwide*. Toronto, Canada: Alfred A. Knopf.

Leatherman, Janie L. 2011. *Sexual Violence and Armed Conflict*. Cambridge, UK, and Malden, MA: Polity Press.

Lee, David, ed. 2015. *Law of Armed Conflict Deskbook*. 5th ed. Charlottesville, VA: International and Operational Law Department, The United States Army Judge Advocate General's Legal Center and School. Accessed October 15, 2015. http://www.loc.gov/rr/frd/Military_Law/pdf/LOAC-Deskbook-2015.pdf.

Lentin, Ronit, ed. 1997. *Gender and Catastrophe*. London and New York: Zed Books.

Lieber, Francis. 1863. *General Orders No. 100: The Lieber Code. Instructions for the Government of Armies of the United States in the Field*. Accessed February 19, 2017. http://avalon.law.yale.edu/19th_century/lieber.asp.

Lilly, J. Robert. 2007. *Taken by Force: Rape and American GIs in Europe during World War II*. Basingstoke, UK, and New York: Palgrave Macmillan.

Lipkes, Jeff. 2007. *Rehearsals: The German Army in Belgium, August 1914*. Leuven, Belgium: Leuven University Press.

Longden, Sean. 2007. *To the Victor the Spoils: Soldiers' Lives from D-Day to VE-Day*. London: Robinson.

MacKinnon, Catherine A. 1993. "Crimes of War, Crimes of Peace." *UCLA Women's Law Journal* 4 (1): 59–86.

Manjoo, Rashida, and Calleigh McRaith. 2011. "Gender-Based Violence and Justice in Conflict and Post-Conflict Areas." *Cornell International Law Journal* 44:11–31.

Meger, Sara. 2016. *Rape Loot Pillage: The Political Economy of Sexual Violence in Armed Conflict*. New York: Oxford University Press.

Meron, Theodor. 1993. "Rape as a Crime under International Humanitarian Law." *The American Journal of International Law* 87 (3): 424–28.

Mitchell, Reid. 1993. *The Vacant Chair: The Northern Soldier Leaves Home*. New York: Oxford University Press.

Morris, Madeline. 1996. "By Force of Arms: Rape, War, and Military Culture." *Duke Law Journal* 45 (4): 651–781.

Murphy, Kim. 2014. *I Had Rather Die: Rape in the Civil War*. Batesville, VA: Coachlight Press.

Naimark, Norman M. 1995. *The Russians in Germany: A History of the Soviet Zone of Occupation, 1945–1949*. Cambridge, MA: Belknap Press.

Ndulo, Muna. 2009. "The United Nations Responses to the Sexual Abuse and Exploitation of Women and Girls by Peacekeepers during Peacekeeping Missions." *Berkeley Journal of International Law* 27 (1): 127–61.

Ni, Aolain Fionnuala, Dina Francesca Haynes, and Naomi Cahn. 2011. *On the Frontlines: Gender, War, and the Post-Conflict Process*. Oxford, UK, and New York: Oxford University Press.

Notar, Susan A. 2006. "Peacekeepers as Perpetrators: Sexual Exploitation and Abuse of Women and Children in the Democratic Republic of the Congo." *Journal of Gender, Social Policy and the Law* 14 (2): 413–29.

Nowrojee, Binaifer. 1996. *Shattered Lives: Sexual Violence during the Rwandan Genocide and Its Aftermath*. New York: Human Rights Watch. Accessed February 19, 2017. https://www.hrw.org/reports/1996/Rwanda.htm.

Oosterveld,Valerie. 2011. "The Gender Jurisprudence of the Special Court for Sierra Leone: Progress in the Revolutionary United Front Judgments." *Cornell International Law Journal* 44 (1): 49–74.

O'Toole, Laura L, Jessica R. Schiffman, and Margie L. Kiter Edwards, eds. 2007. *Gender Violence: Interdisciplinary Perspectives*. New York: New York University Press.

Overy, Richard. 1999. *Russia's War*. London: Penguin.

Phang, Sara Elise. 2008. *Roman Military Service: Ideologies of Discipline in the Late Republic and Early Principate*. New York: Cambridge University Press.

Rittner, Carol, and John K. Roth, eds. 2012. *Rape: Weapon of War and Genocide*. St. Paul, MN: Paragon House.

Schabas, William. 2012. *Unimaginable Atrocities: Justice, Politics, and Rights at the War Crimes Tribunals*. Oxford, UK: Oxford University Press.

Schrijvers, Peter. 2002. *The GI War against Japan: American Soldiers in Asia and the Pacific During World War II*. New York: New York University Press.

Sharlach, Lisa. 2000. "Rape as Genocide: Bangladesh, the Former Yugoslavia, and Rwanda." *New Political Science* 22 (1): 89–102.

Simm, Gabrielle. 2013. *Sex in Peace Operations*. Cambridge, UK: Cambridge University Press.

Special Court for Sierra Leone. 2009. *Prosecutor v. Issa Hassan Sesay, Morris Kallon, and Augustine Gbao*. SCSL-04-15-T. Accessed February 19, 2017. http://www.rscsl.org/Documents/Decisions/RUF/1234/SCSL-04-15-T-1234-searchable.pdf.

Tanaka, Yuki. 2001. *Japan's Comfort Women: Sexual Slavery and Prostitution during World War II and the US Occupation*. London and New York: Routledge.

Totten, Samuel, and Eric Markusen, eds. 2006. *Genocide in Darfur: Investigating the Atrocities in the Sudan*. New York and London: Routledge.

True, Jacqui. 2015. "Winning the Battle but Losing the War on Violence: A Feminist Perspective on the Declining Global Violence Thesis." *International Feminist Journal of Politics* 17 (4): 554–72.

Turshen, Meredeth. 2016. *Gender and the Political Economy of Conflict in Africa: The Persistence of Violence*. Abingdon, UK, and New York: Routledge.

United Nations Human Rights Council. 2015. "Report of the Office of the United Nations High Commissioner for Human Rights on the Human Rights Situation in Iraq in the Light of Abuses Committed by the So-called Islamic State in Iraq and the Levant and Associated Groups." Accessed February 19, 2016. http://www.ohchr.org/EN/HRBodies/HRC/RegularSessions/Session28/Documents/A_HRC_28_18_AUV.doc.

United Nations Security Council. n.d. "Security Council Resolutions—Resolutions Adopted by the Security Council since 1946." Accessed September 23, 2016. http://www.un.org/en/sc/documents/resolutions/.

United Nations War Crimes Commission. n.d. *Law Reports of Trials of War Criminals*. Military Legal Resources. Vols. 1–15. Washington, DC: Library of Congress,

Accessed February 19, 2017. https://www.loc.gov/rr/frd/Military_Law/law-reports -trials-war-criminals.html.

Weaver, Gina Marie. 2010. *Ideologies of Forgetting: Rape in the Vietnam War*. Albany: State University of New York Press.

Yoshiaki, Yoshimi. 2000. *Comfort Women: Sexual Slavery in the Japanese Military during World War II*. New York: Columbia University Press.

Zangana, Haifa. 2009. *City of Widows: An Iraqi Woman's Account of War and Resistance*. New York: Seven Stories Press.

Zawati, Hilmi M. 2014. *Fair Labelling and the Dilemma of Prosecuting Gender-Based Crimes at the International Criminal Tribunals*. Oxford, UK, and New York: Oxford University Press.

Zuckerman, Larry. 2004. *The Rape of Belgium: The Untold Story of World War I*. New York and London: New York University Press.

Primary Documents

Michael M. v. Superior Court of Sonoma County

1981

In Michael M. v. Superior Court of Sonoma County, *the petitioner, Michael M., was 17 and a half when he was found guilty of violating the statutory rape law in California. The law at that time defined* unlawful sexual intercourse *as "an act of sexual intercourse with a female not the wife of the perpetrator, where the female is under the age of 18 years." Michael M. argued that the law was unconstitutional because it violated the Fourteenth Amendment, as only men were guilty of the crime. In a 5–4 decision, the California Supreme Court ruled that California's law did not discriminate on the basis of gender. Since that time, however, California's sexual assault laws have been changed so that they are gender-neutral.*

JUSTICE REHNQUIST announced the judgment of the Court and delivered an opinion, in which THE CHIEF JUSTICE, JUSTICE STEWART, and JUSTICE POWELL joined.

The question presented in this case is whether California's "statutory rape" law, § 261.5 of the Cal.Penal Code Ann. (West Supp. 1981), violates the Equal Protection Clause of the Fourteenth Amendment. Section 261.5 defines unlawful sexual intercourse as "an act of sexual intercourse accomplished with a female not the wife of the perpetrator, where the female is under the age of 18 years." The statute thus makes men alone criminally liable for the act of sexual intercourse.

In July, 1978, a complaint was filed in the Municipal Court of Sonoma County, Cal., alleging that petitioner, then a 17 1/2-year-old male, had had unlawful sexual intercourse with a female under the age of 18, in violation of § 261.5. The evidence adduced at a preliminary hearing showed that, at approximately midnight on June 3, 1978, petitioner and two friends approached Sharon, a 16 1/2-year-old female, and her sister as they waited at a bus stop. Petitioner and Sharon, who had already been drinking, moved away from the others and began to kiss. After being struck in the face for rebuffing petitioner's initial advances, Sharon submitted to sexual intercourse with petitioner. Prior to trial, petitioner sought to set aside the information on both state and federal constitutional grounds, asserting that § 261.5 unlawfully discriminated on the basis of gender.

The trial court and the California Court of Appeal denied petitioner's request for relief, and petitioner sought review in the Supreme Court of California.

The Supreme Court held that "section 261.5 discriminates on the basis of sex, because only females may be victims and only males may violate the section." 25 Cal.3d 608, 611, 601 P.2d 572, 574. The court then subjected the classification to "strict scrutiny," stating that it must be justified by a compelling state interest. It found that the classification was "supported not by mere social convention, but by the immutable physiological fact that it is the female exclusively who can become pregnant." *Ibid.* Canvassing "the tragic human costs of illegitimate teenage pregnancies," including the large number of teenage abortions, the increased medical risk associated with teenage pregnancies, and the social consequences of teenage childbearing, the court concluded that the State has a compelling interest in preventing such pregnancies. Because males alone can "physiologically cause the result which the law properly seeks to avoid," the court further held that the gender classification was readily justified as a means of identifying offender and victim. For the reasons stated below, we affirm the judgment of the California Supreme Court.

As is evident from our opinions, the Court has had some difficulty in agreeing upon the proper approach and analysis in cases involving challenges to gender-based classifications. The issues posed by such challenges range from issues of standing, *see Orr v. Orr,* 440 U.S. 268 (1979), to the appropriate standard of judicial review for the substantive classification. Unlike the California Supreme Court, we have not held that gender-based classifications are "inherently suspect," and thus we do not apply so-called "strict scrutiny" to those classifications. *See Stanton v. Stanton,* 421 U.S. 7 (1975). Our cases have held, however, that the traditional minimum rationality test takes on a somewhat "sharper focus" when gender-based classifications are challenged. *See Craig v. Boren,* 429 U.S. 190, 429 U.S. 210 n.* (1976) (POWELL, J., concurring). In *Reed v. Reed,* 404 U.S. 71 (1971), for example, the Court stated that a gender-based classification will be upheld if it bears a "fair and substantial relationship" to legitimate state ends, while in *Craig v. Boren, supra* at 429 U.S. 197, the Court restated the test to require the classification to bear a "substantial relationship" to "important governmental objectives."

Underlying these decisions is the principle that a legislature may not "make overbroad generalizations based on sex which are entirely unrelated to any differences between men and women or which demean the ability or social status of the affected class."

Parham v. Hughes, 441 U.S. 347, 441 U.S. 354 (1979) (plurality opinion of STEWART, J.). But because the Equal Protection Clause does not "demand that a statute necessarily apply equally to all persons" or require *"things which are different in fact . . . to be treated in law as though they were the same," Rinaldi v.*

Yeager, 384 U.S. 305, 384 U.S. 309 (1966), quoting Tigner v. Texas, 310 U.S. 141, 310 U.S. 147 (1940), this Court has consistently upheld statutes where the gender classification is not invidious, but rather realistically reflects the fact that the sexes are not similarly situated in certain circumstances. Parham v. Hughes, supra; Califano v. Webster, 430 U.S. 313 (1977); Schlesinger v. Ballard, 419 U.S. 498 (1975); Kahn v. Shevin, 416 U.S. 351 (1974). As the Court has stated, a legislature may "provide for the special problems of women." Weinberger v. Wiesenfeld, 420 U.S. 636, 420 U.S. 653 (1975).

Applying those principles to this case, the fact that the California Legislature criminalized the act of illicit sexual intercourse with a minor female is a sure indication of its intent or purpose to discourage that conduct. . . . Precisely why the legislature desired that result is, of course, somewhat less clear. This Court has long recognized that "[i]nquiries into congressional motives or purposes are a hazardous matter," *United States v. O'Brien,* 391 U.S. 367, 391 U.S. 383-384 (1968); *Palmer v. Thompson,* 403 U.S. 217, 403 U.S. 224 (1971), and the search for the "actual" or "primary" purpose of a statute is likely to be elusive. *Arlington Heights v. Metropolitan Housing Dev. Corp.,* 429 U.S. 252, 429 U.S. 265 (1977); *McGinnis v. Royster,* 410 U.S. 263, 410 U.S. 276-277 (1973). Here, for example, the individual legislators may have voted for the statute for a variety of reasons. Some legislators may have been concerned about preventing teenage pregnancies, others about protecting young females from physical injury or from the loss of "chastity," and still others about promoting various religious and moral attitudes towards premarital sex.

The justification for the statute offered by the State and accepted by the Supreme Court of California, is that the legislature sought to prevent illegitimate teenage pregnancies. That finding, of course, is entitled to great deference. *Reitman v. Mulkey,* 387 U.S. 369, 387 U.S. 373-374 (1967). And although our cases establish that the State's asserted reason for the enactment of a statute may be rejected, if it "could not have been a goal of the legislation," *Weinberger v. Wiesenfeld, supra* at 420 U.S. 648, n. 16, this is not such a case.

We are satisfied not only that the prevention of illegitimate pregnancy is at least one of the "purposes" of the statute, but also that the State has a strong interest in preventing such pregnancy. At the risk of stating the obvious, teenage pregnancies, which have increased dramatically over the last two decades, have significant social, medical, and economic consequences for both the mother and her child, and the State.

Of particular concern to the State is that approximately half of all teenage pregnancies end in abortion. And of those children who are born, their illegitimacy makes them likely candidates to become wards of the State.

We need not be medical doctors to discern that young men and young women are not similarly situated with respect to the problems and the risks of sexual intercourse. Only women may become pregnant, and they suffer disproportionately the profound physical, emotional, and psychological consequences of sexual activity. The statute at issue here protects women from sexual intercourse at an age when those consequences are particularly severe.

The question thus boils down to whether a State may attack the problem of sexual intercourse and teenage pregnancy directly by prohibiting a male from having sexual intercourse with a minor female. We hold that such a statute is sufficiently related to the State's objectives to pass constitutional muster.

Because virtually all of the significant harmful and inescapably identifiable consequences of teenage pregnancy fall on the young female, a legislature acts well within its authority when it elects to punish only the participant who, by nature, suffers few of the consequences of his conduct. It is hardly unreasonable for a legislature acting to protect minor females to exclude them from punishment. Moreover, the risk of pregnancy itself constitutes a substantial deterrence to young females. No similar natural sanctions deter males. A criminal sanction imposed solely on males thus serves to roughly "equalize" the deterrents on the sexes.

We are unable to accept petitioner's contention that the statute is impermissibly underinclusive and must, in order to pass judicial scrutiny, be *broadened* so as to hold the female as criminally liable as the male. It is argued that this statute is not *necessary* to deter teenage pregnancy because a gender-neutral statute, where both male and female would be subject to prosecution, would serve that goal equally well. The relevant inquiry, however, is not whether the statute is drawn as precisely as it might have been, but whether the line chosen by the California Legislature is within constitutional limitations. *Kahn v. Shevin*, 416 U.S. at 3 416 U.S. 56, n. 10.

In any event, we cannot say that a gender-neutral statute would be as effective as the statute California has chosen to enact. The State persuasively contends that a gender-neutral statute would frustrate its interest in effective enforcement. Its view is that a female is surely less likely to report violations of the statute if she herself would be subject to criminal prosecution. In an area already fraught with prosecutorial difficulties, we decline to hold that the Equal Protection Clause requires a legislature to enact a statute so broad that it may well be incapable of enforcement.

We similarly reject petitioner's argument that § 261.5 is impermissibly overbroad because it makes unlawful sexual intercourse with prepubescent females, who are, by definition, incapable of becoming pregnant. Quite apart from the fact that the statute could well be justified on the grounds that very young females are particularly susceptible to physical injury from sexual intercourse, *see Rundlett v. Oliver*, 607 F.2d 495 (CA1 1979), it is ludicrous to suggest that the Constitution requires the California Legislature to limit the scope of its rape statute to older teenagers and exclude young girls.

There remains only petitioner's contention that the statute is unconstitutional as it is applied to him because he, like Sharon, was under 18 at the time of sexual intercourse. Petitioner argues that the statute is flawed because it presumes that, as between two persons under 18, the male is the culpable aggressor. We find petitioner's contentions unpersuasive. Contrary to his assertions, the statute does not rest on the assumption that males are generally the aggressors. It is, instead, an attempt by a legislature to prevent illegitimate teenage pregnancy by providing an additional deterrent for men. The age of the man is irrelevant, since young men are as capable as older men of inflicting the harm sought to be prevented.

In upholding the California statute, we also recognize that this is not a case where a statute is being challenged on the grounds that it "invidiously discriminates" against females.

To the contrary, the statute places a burden on males which is not shared by females. But we find nothing to suggest that men, because of past discrimination or peculiar disadvantages, are in need of the special solicitude of the courts. Nor is this a case where the gender classification is made "solely for . . . administrative convenience," as in *Frontiero v. Richardson,* 411 U.S. 677, 411 U.S. 690 (1973) (emphasis omitted), or rests on "the baggage of sexual stereotypes" as in *Orr v. Orr,* 440 U.S. at 440 U.S. 283. As we have held, the statute instead reasonably reflects the fact that the consequences of sexual intercourse and pregnancy fall more heavily on the female than on the male.

Accordingly the judgment of the California Supreme Court is
Affirmed.

Source: *Michael M. v. Superior Court,* 450 U.S. 464 (1981).

Anita Hill's Testimony

Supreme Court Nomination Hearings for Clarence Thomas, Part 4

October 11, 1991

President George H. W. Bush nominated Clarence Thomas to fill a vacancy on the U.S. Supreme Court after Thurgood Marshall decided to retire in 1991. Despite some opposition from civil rights organization and women's groups, Thomas's confirmation hearings began uneventfully. After the hearings moved to the Senate, law professor Anita Hill, who had worked for Thomas when he was the head of the Equal Employment Opportunities Commission, accused him of having sexually harassed her. Though Thomas was confirmed, the controversy is seen as the spark that lit up new debates and policies on sexual harassment. It also led to a record number of women running for and winning legislative seats. The media called 1992 the "Year of the Woman." The following excerpt is from Hill's testimony. The experiences she mentions are typical of sexual harassment cases in which an individual has been repeatedly propositioned and/or threatened by a boss or supervisor.

During this period at the Department of Education, my working relationship with Judge Thomas was positive. I had a good deal of responsibility as well as independence. I thought that he respected my work and that he trusted my judgment. After approximately three months of working together, he asked me to go out with him socially. I declined and explained to him that I thought that it would only jeopardize what, at the time, I considered to be a very good working relationship. I had a normal social life with other men outside of the office. I believed then, as now, that having a social relationship with a person who was supervising my work would be ill-advised. I was very uncomfortable with the idea and told him so.

I thought that by saying "no" and explaining my reasons, my employer would abandon his social suggestions. However, to my regret, in the following few weeks he continued to ask me out on several occasions. He pressed me to justify my reasons for saying "no" to him. These incidents took place in his office or mine. They were in the form of private conversations which would not have been overheard by anyone else.

My working relationship became even more strained when Judge Thomas began to use work situations to discuss sex. On these occasions he would call me into his office for reports on education issues and projects or he might suggest that because of time pressures we go to lunch at a government cafeteria. After a brief discussion of work, he would turn the conversation to discussion of sexual matters. His conversations were very vivid. He spoke about acts that he had seen in pornographic films involving such matters as women having sex with animals and films showing group sex or rape scenes. He talked about pornographic materials depicting individuals with large penises or large breasts involved in various sex acts. On several occasions Thomas told me graphically of his own sexual prowess.

Because I was extremely uncomfortable talking about sex with him at all and particularly in such a graphic way, I told him that I did not want to talk about those subjects. I would also try to change the subject to education matters or to nonsexual personal matters such as his background or beliefs. My efforts to change the subject were rarely successful.

Throughout the period of these conversations, he also from time-to-time asked me for social engagements. My reactions to these conversations was to avoid having them by eliminating opportunities for us to engage in extended conversations. This was difficult because I was his only assistant at the Office for Civil Rights. During the latter part of my time at the Department of Education, the social pressures and any conversation of this offensive kind ended. I began both to believe and hope that our working relationship could be on a proper, cordial and professional base.

When Judge Thomas was made Chairman of the EEOC, I needed to face the question of whether to go with him. I was asked to do so. I did. The work itself was interesting and at that time it appeared that the sexual overtures which had so troubled me had ended. I also faced the realistic fact that I had no alternative job. While I might have gone back to private practice, perhaps in my old firm or at another, I was dedicated to civil rights work and my first choice was to be in that field . . .

For my first months at the EEOC, where I continued as an assistant to Judge Thomas, there were no sexual conversations or overtures. However, during the Fall and Winter of 1982, these began again. The comments were random and ranged from pressing me about why I didn't go out with him to remarks about my personal appearance. I remember his saying that someday I would have to give him the real reason that I wouldn't go out with him. He began to show real displeasure in his tone of voice, his demeanor and his continued pressure for an explanation. He commented on what I was wearing in terms of whether it made me more or less sexually attractive. The incidents occurred in his inner office at the EEOC.

One of the oddest episodes I remember was an occasion in which Thomas was drinking a Coke in his office. He got up from the table at which we were working, went over to his desk to get the Coke, looked at the can, and said, "Who has put a pubic hair on my Coke?" On other occasions he referred to the size of his own penis as being larger than normal and he also spoke on some occasions of the pleasures he had given to women with oral sex.

At this point, late 1982, I began to feel severe stress on the job. I began to be concerned that Clarence Thomas might take it out on me by downgrading me or not giving me important assignments. I also thought that he might find an excuse for dismissing me . . .

In January of 1983, I began looking for another job . . . In February, 1983, I was hospitalized for five days on an emergency basis for an acute stomach pain which I attributed to stress on the job. . . .

In the Spring of 1983, an opportunity to teach law at Oral Roberts University opened up. I agreed to take the job in large part because of my desire to escape the pressures I felt at the EEOC due to Thomas. When I informed him that I was leaving in July, I recall that his response was that now I "would no longer have an excuse for not going out with" him. I told him that I still preferred not to do so. . . .

At some time after that meeting, he asked if he could take me to dinner at the end of my term. When I declined, he assured me that the dinner was a professional courtesy only and not a social invitation. I reluctantly agreed to accept that invitation but only if it was at the very end of a workday. On, as I recall, the last day of my employment at the EEOC in the summer of 1983, I did have dinner with Clarence Thomas. We went directly from work to a restaurant near the office. We talked about the work I had done both at Education and at EEOC. He told me that he was pleased with all of it except for an article and speech that I done [sic] for him when we were at the Office of Civil Rights. Finally, he made a comment which I vividly remember. He said that if I ever told anyone about his behavior toward me it could ruin his career. This was not an apology nor was there any explanation. That was his last remark about the possibility of our going out or reference to his behavior.

Source: Nomination of Judge Clarence Thomas to Be Associate Justice of the Supreme Court of the United States, Hearings before the Committee on the Judiciary, United States Senate, 102nd Congress, 1st Session. J-102-40. Washington, DC: Government Printing Office, 1993, pp. 36–39. Accessed December 21, 2017. https://web.archive.org/web/20071127082050/http://www.gpoaccess.gov/congress/senate/judiciary/sh102-1084pt4/36-40.pdf

The Federal Campus Sexual Assault Victims' Bill of Rights
1992

The Clery Act was first passed in 1990. Since then, it has been amended several times. In 1992, the amendment included the Campus Sexual Assault Victims' Bill of Rights (also known as the Ramstad Act). This act was signed into law by President George H. W. Bush. The law requires that all colleges and universities (public and private) that participate in federal student aid programs provide sexual assault victims certain basic rights, such as the option to notify law enforcement and the right to be informed of counseling services. Schools that violate the law can be fined and lose their eligibility to participate in federal student aid programs. The following is Minnesota Representative Jim Ramstad's discussion of the bill in the House of Representatives in February 1992.

Mr. Speaker, last May I introduced H.R. 2363, the Campus Sexual Assault Victims' Bill of Rights Act. As of today, this measure has received the strong bipartisan support of 176 cosponsors.

This legislation is of vital importance to the thousands of women who are raped on our college and university campuses each year. Mr. Speaker, campus rape victims deserve to be informed of their legal rights. And whether the rape victim chooses to pursue the matter through campus proceedings or the court system, campus officials should provide them reasonable assistance in exercising their rights.

Mr. Speaker, knowing that one in four college women will be the victim of rape or attempted rape during her college career, Congress must take strong action to ensure victims their rights.

Last week, the Senate—without opposition—passed an amendment to the Higher Education Reauthorization Act which is based on the Campus Sexual Assault Victims' Bill of Rights Act.

Mr. Speaker, let us bring the higher education reauthorization bill to the floor as soon as possible so that we can join the Senate in taking this much needed action to protect campus sexual assault victims.

Source: *Congressional Record*, Vol. 138 (Pt. 3), Number 15, p. 3336. February 25, 1992. Washington, DC: U.S. Government Printing Office, 1992. https://www.congress.gov/bill/102nd-congress/senate-bill/1289/text.

The Personal Responsibility and Work Opportunity Reconciliation Act

August 1996

Many solutions have been proposed to curb teen pregnancy. In 1996, President Bill Clinton connected statutory rape laws to welfare-reform measures. The bill he signed into law, the Personal Responsibility and Work Opportunity Reconciliation Act, directed the Justice Department to examine the "link between statutory rape and teen pregnancy." Individual states were also urged to examine and enforce their own statutory rape laws.

SEC. 905. ESTABLISHING NATIONAL GOALS TO PREVENT TEENAGE PREGNANCIES.

(a) IN GENERAL.—Not later than January 1, 1997, the Secretary of Health and Human Services shall establish and implement a strategy for—

(1) preventing out-of-wedlock teenage pregnancies, and
(2) assuring that at least 25 percent of the communities in the United States have teenage pregnancy prevention programs in place.

(b) REPORT.—Not later than June 30, 1998, and annually thereafter, the Secretary shall report to the Congress with respect to the progress that has been made in meeting the goals described in paragraphs (1) and (2) of subsection (a).

SEC. 906. SENSE OF THE SENATE REGARDING ENFORCEMENT OF STATUTORY RAPE LAWS.

(a) SENSE OF THE SENATE.—It is the sense of the Senate that States and local jurisdictions should aggressively enforce statutory rape laws.

(b) JUSTICE DEPARTMENT PROGRAM ON STATUTORY RAPE.—Not later than January 1, 1997, the Attorney General shall establish and implement a program that—

(1)   studies the linkage between statutory rape and teenage pregnancy, particularly by predatory older men committing repeat offenses; and

(2)   educates State and local criminal law enforcement officials on the prevention and prosecution of statutory rape, focusing in particular on the commission of statutory rape by predatory older men committing repeat offenses, and any links to teenage pregnancy.

(c) VIOLENCE AGAINST WOMEN INITIATIVE.—The Attorney General shall ensure that the Department of Justice's Violence Against Women initiative addresses the issue of statutory rape, particularly the commission of statutory rape by predatory older men committing repeat offenses.

Source: "The Personal Responsibility and Work Opportunity Reconciliation Act." Public Law 104–193, August 22, 1996, 104th Congress. Available at https://www.congress.gov/104/plaws/publ193/PLAW-104publ193.pdf.

First Anniversary of the 1996 World Congress against Commercial Sexual Exploitation of Children

ECPAT (End Child Prostitution in Asian Tourism) began with a focus on Asia, but it has grown into an international organization with a global mission. The First World Congress against Commercial Sexual Exploitation of Children was held August 27–31, 1996, in Stockholm. The Congress was hosted by the Government of Sweden, along with ECPAT, UNICEF, and Group for the Convention on the Rights of the Child, an NGO. At the 1996 meeting, 122 nations adopted the Agenda for Action described in the following excerpt from the first annual report.

ECPAT International has great pleasure releasing this first anniversary report on the follow up to the Declaration and Agenda for Action adopted at the World Congress against Commercial Sexual Exploitation of Children The Agenda for Action which was unanimously adopted by all 122 governments represented at the Congress together with Inter-Governmental Organisation (IGO) and Non-Governmental Organisation (NGO) participants on 28 August 1996, provides a framework for the eventual eradication of the sexual exploitation of children worldwide.

The Agenda for Action asks governments in cooperation with IGOs and relevant members of the civil society to work together to face the growing challenge of child prostitution, child pornography and the trafficking of children for sexual purposes. It reiterates its commitment to the rights of the child, bearing in mind the Convention on the Rights of the Child and accords high priority to action. Recognising the globalisation of these issues, it promotes stronger cooperation between States and all sectors of society both at the national and international level.

The Agenda for Action proposes a five pronged approach to the eradication of commercial sexual exploitation of children:

1) The coordination of actions at local, national, the regional and international levels.
2) The taking of preventative measures through the formal and informal education sector, sensitising relevant target groups to their rights and to the issue.
3) The protection of children already caught in the horror of the sex trade through the strengthening or development of relevant laws and policies and the strengthening of law enforcement programmes and international cooperation.
4) The recovery and reintegration of children into society through non-punitive, gender-sensitive support systems and
5) To promote the participation of children, including child victims and their families, so that they are able to express their views to take action to protect children from commercial sexual exploitation.

The Stockholm World Congress decided that the existing international mechanisms, namely the Committee on the Rights of the Child and the Special Rapporteur on the Sale of Children, Child Prostitution and Child Pornography, would provide the framework for following up the implementation of the Agenda for Action. However it became clear soon after the Congress that these existing mechanisms would benefit from wider support from the NGO community. A meeting hosted by the United Nations Children's Fund (UNICEF) in New York in December 1996 at which ECPAT International and the Geneva-based NGO Group for the Convention on the Rights of the Child participated, decided to establish an Advisory Group to the Special Rapporteur and a data-base of information which would contain relevant information on the implementation of the Agenda for Action. With support from UNICEF, ECPAT International agreed to accept the responsibility for establishing and maintaining the data base.

. . .

The first world Congress against the Commercial Sexual Exploitation of Children was held in Stockholm, Sweden, August 27–31, 1996. Official government delegations attended the Congress from 122 countries (see Appendix) and were joined by other delegates representing Non-Governmental Organisations (NGOs) and intergovernmental bodies and the commercial sector. Attendance at the Congress totaled 1,300 persons.

The Congress was called to consider the three areas of commercial sexual exploitation of children listed in the UN Convention on the Rights of the Child:

• the prostitution of children
• child pornography and
• trafficking in children for sexual purposes

On August 28, 1996 the participants unanimously adopted an Agenda for Action which confirmed the commitment of governments "to a global partnership against the commercial sexual exploitation of children". Unfortunately neither the Agenda for Action nor the subsequent Congress statements made any provision for a follow-up mechanism to monitor the actions of governments and NGOs in fulfilling the mandate of the Agenda.

The Congress itself was planned and organised by the Swedish Government in cooperation with three agencies:

- ECPAT, the international NGO working to end child prostitution which initiated the idea of the Congress and approached the Swedish government to organise the Congress
- The United Nations Children's Fund (UNICEF) through its division on Children in Especially Difficult Circumstances (CEDC) which is mandated to work in the area of the commercial sexual exploitation of children.
- The Geneva-based NGO Group for the Convention on the Rights of the Child which represents 41 non-governmental bodies working in the area of children's rights.

On December 12, 13, 1996 a meeting of these three bodies took place at UNICEF headquarters in New York. This meeting considered the need for follow-up to the Congress and agreed on two specific actions:

a) In order to assist the Committee on the Rights of the Child and the Special Rapporteur of the UN Commission on Human Rights on the Sale of Children, Child Prostitution and Child Pornography, it was agreed that an Advisory Group would be established with special responsibility to make recommendations to UN bodies on the commercial sexual exploitation of children. The NGO Group for the Convention on the Rights of the Child agreed to coordinate the functioning of this Advisory Group and they expect to have their first meeting in October 1997.

b) The second agreed initiative was that ECPAT would be asked to establish a major information data-base which will store and share information on developments in all of the countries concerned with this issue. This information will provide ideas and background so that countries and organisations seeking to take action will have a central bank of data immediately available for their use.

United Nations General Assembly: A resolution passed at the 52nd General Assembly, November 1996, on "Prevention and eradication of the sale of children and of their sexual exploitation, including child prostitution and child pornography" welcomed the convening of the Congress in Sweden and described the Agenda for Action as an important contribution to the global efforts aimed at the eradication of such practices. The UN called on all States to implement "on an urgent basis" measures outlined in the Agenda. It makes mention of the need for improving laws and specifically urges the adoption and implementation of extraterritorial laws in the area of child sex abuse.

Source: First Annual Report, World Congress against Commercial Sexual Exploitation of Children, 1996. ECPAT International. http://www.ecpat.org/.

Rape and Murder of Brandon Teena

September 1997

Brandon Teena (born Teena Brandon), a transgender man, was raped by John Lotter and Marvin Nissen in 1993. After Teena reported the rape, the two men killed him. Joann Brandon, Brandon's mother, sued Charles B. Laux, who was the Richardson County, Nebraska, sheriff at the time. She claimed that Laux could have prevented the murder if he had arrested the men after the rape was reported. Brandon's story was the subject of the Academy Award–winning film Boys Don't Cry *(1999), based on the documentary* The Brandon Teena Story *(1998). Below is an excerpt from the Nebraska court case following the murder.*

MEMORANDUM AND ORDER
KOPF, District Judge.
This is a tragic case. Teena Brandon (Brandon), a young woman who dressed like a man, was shot by Defendant John Lotter (Lotter) and stabbed by Defendant Marvin Nissen, also known as Tom Nissen (Nissen), in the early morning hours of December 31, 1993. Brandon died. Lotter and Nissen had conspired to kill Brandon to silence her about a prior sexual assault they had perpetrated upon her.

Plaintiff claims that this conspiracy was motivated by the hatred that Nissen and Lotter held for women who dressed like men. The plaintiff further asserts that the conspiracy to kill Brandon was simply an extension of the conspiracy to rape Brandon because she was a female who dressed like a male.

About six days before her death, and on Christmas Day, Brandon reported to Charles B. Laux (Laux), then a county sheriff, that these men had raped her on Christmas Eve. Brandon told Laux that she would testify against the men. Nevertheless, because Brandon was upset with Laux, she refused two requests for follow-up interviews.

Brandon's mother, who is the personal representative of the estate, has sued Laux claiming that he had knowledge of the conspiracy to deny Brandon her civil rights and did nothing to prevent the murder. Laux did not immediately arrest the men and he did not inform Brandon that he was not going to immediately arrest them. Thus, the plaintiff claims that Laux is liable to the plaintiff pursuant to 42 U.S.C. § 1986 (providing a cause of action for neglect to prevent acts done in furtherance of a conspiracy to interfere with civil rights)

Laux has filed a motion for summary judgment. Among other things, he claims that he is entitled to qualified immunity from suit. After carefully reviewing the undisputed material facts, I find and conclude that I must grant summary judgment in favor of Laux on the defense of qualified immunity. A reasonable officer in the shoes of Laux could have believed that Nissen and Lotter were not about to harm Brandon.

Source: *Brandon v. Lotter*, 976 F. Supp. 872 (D. Neb. 1997) U.S. District Court for the District of Nebraska—976 F. Supp. 872, September 2, 1997.

South African Criminal Law on Sexual Offences
2007

In 2007, the Republic of South Africa replaced its previous rape laws "with a new expanded statutory offence of rape, applicable to all forms of sexual penetration without consent, irrespective of gender." The following is an excerpt from the act, which eliminates marriage to the rape victim as a defense, stipulates the age of consent, and provides leeway on acts committed as a "legitimate cultural practice."

Defences and sentencing

56. (1) Whenever an accused person is charged with an offence under section 3, 4, 5, 6 or 7 it is not a valid defence for that accused person to contend that a marital or other relationship exists or existed between him or her and the complainant.

(2) Whenever an accused person is charged with an offence under—

(a) section 15 or 16, it is, subject to subsection (3), a valid defence to such a charge to contend that the child deceived the accused person into believing that he or she was 16 years or older at the time of the alleged commission of the offence and the accused person reasonably believed that the child was 16 years or older; or

(b) section 16, it is a valid defence to such a charge to contend that both the accused persons were children and the age difference between them was not more than two years at the time of the alleged commission of the offence.

(3) The provisions of subsection (2)(a) do not apply if the accused person is related to the child within the prohibited incest degrees of blood, affinity or an adoptive relationship.

(4) A person ("A") may not be convicted of an offence in terms of section 12 if, at the time when the act of sexual penetration was first committed—

(a) A was below the age of 18 years; and

(b) the other person ("B") exercised power or authority over A or a relationship of trust existed between A and B.

(5) A person may not be convicted of an offence in terms of section 17(4) or (5) or section 23(4) or (5) or section 54, if that person is—

(a) a child; and
(b) not a person contemplated in section 17(1) and (2) or 23(1) and (2), as the case may be.

(6) It is not a valid defense to a charge under section 20(1), in respect of a visual representation that—

(a) the accused person believed that a person shown in the representation that is alleged to constitute child pornography, was or was depicted as being 18 years or older unless the accused took all reasonable steps to ascertain the age of that person; and (b) took all reasonable steps to ensure that, where the person was 18 years or older, the representation did not depict that person as being under the age of 18 years.

(7) If a person is convicted of any offence under this Act, the court that imposes the sentence shall consider as an aggravating factor the fact that the person—

(a) committed the offence with intent to gain financially, or receive any favour, benefit, reward, compensation or any other advantage; or
(b) gained financially, or received any favour, benefit, reward, compensation or any other advantage,

from the commission of such offence.

(8) A person may not be convicted of an offence in terms of section 9 or 22 if that person commits such act in compliance with and in the interest of a legitimate cultural practice.

Inability of children under 12 years and persons who are mentally disabled to consent to sexual acts

57. (1) Notwithstanding anything to the contrary in any law contained, a male or female person under the age of 12 years is incapable of consenting to a sexual act.

(2) Notwithstanding anything to the contrary in any law contained, a person who is mentally disabled is incapable of consenting to a sexual act.

Source: Republic of South Africa, Criminal Law (Sexual Offense and Related Matters) Amendment Act, No. 32, 2007, South Africa Department of Justice Website. http://evaw-global-database.unwomen.org/-/media/files/un%20 women/vaw/full%20text/africa/south%20africa%20%20criminal%20law%20 sexual%20offences%20and%20related%20matters%20amendme.pdf.

Why Don't Rape Victims Report the Crime?

Medical University of South Carolina,

National Crime Victims Research and Treatment Center

February 2007

The authors of this study analyzed the information taken from interviews with 5,000 U.S. women in a national sample. The women interviewed were between the ages of 18 and 86. Of the women in the sample, 2,000 were currently attending college or university within the United States. The object of the study was to determine how many U.S. women had ever been sexually assaulted, and also how many had been sexually assaulted in the year of the study (2006). Other goals included identifying characteristics of different types of rape and determining why women report or do not report when they have been raped.

. . . there is no evidence that rape in America is a smaller problem than it was 15 years ago, and there is no evidence that women are more willing to report rape cases today than they were 15 years ago. Unreported cases cannot be addressed by the criminal justice system, and victims who do not report their rapes do not receive the services that might assist them as they attempt to recover. Despite concerted national efforts to address underreporting over the past 15 years, it appears that the problem still exists and requires our attention.

Our Nation and communities must re-double efforts to understand why victims are reluctant to report, work to reduce barriers to reporting, and sufficiently address their concerns about reporting so that they do actually report. As was the case 15 years ago, the concerns of rape victims provide important insights into why they don't report, including fear of reprisal; concerns about family and friends knowing; fear of bad treatment by the criminal justice system; not knowing how to report; and unclear that a crime occurred or that harm was intended. An obvious first step in reporting any crime to law enforcement, including rape, is a recognition that a crime occurred, or that a rape occurred. Data indicate that only 71 percent of victims in forcible rape cases correctly defined what happened to them as a rape. If a person doesn't know she was raped, no reporting, no access to services or support, no interventions and no apprehension of rapists are likely outcomes.

While 71 percent of forcible rape victims correctly defined what happened to them as a rape, only 45 percent of victims of DAFR [Drug or Alcohol-Facilitated Rape] and IR [Incapacitated Rape] cases did so. Public education about what rape is, along with the important fact that a victim's use of alcohol or other drugs prior to a rape does not change the definition or act of rape, is needed. Such education should target whole communities, not just potential victims.

Source: Report submitted to the U.S. Department of Justice by Dean G. Kilpatrick, Heidi S. Resnick, Kenneth J. Ruggiero, Lauren M. Conoscenti, and Jenna

McCauley. *Drug-facilitated, Incapacitated, and Forcible Rape: A National Study.* February 1, 2007, p. 62. Medical University of South Carolina, National Crime Victims Research and Treatment Center. https://www.ncjrs.gov/pdffiles1/nij /grants/219181.pdf.

Rape as a Weapon of War

U.S. Senate Subcommittee on Human Rights and the Law

April 1, 2008

On April 1, 2008, the U.S. Senate Subcommittee on Human Rights and the Law held a hearing that included testimony of witnesses to rape in conflict areas. The hearing was preceded by a video of clips from the documentary film The Greatest Silence: Rape in the Congo *by filmmaker Lisa Jackson, whose testimony is excerpted elsewhere in this volume. Below are excerpts from Senator Richard Durbin's opening remarks and an excerpt from the testimony of Dr. Denis Mukwege, director of the Panzi Hospital in the Democratic Republic of Congo, who describes the physical and psychological problems faced by the survivors of rape, as well as the challenges of treating them.*

Senator Durbin

It is appalling that today women and girls are being raped in conflict situations around the world. It reflects our collective failure to stop the use of women's bodies as a battleground.

The scale of this problem is daunting. A recent report documented conflict-related sexual violence in 51 countries in Africa, the Americas, Asia, Europe, and the Middle East in the last two decades.

Wartime rape is not inevitable. The widespread prevalence of sexual violence in recent conflicts results in part from the lack of accountability for those who commit the rape.

Government and rebel forces violate human rights and these poor people with impunity, perpetuating the stigma that surrounds these crimes.

Historically, wartime sexual violence was tolerated as unfortunate but unavoidable.

Throughout the 20th century, rape and other forms of sexual violence were included in increasingly specific terms in international agreements on the conduct of war. Prejudice and misconceptions meant these crimes were initially framed as private acts violating family dignity and honor, rather than the violent public crimes that they are.

As noted in the video we just watched, the Yugoslav and Rwanda Tribunals made significant progress by prosecuting perpetrators of sexual violence. That we have moved beyond the not-so-distant debate about whether sexual violence in conflict is a war crime is an important forward step.

Despite these developments, wartime sexual violence and the experience of those women and men who survive it remain invisible far too often.

During today's hearing, we are going to discuss the legal options for holding accountable those who use rape as a military tactic. While a growing number of perpetrators of wartime sexual violence have been prosecuted, a much larger number have escaped accountability. The average wartime rapist runs very little risk of being prosecuted.

The United States and other countries must play a greater role. I am sorry to say that if a foreign warlord who engaged in mass rape came to the United States of America today, he would probably be beyond the reach of our laws. It is not a crime under U.S. law for a non-U.S. national to perpetrate sexual violence in conflict against non-U.S. nationals, so the U.S. Government is unable to prosecute such perpetrators of wartime rape who end up in our country.

There is also no U.S. law prohibiting crimes against humanity, one of the most serious human rights violations, which includes mass rape and other forms of sexual violence.

And we must make it clear that genocide and torture, two of the most serious human rights violations that are a crime under U.S. law, can include wartime sexual violence.

These loopholes have real consequences. For example, take the case of Emmanuel "Chuckie" Taylor, son of the warlord Charles Taylor, whom the Justice Department is prosecuting under the torture statute. As the head of the notorious Anti-Terrorist Unit of the Liberian Government, Chuckie Taylor was implicated in wartime rapes committed by the ATU, but it is unlikely that he could be prosecuted for these crimes against humanity in the United States.

Another example is Marko Boskic, who found safe haven in our country after reportedly participating in the execution of men and boys in the Srebrenica massacre. Under current law, the United States was unable to prosecute Boskic for his crimes against humanity and charged him only with visa fraud.

In addition to punishing individual perpetrators, governments that tolerate and fail to take steps to stop wartime sexual violence must be held accountable for their actions. At the very least, we should ensure that U.S. tax dollars do not fund state armies that fail to prevent their forces from engaging in mass rape.

We must work to end the use of rape as a weapon of war, but as long as the practice persists, we should support programs that provide protection, medical care, psychological services and legal remedies to survivors of wartime sexual violence.

As I have said so many times and I will repeat again today, this Subcommittee will focus on legislation, not lamentation.

We must end impunity for wartime sexual violence. I look forward to working with the members of this Subcommittee to ensure that our laws hold accountable those who use rape as a weapon of war. . . .

Statement of Denis Mukwege, M.D., Director, Panzi General Referral Hospital, Bukavu, South Kivu, Democratic Republic of Congo, Accompanied by Jean Moorhead, Interpreter

. . . The word "rape" or "sexual violence" cannot fully translate the horror that hundreds of thousands of women are living in this part of the world. My testimony refers to my daily contacts with these victims in the hospital, and the thousands of women whom we treat.

It is important to point out that this sexual terrorism is done in a methodical manner and according to the method of terror each armed group uses against their victims. Generally, the victims are raped by several men at a time, one after another; in public, in front of parents, husbands, children, or neighbors; rape is followed by mutilations or other corporal torture; sexual slavery often goes on for months; and there are all sorts of psychological torture.

On arriving at the hospital, women victims complain of physical, psychological, and social problems, and they show sexually transmissible infections, especially chlamydia, which is a source of chronic abdominal pain and results in sterility; HIV infection, accompanied by opportunistic diseases; genital lesions ranging from simple wounds to complicated genital lesions stopping urinary or digestive function such as urogenital and recto-genital fistulas; fibrosis of the vagina, et cetera.

It goes without saying that this woman, who has become incapable of fully using her capacities as a woman because all possibility of motherhood is taken away from her, and in addition is weakened by AIDS, hopes in her pain for an easy death. And we are all witnesses that this is voluntary murder.

The woman is deeply humiliated, and this brings on behavioral difficulties which can result in suicide, disinterest in living, not caring for anything, and aggressiveness. These women are often rejected by their own family and their husbands. This exclusion and isolation can worsen the behavioral problems which were mentioned before.

This results in a breakup of the family, and often the woman or girl victim is excluded and condemned instead of the rapist. The result is the destruction of potential mothers and the spread of HIV on a large scale, which brings about the disappearance of the population without the capacity of the population renewing itself.

The analysis of this phenomenon shows that the rapists are not doing this to satisfy some kind of sexual desire, but simply want to destroy the woman. They want to destroy life.

This sadistic desire to destroy pertains not only to the woman, but to her whole family and the whole community. This situation is so much more serious because it does not concern 10,000 women but, according to estimates, several hundred thousand women . . .

Chairman Durbin: Dr. Mukwege, thank you very much for that moving testimony. When I visited DOCS Hospital in Goma, and asked about the doctors who were there, they told me that there was one surgeon for every 1 million people. And I asked them what these doctors were paid, and I was told that they work for the government and that they were paid $600 a month, when they were paid. Can you tell me if the circumstances at your hospital are similar?

Dr. Mukwege: The situation of doctors in the Congo today is catastrophical. I have worked for almost 25 years in this area, in this region, as the only gynecologist. It is practically impossible to find a gynecologist who will come and work under these conditions. They prefer to go to South Africa or other countries where they are better paid and treated. And to get around this problem, I have trained some of my colleagues, doctors, in gynecological and obstetrical interventions to be able to help me to work in the hospital.

Chairman Durbin: May I ask you this? You have spoken to us graphically about the physical damage being done to the victims. Would you speak for a moment about the psychological element? What I found in many of these women in Goma was rejection by their families, by their tribes, by all of their friends. They were alone after they had been victimized. You have given us examples of women who have been victimized. Are these women welcomed back to some part of their background, their family, their community, their village? What is their future after the surgery?

Dr. Mukwege: After surgery, we come up against two types of problems. The first group are women who are cured physically and who do not have AIDS. It is easier to reconciliate this group of women with their families, and, with the help of churches and NGO's, we make many efforts to reconcile these women with their families. There has been a favorable change today in the way that people look at the women, and we have been working with the churches not to condemn these women. And this has led to an acceptance on the part of the community and the families of these women.

But even if the woman does not have AIDS or she is not very sick, when the rapist gives a child to the woman he rapes, it is hard for the family to accept the child, and for the community also. And we have been trying to work with the family to accept the child, because when the father of the child has killed the whole family, it is absolutely difficult for the family or the community to accept the child.

We have a problem because with very young girls, many of them are incurable, 13, 14 years old. The bladder was destroyed. The rectum was destroyed. The vagina was destroyed. And in that state it is hard to cure them. So they cannot go home because when they go home, they do not smell good because they are incontinent, and they always come back to the hospital. And it is a problem because we keep these young women.

They never want to leave the hospital. They always find a reason to stay at the hospital, and it is hard for the hospital because the hospital cannot keep all these women. And that is a big problem for us. They always find a reason to come back and stay there.

Source: U.S. Senate Subcommittee on Human Rights and the Law. Committee on the Judiciary. Senate Hearing 110-581. *Rape as a Weapon of War: Accountability for Sexual Violence in Conflict.* Washington, DC: U.S. Government Printing Office, 2008.

Testimony of Lisa F. Jackson

U.S. Senate Subcommittee on Human Rights and the Law

April 1, 2008

On April 1, 2008, the Senate Committee on the Judiciary held a hearing before the Subcommittee on Human Rights and the Law that included the testimony of several witnesses to sexual violence in conflict areas. An excerpt from documentary filmmaker Lisa Jackson's testimony follows. Jackson also disclosed that she was a survivor of a gang rape in New York City. As she notes, women are not safe from sexual violence in peacetime or in war. In 2016, the International Criminal Court (ICC) found former Congolese vice president Jean-Pierre Bemba guilty of using sexual violence as a weapon of war.

. . . I am honored to be asked to come before you to describe from my own perspective some of what I witnessed and heard in the months that I spent in the Eastern DR Congo in 2006 and 2007 shooting a documentary film. During that time I interviewed many women and girls who had survived sexual violence. I talked with peacekeepers, priests, doctors, activists, international aid workers and, most chillingly of all, with a dozen self-confessed rapists, uniformed soldiers in the Congolese army who boasted to my camera about the dozens of women they had raped. What I heard in the Congo has altered the course of my own life, and I hope I can convey to you here today even a small sense of the profound impact that the women—and men—of the Congo had on me.

I want to add a personal note: in 1976, here in Washington, DC, I myself was gang-raped. The three men who attacked me that night in Georgetown were never found and the statute of limitations on the crime expired long ago. I shared my story with the raped women I met in the Congo and they all asked about the war that was happening in my country. I explained to them that even in peacetime, women are not safe.

And while I'm grateful that the Subcommittee has taken on this formidable issue of sexual violence in conflict, it is a bit stunning that it has taken until mid-2008 for this subject to be addressed in these halls. The past century offers too many examples of rape being used as a weapon of war: the Japanese rapes during the 1937 occupation of Nanking, an estimated 200,000 women raped by Pakistani soldiers during the battle for Bangladeshi independence in 1971, the horrors of Bosnia and its infamous rape hotels, Rwanda with half a million rapes on top of the genocide deaths, the systematic raping of women by the Janjaweed in Darfur. . . . The title of my film is "The Greatest Silence", taken from the opening of line of a survey cowritten, in 2002, by Ellen Johnson Sirleaf, the president of Liberia: "Violence against women in conflict is one of history's greatest silences." And, sadly, history proves she is right.

But even in the context of this horrifying litany of the suffering of women in war, what has been happening in the Democratic Republic of Congo in the last 10 years is beyond the pale of any historical precedent. Congo's war is a war against women, a war in which women's bodies have become the battleground, where no woman is safe. Hundreds of thousands of women and girls have been intentionally and systematically targeted, gang raped, mutilated, forcibly abducted for many months to vast inaccessible forest areas and used as sexual slaves. They are attacked by armed militias from Uganda and Burundi, by Hutu genocidaires who fled from justice in Rwanda, by warlords and their thugs, and by members of the very army and police forces that are supposed to protect them. United Nations peacekeepers have also committed rape and sexual exploitation. It is a femicide, pure and simple, and it is my hope that what you hear today will move this august body to action. . . .

I first went to South Kivu, a province in the eastern DRC, in the spring of 2006, to investigate what was happening there for a documentary film about the fate of women and girls in conflict. I went in search of rape survivors who might tell me their stories and I found many dozens of raped women, women of all ages, too many women who at times would line up for hours, waiting until after the light disappeared and my camera could no longer record an image, waiting to talk to me, waiting to tell their stories to someone who would listen to them without judgment, hoping that I would relay their stories to a world that seemed indifferent to their horrific plight. I talked to them in their hospital beds, sitting on dirt floors in their mud huts, on the hard benches of a parish church, in the offices of NGOs where a few lucky ones had found skills training and shelter. These women might be just statistics to some, but to me they have names, faces, lives and stories that I will never forget.

Muhindo, a somber, dignified woman of 52 with five children, had been kidnapped from her home, dragged into the bush by soldiers from a Rwandan armed group who held her captive for two months. They used her as a sex slave, raped her daily, and forced her to carry their loads, cook their food and wash their clothes.

Veranda is 35 years old and has survived two attacks; she was first raped by Rwandese militia—the Interahamwe group—and again by thieves dressed in Congolese Army uniforms.

Safi lives in the hills above Bunyakiri and was raped at age 11 while her home was being looted by soldiers. Her huge eyes still have a slightly stunned look as she tells me that when she grows up she hopes to be a nun.

Maria Namafu was 70 years old when she was raped by three soldiers. When she told them "I am an old woman" they said "you're not too old for us."

Faida was kidnapped from her home in Bunyakiri, enslaved and raped repeatedly by Interahamwe soldiers. She died from the resulting infections in 2007.

These are five out of literally hundreds of thousands of victims. Why is it that we know so very little about these women? . . . And why is it that rape in conflict is so infrequently prosecuted in the world's courts for being the heinous crime of war that it is? Where is the outrage? Perhaps there is some explanation in a comment made to me by a colonel in the UN peacekeeping force when I asked him about rape in the Congo. His candor somewhat surprised me:

> I think we're all very ignorant of it. I think it's an issue that we want to push to one side. I don't think, as a human, I feel particularly comfortable sitting and talking about it here, for example. But it happens here on a huge scale and I agree, it is not spoken about.

. . .

Rape survivors face emotional torment, psychological damage, crippling physical injuries, disease, social ostracism and many other consequences that can devastate their lives and the lives of their families I think about Marie Jeanne M'wamasoro, a 34-year-old mother of eight, who was raped by five members of a Rwandan armed group when she was six months pregnant. She has been abandoned by her husband who tells their children that she wanted to be raped. She knows that she is stigmatized for life and says to me, with tears spilling over: "My heart is broken. I know that wherever I go people will say 'that woman was raped.'" And Imakile Furha who is now 18 years old and was raped at age 15 by two members of a Rwandan armed group who broke into her home in the middle of the night. She has a daughter, Lumiere, from those rapes, and she lives with a burden no teenager should have to bear: "There is nothing I can do about the past. But sometimes I spend my days crying. I really don't have a plan for the future. I hope that by the grace of God I will find someone who will marry me."

The lives of these women—and their children—have been forever altered, and some of them destroyed. What I am going to read to you now is a transcription of one survivor's incredible soliloquy. She was part of a group of women who had been kidnapped and held as sex slaves. She stood up, unprompted, spoke directly to my camera and told me:

> I am very thankful, because we believe that with your arrival here we will get help. The same painful thing has happened to every woman in this room. They have taken our belongings. We were raped by twenty men at the same time. Our bodies are suffering. They have taken their guns and put them inside of us. They kill our children and then they tell us to eat those children. If a woman is pregnant they make your children stand on your belly so that you will abort. Then they take the blood from your womb and put it in a bowl and tell you to drink it. When we were living in the forest it wasn't just one man. Every soldier can have sex with you. We got pregnant there. We gave birth in the forest, alone, like animals, without food or medicine. We are all alone—our husbands have been killed, or they have denied us. Even our families have denied us. We don't know what to do, where to go.

When she finished speaking, she turned to the wall, covered her face, and wept. Her story was no exaggeration. . . .

I interviewed soldiers, members of the national Congolese army, who talked brazenly to me about the rapes they had committed. They were practically swaggering, describing their reasons and methods of rape without shame, guilt or even a hint of remorse, because they knew that in Congo's culture of impunity they would face no reprisals for their crimes. . . .

In my 30 years of filmmaking, interviewing these soldiers was the single, most devastating moment I had ever experienced. I had just recorded men confessing to unspeakable crimes and when the interviews were over they just melted back into the forest. There was no one around to arrest them, they were not talking to me from a jail cell. And as they vanished into the bush I thought to myself, who will be their next victims?

. . . The widespread rape and sexual violence is fuelled by a pervasive culture of impunity that the Government of Congo seems unwilling or unable to combat. . . .

Yes, the government passed a sweeping new law last year regarding sexual violence, a law that, for instance, finally made rape with guns and sticks a crime, but I heard over and over again stories about the futility of enforcement, about rapists who would pay a bribe of 3 or 4 dollars and walk free, about jails with no locks on the cell doors, about sex crime units with—literally—a staff of one, and about women who face brutal reprisals if they speak out about the crimes perpetrated against them or dare to denounce their attackers. They are left to bear the pain alone, without the solace of peace, or the possibility of justice.

As one women's advocate in Kinshasa said to me:

> The rapists of yesterday have today become the authorities and they encourage sexual violence because for them it has become a lifestyle. That is why the violence doesn't end.

. . . We cannot speak of peace in Congo while rampant sexual violence continues unabated and a war continues to rage against women and girls. In the face of the government's impotence or unwillingness to intervene, the international community must act to bring an end to these deplorable crimes. . . .

Source: U.S. Senate Subcommittee on Human Rights and the Law. Committee on the Judiciary. Senate Hearing 110-581. *Rape as a Weapon of War: Accountability for Sexual Violence in Conflict.* Washington, DC: U.S. Government Printing Office, 2008.

Remarks by President Barack Obama at Reception Commemorating the Enactment of the Matthew Shepard and James Byrd, Jr., Hate Crimes Prevention Act

October 28, 2009

In 1998, near Laramie, Wyoming, student Matthew Shepard was tortured and murdered. It was widely reported that Shepard's assailants attacked him because he was gay. James Byrd Jr.'s murder also happened in 1998, in Jasper, Texas. Byrd was an African American man who was dragged behind a truck by white supremacists and then beheaded. The Matthew Shepard and James Byrd, Jr., Hate Crimes Prevention Act, commonly known as the Matthew Shepard Act and passed in 2009, expands the previous federal hate crime law to include crimes motivated by the victim's—or perception of the victim's—sexual orientation, gender identity, or disability, as well as by race, religion, and national origin. Below, President Barack Obama commemorates his signing the act into law.

THE PRESIDENT [Barack Obama]: Thank you so much, everybody. Thank you so much, and welcome to the White House. . . .

To all the activists, all the organizers, all the people who helped make this day happen, thank you for your years of advocacy and activism, pushing and protesting that made this victory possible.

You know, as a nation we've come far on the journey towards a more perfect union. And today, we've taken another step forward. This afternoon, I signed into law the Matthew Shepard and James Byrd, Jr. Hate Crimes Prevention Act . . .

This is the culmination of a struggle that has lasted more than a decade. Time and again, we faced opposition. Time and again, the measure was defeated or delayed. Time and again we've been reminded of the difficulty of building a nation in which we're all free to live and love as we see fit. But the cause endured and the struggle continued, waged by the family of Matthew Shepard, by the family of James Byrd, by folks who held vigils and led marches, by those who rallied and organized and refused to give up, by the late Senator Ted Kennedy who fought so hard for this legislation . . . and all who toiled for years to reach this day.

You understood that we must stand against crimes that are meant not only to break bones, but to break spirits—not only to inflict harm, but to instill fear. You understand that the rights afforded every citizen under our Constitution mean nothing if we do not protect those rights—both from unjust laws and violent acts. And you understand how necessary this law continues to be.

In the most recent year for which we have data, the FBI reported roughly 7,600 hate crimes in this country. Over the past 10 years, there were more than 12,000 reported hate crimes based on sexual orientation alone. And we will never know how many incidents were never reported at all.

And that's why, through this law, we will strengthen the protections against crimes based on the color of your skin, the faith in your heart, or the place of your birth. We will finally add federal protections against crimes based on gender, disability, gender identity, or sexual orientation. . . . And prosecutors will have new tools to work with states in order to prosecute to the fullest those who would perpetrate such crimes. Because no one in America should ever be afraid to walk down the street holding the hands of the person they love. No one in America should be forced to look over their shoulder because of who they are or because they live with a disability.

At root, this isn't just about our laws; this is about who we are as a people. This is about whether we value one another—whether we embrace our differences, rather than allowing them to become a source of animus. It's hard for any of us to imagine the mind-set of someone who would kidnap a young man and beat him to within an inch of his life, tie him to a fence, and leave him for dead. It's hard for any of us to imagine the twisted mentality of those who'd offer a neighbor a ride home, attack him, chain him to the back of a truck, and drag him for miles until he finally died.

But we sense where such cruelty begins: the moment we fail to see in another our common humanity—the very moment when we fail to recognize in a person the same fears and hopes, the same passions and imperfections, the same dreams that we all share.

We have for centuries strived to live up to our founding ideal, of a nation where all are free and equal and able to pursue their own version of happiness. Through conflict and tumult, through the morass of hatred and prejudice, through periods of division and discord we have endured and grown stronger and fairer and freer. And at every turn, we've made progress not only by changing laws but by changing hearts, by our willingness to walk in another's shoes, by our capacity to love and accept even in the face of rage and bigotry.

In April of 1968, just one week after the assassination of Martin Luther King, as our nation mourned in grief and shuddered in anger, President Lyndon Johnson signed landmark civil rights legislation. This was the first time we enshrined into law federal protections against crimes motivated by religious or racial hatred—the law on which we build today.

As he signed his name, at a difficult moment for our country, President Johnson said that through this law "the bells of freedom ring out a little louder." That is the promise of America. Over the sounds of hatred and chaos, over the din of grief and anger, we can still hear those ideals—even when they are faint, even when some would try to drown them out. At our best we seek to make sure those ideals can be heard and felt by Americans everywhere. And that work did not end in 1968. It certainly does not end today. But because of the efforts of the folks in this room—particularly those family members who are standing behind me—we can be proud that that bell rings even louder now and each day grows louder still.

Source: Office of the Press Secretary, The White House. "Remarks by the President at Reception Commemorating the Enactment of the Matthew Shepard and James Byrd, Jr. Hate Crimes Prevention Act," October 28, 2009. https://obamawhitehouse.archives.gov/the-press-office/remarks-president-reception-commemorating-enactment-matthew-shepard-and-james-byrd-.

A Police Commissioner Shares a Lesson

U.S. Senate Hearing on "Rape in the United States: The Chronic Failure to Report and Investigate Rape Cases"

September 14, 2010

On September 14, 2010, a U.S. Senate committee chaired by Senator Arlen Specter held a hearing entitled "Rape in the United States: The Chronic Failure to Report and Investigate Rape Cases." Witnesses from a variety of fields, including politics, law, and nonprofit organizations, testified. The following is the testimony of Charles H. Ramsey, then the Philadelphia police commissioner, on how the Philadelphia police department has changed its practices to better investigate rape and to help victims of rape.

Good Morning Chairman Specter, Senator Graham, and invited speakers and guests. Thank you for this opportunity to appear before you today to discuss this critically important issue. Having had 42 years in law enforcement, I have witnessed many important changes in how rape and sexual assault are reported and handled by police departments in three cities: first in Chicago for 30 years, then as Chief of the Metropolitan Police Department here in Washington, DC, for nine years, and now as Police Commissioner in Philadelphia. Additionally, I currently serve as the President of the Police Executive Research Forum (PERF), the First Vice President of Major Cities Chiefs and as a member of the executive committee of the International Association of Chiefs of Police.

I'd like to begin by thanking a trusted colleague, tireless advocate and friend in Carol Tracy, who testified before me and summarized the incidents in

Philadelphia in 1999 that led to dramatic changes in the Department. I firmly believe that partnerships between law enforcement agencies and our social service, prevention and victim advocacy counterparts are absolutely essential in addressing some of the most pressing issues that confront us.

I will be brief in this testimony, and share with you the most relevant lessons learned from our history in the Philadelphia Police Department of how rape has been reported and investigated. The deliberate downgrading of rape cases in the Philadelphia Police Department in the late 1990s, brought to light by the excellent investigative work of the *Philadelphia Inquirer,* exposed a widespread hidden practice. There was no one person, or unit responsible; **it was a pervasive and systemic failure**. Consequently, it took a comprehensive and relentless approach to address this failure. Under then Police Commissioner, John Timoney, many important corrective actions were taken at all levels: from training, report writing and interviewing, to coding and follow-up investigation. It also required changing leadership, adjusting staffing levels, accepting oversight and establishing partnerships with advocacy groups.

The Department has had the same commander of the now Special Victims Unit (SVU), since the year 2000, at which time a number of seasoned investigators were also transferred into the unit to increase our staffing levels. Our partners have also remained in their positions in the advocacy groups. Carol Tracy has been with the Women's Law Project since these changes were implemented, and once a year, she and her peers from other organizations, come to the SVU office and pore over between 300 to 400 cases selected at random. They have complete access to our files and our personnel. This is just the formal component of their annual review, but on a daily basis, these organizations are in constant communication with police personnel from SVU. They have established a long-term relationship, one which has built trust and confidence in what was a broken system. I credit all the personnel in SVU and our advocacy groups for their persistence and their dedication to their jobs, and to the thousands of people they've helped deal with such painful acts of violence and trauma. I cannot overstate the importance of this collaboration in charting a new course of direction in how rape was, and is reported and investigated by our Department.

The Philadelphia Police Department put measures into place that thus far have been helpful in re-establishing trust, and promoting a culture that treats victims of rape with dignity and respect. There will always be ways in which we can better the process, and we are committed to continuous improvement as a core principle for how we will move into the future. It's now been over ten years since these practices have been exposed, and seemingly, we have sustained these changes for the better. Sustainability cannot be overlooked as we discuss implementing long-term procedural and cultural changes.

Fostering collaboration amongst governmental organizations, police departments, courts, and advocacy and prevention groups is critical in ensuring that we work with victims of rape and sexual assault in a manner that is compassionate, and under a process that is transparent. We must all be advocates for anyone who has been impacted by this kind of violence. If there are lessons to be learned from our Department, I would urge others to focus on this aspect of how we report and investigate rape and sexual assault. Don't do it alone—Invite your stakeholders to be a part of this process, and work together in treating rape and sexual assault from a holistic perspective. Our partnerships have strengthened every part of the process, from reporting each case of sexual assault, irrespective of the circumstances, to a thorough investigation by well-trained specialized detectives, and finally to working with our medical and mental health providers in minimizing the trauma experienced by victims of the heinous crime.

A crisis is often a catalyst for real and systemic change—such was the case for Philadelphia. Police departments can also learn from each other, and organizations like PERF can facilitate that transfer of knowledge. . . .

Source: Testimony of Police Commissioner Charles H. Ramsey, Philadelphia Police Department. "Rape in the United States: The Chronic Failure to Report and Investigate Rape Cases, September 14, 2010." Hearing before the Senate Committee on the Judiciary Subcommittee on Crime and Drugs, Washington, D.C. Available at https://www.judiciary.senate.gov/imo/media/doc/09-14-10% 20Ramsey%20Testimony.pdf.

Dear Colleague Letter

The Office of Civil Rights,

U.S. Department of Education

April 4, 2011

In April of 2011, the Office of Civil Rights (OCR), under the U.S. Department of Education, released a "Dear Colleague" letter to colleges, universities, and schools across the country. The aim of the letter, signed by Assistant Secretary of Civil Rights Russlynn Ali, was to inform and remind schools that Title IX covers sexual violence, including sexual harassment. Though the 19-page letter did not actually establish new regulations, it did provide clarification for mandates that colleges had found confusing. In addition, the distribution of the letter indicated that the OCR would be cracking down on Title IX violations. Because of the letter, many colleges revisited and made changes to their sexual violence policies and procedures. However, some have found parts of the letter's guidance—such as the direction to adapt a "preponderance of evidence" standard—controversial, as they feel it does not provide defendants adequate due process. Below is an excerpt from the letter.

In 2015, a related "Dear Colleague" letter reminded schools receiving federal funds that they need to appoint a Title IX Coordinator to ensure compliance with all legal obligations outlined in Title IX.

April 4, 2011

Dear Colleague:

Education has long been recognized as the great equalizer in America. The U.S. Department of Education and its Office for Civil Rights (OCR) believe that providing all students with an educational environment free from discrimination is extremely important. The sexual harassment of students, including sexual violence, interferes with students' right to receive an education free from discrimination and, in the case of sexual violence, is a crime.

Title IX of the Education Amendments of 1972 (Title IX), 20 U.S.C. §§ 1681 *et seq.*, and its implementing regulations, 34 C.F.R. Part 106, prohibit discrimination on the basis of sex in education programs or activities operated by recipients of Federal financial assistance. Sexual harassment of students, which includes acts of sexual violence, is a form of sex discrimination prohibited by Title IX. In order to assist recipients, which include school districts, colleges, and universities (hereinafter "schools" or "recipients") in meeting these obligations, this letter explains that the requirements of Title IX pertaining to sexual harassment also cover sexual violence, and lays out the specific Title IX requirements applicable to sexual violence. Sexual violence, as that term is used in this letter, refers to physical sexual acts perpetrated against a person's will or where a person is incapable of giving consent due to the victim's use of drugs or alcohol. An individual also may be unable to give consent due to an intellectual or other disability. A number of different acts fall into the category of sexual violence, including rape, sexual assault, sexual battery, and sexual coercion. All such acts of sexual violence are forms of sexual harassment covered under Title IX.

The statistics on sexual violence are both deeply troubling and a call to action for the nation. A report prepared for the National Institute of Justice found that about 1 in 5 women are victims of completed or attempted sexual assault while in college. The report also found that approximately 6.1 percent of males were victims of completed or attempted sexual assault during college. According to data collected under the Jeanne Clery Disclosure of Campus Security and Campus Crime Statistics Act (Clery Act), 20 U.S.C. § 1092(f), in 2009, college campuses reported nearly 3,300 forcible sex offenses as defined by the Clery Act. This problem is not limited to college. During the 2007-2008 school year, there were 800 reported incidents of rape and attempted rape and 3,800 reported incidents of other sexual batteries at public high schools. Additionally, the likelihood that a woman with intellectual disabilities will be sexually assaulted is estimated to be significantly higher than the general population.

The Department is deeply concerned about this problem and is committed to ensuring that all students feel safe in their school, so that they have the opportunity to benefit fully from the school's programs and activities.

This letter begins with a discussion of Title IX's requirements related to student-on-student sexual harassment, including sexual violence, and explains schools' responsibility to take immediate and effective steps to end sexual harassment and sexual violence. These requirements are discussed in detail in OCR's *Revised Sexual Harassment Guidance* issued in 2001 (*2001 Guidance*). This letter supplements the *2001 Guidance* by providing additional guidance and practical examples regarding the Title IX requirements as they relate to sexual violence. This letter concludes by discussing the proactive efforts schools can take to prevent sexual harassment and violence, and by providing examples of remedies that schools and OCR may use to end such conduct, prevent its recurrence, and address its effects. Although some examples contained in this letter are applicable only in the postsecondary context, sexual harassment and violence also are concerns for school districts. The Title IX obligations discussed in this letter apply equally to school districts unless otherwise noted.

Title IX Requirements Related to Sexual Harassment and Sexual Violence

Schools' Obligations to Respond to Sexual Harassment and Sexual Violence

Sexual harassment is unwelcome conduct of a sexual nature. It includes unwelcome sexual advances, requests for sexual favors, and other verbal, non-verbal, or physical conduct of a sexual nature. Sexual violence is a form of sexual harassment prohibited by Title IX.

As explained in OCR's *2001 Guidance*, when a student sexually harasses another student, the harassing conduct creates a hostile environment if the conduct is sufficiently serious that it interferes with or limits a student's ability to participate in or benefit from the school's program. The more severe the conduct, the less need there is to show a repetitive series of incidents to prove a hostile environment, particularly if the harassment is physical. Indeed, a single or isolated incident of sexual harassment may create a hostile environment if the incident is sufficiently severe. For instance, a single instance of rape is sufficiently severe to create a hostile environment.

Title IX protects students from sexual harassment in a school's education programs and activities. This means that Title IX protects students in connection with all the academic, educational, extracurricular, athletic, and other programs of the school, whether those programs take place in a school's facilities, on a school bus, at a class or training program sponsored by the school at another location, or elsewhere. For example, Title IX protects a student who is sexually assaulted by a fellow student during a school-sponsored field trip.

If a school knows or reasonably should know about student-on-student harassment that creates a hostile environment, Title IX requires the school to take immediate action to eliminate the harassment, prevent its recurrence, and address its effects. Schools also are required to publish a notice of nondiscrimination and to adopt and publish grievance procedures. Because of these requirements, which are discussed in greater detail in the following section, schools need to ensure that their employees are trained so that they know to report harassment to appropriate school officials, and so that employees with the authority to address harassment know how to respond properly. Training for employees should include practical information about how to identify and report sexual harassment and violence. OCR recommends that this training be provided to any employees likely to witness or receive reports of sexual harassment and violence, including teachers, school law enforcement unit employees, school administrators, school counselors, general counsels, health personnel, and resident advisors.

Schools may have an obligation to respond to student-on-student sexual harassment that initially occurred off school grounds, outside a school's education program or activity. If a student files a complaint with the school, regardless of where the conduct occurred, the school must process the complaint in accordance with its established procedures. Because students often experience the continuing effects of off-campus sexual harassment in the educational setting, schools should consider the effects of the off-campus conduct when evaluating whether there is a hostile environment on campus. For example, if a student alleges that he or she was sexually assaulted by another student off school grounds, and that upon returning to school he or she was taunted and harassed by other students who are the alleged perpetrator's friends, the school should take the earlier sexual assault into account in determining whether there is a sexually hostile environment. The school also should take steps to protect a student who was assaulted off campus from further sexual harassment or retaliation from the perpetrator and his or her associates. . . .

Procedural Requirements Pertaining to Sexual Harassment and Sexual Violence

Recipients of Federal financial assistance must comply with the procedural requirements outlined in the Title IX implementing regulations. Specifically, a recipient must:

(A) Disseminate a notice of nondiscrimination;
(B) Designate at least one employee to coordinate its efforts to comply with and carry out its responsibilities under Title IX; and
(C) Adopt and publish grievance procedures providing for prompt and equitable resolution of student and employee sex discrimination complaints. . . .

Prompt and Equitable Requirements

As stated in the *2001 Guidance*, OCR has identified a number of elements in evaluating whether a school's grievance procedures provide for prompt and equitable resolution of sexual harassment complaints. These elements also apply to sexual violence complaints because, as explained above, sexual violence is a form of sexual harassment. OCR will review all aspects of a school's grievance procedures, including the following elements that are critical to achieve compliance with Title IX:

- Notice to students, parents of elementary and secondary students, and employees of the grievance procedures, including where complaints may be filed;
- Application of the procedures to complaints alleging harassment carried out by employees, other students, or third parties;
- Adequate, reliable, and impartial investigation of complaints, including the opportunity for both parties to present witnesses and other evidence;
- Designated and reasonably prompt time frames for the major stages of the complaint process;
- Notice to parties of the outcome of the complaint; and
- An assurance that the school will take steps to prevent recurrence of any harassment and to correct its discriminatory effects on the complainant and others, if appropriate.

As noted in the *2001 Guidance*, procedures adopted by schools will vary in detail, specificity, and components, reflecting differences in the age of students, school sizes and administrative structures, State or local legal requirements, and past experiences. Although OCR examines whether all applicable elements are addressed when investigating sexual harassment complaints, this letter focuses on those elements where our work indicates that more clarification and explanation are needed, including:

(A) *Notice of the Grievance Procedures*

The procedures for resolving complaints of sex discrimination, including sexual harassment, should be written in language appropriate to the age of the school's students, easily understood, easily located, and widely distributed. OCR recommends that the grievance procedures be prominently posted on school Web sites; sent electronically to all members of the school community; available at various locations throughout the school or campus; and summarized in or attached to major publications issued by the school, such as handbooks, codes of conduct, and catalogs for students, parents of elementary and secondary students, faculty, and staff.

(B) *Adequate, Reliable, and Impartial Investigation of Complaints*

OCR's work indicates that a number of issues related to an adequate, reliable, and impartial investigation arise in sexual harassment and violence complaints. In some cases, the conduct may constitute both sexual harassment under Title IX and criminal activity. Police investigations may be useful for fact-gathering; but because the standards for criminal investigations are different, police investigations or reports are not determinative of whether sexual harassment or violence violates Title IX. Conduct may constitute unlawful sexual harassment under Title IX even if the police do not have sufficient evidence of a criminal violation. In addition, a criminal investigation into allegations of sexual violence does not relieve the school of its duty under Title IX to resolve complaints promptly and equitably.

A school should notify a complainant of the right to file a criminal complaint, and should not dissuade a victim from doing so either during or after the school's internal Title IX investigation. For instance, if a complainant wants to file a police report, the school should not tell the complainant that it is working toward a solution and instruct, or ask, the complainant to wait to file the report.

Schools should not wait for the conclusion of a criminal investigation or criminal proceeding to begin their own Title IX investigation and, if needed, must take immediate steps to protect the student in the educational setting. For example, a school should not delay conducting its own investigation or taking steps to protect the complainant because it wants to see whether the alleged perpetrator will be found guilty of a crime. Any agreement or Memorandum of Understanding (MOU) with a local police department must allow the school to meet its Title IX obligation to resolve complaints promptly and equitably. Although a school may need to delay temporarily the fact-finding portion of a Title IX investigation while the police are gathering evidence, once notified that the police department has completed its gathering of evidence (not the ultimate outcome of the investigation or the filing of any charges), the school must promptly resume and complete its fact-finding for the Title IX investigation. Moreover, nothing in an MOU or the criminal investigation itself should prevent a school from notifying complainants of their Title IX rights and the school's grievance procedures, or from taking interim steps to ensure the safety and well-being of the complainant and the school community while the law enforcement agency's fact-gathering is in progress. OCR also recommends that a school's MOU include clear policies on when a school will refer a matter to local law enforcement.

As noted above, the Title IX regulation requires schools to provide equitable grievance procedures. As part of these procedures, schools generally conduct investigations and hearings to determine whether sexual harassment or violence occurred. In addressing complaints filed with OCR under Title IX, OCR reviews a school's procedures to determine whether the school is using a preponderance of the evidence standard to evaluate complaints. The Supreme

Court has applied a preponderance of the evidence standard in civil litigation involving discrimination under Title VII of the Civil Rights Act of 1964 (Title VII), 42 U.S.C. §§ 2000e *et seq.* Like Title IX, Title VII prohibits discrimination on the basis of sex. OCR also uses a preponderance of the evidence standard when it resolves complaints against recipients. For instance, OCR's Case Processing Manual requires that a noncompliance determination be supported by the preponderance of the evidence when resolving allegations of discrimination under all the statutes enforced by OCR, including Title IX. OCR also uses a preponderance of the evidence standard in its fund termination administrative hearings. Thus, in order for a school's grievance procedures to be consistent with Title IX standards, the school must use a preponderance of the evidence standard (*i.e.*, it is more likely than not that sexual harassment or violence occurred). The "clear and convincing" standard (*i.e.*, it is highly probable or reasonably certain that the sexual harassment or violence occurred), currently used by some schools, is a higher standard of proof. Grievance procedures that use this higher standard are inconsistent with the standard of proof established for violations of the civil rights laws, and are thus not equitable under Title IX. Therefore, preponderance of the evidence is the appropriate standard for investigating allegations of sexual harassment or violence.

Throughout a school's Title IX investigation, including at any hearing, the parties must have an equal opportunity to present relevant witnesses and other evidence. The complainant and the alleged perpetrator must be afforded similar and timely access to any information that will be used at the hearing. For example, a school should not conduct a pre-hearing meeting during which only the alleged perpetrator is present and given an opportunity to present his or her side of the story, unless a similar meeting takes place with the complainant; a hearing officer or disciplinary board should not allow only the alleged perpetrator to present character witnesses at a hearing; and a school should not allow the alleged perpetrator to review the complainant's statement without also allowing the complainant to review the alleged perpetrator's statement.

While OCR does not require schools to permit parties to have lawyers at any stage of the proceedings, if a school chooses to allow the parties to have their lawyers participate in the proceedings, it must do so equally for both parties. Additionally, any school-imposed restrictions on the ability of lawyers to speak or otherwise participate in the proceedings should apply equally. OCR strongly discourages schools from allowing the parties personally to question or cross examine each other during the hearing. Allowing an alleged perpetrator to question an alleged victim directly may be traumatic or intimidating, thereby possibly escalating or perpetuating a hostile environment. OCR also recommends that schools provide an appeals process. If a school provides for appeal of the findings or remedy, it must do so for both parties. Schools must maintain documentation of all proceedings, which may include written find-ings of facts, transcripts, or audio recordings.

All persons involved in implementing a recipient's grievance procedures (*e.g.*, Title IX coordinators, investigators, and adjudicators) must have training or experience in handling complaints of sexual harassment and sexual vio-lence, and in the recipient's grievance procedures. The training also should include applicable confidentiality requirements. In sexual violence cases, the fact-finder and decision-maker also should have adequate training or knowl-edge regarding sexual violence. Additionally, a school's investigation and hear-ing processes cannot be equitable unless they are impartial. Therefore, any real or perceived conflicts of interest between the fact-finder or decision-maker and the parties should be disclosed.

Public and state-supported schools must provide due process to the alleged perpetrator. However, schools should ensure that steps taken to accord due process rights to the alleged perpetrator do not restrict or unnecessarily delay the Title IX protections for the complainant.

(C) *Designated and Reasonably Prompt Time Frames*

OCR will evaluate whether a school's grievance procedures specify the time frames for all major stages of the procedures, as well as the process for extending timelines. Grievance procedures should specify the time frame within which: (1) the school will conduct a full investigation of the complaint; (2) both parties receive a response regarding the outcome of the complaint; and (3) the parties may file an appeal, if applicable. Both parties should be given periodic status updates. Based on OCR experience, a typical investigation takes approximately 60 calendar days following receipt of the complaint. Whether OCR considers complaint resolutions to be timely, however, will vary depending on the com-plexity of the investigation and the severity and extent of the harassment. For example, the resolution of a complaint involving multiple incidents with multi-ple complainants likely would take longer than one involving a single incident that occurred in a classroom during school hours with a single complainant.

(D) *Notice of Outcome*

Both parties must be notified, in writing, about the outcome of both the com-plaint and any appeal, *i.e.*, whether harassment was found to have occurred. OCR recommends that schools provide the written determination of the final outcome to the complainant and the alleged perpetrator concurrently. Title IX does not require the school to notify the alleged perpetrator of the outcome before it notifies the complainant.

Due to the intersection of Title IX and FERPA requirements, OCR recognizes that there may be confusion regarding what information a school may disclose to the complainant. FERPA generally prohibits the nonconsensual disclosure of personally identifiable information from a student's "education record." However, as stated in the 2001 Guidance, FERPA permits a school to disclose to the harassed student information about the sanction imposed upon a student who was found to have engaged in harassment when the sanction directly relates to the harassed student. This includes an order that the harasser stay away from the harassed student, or that the harasser is prohibited from attending school for a period of time, or transferred to other classes or another residence hall. Disclosure of other information in the student's "education record," including information about sanctions that do not relate to the harassed student, may result in a violation of FERPA. . . .

Steps to Prevent Sexual Harassment and Sexual Violence and Correct Its Discriminatory Effects on the Complainant and Others

Education and Prevention

In addition to ensuring full compliance with Title IX, schools should take proactive measures to prevent sexual harassment and violence. OCR recommends that all schools implement preventive education programs and make victim resources, including comprehensive victim services, available. Schools may want to include these education programs in their (1) orientation programs for new students, faculty, staff, and employees; (2) training for students who serve as advisors in residence halls; (3) training for student athletes and coaches; and (4) school assemblies and "back to school nights." These programs should include a discussion of what constitutes sexual harassment and sexual violence, the school's policies and disciplinary procedures, and the consequences of violating these policies.

The education programs also should include information aimed at encouraging students to report incidents of sexual violence to the appropriate school and law enforcement authorities. Schools should be aware that victims or third parties may be deterred from reporting incidents if alcohol, drugs, or other violations of school or campus rules were involved. As a result, schools should consider whether their disciplinary policies have a chilling effect on victims' or other students' reporting of sexual violence offenses. For example, OCR recommends that schools inform students that the schools' primary concern is student safety, that any other rules violations will be addressed separately from the sexual violence allegation, and that use of alcohol or drugs never makes the victim at fault for sexual violence.

OCR also recommends that schools develop specific sexual violence materials that include the schools' policies, rules, and resources for students, faculty, coaches, and administrators. Schools also should include such information in their employee handbook and any handbooks that student athletes and members of student activity groups receive. These materials should include where and to whom students should go if they are victims of sexual violence. These materials also should tell students and school employees what to do if they learn of an incident of sexual violence. Schools also should assess student activities regularly to ensure that the practices and behavior of students do not violate the schools' policies against sexual harassment and sexual violence.

Remedies and Enforcement

As discussed above, if a school determines that sexual harassment that creates a hostile environment has occurred, it must take immediate action to eliminate the hostile environment, prevent its recurrence, and address its effects. In addition to counseling or taking disciplinary action against the harasser, effective corrective action may require remedies for the complainant, as well as changes to the school's overall services or policies. Examples of these actions are discussed in greater detail below.

Title IX requires a school to take steps to protect the complainant as necessary, including taking interim steps before the final outcome of the investigation. The school should undertake these steps promptly once it has notice of a sexual harassment or violence allegation. The school should notify the complainant of his or her options to avoid contact with the alleged perpetrator and allow students to change academic or living situations as appropriate. For instance, the school may prohibit the alleged perpetrator from having any contact with the complainant pending the results of the school's investigation. When taking steps to separate the complainant and alleged perpetrator, a school should minimize the burden on the complainant, and thus should not, as a matter of course, remove complainants from classes or housing while allowing alleged perpetrators to remain. In addition, schools should ensure that complainants are aware of their Title IX rights and any available resources, such as counseling, health, and mental health services, and their right to file a complaint with local law enforcement.

Schools should be aware that complaints of sexual harassment or violence may be followed by retaliation by the alleged perpetrator or his or her associates. For instance, friends of the alleged perpetrator may subject the complainant to name-calling and taunting. As part of their Title IX obligations, schools must have policies and procedures in place to protect against retaliatory harassment. At a minimum, schools must ensure that complainants and their parents, if appropriate, know how to report any subsequent problems, and should follow-up with complainants to determine whether any retaliation or new incidents of harassment have occurred.

When OCR finds that a school has not taken prompt and effective steps to respond to sexual harassment or violence, OCR will seek appropriate remedies

for both the complainant and the broader student population. When conducting Title IX enforcement activities, OCR seeks to obtain voluntary compliance
from recipients. When a recipient does not come into compliance voluntarily,
OCR may initiate proceedings to withdraw Federal funding by the Department
or refer the case to the U.S. Department of Justice for litigation.

Schools should proactively consider the following remedies when determining how to respond to sexual harassment or violence. These are the same types
of remedies that OCR would seek in its cases.

Depending on the specific nature of the problem, remedies for the complainant might include, but are not limited to:

- providing an escort to ensure that the complainant can move safely between
  classes and activities;
- ensuring that the complainant and alleged perpetrator do not attend the same
  classes;
- moving the complainant or alleged perpetrator to a different residence hall or, in
  the case of an elementary or secondary school student, to another school within
  the district;
- providing counseling services;
- providing medical services;
- providing academic support services, such as tutoring;
- arranging for the complainant to re-take a course or withdraw from a class without penalty, including ensuring that any changes do not adversely affect the complainant's academic record; and
- reviewing any disciplinary actions taken against the complainant to see if there is
  a causal connection between the harassment and the misconduct that may have
  resulted in the complainant being disciplined.

Remedies for the broader student population might include, but are not
limited to:

Counseling and Training

- offering counseling, health, mental health, or other holistic and comprehensive
  victim services to all students affected by sexual harassment or sexual violence,
  and notifying students of campus and community counseling, health, mental
  health, and other student services;
- designating an individual from the school's counseling center to be "on call" to
  assist victims of sexual harassment or violence whenever needed;
- training the Title IX coordinator and any other employees who are involved in
  processing, investigating, or resolving complaints of sexual harassment or sexual
  violence, including providing training on:

  o the school's Title IX responsibilities to address allegations of sexual harassment
    or violence

- how to conduct Title IX investigations
- information on the link between alcohol and drug abuse and sexual harassment or violence and best practices to address that link;

- training all school law enforcement unit personnel on the school's Title IX responsibilities and handling of sexual harassment or violence complaints;
- training all employees who interact with students regularly on recognizing and appropriately addressing allegations of sexual harassment or violence under Title IX; and
- informing students of their options to notify proper law enforcement authorities, including school and local police, and the option to be assisted by school employees in notifying those authorities.

Development of Materials and Implementation of Policies and Procedures

- developing materials on sexual harassment and violence, which should be distributed to students during orientation and upon receipt of complaints, as well as widely posted throughout school buildings and residence halls, and which should include:

  - what constitutes sexual harassment or violence
  - what to do if a student has been the victim of sexual harassment or violence
  - contact information for counseling and victim services on and off school grounds
  - how to file a complaint with the school
  - how to contact the school's Title IX coordinator
  - what the school will do to respond to allegations of sexual harassment or violence, including the interim measures that can be taken

- requiring the Title IX coordinator to communicate regularly with the school's law enforcement unit investigating cases and to provide information to law enforcement unit personnel regarding Title IX requirements;
- requiring the Title IX coordinator to review all evidence in a sexual harassment or sexual violence case brought before the school's disciplinary committee to determine whether the complainant is entitled to a remedy under Title IX that was not available through the disciplinary committee;
- requiring the school to create a committee of students and school officials to identify strategies for ensuring that students:

  - know the school's prohibition against sex discrimination, including sexual harassment and violence
  - recognize sex discrimination, sexual harassment, and sexual violence when they occur
  - understand how and to whom to report any incidents

- know the connection between alcohol and drug abuse and sexual harassment or violence
- feel comfortable that school officials will respond promptly and equitably to reports of sexual harassment or violence;

- issuing new policy statements or other steps that clearly communicate that the school does not tolerate sexual harassment and violence and will respond to any incidents and to any student who reports such incidents; and
- revising grievance procedures used to handle sexual harassment and violence complaints to ensure that they are prompt and equitable, as required by Title IX.

School Investigations and Reports to OCR

- conducting periodic assessments of student activities to ensure that the practices and behavior of students do not violate the school's policies against sexual harassment and violence;
- investigating whether any other students also may have been subjected to sexual harassment or violence;
- investigating whether school employees with knowledge of allegations of sexual harassment or violence failed to carry out their duties in responding to those allegations;
- conducting, in conjunction with student leaders, a school or campus "climate check" to assess the effectiveness of efforts to ensure that the school is free from sexual harassment and violence, and using the resulting information to inform future proactive steps that will be taken by the school; and
- submitting to OCR copies of all grievances filed by students alleging sexual harassment or violence, and providing OCR with documentation related to the investigation of each complaint, such as witness interviews, investigator notes, evidence submitted by the parties, investigative reports and summaries, any final disposition letters, disciplinary records, and documentation regarding any appeals.

Conclusion

The Department is committed to ensuring that all students feel safe and have the opportunity to benefit fully from their schools' education programs and activities. As part of this commitment, OCR provides technical assistance to assist recipients in achieving voluntary compliance with Title IX.

If you need additional information about Title IX, have questions regarding OCR's policies, or seek technical assistance, please contact the OCR enforcement office that serves your state or territory. The list of offices is available at http://wdcrobcolp01.ed.gov/CFAPPS/OCR/contactus.cfm. Additional information about addressing sexual violence, including victim resources and information for schools, is available from the U.S. Department of Justice's Office on Violence Against Women (OVW) at http://www.ovw.usdoj.gov/.

Thank you for your prompt attention to this matter. I look forward to continuing our work together to ensure that all students have an equal opportunity to learn in a safe and respectful school climate.

Sincerely,

Russlynn Ali

Assistant Secretary for Civil Rights

Source: U.S. Department of Education. http://www2.ed.gov/about/offices/list /ocr/letters/colleague-201104.html.

Testimony of Esmeralda Soto on Sexual Assault in an Immigrant Detention Center, Prepared for the U.S. Senate Judiciary Committee Hearing on the Violence Against Women Act (VAWA)

July 13, 2011

The Prison Rape Elimination Act (PREA) of 2003 did not apply to immigrants in the custody of Immigration and Customs Enforcement (ICE). Esmeralda Soto (formerly known as Mayra Soto), a transwoman who immigrated to the United States, testified in a hearing before the National Prison Rape Elimination Commission (December 13, 2006). Her written testimony was used by Just Detention International in 2011 as part of its evidence on why the PREA should include those held in immigration detention sites. The Justice Department has since ruled that the law applies to those held in ICE facilities, though some immigrant rights organizations believe individuals held in private facilities are still at risk. Immigration detainees are particularly vulnerable to sexual abuse because they do not have the same rights as citizens, and they may be isolated by their cultural beliefs and language barriers. Immigrants held by ICE also fear they will be deported if they complain. LGBT individuals are often targets of sexual abuse, as are youths and those with mental or physical disabilities.

On December 19, 2003, a few days after being transferred to the San Pedro detention center, I was taken to see my lawyer. Because she was with another client at the time, I was placed in a locked holding cell. While I waited in the cell an immigration officer came in with his pants unzipped and told me that "I was going to suck him off." He checked the hall to make sure nobody was around, then re-entered the cell and forced me to perform oral sex. Once he was done, he put his finger to his mouth and ordered me not to tell anyone. He had ejaculated in my mouth, on my red detention uniform, and on the floor. . . . To this day, the thought of what that immigration officer did to me makes me nauseous and fills me with fear, disgust and anger. It is difficult to comprehend how a federal employee who was supposed to maintain a secure environment for me while I was detained could abuse his authority in such a flagrant and appalling manner. In the holding room by myself, I had not felt unsafe because I knew my lawyer was in the next room and there was an officer patrolling in the hallway. Little did I know that the person I needed to fear was an officer who was supposed to keep me safe, and that he would feel so confident that he could get away with raping me that he would do it with my legal counsel so close by.

After the assault, I was returned to the cell with the other transgender women. I immediately began to notice an air of hostility from the immigrations officers in the unit. They treated me as if I was a liar and blamed me for the dismissal of their coworker. I repeatedly asked to see a counselor because I needed to vent what I was feeling. I literally felt like I was going to explode. The officers continuously ignored or humiliated me, and looked upon me with what I felt was pure hatred. Meanwhile, the memory of the assault was killing me inside. I lost my appetite and could hardly stomach any food. I quit sleeping altogether and I slipped further and further into depression. Finally when I threatened to commit suicide, one of the other transgender detainees in the cell pleaded with an officer and convinced him that I desperately needed help. Because there are no mental health providers at the San Pedro facility I was taken to the El Centro Detention Facility near San Diego, California. Unfortunately, I was still not given counseling, or any lasting relief. The psychologist simply gave me three tranquilizers and sent me back to San Pedro. Eventually, the nurse at San Pedro did manage to prescribe me anti-depressants, and I was given sleeping aids.

Due to the negative attitudes that officials at the facility had taken toward me, my biggest fear at this point was that my application for asylum would be denied and I'd be deported back to Mexico. I felt a constant pressure to retract my complaint against the officer, but I really did not want to give in. I wanted to remain strong and show that I was not going to let myself be taken advantage of. . . . I was eventually able to see a judge in my case and she granted me "withholding of removal." Today I live in Santa Ana, California, and am still struggling to let go of the horrible experiences I had at the San Pedro Service Processing Center.

Source: Testimony of Mayra Soto. The Elimination of Prison Rape: Immigration Facilities and Personnel/Staffing/Labor Relations, Hearing before the National Prison Rape Elimination Commission on December 13, 2006, https:// justdetention.org/wp-content/uploads/2015/10/JDI-Advocates-to-Stop-Sexual -Abuse-in-Immigration-Detention.pdf.

Note: Since testifying before the commission, Ms. Soto has changed her first name. Her testimony was used by Just Detention International in 2011.

The Clery Act, Amended

2013

The Jeanne Clery Disclosure of Campus Security Policy and Crime Statistics Act, more commonly known as the Clery Act, was first passed in 1990. It was named for Jeanne Clery, who was raped and murdered by a fellow student in her dorm room at Lehigh College in Bethlehem, Pennsylvania, on April 5, 1986. This federal law requires colleges to report all campus crimes. Under this act, colleges must also warn the school community of any public safety risks. The act has been reauthorized several times. In 2013, the Violence Against Women and Department of Justice Reauthorization Act (VAWA) amended the Clery Act to include new definitions of dating violence, domestic violence, and stalking, as well as the policies and procedures that colleges must follow regarding these crimes.

. . . Each eligible institution participating in any program under this subchapter and part C of subchapter I of chapter 34 of title 42, other than a foreign institution of higher education, shall on August 1, 1991, begin to collect the following information with respect to campus crime statistics and campus security policies of that institution, and beginning September 1, 1992, and each year thereafter, prepare, publish, and distribute, through appropriate publications or mailings, to all current students and employees, and to any applicant for enrollment or employment upon request, an annual security report containing at least the following information with respect to the campus security policies and campus crime statistics of that institution:

(A) A statement of current campus policies regarding procedures and facilities for students and others to report criminal actions or other emergencies occurring on campus and policies concerning the institution's response to such reports.

(B) A statement of current policies concerning security and access to campus facilities, including campus residences, and security considerations used in the maintenance of campus facilities.

(C) A statement of current policies concerning campus law enforcement . . .

(D) A description of the type and frequency of programs designed to inform students and employees about campus security procedures and practices and to encourage students and employees to be responsible for their own security and the security of others.

(E) A description of programs designed to inform students and employees about the prevention of crimes.

(F) Statistics concerning the occurrence on campus, in or on noncampus buildings or property, and on public property during the most recent calendar year, and during the 2 preceding calendar years for which data are available—

(i) of the following criminal offenses reported to campus security authorities or local police agencies:
(I)   murder;

(II)   sex offenses, forcible or nonforcible;

(III)   robbery;

(IV)   aggravated assault;

(V)   burglary;

(VI)   motor vehicle theft;

(VII)   manslaughter;

(VIII) arson;

(IX)   arrests or persons referred for campus disciplinary action for liquor
        law violations, drug-related violations, and weapons possession . . .

Source: Jeanne Clery Disclosure of Campus Security Policy and Campus Crime
Statistics Act. 20 U.S.C. § 1092(f) (1990, amended in 1991, 1992, 1998, 2000,
2008). Amendments to the Clery Act in 2013 can be found in Section 304 of the
2013 Violence Against Women and Department of Justice Reauthorization Act
(VAWA). https://www.gpo.gov/fdsys/pkg/BILLS-113s47pcs/pdf/BILLS-113s47
pcs.pdf.

Note: Additional information about the Clery Act, including compliance
resources and Clery Act statistics, can be found on the Jeanne Clery Act Information website: www.cleryact.info.

The Campus Sexual Violence Elimination Act

March 2013

The Campus Sexual Violence Elimination Act ("Campus SaVE Act") was enacted in
March 2013, as part of the Violence Against Women Reauthorization Act of 2013.
The Campus SaVE Act, which amended the Clery Act, requires colleges to include in
their reporting any incidents of domestic violence, dating violence, and stalking. In
addition, the SaVE Act requires schools to provide services for students who have been
sexually assaulted and to provide "primary prevention and awareness programs" for
students and employees. In other words, it is not enough to have a policy; under the
act, schools must also have actual prevention programs. The act went into effect on
July 1, 2015. Representative Carolyn Maloney of New York introduced the Campus
SaVE Act in the House of Representatives; her introduction follows.

Mr. Speaker, today, I am proud to introduce the Campus Sexual Violence
Elimination (SaVE) Act. This bill will close a gap in current law by requiring
universities and colleges to spell out their policies on sexual assault, stalking,
dating violence, and domestic violence generally. By requiring transparency
out of these institutions, this bill will increase awareness for the victimization
students face every day on our college campuses.

Sexual and dating violence is a serious problem on our college campuses.
Over 13 percent of female undergrads have reported being stalked while at

school and one out of every five women in college have reported being sexually assaulted. While these statistics are shocking, what's even more shocking is that only a fraction of these incidents are reported. When these instances of abuse go unreported, our nation's female undergraduate victims never get the support they need.

The Campus SaVE Act would close the gap in current law by requiring institutions of higher education to clearly explain their policies on dating violence, sexual assault, stalking, and domestic violence. Institutions will be required to include in their annual security reports statistics on domestic violence, dating violence, and stalking that were reported to campus police or local police agencies. It will also promote prevention and bystander responsibility by requiring these institutions to develop clear statements of policy regarding domestic violence, dating violence, sexual assault, and stalking prevention programs. Campus SaVE ensures that victims get the help they need by requiring schools to provide clear statements regarding their procedures followed when a case of domestic violence, dating violence, sexual assault, or stalking is reported and provide victims an explanation of their rights in writing.

Young people should be able to focus on finding their intellectual passion during these years, not dealing with the mental and physical exhaustion of abuse. The Campus Sexual Violence Elimination Act will help ensure our college campuses and universities are safer and I urge my colleagues to support it.

Source: *Congressional Record*, Vol. 159, Number 26, p. E179. February 25, 2013. Washington, DC: U.S. Government Printing Office, 2013.

Statement of Ms. Brigette McCoy, Former Specialist, U.S. Army

U.S. Senate

March 13, 2013

On March 13, 2013, several victims of sexual assault and abuse in the U.S. military gave statements before a U.S. Senate subcommittee. The Subcommittee on Personnel (Committee on Armed Forces) was chaired by Senator Kirsten Gillibrand. The following excerpted testimony is from Brigette McCoy, who served in the U.S. Army from 1987 to 1991.

Thank you very much for having me here today. I have deep gratitude towards those who have worked tirelessly for our voices to be heard and to those here listening with compassionate and open hearts poised to make positive changes toward these matters at hand, changes that need to come from the root.

I am a Gulf War-era, service-connected, disabled veteran.

I was raped during military service and during my first assignment. That was 1988. I was 18 years old. It was 2 weeks before my 19th birthday. This happened in a foreign country, away from American soil, while I was stationed in Germany.

I did not report it for reasons which will become clear as I tell my story. That would not be the last time I would be assaulted or harassed. This is my story, but it is not mine alone. More than 19,000 men and women every year share similar stories.

That year, the year that I was raped, that same year I was raped again by another soldier in my unit.

Another year, I was sexually harassed by a commissioned officer in my unit.

Between 1990 and 1991, another NCO [non-commissioned officer] in my unit began to harass me through inappropriate touching, words, and behavior. This NCO then requested from my command that I be moved to work directly for him in a work environment where there was no access, closed and window-less, key entry coded vault. Upon receiving my new shift schedule, I can only compare the anguish of this entrapment to discovering your child has been constantly molested by a person of authority. I was at mental and emotional collapse.

A senior woman NCO in my unit helped me to write a written statement to present to my command and to file a formal complaint, a complaint that my command answered with no official hearing, no written response, and it was only answered later with a verbal response from my first sergeant who asked me what did I want and that I had misunderstood this NCO's intentions toward me.

The only thing that I wanted at that time was two basic things. One was an apology and for the harassment to stop. That was all.

I did not know what was happening, and at no time did anyone ever move forward with my formal complaint. Nor was anyone willing to discuss the process with me. They did, however, remove me from his team and his formal apology consisted of him driving by me on base, rolling down his window, and saying to me sorry.

So after that in the days that followed, I was verbally and socially harassed, put on extra duties that conflicted with my medical profile, and socially isolated. Eventually I was given a choice to either get out or to face possible UCMJ [United States Code of Military Justice] action myself.

Most women who are victims of sexual harassment or abuse are threatened and charged with UCMJ action. So I felt I had no choice. I was literally terrified, and so in that terrified position, I was paralyzed and I just chose to get out because that was the option that was given to me.

Within a week, I had orders out of Germany and I was escorted by two NCOs to my plane and that was it. My career was over.

Please note that in unit I was not the only one that was sexually assaulted or sexually harassed. Many women came to me and said they had had the same situation happen, but they never told me who in fact did this.

Returning to the United States and civilian life was difficult, and I had a lot of false starts. I had a lot of negative behaviors that carried from the military. I was anxious and overly protective. I became suicidal and attempted suicide. I went through severe depression and had multiple severe medical illnesses and was unable to carry on the rigors of work for which I was highly trained. I repeatedly moved from place to place and was homeless and medically disabled, but not even the Department of Veterans Affairs (VA) would recognize this and help me until some 2 decades later. . . .

I grieved because I felt I was the lucky one. I left my unit alive with an honorable discharge. Although discombobulated and scared for my life and my future, many leave with less than honorable discharges and personality disorders on their records, further hindering them from applying for medical treatment and medical claims. . . .

22 years later almost to the day of my early expiration of term of service, I was awarded veteran service compensation and service connection for military sexual trauma (MST). . . . Why did I have to be violated again through the process of asking for help and seeking claim status? . . .

I have to say I no longer have any faith or hope that the military chain of command will consistently prosecute, convict, sentence, and carry out the sentencing of sexual predators in uniform without absconding justice somehow. Only 8 percent of them are prosecuted. How many are relieved of their duties, their pensions, their careers? How many of them are placed on the national registry as sex offenders before they are returned to civilian life? Even asking that, what happens to the 92 percent that were not sentenced or prosecuted?

Let's not allow sexual predators who happen to wear a uniform the opportunity to become highly trained, highly degreed, military decorated sexual predators. Let's make sure they are convicted and dishonorably discharged and listed on the national registry. Let's do this before they go on notice in our communities to further harm our service members, our community, and our family members.

Sexual assault and trauma has deep and broad roots in the military. Let's not just pluck a few leaves and trim the branch. Let's deal with this from the roots. Please make it stop.

Source: Testimony of Brigette McCoy. "Testimony on Sexual Assaults in the Military." Senate Hearing 113-303. Hearing Before the Subcommittee on Personnel of the Committee on Armed Services, United States Senate, One Hundred Thirteenth Congress, First Session, March 13, 2013. Washington, DC: U.S. Government Printing Office, 2014. https://www.gpo.gov/fdsys/pkg/CHRG-113shrg88340/html/CHRG-113shrg88340.htm.

Sexual Assault in the Military

U.S. Commission on Civil Rights

September 2013

The National Defense Authorization Act (NDAA) requires the secretary of defense to prepare an annual fiscal year report on sexual assault involving members of the military and submit it to the Committee on Armed Services of the Senate and House of Representatives. In addition, other reports are commissioned by other government offices and services. In 2013, the U.S. Commission on Civil Rights examined sexual assault within the U.S. Armed Services. The following is the Executive Summary from this report, released in September 2013.

Executive Summary

The U.S. Commission on Civil Rights chose to focus on sexual assault in the U.S. military for its annual 2013 Statutory Enforcement Report. This report examines how the Department of Defense and its Armed Services—the Army, Navy, Marine Corps, and Air Force (the Services)—respond to Service members who report having been sexually assaulted ("victims") and how it investigates and disciplines Service members accused of perpetrating sexual assault ("perpetrators"). This report also reviews how the military educates Service members and trains military criminal investigators and military lawyers about sexual assault offenses. The topic is both relevant and timely, as Congress is currently considering ways to address this issue.

The Commission has authority to examine questions related to sexual assault in the military because the issues involve both sex discrimination and the denial of equal protection in the administration of justice. The issue of sex discrimination involves female Service members, who represent 14 percent of the military population, but are disproportionately likely to be victims at a rate five times that of their male counterparts. The questions related to a possible denial of equal protection in the administration of justice led the Commission to examine cases in which sexual assault victims, as well as Service members accused of sexual assault, claim unfair treatment in the military justice system.

Through this report, the Commission sheds light on the scope, response, investigation, and discipline of sexual assault in the U.S. military. The Commission held a briefing on January 11, 2013 to hear the testimony of military officials, scholars, advocacy groups, and practitioners on the topic of sexual assault in the military. In response to written questions from the Commission, the Department of Defense and its Armed Services provided documents and other materials, including data on investigated sexual assault allegations, which the Commission analyzed. The results of these efforts are memorialized in this report.

The report reveals that the Department of Defense may benefit from greater data collection to better understand trends in sexual assault cases and to implement improvements in future initiatives. Although the Department of Defense has already implemented policies to reduce sexual and sexist material from the military workplace in an effort to reduce sexual harassment, the effects of such recent efforts have yet to be measured. The Department of Defense also has a plan to standardize sexual assault response and prevention training across the Services to promote best practices. There will be a need to track the success of such policies over time. Greater commander accountability for leadership failures to implement such policies, especially in cases where victims claim sexual assault at the hands of superiors within the chain of command, should also be considered. Without increased data collection, however, it is difficult to measure the effects of any new changes the military chooses to implement.

Source: U.S. Commission on Civil Rights. "Sexual Assault in the Military: 2013 Statutory Enforcement Report." http://www.usccr.gov/pubs/09242013 _Statutory_Enforcement_Report_Sexual_Assault_in_the_Military.pdf.

Title IX Rights for Students Who Have Experienced Sexual Violence

2014

Title IX is part of the Education Amendments of 1972. It applies to all colleges and universities—public and private—that receive federal funds. Although Title IX is often thought of as a law that enacted equal opportunities for women and men in athletics, it applies to all aspects of education. The following document, prepared by the Office of Civil Rights, explains how Title IX covers the rights of students who have experienced sexual assault on campus.

Know Your Rights: Title IX Requires Your School to Address Sexual Violence

Title IX of the Education Amendments of 1972 prohibits sex discrimination—which includes sexual violence—in educational programs and activities. All public and private schools, school districts, colleges, and universities receiving federal funds must comply with Title IX. If you have experienced sexual violence, here are some things you should know about your Title IX rights:

Your School Must Respond Promptly and Effectively to Sexual Violence

- You have the right to report the incident to your school, have your school investigate what happened, and have your complaint resolved promptly and equitable.
- You have the right to choose to report an incident of sexual violence to campus or local law enforcement. But a criminal investigation does not relieve your school of its duty under Title IX to respond promptly and effectively.

- Your school must adopt and publish procedures for resolving complaints of sex discrimination, including sexual violence. Your school may use student disciplinary procedures, but any procedures for sexual violence complaints must afford you a prompt and equitable resolution.
- Your school should ensure that you are aware of your Title IX rights and any available resources, such as victim advocacy, housing assistance, academic support, counseling, disability services, health and mental health services, and legal assistance.
- Your school must designate a Title IX coordinator and make sure all students and employees know how to contact him or her. The Title IX coordinator should also be available to meet with you.
- All students are protected by Title IX, regardless of whether they have a disability, are international or undocumented, and regardless of their sexual orientation and gender identity.

Your School Must Provide Interim Measures as Necessary

- Your school must protect you as necessary, even before it completes any investigation. Your school should start doing this promptly once the incident is reported.
- Once you tell your school about an incident of sexual violence, you have the right to receive some immediate help, such as changing classes, dorms, or transportation. When taking these measures, your school should minimize the burden on you.
- You have the right to report any retaliation by school employees, the alleged perpetrator, and other students, and your school should take strong responsive action if it occurs.

Your School Should Make Known Where You Can Find Confidential Support Services

- Your school should clearly identify where you can go to talk to someone confidentially and who can provide services like advocacy, counseling, or academic support. Some people, such as counselors or victim advocates, can talk to you in confidence without triggering a school's investigation.
- Because different employees have different reporting obligations when they find out about sexual violence involving students, your school should clearly explain the reporting obligations of all school employees.
- Even if you do not specifically ask for confidentiality, your school should only disclose information to individuals who are responsible for handling the school's response to sexual violence. Your school should consult with you about how to best protect your safety and privacy.

Your School Must Conduct an Adequate, Reliable, and Impartial Investigation

- You have the right to be notified of the timeframes for all major stages of the investigation.
- You have the right to present witnesses and evidence.

- If the alleged perpetrator is allowed to have a lawyer, you have the right to have one too.
- Your school must resolve your complaint based on what they think is more likely than not to have happened (this is called a preponderance-of-the-evidence standard of proof). Your school cannot use a higher standard of proof.
- You have the right to be notified in writing of the outcome of your complaint and any appeal, including any sanctions that directly relate to you.
- If your school provides for an appeal process, it must be equally available for both parties.
- You have the right to have any proceedings documented, which may include written findings of fact, transcripts, or audio recordings.
- You have the right not to "work it out" with the alleged perpetrator in mediation. Mediation is not appropriate in cases involving sexual assault.

Your School Must Provide Remedies as Necessary

- If an investigation reveals that sexual violence created a hostile environment, your school must take prompt and effective steps reasonably calculated to end the sexual violence, eliminate the hostile environment, prevent its recurrence, and, as appropriate, remedy its effects.
- Appropriate remedies will generally include disciplinary action against the perpetrator, but may also include remedies to help you get your education back on track (like academic support, retaking a class without penalty, and counseling). These remedies are in addition to any interim measures you received.
- Your school may also have to provide remedies for the broader student population (such as training) or change its services or policies to prevent such incidents from repeating.

If you want to learn more about your rights, or if you believe that your school is violating federal law, you may contact the U.S. Department of Education, Office for Civil Rights, at (800) 421-3481 or ocr@ed.gov. If you wish to fill out a complaint form online, you may do so at http://www.ed.gov/ocr/complaintintro.html.

Source: U.S. Department of Education, Office for Civil Rights. "Know Your Rights: Title IX Requires Your School to Address Sexual Violence." https://www2.ed.gov/about/offices/list/ocr/docs/know-rights-201404-title-ix.pdf.

"Yes Means Yes" Bill: California SB 967

February 10, 2014

California Law SB 967, known as the "Yes Means Yes" Bill, requires affirmative response for sexual activity. This means that someone who is unconscious, drunk, or drugged cannot consent to sex. Under the law, all postsecondary schools—public and private—that receive financial aid must apply the standards. The following are the summary of the law and the section that describes affirmative consent.

An act to add Section 67386 to the Education Code, relating to Student Safety. [Approved by Governor September 28, 2014. Filed with Secretary of State September 28, 2014.]

SB 967, de León. Student safety: sexual assault.

Existing law requires the governing boards of each community college district, the Trustees of the California State University, the Regents of the University of California, and the governing boards of independent postsecondary institutions to adopt and implement written procedures or protocols to ensure that students, faculty, and staff who are victims of sexual assault on the grounds or facilities of their institutions receive treatment and information, including a description of on-campus and off-campus resources.

This bill would require the governing boards of each community college district, the Trustees of the California State University, the Regents of the University of California, and the governing boards of independent postsecondary institutions, in order to receive state funds for student financial assistance, to adopt policies concerning sexual assault, domestic violence, dating violence, and stalking that include certain elements, including an affirmative consent standard in the determination of whether consent was given by a complainant. The bill would require these governing boards to adopt certain sexual assault policies and protocols, as specified, and would require the governing boards, to the extent feasible, to enter into memoranda of understanding or other agreements or collaborative partnerships with on-campus and community-based organizations to refer students for assistance or make services available to students. The bill would also require the governing boards to implement comprehensive prevention and outreach programs addressing sexual assault, domestic violence, dating violence, and stalking. By requiring community college districts to adopt or modify certain policies and protocols, the bill would impose a state-mandated local program.

The California Constitution requires the state to reimburse local agencies and school districts for certain costs mandated by the state. Statutory provisions establish procedures for making that reimbursement.

This bill would provide that, if the Commission on State Mandates determines that the bill contains costs mandated by the state, reimbursement for those costs shall be made pursuant to these statutory provisions.

THE PEOPLE OF THE STATE OF CALIFORNIA DO ENACT AS FOLLOWS:
SECTION 1. Section 67386 is added to the Education Code, to read:
67386. (a) In order to receive state funds for student financial assistance, the governing board of each community college district, the Trustees of the California State University, the Regents of the University of California, and the governing boards of independent postsecondary institutions shall adopt a policy concerning sexual assault, domestic violence, dating violence, and stalking, as defined in the federal Higher Education Act of 1965 (20 U.S.C. Sec. 1092(f))

involving a student, both on and off campus. The policy shall include all of the following:

(1) An affirmative consent standard in the determination of whether consent was given by both parties to sexual activity. "Affirmative consent" means affirmative, conscious, and voluntary agreement to engage in sexual activity. It is the responsibility of each person involved in the sexual activity to ensure that he or she has the affirmative consent of the other or others to engage in the sexual activity. Lack of protest or resistance does not mean consent, nor does silence mean consent. Affirmative consent must be ongoing throughout a sexual activity and can be revoked at any time. The existence of a dating relationship between the persons involved, or the fact of past sexual relations between them, should never by itself be assumed to be an indicator of consent.

(2) A policy that, in the evaluation of complaints in any disciplinary process, it shall not be a valid excuse to alleged lack of affirmative consent that the accused believed that the complainant consented to the sexual activity under either of the following circumstances:

  (A) The accused's belief in affirmative consent arose from the intoxication or recklessness of the accused.
  (B) The accused did not take reasonable steps, in the circumstances known to the accused at the time, to ascertain whether the complainant affirmatively consented.

(3) A policy that the standard used in determining whether the elements of the complaint against the accused have been demonstrated is the preponderance of the evidence.

(4) A policy that, in the evaluation of complaints in the disciplinary process, it shall not be a valid excuse that the accused believed that the complainant affirmatively consented to the sexual activity if the accused knew or reasonably should have known that the complainant was unable to consent to the sexual activity under any of the following circumstances:

  (A) The complainant was asleep or unconscious.
  (B) The complainant was incapacitated due to the influence of drugs, alcohol, or medication, so that the complainant could not understand the fact, nature, or extent of the sexual activity.
  (C) The complainant was unable to communicate due to a mental or physical condition.

(b) In order to receive state funds for student financial assistance, the governing board of each community college district, the Trustees of the California State University, the Regents of the University of California, and the governing boards of independent postsecondary institutions shall adopt detailed and victim-centered policies and protocols regarding sexual assault, domestic violence, dating violence, and stalking involving a student that comport with best practices and current professional standards. . . .

Source: California Senate Bill No. 967, Chapter 748. "An act to add Section 67386 to the Education Code, relating to student safety." Available at https://leginfo.legislature.ca.gov/faces/billNavClient.xhtml?bill_id=201320140SB967.

A Male Survivor of Military Sexual Trauma

Testimony of Brian K. Lewis

March 2014

In March 2014, several survivors of military sexual assault testified before a U.S. Senate committee chaired by Senator Kirsten E. Gillibrand. Senator Gillibrand was also one of the sponsors of the Military Justice Improvement Act, which was introduced to the Senate in 2013. As of May 2017, the bill has not been passed. The following testimony is from Brian K. Lewis, a former U.S. Navy petty officer third class, who was sexually assaulted while in service.

Chairman Gillibrand and Ranking Member Graham, members of the subcommittee, thank you for holding this hearing today on sexual assault in our military. I am humbled to be sitting here today before you as the first male survivor to testify in front of Congress on this very important issue, and thank you for allowing that privilege to me. . . .

I enlisted in the Navy in 1997 and advanced to the rank of petty officer third class. During my tour on the USS Frank Cable, I was raped by a superior NCO. I was ordered by my command not to report this crime.

After this crime had taken place, I was misdiagnosed with a personality disorder by the current director of the Defense Centers of Excellence for Psychological Health and Traumatic Brain Injury. I filed retaliation claims to no avail. I was given a general discharge for a personality disorder in August 2001.

My petition to change my discharge from a general discharge for a personality disorder to a medical retirement for PTSD was denied by the Board for Correction of Naval Records. I carry that discharge as an official and permanent symbol of shame on top of the physical attack, the retaliation, and the aftermath. I fear it will be discussed when I apply for law school, when I apply to be admitted to the bar, even when I apply for a job . . .

I am here today because I am not alone. My story is all too common. Protect our Defenders regularly hears from Active Duty personnel seeking help as they are being denied opportunities to report, generally retaliated against, diagnosed with errant medical diagnoses, or being charged with collateral misconduct after reporting the attack. The culture of victim-blaming and retaliation while failing to punish the perpetrator must end.

DOD [Department of Defense] regularly acknowledges this crisis. They estimate 19,000 sexual assaults occur each year and 86 percent of victims do not report mostly out of fear of retaliation. Of those 19,000 victims, about 10,700 are men and 8,300 are women. To translate this into percentages, about 56 percent of estimated victims in our military are men. This is the part of the crisis that DOD does not acknowledge.

Now, just what can we do to stop sexual assault in our military? First, we must recognize that rape is not just about sex. It is about violence, power, and sometimes about abuse of authority. General Franklin's recent action to set aside the guilty verdict against Lieutenant Colonel Wilkerson of aggravated sexual assault is yet another example of an abuse of authority taken by a commander that will have a chilling effect on military judges, prosecutors, and juries and inhibit victims from coming forward. A system that elevates a single individual's authority and discretion over the rule of law often precludes justice and hinders it long into the future.

Colonel Wilkerson's victim has been in contact with Protect our Defenders, and she wants you to know, quote, I endured 8 months of public humiliation and investigations. Why bother to put the investigators, prosecutors, judge, jury, and me through this if one person can set aside justice with the swipe of a pen? . . .

Reforms to date, have clearly not successfully addressed this epidemic because they have targeted the symptoms without addressing the root cause, which is that the military justice system is fraught with inherent personal bias, conflicts of interest, abuse of authority, and too often a low regard for the victim. Whereas civilians have the constitutional protections of an independent judicial system, servicemembers do not. Servicemembers must report an assault to their commanders. However, if those commanders take action and prove that an assault occurred, they also prove a failure of their own leadership. Congress has put commanders in charge of violent sexual crime from victim care, through the legal and investigative processes, through adjudication, and post-trial. Commanders have too often failed to care for the victim or prosecute the perpetrator. They have failed to end this longstanding epidemic.

We also need to ensure that prevention efforts are inclusive of male servicemembers. The majority of prevention efforts are targeted toward females. As I demonstrated, men are a majority of the victims in our military. We cannot marginalize male survivors and send a message that men cannot be raped and therefore are not real survivors.

Survivors of MST also need a fair review of their discharges. The military has shoved many survivors out the back door with inaccurate, misleading, and very harmful, almost weaponized medical diagnoses like personality disorders that affect their benefits and future employment opportunities. We need to establish a system separate and apart from the boards for correction of military

records to examine these discharges and grant survivors the medical retire-
ments they are due from DOD. Currently the correction boards only change
about 10 percent of their discharges. These discharges make it much harder for
veterans to find meaningful employment, often re-victimize the veteran, make
it impossible often for these veterans to use their earned education benefits.

In conclusion, this epidemic has not successfully been addressed in decades
of review and reform by DOD or by Congress. Some of the reasons for this
include men being invisible and ignored as survivors of MST, inherent bias and
conflict of interest present in a broken military justice system. The reporting,
investigation, prosecution, and adjudication of sexual assault must be taken
out of the chain of command and into an independent office with professional
military and civilian oversight.

The established discharge review process is a rubber stamp that causes lifelong harm and needs overhaul badly. It is another way that DOD fails us.

Congressional legislation created these systems that are inherently biased,
unfair, and do not work. It is now Congress' duty to pass legislation so servicemembers can receive justice that is fair, impartial, and finally addresses
the military's epidemic of sexual assault. It should also be noted that a lot of
survivors, as the other panelists have said, do not come home. There are people
like Harry Goodwin and so many others that do not survive from their sexual
assaults, and we need to do this in memory of them.

Source: Testimony of Brian K. Lewis. "Testimony on Sexual Assaults in the
Military." Senate Hearing 113-303. Hearing before the Subcommittee on Personnel of the Committee on Armed Services, United States Senate, One Hundred Thirteenth Congress, First Session, March 13, 2013. Washington, DC:
U.S. Government Printing Office, 2014. https://www.gpo.gov/fdsys/pkg/CHRG
-113shrg88340/html/CHRG-113shrg88340.htm.

"Not Alone" Report

Task Force to Protect Students from Sexual Assault

April 2014

*In January 2014, President Barack Obama called for the creation of a White House
Task Force to Protect Students from Sexual Assault. Citing the alarming statistics on
the prevalence of sexual assault on college campuses, Obama directed the Office of the
Vice President and the White House Council on Women and Girls to lead an effort to
develop a coordinated federal response to campus sexual assault through the creation
of a task force.*

*Launched in connection with the Task Force to Protect Students from Sexual
Assault, the website www.changingourcampus.org (formerly www.notalone.gov)*

includes resources on how to respond to and prevent sexual assault. It includes data and resources for students and schools. Additionally, the task force released its first report in April 2014.

Executive Summary

Why We Need to Act

One in five women is sexually assaulted in college. Most often, it's by someone she knows – and also most often, she does not report what happened. Many survivors are left feeling isolated, ashamed or to blame. Although it happens less often, men, too, are victims of these crimes.

The President created the Task Force to Protect Students From Sexual Assault to turn this tide. As the name of our new website—NotAlone.gov—indicates, we are here to tell sexual assault survivors that they are not alone. And we're also here to help schools live up to their obligation to protect students from sexual violence.

Over the last three months, we have had a national conversation with thousands of people who care about this issue. Today, we offer our first set of action steps and recommendations.

1. Identifying the Problem: Campus Climate Surveys

The first step in solving a problem is to name it and know the extent of it—and a campus climate survey is the best way to do that. We are providing schools with a toolkit to conduct a survey—and we urge schools to show they're serious about the problem by conducting the survey next year. The Justice Department, too, will partner with Rutgers University's Center on Violence Against Women and Children to pilot, evaluate and further refine the survey—and at the end of this trial period, we will explore legislative or administrative options to require schools to conduct a survey in 2016.

2. Preventing Sexual Assault—and Engaging Men

Prevention programs can change attitudes, behavior—and the culture. In addition to identifying a number of promising prevention strategies that schools can undertake now, we are also researching new ideas and solutions. But one thing we know for sure: we need to engage men as allies in this cause. Most men are not perpetrators—and when we empower men to step in when someone's in trouble, they become an important part of the solution.

As the President and Vice President's new Public Service Announcement puts it: if she doesn't consent—or can't consent—it's a crime. And if you see it happening, help her, don't blame her, speak up. We are also providing schools with links and information about how they can implement their own bystander intervention programs on campus.

3. Effectively Responding When a Student Is Sexually Assaulted

When one of its students is sexually assaulted, a school needs to have all the pieces of a plan in place. And that should include:

Someone a survivor can talk to in confidence

While many victims of sexual assault are ready to file a formal (or even public) complaint against an alleged offender right away—many others want time and privacy to sort through their next steps. For some, having a confidential place to go can mean the difference between getting help and staying silent.

Today, we are providing schools with a model reporting and confidentiality protocol—which, at its heart, aims to give survivors more control over the process. Victims who want their school to fully investigate an incident must be taken seriously—and know where to report. But for those who aren't quite ready, they need to have—and know about—places to go for confidential advice and support.

That means a school should make it clear, up front, who on campus can maintain a victim's confidence and who can't—so a victim can make an informed decision about where best to turn. A school's policy should also explain when it may need to override a confidentiality request (and pursue an alleged perpetrator) in order to help provide a safe campus for everyone. Our sample policy provides recommendations for how a school can strike that often difficult balance, while also being ever mindful of a survivor's well-being.

New guidance from the Department of Education also makes clear that on-campus counselors and advocates—like those who work or volunteer in sexual assault centers, victim advocacy offices, women's and health centers, as well as licensed and pastoral counselors—can talk to a survivor in confidence. In recent years, some schools have indicated that some of these counselors and advocates cannot maintain confidentiality. This new guidance clarifies that they can.

A comprehensive sexual misconduct policy

We are also providing a checklist for schools to use in drafting (or reevaluating) their own sexual misconduct policies. Although every school will need to tailor a policy to its own needs and circumstances, all schools should be sure to bring the key stakeholders—including students—to the table. Among other things, this checklist includes ideas a school could consider in deciding what is—or is not—consent to sexual activity. As we heard from many students, this can often be the essence of the matter—and a school community should work together to come up with a careful and considered understanding.

Trauma-informed training for school officials

Sexual assault is a unique crime: unlike other crimes, victims often blame themselves; the associated trauma can leave their memories fragmented;

and insensitive or judgmental questions can compound a victim's distress. Starting this year, the Justice Department, through both its Center for Campus Public Safety and its Office on Violence Against Women, will develop trauma-informed training programs for school officials and campus and local law enforcement.

The Department of Education's National Center on Safe and Supportive Learning Environments will do the same for campus health centers. This kind of training has multiple benefits: when survivors are treated with care and wisdom, they start trusting the system, and the strength of their accounts can better hold offenders accountable.

Better school disciplinary systems

Many sexual assault survivors are wary of their school's adjudication process—which can sometimes subject them to harsh and hurtful questioning (like about their prior sexual history) by students or staff unschooled in the dynamics of these crimes. Some schools are experimenting with new models—like having a single, trained investigator do the lion's share of the fact-finding—with very positive results. We need to learn more about these promising new ideas. And so starting this year, the Justice Department will begin assessing different models for investigating and adjudicating campus sexual assault cases with an eye toward identifying best practices.

The Department of Education's new guidance also urges some important improvements to many schools' current disciplinary processes: questions about the survivor's sexual history with anyone other than the alleged perpetrator should not be permitted; adjudicators should know that the mere fact of a previous consensual sexual relationship does not itself imply consent or preclude a finding of sexual violence; and the parties should not be allowed to personally cross-examine each other.

Partnerships with the community

Because students can be sexually assaulted at all hours of the day or night, emergency services should be available 24 hours a day, too. Other types of support can also be crucial—like longer-term therapies and advocates who can accompany survivors to medical and legal appointments. Many schools cannot themselves provide all these services, but in partnership with a local rape crisis center, they can. So, too, when both the college and the local police are simultaneously investigating a case (a criminal investigation does not relieve a school of its duty to itself investigate and respond), coordination can be crucial. So we are providing schools with a sample agreement they can use to partner with their local rape crisis center—and by June, we will provide a similar sample for forging a partnership with local law enforcement.

4. Increasing Transparency and Improving Enforcement

More transparency and information

The government is committed to making our enforcement efforts more transparent—and getting students and schools more resources to help bring an end to this violence. As part of this effort, we will post enforcement data on our new website—NotAlone.gov—and give students a roadmap for filing a complaint if they think their school has not lived up to its obligations.

Among many other things on the website, sexual assault survivors can also locate an array of services by typing in their zip codes, learn about their legal rights, see which colleges have had enforcement actions taken against them, get "plain English" definitions of some complicated legal terms and concepts; and find their states' privacy laws. Schools and advocates can access federal guidance, learn about relevant legislation, and review the best available evidence and research. We invite everyone to take a look.

Improved Enforcement

Today, the Department of Education's Office for Civil Rights (OCR) is releasing a 52-point guidance document that answers many frequently asked questions about a student's rights, and a school's obligations, under Title IX. Among many other topics, the new guidance clarifies that Title IX protects all students, regardless of their sexual orientation or gender identity, immigration status, or whether they have a disability. It also makes clear that students who report sexual violence have a right to expect their school to take steps to protect and support them, including while a school investigation is pending. The guidance also clarifies that recent amendments to the Clery Act do not alter a school's responsibility under Title IX to respond to and prevent sexual violence. OCR is also strengthening its enforcement procedures in a number of ways—by, for example, instituting time limits on negotiating voluntary resolution agreements and making clear that schools should provide survivors with interim relief (like changing housing or class schedules) pending the outcome of an OCR investigation. And OCR will be more visible on campus during its investigations, so students can help give OCR a fuller picture about what's happening and how a school is responding.

The Departments of Education and Justice, which both enforce Title IX, have entered into an agreement to better coordinate their efforts—as have the two offices within the Department of Education charged with enforcing Title IX and the Clery Act.

Next Steps

This report is the first step in the Task Force's work. We will continue to work toward solutions, clarity, and better coordination. We will also review the various laws and regulations that address sexual violence for possible regulatory or statutory improvements, and seek new resources to enhance enforcement. Also, campus law enforcement officials have special expertise to offer—and they should be tapped to play a more central role. We will also consider how our recommendations apply to public elementary and secondary schools—and what more we can do to help there.

* * *

The Task Force thanks everyone who has offered their wisdom, stories, expertise, and experiences over the past 90 days. Although the problem is daunting and much of what we heard was heartbreaking, we are more committed than ever to helping bring an end to this violence.

Source: "Not Alone: The First Report of the White House Task Force to Protect Students from Sexual Assault," April 2014. https://www.justice.gov/ovw/page /file/905942/download.

Paroline v. United States

April 2014

In this complicated case, a woman who had been sexually abused as a child by her uncle—who was convicted of the crime—learned later that images of her abuse were available on the Internet. The uncle, Doyle Randall Paroline, who pleaded guilty to possessing images of child pornography, possessed two images of the woman known as "Amy." Amy sought restitution from Paroline, though an unknown number of people may also possess images of her. In her victim statement, Amy told the court how she still suffered. Under § 2259 of the Mandatory Victim Restitution Act, victims are entitled to restitution, but the amount and how it should be determined are left to the courts. Although Paroline admitted to having images, they were only two images, and therefore the question arose whether he should pay the full victim's restitution. Below is the excerpted majority opinion delivered by Chief Justice John Roberts of the U.S. Supreme Court. The opinion did not solve the problem. It has left district courts with a struggle to determine in each case how to apply restitution in child pornography cases. The Amy and Vicky Child Pornography Victim Restitution Improvement Act of 2015 was introduced to deal with some of the issues of this case. It was introduced again to the Senate by Senator Orrin G. Hatch on November 16, 2017, and referred to the Committee on the Judiciary.

Supreme Court of the United States
   DOYLE RANDALL PAROLINE, PETITIONER v. UNITED STATES, ET AL.
   No. 12-8561

On Writ of Certiorari to the United States Court of Appeals for the Fifth Circuit.

Argued January 22, 2014, Decided April 23, 2014 OCTOBER TERM, 2013 [**719] [*1713]

Syllabus

The respondent victim in this case was sexually abused as a young girl in order to produce child pornography. When she was 17, she learned that images of her abuse were being trafficked on the Internet, in effect repeating the original wrongs, for she knew that her humiliation and hurt would be renewed well into the future as thousands of additional wrongdoers witnessed those crimes. Petitioner Paroline pleaded guilty in federal court to possessing images of child pornography, which included two of the victim, in violation of **18 U.S.C. § 2252**. The victim then sought restitution under § 2259, requesting nearly $3 million in lost income and about $500,000 in future treatment and counseling costs. The District Court declined to award restitution, concluding that the Government had not met its burden of proving what losses, if any, were proximately caused by Paroline's offense. The victim sought a writ of mandamus, asking the Fifth Circuit to direct the District Court to order Paroline to pay restitution. Granting the writ on rehearing en banc, the Fifth Circuit held, *inter alia*, that § 2259 did not limit restitution to losses proximately caused by the defendant, and that each defendant who possessed the victim's images should be made liable for the victim's entire losses from the trade in her images.

. . .

KENNEDY, J., delivered the opinion of the Court, in which GINSBURG, BREYER, ALITO, and KAGAN, JJ., joined. ROBERTS, C. J., filed a dissenting opinion, in which SCALIA and THOMAS, JJ., joined. SOTOMAYOR, J., filed a dissenting opinion.

JUSTICE KENNEDY delivered the opinion of the Court.

This case presents the question of how to determine the amount of restitution a possessor of child pornography must pay to the victim whose childhood abuse appears in the pornographic materials possessed. The relevant statutory provisions are set forth at **18 U.S.C. § 2259**. Enacted as a component of the Violence Against Women Act of 1994, **§ 2259** requires district courts to award restitution for certain federal criminal offenses, including child-pornography possession.

Petitioner Doyle Randall Paroline pleaded guilty to such an offense. He admitted to possessing between 150 and 300 images of child pornography, which included two that depicted the sexual exploitation of a young girl, now a young woman, who goes by the pseudonym "Amy" for this litigation. The question is what causal relationship must be established between the defendant's conduct and a victim's losses for purposes of determining the right to, and the amount of, restitution under **§ 2259**.

I

Three decades ago, this Court observed that "the exploitive use of children in the production of pornography has become a serious national problem." *New York v. Ferber*, **458 U.S. 747, 749** (1982). . . . The demand for child pornography harms children in part because it drives production, which involves child abuse. The harms caused by child pornography, however, are still more . . . extensive because child pornography is "a permanent record" of the . . . depicted child's abuse, and "the harm to the child is exacerbated by [its] circulation." Because child pornography is now traded with ease on the Internet, "the number of still images and videos memorializing the sexual assault and other sexual exploitation of children, many very young in age, has grown exponentially." United States Sentencing Comm'n, P. Saris et al., Federal Child Pornography Offenses 3 (2012) (hereinafter Sentencing Comm'n Report).

One person whose story illustrates the devastating harm caused by child pornography is the respondent victim in this case. When she was eight and nine years old, she was sexually abused by her uncle in order to produce child pornography. Her uncle was prosecuted, required to pay about $6,000 in restitution, and sentenced to a lengthy prison term. The victim underwent an initial course of therapy beginning in 1998 and continuing into 1999. By the end of this period, her therapist's notes reported that she was 'back to normal'; her involvement in dance and other age-appropriate activities, and the support of her family, justified an optimistic assessment. [App. 70-71.] Her functioning appeared to decline in her teenage years, however; and a major blow to her recovery came when, at the age of 17, she learned that images of her abuse were being trafficked on the Internet. [*Id.*, at 71.] The digital images were available nationwide and no doubt worldwide. Though the exact scale of the trade in her images is unknown, the possessors to date easily number in the thousands. The knowledge that her images were circulated far and wide renewed the victim's trauma and made it difficult for her to recover from her abuse. As she explained in a victim impact statement submitted to the District Court in this case:

"Every day of my life I live in constant fear that someone will see my pictures and recognize me and that I will be humiliated all over again. It hurts me to know someone is looking at them—at me—when I was just a little girl being abused for the camera. I did not choose to be there, but now I am there forever in pictures that people are using to do sick things. I want it all erased. I want it all stopped. But I am powerless to stop it just like I was powerless to stop my uncle. . . . My life and my feelings are worse now because the crime has never really stopped and will never really stop. . . . It's like I am being abused over and over and over again." [*Id.*, at 60-61.]

The victim says in her statement that her fear and trauma make it difficult for her to trust others or to feel that she has control over what happens to her. [*Id.*, at 63.]

The full extent of this victim's suffering is hard to grasp. Her abuser took away her childhood, her self-conception of her innocence, and her freedom from the kind of nightmares and memories that most others will never know. These crimes were compounded by the distribution of images of her abuser's horrific acts, which meant the wrongs inflicted upon her . . . were in effect repeated; for she knew her humiliation and hurt were and would be renewed into the future as an ever-increasing number of wrongdoers witnessed the crimes . . . committed against her.

Petitioner Paroline is one of the individuals who possessed this victim's images. In 2009, he pleaded guilty in federal court to one count of possession of material involving the sexual exploitation of children in violation of **18 U.S.C. § 2252. 672 F. Supp. 2d 781, 783** (ED Tex. 2009). Paroline admitted to knowing possession of between 150 and . . . 300 images of child pornography, two of which depicted the respondent victim. . . . The victim sought restitution under **§ 2259**, . . . asking for close to $3.4 million, consisting of nearly $3 million in lost income and about $500,000 in future treatment and counseling costs. [App. 52, 104.] She also sought attorney's fees and costs. **672 F. Supp. 2d, at 783.** The parties submitted competing expert reports. They stipulated that the victim did not know who Paroline was and that none of her claimed losses flowed from any specific knowledge about him or his offense conduct. . . .

After briefing and hearings, the District Court declined to award restitution. **672 F. Supp. 2d, at 793.** The District Court observed that "everyone involved with child pornography—from the abusers and producers to the end-users and possessors—contribute[s] to [the victim's] ongoing harm."
. . .

As a general matter, to say one event proximately caused another is a way of making two separate but related assertions. First, it means the former event caused the latter. This is known as actual cause or cause in fact. . . .

Every event has many causes . . . and only some of them are proximate, as the law uses that term. So to say that one event was a proximate cause of another means that it was not just any cause, but one with a sufficient connection to the result. The idea of proximate cause, as distinct from actual cause or cause in fact, defies easy summary. It is "a flexible concept," . . .

. . . All parties agree **§ 2259** imposes some causation requirement. The statute defines a victim as "the individual harmed as a result of a commission of a crime under this chapter." . . . And a straightforward reading of **§ 2259(c)** indicates that the term "a crime" refers to the offense of conviction. . . . So if the defendant's offense conduct did not cause harm to an individual, that individual is by definition not a "victim" entitled to restitution under **§ 2259**.

As noted above, **§ 2259** requires a court to order restitution for "the full amount of the victim's losses," **§ 2259(b)(1)**, which the statute defines to include "any costs incurred by the victim" for six enumerated categories of expense, § 2259(b)(3). The reference to "costs incurred by the victim" is most naturally understood as costs stemming from the source that qualifies an individual as a "victim" in the first place—namely, ones arising "as a result of" the offense. Thus, as is typically the case with criminal restitution, § 2259 is intended to compensate victims for losses caused by the offense of conviction. See **id., at 416**. This is an important point, for it means the central concern of the causal inquiry must be the conduct of the particular defendant from whom restitution is sought.

But there is a further question whether restitution under § 2259 is limited to losses proximately caused by the offense. As noted, a requirement of proximate cause is more restrictive than a requirement of factual cause alone. Even if § 2259 made no express reference to proximate causation, the Court might well hold that a showing of proximate cause was required. . . .

Here, however, the interpretive task is easier, for the requirement . . . of proximate cause is in the statute's text. The statute enumerates six categories of covered losses. § 2259(b)(3). These include certain medical services, § 2259(b)(3)(A); physical and occupational therapy, § 2259(b)(3)(B); transportation, temporary housing, and child care, § 2259(b)(3)(C); lost income, § 2259(b)(3)(D); attorney's fees and costs, § 2259(b)(3)(E); and a final catchall category for "any other losses suffered by the victim as a proximate result of the offense," § 2259(b)(3)(F).

The victim argues that because the "proximate result" language appears only in the final, catchall category of losses set forth at § 2259(b)(3)(F), the statute has no proximate-cause requirement for losses falling within the prior enumerated categories. [*1721] She justifies this reading of § 2259(b) in part on the grammatical rule of the last antecedent, "according to which a limiting clause or phrase . . . should ordinarily be read as modifying only the noun or phrase that it immediately follows." *Barnhart v. Thomas*, **540 U.S. 20, 26** (2003). But that rule is "not an absolute and can assuredly be overcome by other indicia of meaning." **Ibid.** The Court has not applied it in a mechanical way where it would require accepting "unlikely premises." *United States v. Hayes*, **555 U.S. 415, 425** (2009).

Other canons of statutory construction, moreover, work against the reading the victim suggests . . .

The victim says that if Congress had wanted to limit the losses recoverable under § 2259 to those proximately caused by the offense, it could have written the statute the same way it wrote § 2327, which provides for restitution to victims of telemarketing fraud.

Reading the statute to impose a general proximate-cause limitation accords with common sense. As noted above, proximate cause forecloses . . . liability in situations where the causal link between conduct and result is so attenuated that the so-called consequence is more akin to mere fortuity. For example, suppose the traumatized victim of a Chapter 110 offender needed therapy and had a car accident on the way to her therapist's office. The resulting medical costs, in a literal sense, would be a factual result of the offense. But it would be strange indeed to make a defendant pay restitution for these costs. The victim herself concedes Congress did not intend costs like these to be recoverable under § 2259. . . .

The victim may be right that the concept of proximate cause is not necessary to impose sensible limitations on restitution for remote consequences. But one very effective way, and perhaps the most obvious way, of excluding costs like those arising from the hypothetical car accident described above would be to incorporate a proximate-cause limitation into the statute. Congress did so, and for reasons given above the proximate-cause requirement applies to all the losses described in § 2259. Restitution is therefore proper under § 2259 only to the extent the defendant's offense proximately caused a victim's losses.

III

There remains the difficult question of how to apply the statute's causation requirements in this case. The problem stems from the somewhat atypical causal process underlying the losses the victim claims here. It is perhaps simple enough for the victim to prove the aggregate losses, including the costs of psychiatric treatment and lost income, that stem from the ongoing traffic in her images as a whole. (Complications may arise in disaggregating losses sustained as a result of the initial physical abuse, but those questions may be set aside for present purposes.) These losses may be called, for convenience's sake, a victim's "general losses." The difficulty is in determining the "full amount" of those general losses, if any, that are the proximate result of the offense conduct of a particular defendant who is one of thousands who have possessed and will in the future possess the victim's images but who has no other connection to the victim.

In determining the amount of general losses a defendant must pay under § 2259 the ultimate question is how much of these losses were the "proximate result," § 2259(b)(3)(F), of that individual's offense. But the most difficult aspect of this inquiry concerns . . . the threshold requirement of causation in fact. To be sure, the requirement of proximate causation, as distinct from mere causation in fact, would prevent holding any possessor liable for losses caused in only a remote sense. But the victim's costs of treatment and lost income resulting from the trauma of knowing that images of her abuse are . . . being viewed over and over are direct and foreseeable results of child-pornography crimes, including possession, assuming the prerequisite of factual causation is satisfied. The primary problem, then, is the proper standard of causation in fact.

A

The traditional way to prove that one event was a factual cause of another is to show that the latter would not have occurred "but for" the former. . . .

In this case, however, a showing of but-for causation cannot be made. The District Court found that the Government failed to prove specific losses caused by Paroline in a but-for sense and recognized that it would be "incredibly difficult" to do so in a case like this. **672 F. Supp. 2d, at 791-793.** That finding has a solid foundation in the record, and it is all but unchallenged in this Court. . . . From the victim's perspective, Paroline was just one of thousands of anonymous possessors. To be sure, the victim's precise degree of trauma likely bears a relation to the total number of offenders; it would probably be less if only 10 rather than thousands had seen her images. But it is not possible to prove that her losses would be less (and by how much) but for one possessor's individual role in the large, loosely connected network through which her images circulate. See Sentencing Comm'n Report, at ii, xx. Even without Paroline's offense, thousands would have viewed and would in the future view the victim's images, so it cannot be shown that her trauma and attendant losses would have been any different but for Paroline's offense. That is especially so given the parties' stipulation that the victim had no knowledge of Paroline. . . .

Recognizing that losses cannot be substantiated under a but-for approach where the defendant is an anonymous possessor of images in wide circulation on the Internet, the victim and the Government urge the Court to read **§ 2259** to require a less restrictive causation standard, at least in this and similar child-pornography cases. They are correct to note that courts have departed from the but-for standard where circumstances warrant, especially where the combined conduct of multiple wrongdoers produces a bad outcome. . . .

. . . . Paroline's possession of two images of the victim was surely not sufficient to cause her entire losses from the ongoing trade in her images. Nor is there a practical way to isolate some subset of the victim's general losses that Paroline's conduct alone would have been sufficient to cause. . . .

. . . The striking outcome of this reasoning—that each possessor of the victim's images would bear the consequences of the acts of the many thousands who possessed those images—illustrates why the Court has been reluctant to adopt aggregate causation logic in an incautious manner, especially in interpreting criminal statutes where there is no language expressly suggesting Congress intended that approach. . . .

Contrary to the victim's suggestion, this is not akin to a case in which a "gang of ruffians" collectively beats a person, or in which a woman is "gang raped by five men on one night or by five men on five sequential . . . nights." . . . First, this case does not involve a set of wrongdoers acting in concert . . . Paroline had no contact with the overwhelming majority of the offenders for whose actions the victim would hold him accountable. Second, adopting the victim's approach would make an individual possessor liable for the combined consequences of the acts of not just 2, 5, or even 100 independently acting offenders; . . . but instead, a number that may reach into the tens of thousands. . . .

It is unclear whether it could ever be sensible to embrace the fiction that this victim's entire losses were the "proximate result," § 2259(b)(3)(F), of a single possessor's offense. Paroline's contribution to the causal process underlying the victim's losses was very minor, both compared to the combined . . . acts of all other relevant offenders, and in comparison to the contributions of other individual offenders, particularly distributors (who may have caused hundreds or thousands of further viewings) and the initial producer of the child pornography. . . .

. . . The reality is that the victim's suggested approach would amount to holding each possessor of her images liable for the conduct of thousands of other independently acting possessors and distributors, . . . with no legal or practical avenue for seeking contribution. That approach is so . . . severe it might raise questions under the Excessive Fines Clause of the **Eighth Amendment**. . . .

B

The contention that the victim's entire losses from the ongoing trade in her images were "suffered . . . as a proximate result" of Paroline's offense for purposes of § 2259 must be rejected. But that does not mean the broader principles underlying the aggregate causation theories the Government and the victim cite are irrelevant to determining the proper outcome in cases like this. The cause of the victim's general losses is the trade in her images. And Paroline is a part of that cause, for he is one of those who viewed her images. While it is not possible to identify a discrete, readily definable incremental loss he caused, it is indisputable that he was a part of the overall phenomenon that caused her general losses. Just as it undermines the purposes of tort law to turn away plaintiffs harmed by several wrongdoers, it would undermine the remedial and penological purposes of § 2259 to turn away victims in cases like this.

With respect to the statute's remedial purpose, there can be no question that it would produce anomalous results to say that no restitution is appropriate in these circumstances. It is common ground that the victim suffers continuing and grievous harm as a result of her knowledge that a large, indeterminate number of individuals have viewed and will in the future view images of the sexual abuse she endured . . . Harms of this sort are a major reason why child pornography is outlawed. See *Ferber*, **458 U.S., at 759**. The unlawful conduct of everyone who reproduces, distributes, or possesses the images of the victim's abuse—including Paroline . . . —plays a part in sustaining and aggravating this tragedy. And there can be no doubt Congress wanted victims to receive restitution for harms like this. The law makes restitution "mandatory," § 2259(b)(4), for child-pornography offenses under Chapter 110, . . . language that indicates Congress' clear intent that victims of child pornography be compensated by the perpetrators who contributed to their anguish. It would undermine this intent to apply the statute in a way that . . . would render it a dead letter in child-pornography prosecutions of this type.

Denying restitution in cases like this would also be at odds with the penological purposes of § 2259's mandatory restitution scheme. In a sense, every viewing of child pornography is a repetition of the victim's abuse. One reason to make restitution mandatory for crimes like this is to impress upon offenders that their conduct produces concrete and devastating harms for real, identifiable victims . . . It would be inconsistent with this purpose to apply the statute in a way that leaves offenders with the mistaken impression that child-pornography possession (at least where the images are in wide circulation) is a victimless crime.

If the statute by its terms required a showing of strict but-for causation, these purposes would be beside the point. But the text of the statute is not so limited. Although Congress limited restitution to losses that are the "proximate result" of the defendant's offense, such unelaborated causal language by no means requires but-for causation by its terms . . . As the authorities the Government and the victim cite show, the availability of alternative causal standards where circumstances warrant is, no less than the but-for test itself as a default, part of the background legal tradition against which Congress has legislated, cf. **id., at ___ (slip op., at 10)**. It would be unacceptable to adopt a causal standard so strict that it would undermine congressional intent where neither the plain text of the statute nor legal tradition demands such an approach.

In this special context, where it can be shown both that a defendant possessed a victim's images and that a victim has outstanding losses caused by the continuing traffic in those images but where it is impossible to trace a particular amount of those losses to the individual defendant by recourse to a more traditional causal inquiry, a court applying **§ 2259** should order restitution in an amount that comports with the defendant's relative role in the causal process that underlies the victim's general losses. The amount would not be severe in a case like this, given the nature of the causal connection between the conduct of a possessor like Paroline and the entirety . . . of the victim's general losses from the trade in her images, which are the product of the acts of thousands of offenders. It would not, however, be a token or nominal amount. The required restitution would be a reasonable and circumscribed award imposed in recognition of the indisputable role of the offender in the causal process underlying the victim's losses and suited to the relative size of that causal role. This would serve the twin goals of helping the victim achieve eventual restitution for all her child-pornography losses and impressing upon offenders the fact that child-pornography crimes, even simple possession, affect real victims.

There remains the question of how district courts should go about determining the proper amount of restitution. . . . At a general level of abstraction, a court must assess as best it can from available . . . evidence the significance of the individual defendant's conduct in light of the broader causal process that produced the victim's losses. This cannot be a precise mathematical inquiry and involves the use of discretion and sound judgment. But that is neither unusual nor novel, either in the wider context of criminal sentencing or in the more specific domain of restitution . . . Assessing an individual defendant's role in the causal process behind a child-pornography victim's losses does not involve a substantially different or greater exercise of discretion.

There are a variety of factors district courts might consider in determining a proper amount of restitution, and it is neither necessary nor appropriate to prescribe a precise algorithm for determining the proper restitution amount at this point in the law's development. Doing so would unduly constrain the decisionmakers closest to the facts of any given case. But district courts might, as a starting point, determine the amount of the victim's losses caused by the continuing traffic in the victim's images (excluding, of course, any remote losses like the hypothetical car accident described above, see *supra*, at 10), then set an award of restitution in consideration of factors that bear on the relative causal significance of the defendant's conduct in producing those losses. These could include the number of past criminal defendants found to have contributed to the victim's general losses; reasonable predictions of the number of future offenders likely to be caught and convicted for crimes contributing to the victim's general losses; any available and reasonably reliable estimate of the broader number of offenders involved (most of whom will, of course, never be caught or . . . convicted); whether the defendant reproduced or distributed images of the victim; whether the defendant had any connection to the initial production of the images; how many images of the victim the defendant possessed; and other facts relevant to the defendant's relative causal role. . . .

These factors need not be converted into a rigid formula, especially if doing so would result in trivial restitution orders. They should rather serve as rough guideposts for determining an amount that fits the offense. The resulting amount fixed by the court would be deemed the amount of the victim's general losses that were the "proximate result of the offense" for purposes of § 2259, and thus the "full amount" of such losses that should be awarded. The court could then set an appropriate payment schedule in consideration of the defendant's financial means. See § 3664(f)(2).

The victim says this approach is untenable because her losses are "indivisible" in the sense that term is used by tort law. . .

. . . that this approach would consign her to "piecemeal" restitution and leave her to face "decades of litigation that might never lead to full recovery," Brief for Respondent Amy 57, which "would convert Congress's promise to child pornography victims into an empty gesture," *id.*, at 66. But Congress has not promised victims full and swift restitution at all costs. To be sure, the statute states a strong restitutionary purpose; but that purpose cannot be twisted into a license to hold a defendant liable for an amount drastically out of proportion to his own individual causal relation to the victim's losses.

Furthermore, an approach of this sort better effects the need to impress upon defendants that their acts are . . . not irrelevant or victimless. . . . Of course the victim should someday collect restitution for all her child-pornography losses, but it makes sense to spread payment among a larger number of offenders in amounts more closely in proportion to their respective causal roles and their own circumstances so that more are made aware, through the concrete mechanism of restitution, of the impact of child-pornography possession on victims.

C

. . . courts can only do their best to apply the statute as written in a workable manner, faithful to the competing principles at stake: that victims should be compensated and that defendants should be held to account for the impact of their conduct on those victims, but also that defendants should be made liable for the consequences and gravity of their own conduct, not the conduct of others. District courts routinely exercise . . . wide discretion both in sentencing as a general matter and more specifically in fashioning restitution orders. There is no reason to believe they cannot apply the causal standard defined above in a reasonable manner without further detailed guidance at this stage in the law's elaboration. . . .

The Fifth Circuit's interpretation of the requirements of § 2259 was incorrect. The District Court likewise erred in requiring a strict showing of but-for causation. The judgment of the Court of Appeals is vacated, and the case is remanded for further proceedings consistent with this opinion.

It is so ordered.

Source: *Paroline v. United States*, 572 U.S. ___ (2014). https://www.supremecourt.gov/opinions/13pdf/12-8561_7758.pdf.

Statement of Laurie Dishman

Senate Hearing for the Cruise Passenger Protection Act

July 23, 2014

The excerpt below is from Laurie Dishman's testimony in support of a Cruise Passenger Protection Act. Dishman's testimony highlights an experience that few people consider: sexual assault by a stranger while on vacation. It also illuminates the problems that U.S. citizens may face when traveling outside of the United States. Versions of this bill were introduced in Congress in 2013 and 2015, but they did not pass. A Senate bill was introduced on June 29, 2017.

. . . It is quite an honor and a privilege to be here today, Senator Rockefeller, I am a cruise ship rape victim. I have an experience to tell you about. A cruise line employee raped me during a vacation on a Royal Caribbean cruise to Mexico. The crew member was working as a security guard in a disco on the ship. He approached me and asked me my name and cabin number. He later snuck down to my cabin and forced his way in. I resisted and struggled. He strangled me and raped me. I awoke with ligature marks around my neck. He impacted my tampon during the violent rape.

I did not know what to do.

I did not know who to turn to.

There were no police on the ship, I learned. I was hesitant to call and report the crime to the security department because a crew member wearing a security badge has just raped me. No one explained any rape protocols to me.

No one provided me with a statement of my rights. I was unaware if I even had any rights.

Just three days earlier, I was looking forward to this cruise. The glossy color brochures advertised an "adventure every day" and an "experience to remember." I was celebrating my birthday, as well as thirty years of friendship with my best friend, Michelle. I've known Michelle since we were both five years old. I was so excited.

But in the evening, I found myself in the middle of a nightmare. Michelle called the purser's desk to report the crime. A security officer and the head purser (both men) appeared at our cabin door. They sat on the bed where the rape occurred. I told them what happened, but they insisted that I prepare a written statement and sign it. They left without securing the cabin or taking me to the ship infirmary.

After I had finished my statement, the security officer took me and Michelle to the infirmary. A doctor (a man) handed me two large, black trash bags. He told us to return to the cabin and collect evidence. Michelle and I returned to the cabin. We tried to preserve hair and other items by carefully folding the sheets and pillowcases and placing them into the bags. We returned to the infirmary along the public hallways. We then watched the nurses take everything out of the trash bags, unfold the sheets and put everything into other bags.

It was a painful and humiliating ordeal.

The ship doctor eventually performed a rape kit and examined my neck, but failed to administer anti-retroviral medications to me. The procedures seemed disorganized and unprofessional. None of the medical staff were U.S. citizens. The experience was degrading.

I was returned to my cabin after the ordeal in the ship infirmary. I was traumatized to be back at the scene of the crime. I could not take my eyes off of the mattress where the crime occurred, stripped of its sheets, covers and pillow cases. The mattress seemed naked and dirty to me. It looked like I felt. I could not stop thinking about what had just happened to me over and over again.

I did not know what would happen next.

I just wanted to close my eyes and go home.

I was eventually instructed to meet with officers in an office where the questioning continued. Like the Security Officer, Head Purser, and cruise ship doctor, the officers were all men.

I was eventually given three options: (1) get off the ship when it reached Mexico and report the crime to the Mexican police; (2) stay on the cruise ship and report the crime to the FBI when the ship returned to port in Los Angeles; or (3) fly back to L.A. and report the rape to the FBI.

I opted to fly back to Los Angeles as soon as I could get off of the ship.

Once in L.A, I was questioned extensively by the FBI. They photographed the bruising around my neck.

Two days later the FBI boarded the ship when it returned to port, together with the cruise line defense lawyers. The crew member denied even going into my cabin. He did not pass a polygraph. But the FBI said it was just a "she said / he said" situation and declined to arrest him. The Department of Justice declined to prosecute on the same day.

The cruise ship then set sail again, full of passengers and the rapist onboard.

Two days later, I learned, the crew member changed his story. He claimed he had a romantic, consensual encounter with me. It was only then that the cruise line confined him in a cabin and put a security guard at his door. It was only then that the cruise line terminated him and flew him home to Trinidad.

With nowhere to turn, I hired a maritime lawyer in Miami. Why Miami? Because even though I live in Sacramento, and the cruise left from L.A., and the crime occurred in international waters heading to Mexico, the cruise line passenger ticket says that all passengers have to file suit in Miami. I subsequently learned that there are virtually no passenger rights at all contained in the cruise line tickets—only limitations, exclusions, disclaimers, and other fine print which act as a protective shield for the benefit of the cruise industry.

My attorney found out many things that surprised and angered me.

The "security guard" was actually a janitor, who the cruise line called a "cleaning specialist." He was paid less than $550 a month. He was assigned to act in the "security" department because the cruise ship has a limited number of legitimate guards on its staff. He had no training or experience at all as a security guard.

Moreover, the Royal Caribbean records my attorney uncovered revealed an employee history which included lying, falsification of records, insubordination, anger management problems and sexual harassment of girls (who were passengers) during prior cruises. We also learned that on the night in question, witnesses observed him drinking beers given to him by the cruise line bartenders in the disco.

My attorney obtained reports from Royal Caribbean, pursuant to court orders, stating that the cruise line had studied the problem of sexual assaults on their ships as far back as 1999. The outside experts retained by the cruise line concluded that sexual misconduct occurred "frequently and the victims had no advocates to support them." But the cruise line ignored what their own experts concluded, telling the public that such crimes are "rare."

The cruise industry has grown tremendously in the last ten years. There will be more and more crimes as the industry grows . . .

Notwithstanding our best efforts in the past, there remain serious shortcomings in the reporting of crimes and the protection of families whose choose to spend their vacations on cruise ships. Let me provide this committee with a few examples:

- There is substantial under-reporting of crimes on cruise ships. For example, in 2011, there were 563 alleged crimes reported by the cruise lines but only 105 publicly disclosed.
- Few cruise ship crimes are investigated and prosecuted. In 2012, the FBI opened only 18 cases and there were only four convictions.
- The cruise lines do not disclose when a crime involves a minor . . .
- The medical care on cruise ships is often substandard. . . . Most cruise lines claim that ship doctors are "independent contractors" for whom they are not liable. Few consumers understand this, until it is too late.

. . .

The cruise industry is strong and vibrant . . .

Cruise consumers, on the other hand, have virtually no rights or protections. I know this first-hand. I know exactly how it feels to have no rights and to be victimized by the cruise line a second time after their employee assaulted me.

Certainly our Congress can require such a powerful industry to:

- timely and accurately report crimes against cruise ship guests;
- provide a clear and accurate statement of our rights embodied in a ticket without incomprehensible legal mumbo-jumbo;
- hire competent medical providers; and
- provide protection under a consumer agency which will help us in our time of need.

Source: Testimony of Laurie Dishman, "The Cruise Passenger Protection Act (S. 1340): Improving Consumer Protections for Cruise Passengers," Hearing before the Committee on Commerce, Science, and Transportation, United States Senate, One Hundred Thirteenth Congress, Second Session, July 23, 2014. https://www.gpo.gov/fdsys/pkg/CHRG-113shrg91521/html/CHRG-113 shrg91521.htm.

Human Trafficking in American Schools

U.S. Department of Education, Office of Safe and Healthy Students

January 2015

This excerpt from a report written under a grant from the U.S. Department of Education focuses on child sex trafficking and child labor trafficking. The author points out that in 2012, an estimated 26 percent of 20.9 million human trafficking victims were children. Schools are often safe havens for these children, and school personnel— including teachers, administrations, maintenance workers, bus drivers, and others— can and should be advocates for children. However, the author argues, this is a broad issue that requires community involvement as well.

Child trafficking is not solely a school issue; it is a community issue that impacts schools. Therefore, it is recommended that all members of the community play a role in protecting students.

To prevent the trafficking of children, community members first need to admit the problem exists and then commit to educating other community members and increasing awareness of the impact of the problem. Standing up to child trafficking also means equipping leaders with the resources to have an authentic dialog about the issue—including demand—in their neighborhoods, jurisdictions, constituencies, or school districts and giving these leaders the tools to work toward solutions.

Historically, law enforcement and probation departments across the nation have been the primary systems addressing the complex needs of survivors of child sex trafficking. Through sting operations, crackdowns on gangs, and curfew sweeps, a law enforcement agency may be the first agency to interact with a sex trafficking victim. Today, child welfare systems and runaway and homeless youth programs are increasingly elevating their responses to child trafficking. It is strongly recommended that each community develop cross-system mechanisms and infrastructure for collaboration among public agencies and other stakeholders, while building upon the structures, processes, and relationships already in place.

Schools should partner with their school boards, service providers, governmental agencies, and local law enforcement partners to identify the nature, scope, and prevalence of child trafficking in their communities. By getting other partners involved, schools will create safer campuses and increase the chances for academic, social, and psychological student success. These same partners should work collaboratively to develop a comprehensive prevention awareness program targeted at students and parents, alerting them to the nature and danger of child trafficking, as well as to develop protocols for dealing with the crime and providing services to victims.

Source: "Human Trafficking in America's Schools," American Institutes for Research, under contract with the U.S. Department of Education, Office of Safe and Healthy Students, Washington, D.C., 2015. https://safesupportivelearning .ed.gov/human-trafficking-americas-schools/community-involvement.

Testimony of Holly Austin Smith, Child Sex Trafficking Survivor

U.S. Senate

February 24, 2015

The Justice for Victims of Trafficking Act of 2015, which provides protection and services to survivors of sex trafficking, became a public law on May 29, 2015. It aids child survivors by amending the Victims of Child Abuse Act of 1990 to include human trafficking, as well as the production of child pornography. Among other provisions, the bill establishes the Domestic Trafficking Victim's Fund, which distributes money to states to assist in fighting trafficking and to provide aid and assistance to survivors. The following is an excerpt from the testimony of Holly Austin Smith, a child sex trafficking survivor, in support of the bill during Senate Judiciary hearings on February 24, 2015. She is also the author of the book Walking Prey: How America's Youth Are Vulnerable to Sex Slavery.

Thank you, Chairman Grassley, Senator Leahy and other members of the Committee for holding this important hearing.

When I was fourteen years old, I was coerced into prostitution by a man I had met at a local shopping mall in New Jersey. This man exploited a young teen girl who had just graduated eighth grade middle school and was afraid of going into high school, so afraid that she agreed to run away from home. This man promised a glamorous new life; he told the girl she could travel across the country, meet famous people, and live in Los Angeles, California. What he delivered, however, was very different. He took the girl to Atlantic City, ordered her to prostitute, and intimidated her into cooperation. She was sold to the first buyer for $200, a man who told the girl that she reminded him of his granddaughter.

When I was arrested by law enforcement for prostitution, I was made to feel like a criminal, like a juvenile delinquent. I felt stupid, ashamed, and ostracized by society. Days later, alone in my bedroom, I felt so abandoned, so forsaken by society, that I attempted suicide. I wish I could travel back in time to tell this young girl that, years later, advocates and legislators all across the country would be standing up for her, that they would demand better protection and services for kids like her.

Had there been a Justice for Victims of Trafficking Act or Stop Exploitation Through Trafficking Act in 1992, perhaps law enforcement would have immediately recognized that I was a victim, not a criminal. Perhaps they would have assigned a victim's advocate to accompany me through the process of cooperating with and providing testimony to detectives. Perhaps funds from the proposed Domestic Trafficking Victims' Fund could have enabled me to immediately enter effective aftercare treatment and remain there until I fully understood that what had happened to me was not my fault. Perhaps my healing process could have been easier, faster. And perhaps my family and I could have had an easier transition. Even though these protections weren't available to me, they can be made available to victims today. With effective and well-informed legislation and services, victims can heal, overcome, and achieve their greatest dreams and highest potential.

However, without effective services, it is very difficult to heal. This is why I encourage legislators to include provisions that authorize resources for services for all victims of human trafficking and child exploitation—girls, boys, men, and women. Without effective services, victims may return to exploitative situations and youth may be returned to abusive situations from which they had originally run. While youth may escape juvenile detention, they may not escape continued abuse or sexual exploitation. This is particularly true in states implementing safe harbor protections where law enforcement cannot adequately respond without well-resourced service providers trained to work with child victims of commercial sexual exploitation.

In order to create effective anti-trafficking bills, solutions, and services for victims, I encourage legislators and advocates to consult with many survivors having diverse experiences – no single experience can represent all situations of sex or labor trafficking. Male, female, and transgendered survivors; survivors who were children when exploited and those who were adults; and survivors who were U.S. citizens and foreign nationals when exploited – each survivor has a different experience, a different perspective, and a different insight into effective programs that can prevent exploitation, protect victims, and prosecute traffickers and other exploiters. This is why I support the Human Trafficking Survivors Empowerment Act, which would create a survivors-led U.S. Advisory Council on Human Trafficking to review federal government policy and programs on human trafficking. It is so important that survivors play a role in finding the solutions to prevent and end sex and labor trafficking.

Many survivors, including myself, agree that policies on prevention should be one of our highest priorities, which is why it should also be a priority for policymakers. In my book, *Walking Prey: How America's Youth Are Vulnerable to Sex Slavery,* I discuss many predisposing risk factors that can increase a child's vulnerability to a sex trafficker's tactics, as well as community risk factors that can increase the likelihood of crossing paths with a trafficker or other exploiter. With effective community programs, we can prevent human trafficking and child exploitation from happening in the first place. One predisposing factor I mention in Walking Prey is being a youth with minority status, including LGBTQ youth

Nikolaos Al-Khadra is a male advocate from Chicago who identifies as a survivor of sex trafficking and commercial sexual exploitation. Nik says he was forced into prostitution at the age of seventeen; he had been ordered to leave home after accepting his identity as a gay male. "I grew up with [a lot] of emotional and physical abuse," Nik states in a personal email. He describes a home life in which his father regularly attempted to "'beat the gay out'" of him. He writes: "I drove to the gay area of Chicago. I had parked my car, met some other kids who were hanging out on a street named Halsted. I had went back to my car to get something not paying attention and was snatched from my car."

Nik then describes a hellish experience of forced drug use and forced prostitution. He says: "I think with the obvious signs of just leaving home, my personal bags in the car and being oblivious to my surroundings [I was vulnerable] . . . These men are predators [who] prey on kids like myself who were either like me throw-away youth or runaway." After managing to escape, Nik says he then returned to "'Boystown'" and "networked" with others on the street. He says this ultimately led him to illegal escort agencies through which he was exploited for sex in order to survive.

Nik writes: "There really needs to be more programs for LGBTQ youth who become homeless over parents attitudes [toward their] child's sexuality. I think being beat down mentally all throughout my childhood was why I stayed years in the sex trade."

If Nik was in the room, he would tell you that the Runaway and Homeless Youth and Trafficking Prevention Act (RHYPTA) is a necessary step toward preventing sex trafficking and protecting runaway and homeless youth. And I would agree. . . .

Source: Testimony of Holly Austin Smith, "Human Trafficking in the United States: Protecting the Victims," United States Senate, Committee on the Judiciary, February 24, 2015. https://www.judiciary.senate.gov/imo/media/doc/02-24-15%20Smith%20Testimony.pdf.

Hearing on the Rape Kit Backlog

Testimony of Scott Berkowitz of the Rape, Abuse & Incest National Network (RAINN)

U.S. Senate Judiciary Committee Subcommittee on the Constitution

May 20, 2015

In the following excerpt from Scott Berkowitz's testimony, he explains what rape kits are and why it is important for Congress to make certain that funds are allocated to

get rape kits tested. In his testimony, Berkowitz asserts that though the 2004 Debbie
Smith DNA Backlog grant program was authorized (and re-authorized in 2014) to
provide funds to the states, it has not been funded at the authorization level, nor are
all the funds going for labs and rape kit testing.

My name is Scott Berkowitz, and I am the founder and president of the Rape,
Abuse & Incest National Network, or RAINN. RAINN, the nation's largest
anti-sexual violence organization, founded and operates the National Sexual
Assault Hotline (NSAH) in partnership with more than 1,000 local sexual assault
service providers across the U.S. The NSAH, which has helped more than 2.1
million survivors of sexual assault by telephone and through online chat, serves
as the nation's primary resource for victims of sexual violence. RAINN also operates, on behalf of the Department of Defense, the DoD Safe Helpline, which
provides services to members of the US military affected by sexual assault.

. . . Rapists tend to be serial criminals, striking more than once and assaulting more than one victim in the course of their criminal careers. Forensic DNA,
which enables law enforcement to identify sexual predators early on and stop
them in their tracks, is not only important to attain justice for those who have
already been harmed, it is one of the most effective rape prevention tools that
we have available. . . .

Congress made the processing of forensic DNA a national priority by passing the DNA Analysis Backlog Elimination Act. It expanded its commitment—
specifically in regards to rape kits—through enactment of the Debbie Smith
Act in 2004. That act, which RAINN worked hard, in partnership with Debbie Smith and other advocates, to get passed and reauthorized, established
the nation's first and largest anti-rape kit backlog program. In 2013, Congress
passed a key amendment to this landmark law to require, for the first time,
support law enforcement audits of their so-called "hidden" backlogs of unsub-
mitted forensic evidence, and to make sure that a higher percentage of the DNA
funding dollars goes directly to what matters most: testing rape kits and making sure labs have the capacity to meet demand. Before I discuss the incredible
advancements we've witnessed in both

. . . Each rape kit, in actuality, represents a victim—a victim who chose to
endure an invasive, hours-long examination. Often starting just minutes or
hours after the sexual assault, this victim will stand over a sheet and lie on a
table to allow evidence—a ripped fingernail, a piece of torn clothing, anything
his or her attacker might have left behind—to fall, be scraped or removed from
their body. A medical professional (ideally, but not always, a trained sexual
assault nurse examiner) will examine and photograph the victim's genitals for
evidence of trauma. The victim's buttocks, armpits, breasts, and mouth will be
wiped and swabbed in the hope that a strand of hair, a bit of dried blood, or a
drop of semen or spit might be recovered.

Once collected, in the event that a victim decides to report the crime to law enforcement, the items in that box will, if the system is working as it should, go to a laboratory for DNA analysis. Unfortunately, it is often at this stage that the system breaks down. Hundreds of thousands of kits, it is estimated, have never reached a lab. Instead, they became part of what we call the "hidden backlog," warehoused in evidence rooms and, often, never seen again.

. . . Since it was first authorized in 2004, the Debbie Smith DNA backlog Grant program has provided states the help and resources they desperately need to carry out DNA analyses of backlogged evidence, particularly rape kits. The law, which was just renewed for another five years with overwhelming bi-partisan Congressional support, is authorized at the level of $151 million per year. Yet, consistently, the program has been funded below that authorization level—for the last several years at the level of $117 million.

Even worse, only about 65% of that $117 million, on average from FY11 through FY14, is actually being spent on Debbie Smith backlog testing and capacity building purposes. That means, out of $476 million appropriated in that period, about $309 million went to testing and lab capacity. Further, this trend actually shows signs of worsening, not improving: according to DOJ's figures, from FY11 to FY13, the amount of DNA money that allocated to administrative and program support costs rose by 94%, or approximately $6.8 million, after excluding costs imposed by sequestration, while the amount spent on Debbie Smith Act backlog reduction grants decreased by 16%, or about $14.2 million per year.

While spending 65% of DNA funds on testing is an improvement over some prior years, it still falls short of the 75% floor that Congress mandated in the SAFER Act, and the president signed into law, more than two years ago.

We hope that all members of the Judiciary Committee will urge appropriators to rectify this in the FY16 budget. We believe that Congressional intent on this point is clear: the law mandates that not less than 75% of the funding available for the purposes of the Debbie Smith Act shall support testing and capacity enhancement; and an additional 5–7%, as required by the SAFER Act, must be made available for law enforcement evidence audits. Clearer appropriations language would result in testing thousands of additional kits without any additional federal spending.

This need is urgent: As law enforcement increasingly accounts for the hidden backlogs, states will be grappling with higher-than-ever demand for critical forensic DNA casework. Already, according to NIJ, public crime labs processed 10% more DNA cases in 2011 than in 2009, while demand for such tests grew by 16%. We can't afford to have funds siphoned away from the Debbie Smith Act purpose areas, however worthy those other goals are.

This need is time-sensitive: Without accelerated testing of backlogged cases, many victims will lose their chance at justice. Among the 43 states that still have a statute of limitations on felony sex crimes, D.C. and 16 states, including Ohio and Rhode Island, do not make an exception for when DNA evidence is available. It is heartbreaking when we hear about a victim who is unable to secure justice against her rapist, even after a CODIS [the FBI's Combined DNA Index System] hit identifies the assailant, because the statute of limitations has already run out.

In addition to improving the funding process to favor testing and audits, the SAFER Act requires increased transparency around local backlogs. Grant recipients are required to disclose the number of kits discovered, testing status, status of the cases' statute of limitations, and the state's plan for those kits that have been discovered. The attorney general, under SAFER, is required to share these findings with the American public. Unfortunately, more than two years after SAFER became law, NIJ has yet to release a grant solicitation for law enforcement agencies to conduct audits. Also, the law required the development of national protocols and policies related to rape kit evidence processing and testing. These were due no later than September, 2014, but as of this date have not been released.

Source: Written testimony of Scott Berkowitz, "Hearing on the Rape Kit Backlog." U.S. Senate Judiciary Committee, Subcommittee on the Constitution, May 20, 2015. Mr. Berkowitz's complete testimony is available at https://www.judiciary.senate.gov/imo/media/doc/05-20-15%20Berkowitz%20Testimony.pdf.

Technology and Legislation in Fighting Crime: A Survivor Speaks

Testimony of Natasha S. Alexenko

June 18, 2015

Debbie Smith was kidnapped and raped in 1989. It took over six years for her attacker's DNA sample to be found in the state of Virginia's backlog and put into a national database. He was then identified and convicted. Debbie Smith became an advocate for improving and funding DNA testing. The Debbie Smith Act of 2004, which was reauthorized in 2014, provides federal funding to reduce the DNA backlog in criminal investigations. Other bills have been passed or advanced to improve DNA testing, to standardize systems, and to allow DNA information to pass more rapidly into the national database—the Combined DNA Index System (CODIS). Natasha Alexenko, a rape survivor, spoke before the U.S. House Judiciary Subcommittee on Crime and Terrorism in support of the Rape DNA Act of 2016.

When I was 20 years old, I was kidnapped while walking home to my apartment in New York City. This stranger, a man I had never met before, violently raped, sodomized and robbed me at gunpoint. When I finally escaped and thankfully found myself in my apartment, my roommate insisted that I go to the hospital for a rape kit. The medical team at the hospital was aware of the fact that my body was a crime scene. Great care was taken into collecting the evidence necessary to find my perpetrator. Unbeknownst to me, my rape kit was not immediately tested. My rape kit was sitting on a shelf in a county storage facility collecting dust along with 17,000 other kits for 9 ½ years. This was primarily because forensic DNA and the associated DNA databases were still in their infancy. In 2003, my kit was finally taken out of storage and tested. In order to stop the clock on the statute of limitations, I testified before a Grand Jury and the DNA in my rape kit was indicted.

Exactly 14 long years to the day I was attacked, the man that threatened to end my life was identified in CODIS. The DNA in my rape kit belonged to a serial offender by the name of Victor Rondon, a man who had made a career out of his criminal activities. Ironically, while being given a citation in Las Vegas for jaywalking, he assaulted the police officer. Rondon was extradited back to New York when it was discovered that he was on parole for a 1993 conviction of the illegal possession of a 9 mm semi automatic weapon. This was the very weapon he used to threaten to kill me with. Although Rondon had committed other crimes including pandering, assault and drug trafficking while on his 14-year nationwide crime spree, this was the first time anyone bothered to upload his DNA into CODIS.

Victor Rondon is currently behind bars thanks to the dedication of law enforcement and prosecutors in Manhattan County, New York. I am humbled to tell you that I testified against him on behalf of the people of New York. As I sat on the witness stand, ready to testify, I was face to face with Victor Rondon for the first time since my attack 15 years earlier. It was as though time stood still and I fainted at the sight of him. I was able to regain my composure because, for the first time, I felt empowered to set things right. My testimony supplemented the DNA evidence, putting this violent criminal behind bars until 2057, where he can no longer be a burden on law enforcement and society. Time MATTERS. I am not a law enforcement professional, nor a scientist. I do not possess a law degree, and cannot speak to the specific language or provisions in H.R. 320. What I can tell you, as a survivor of sexual assault, is that DNA testing is essential. And time matters. For nearly 15 years I was on a constant state of high alert knowing that this violent criminal was walking the streets. During those years, I felt helpless and guilty for not being able to put this monster behind bars, fully aware that he was likely harming others.

. . . For the last four years, I have been directly involved with nationwide efforts to address the thousands of rape kits that are being found in police evidence rooms throughout the country. These kits sit in the quiet darkness, alone and forgotten—gathering dust and marking time, as the statute of limitations slowly tolls for some of the cases. . .The Debbie Smith Act provides much needed resources to our nation's forensic crime laboratories as they struggle to keep up with the important work of DNA analysis, including rape kits. . . .

But today I am here to talk about the other side of the DNA database system, and crucial new technologies that may reduce the amount of time needed to bring answers to victims of crime. As we make such strong strides to reducing the backlog of untested rape kits, it is important that we not forget that a database full of evidence only has limited value. This evidence must be matched against a perpetrator. To this end, the FBI has established, with congressional authority, the CODIS database, which includes DNA profiles of persons convicted and arrested for crimes, as state laws allow. Delays in analyzing, entering and searching offender profiles against the database of DNA evidence will result in missed opportunities to identify criminals, including rapists. I am living proof of this.

One of a survivor's greatest fears is that the rapist will return or will harm others. Until they are arrested and locked away for their crime, they are free to create additional victims and burden law enforcement and taxpayers. If we have the technology available to identify these perpetrators the FIRST time that they come into law enforcement custody—it is imperative that we do so. It is the responsible thing to do for the safety of the general public. Checking CODIS for possible matches is important if we intend to maximize the value of the DNA evidence that is so painstakingly collected from the bodies of victims . . .

As the process for realizing the potential of RAPID DNA technology moves forward, I know we will be mindful of not rushing a technology ahead of stringent quality standards. Certainly, the FBI is working on this, and I sincerely hope that Congress will ensure that the important work of these groups can continue. I hope that the FBI and its partners in the forensic community will work with all due speed to develop these standards. The important progress being made at jurisdictions throughout the country on rape kit backlogs, through programs such as the Debbie Smith Act and the Sexual Assault Kit Initiative, must not be impeded.

Catching rapists and other repeat violent criminals matters. It matters to victims of crime who still await justice, and it matters to those unsuspecting citizens who may be tomorrow's victims. Laboratories in this country still define a "backlog" as anything older than 30 days. And as a victim of rape, I can tell you that 30 days is still a long time to wait. We should not be satisfied with a backlog of 30 days, not when this definition has been static for so many years. We should do better. We owe to the people. We CAN do better. And with RAPID, we can. . . .

Source: Testimony of Natasha S. Alexenko, "Rapid DNA Technology—HR 320," U.S. House Judiciary Subcommittee on Crime and Terrorism," June 18, 2015. https://judiciary.house.gov/wp-content/uploads/2016/02/Testimony-of-Natasha-Alexenko.pdf.

Vice President Joe Biden

It's On Us to Stop Campus Sexual Assault

November 9, 2015

Joe Biden, then U.S. vice president, wrote the following op-ed piece, which appeared in several college newspapers during the It's On Us Week of Action in November 2015. In the article, Biden calls on colleges, universities, students, and the public to take action to recognize and prevent sexual assault on campus. The op-ed was published just a few months after a major campus rape case was tried in California, in which the perpetrator was sentenced to only six months in jail and three months of probation.

Twenty-one years ago, I wrote the Violence Against Women Act to end the scourge of violence against women and hold perpetrators accountable. It's been a great success, but even one attack is one too many.

So I held a number of calls with hundreds of students, administrators, advocates, and survivors and asked what we can do to make colleges safer. The overwhelming answer—get men involved.

So President Obama and I started *It's On Us*—to wake-up our colleges and universities—and the country—to the epidemic of sexual violence on their campuses.

Over the past year, we've gotten celebrities, major companies, sports leagues, and leading broadcasters to participate in public service announcements and display logos and information, showing how everyone can help prevent these heinous crimes from ever happening.

One thing students can do is take the *It's On Us* pledge. Over 250,000 students have already pledged:

1. To intervene instead of being a bystander.
2. To recognize that any time consent is not—or cannot—be given, it is sexual assault and it is a crime.
3. To do everything you can to create an environment where sexual assault is unacceptable, and all survivors are supported.

The response has been overwhelming. More than 300 campuses have hosted over 1,000 *It's On Us* events, and nearly 300 colleges and universities have created their own *It's On Us* public service announcements, reaching millions of people online and at football and basketball games.

But this year, we want to do even more. That's why between November 8th to November 14th, I'm traveling across the country calling for a Week of Action to get more students involved.

This week, the University of Wisconsin is hosting an It's On Us flag football game with student athletes, members of Greek organizations, and other student groups. At Stonehill College in Massachusetts, students, faculty, and staff are wearing nametags that say how they have been affected by sexual assault: "I am a survivor," and "I will not be a passive bystander." Middle Tennessee State University is hosting discussions in the student center and online about consent and stopping sexual violence.

In addition to taking the pledge, consider other steps:

- Organize drives to get more students to take the *It's On Us* Pledge.
- Ask businesses, libraries, hospitals to display an *It's On Us* logo.
- Encourage sports teams, fraternities, sororities, bands, and other student organizations to get involved.
- Hold press conferences and roundtables with school administrators and community leaders about campus sexual assault.
- Use social media to spread the word using #ItsonUs.

You have to demand that your Universities be held accountable. President Obama and I have made it crystal clear that schools that fail in this responsibility are in violation of Title IX and risk federal investigation and financial penalties. And each of you can make it clear that you expect nothing less.

I also encourage your colleges to partner with local rape crisis centers, local law enforcement, and women's health centers to coordinate a robust community response and ensure that victims are supported in every way possible.

We have more to do to change the culture that asks the wrong questions, like Why were you there? What were you wearing? Were you drinking?

We have to ask the right questions—What made him think that he could do what he did without my consent? Why on Earth did no one stop him instead of standing by? What can we do to make sure everyone has the courage to speak up, intervene, prevent and end sexual assault once and for all?

You know that survivors are not statistics. They're our sisters; they're our classmates; they're our friends. They're at every university, every college, in every community—large and small. For all of them, everywhere, we can and we must end sexual and dating violence on campus.

But we can't do it without you. Visit **www.itsonus.org** to find out what you can do during this Week of Action and throughout the school year.

It's on me. It's on you. It's on us—and it's within our power to end sexual violence on campus once and for all.

Source: The White House, Office of the Vice President, Briefing Room Statement, "Vice President Joe Biden Op-Ed: It's On Us to Stop Campus Sexual Assault." November 9, 2015. https://obamawhitehouse.archives.gov/the-press-office /2015/11/09/vice-president-joe-biden-op-ed-its-us-stop-campus-sexual -assault.

Testimony of Nadia Murad Basee Taha, a Yazidi Victim of Sexual Slavery

United Nations Security Council

December 16, 2015

On December 16, 2015, Nadia Murad Basee Taha, a Yazidi woman, testified in front of the United Nations Security Council. She had endured sexual slavery after she was captured by the Islamic State of Iraq and Syria (ISIS, also called Daesh). She asserts that ISIS is guilty of genocide, and that the militant group intends to eliminate all signs of Yazidi culture through murder, rape, and destruction. Since escaping, she has become a human rights activist and a United Nations goodwill ambassador. In this excerpt, she describes her capture and escape attempts.

It is with great sadness, gratitude and hope that I address the Security Council. As a Yazidi survivor, I am a descendant of one of the world's oldest religions, which is today threatened with extinction. I am here to talk about the practices against us by what is called the Islamic State/Daesh—trafficking in persons, sexual enslavement of women, recruitment of children in war, displacement and the genocide of our society. I am here to tell the Council my story, of what happened to my society, which has lost hope for life and is now moving into unknown territory. I am also here to tell the Council about the more than 3,400 women and children who have been abducted. I am here to tell the Council about this global terrorist organization, the Islamic State, which is trying to destroy our culture and take away our freedom. I am here to talk about the nightmare that, just overnight, turned the life of an entire community upside-down.

Prior to 3 August 2014, I was living with my family, my brothers and sisters in the pretty, quiet village of Kocho. But then the Islamic State attacked our region, and we found ourselves facing a true genocide. . . . Their aim was to eliminate all Yazidi existence under the pretext that—according to them—we were infidels. The Islamic State did not just come to kill us, women and girls, but to take us as war booty and merchandise to be sold in markets for a bit of money, or even for free. Those crimes were not committed without design, they were part of a premeditated policy. The Islamic State came with the sole aim of destroying the Yazidi identity through force, rape, recruitment of children and destruction of all of our temples, which they took control of. All of this can be interpreted only as an act of genocide against our identity, in particular against Yazidi women. Rape was used to destroy women and girls and to ensure that they could never again lead a normal life.

On 15 August, elements from the Islamic State summoned us to the village school. They separated the men from the women and children. I saw them from the second floor of the school as they took away the men and killed them. Six of my brothers were killed, while three survived the mass killing. We, the women and children, were taken by bus from the school to another area. They humiliated us along the way and touched us in a shameful way. They took me to Mosul with more than 150 other Yazidi families. There were thousands of families in a building there, including children who were given away as gifts. One of the men came up to me. He wanted to take me. I looked down at the floor. I was absolutely terrified. When I looked up, I saw a huge man. He was like a monster. I cried out that I was too young and he was huge. He kicked and beat me. A few minutes later, another man came up to me. I was still looking at the floor. I saw that he was a little smaller. I begged for him to take me. I was terribly afraid of the first man. The man who took me asked me to change my religion. I refused. One day, he came and asked me for my hand in what they called "marriage". I said that I was ill; most women were menstruating because they were so scared. A few days later, this man forced me to get dressed and put on my makeup. Then, on that terrible night, he did it.

He forced me to serve in his military company. He humiliated me daily. He forced me to wear clothes that barely covered my body. I was not able to take any more rape and torture. I decided to flee, but one of the guards stopped me. That night he beat me. He asked me to take my clothes off. He put me in a room with guards, who proceeded to commit their crime until I fainted.

I was finally able to escape three months after my abduction. I currently live in Germany. Thankfully, Germany provided me with the necessary medical attention, for which I thank that country . . .

I am asking the Council today to find solutions to the issue of genocide before the International Criminal Court. . . .

Source: Testimony of Nadia Murad Basee Taha, United Nations Security Council Session on "Trafficking in Persons in Situations of Conflict," December 16, 2015. S/PV.7585, pp. 6–7. http://www.securitycouncilreport.org/atf/cf/%7B65B FCF9B-6D27-4E9C-8CD3-CF6E4FF96FF9%7D/s_pv_7585.pdf.

United Nations Under-Secretary-General Zainab Hawa Bangura

Remarks on Conflict-Related Sexual Violence in Syria

February 4, 2016

At a conference in London on February 4, 2016, the United Nations under-secretary-general Zainab Hawa Bangura made the following remarks on conflict-related sexual violence in Syria. She urges other nations to prioritize treatment for rape victims and to provide safe havens for refugees.

Distinguished Guests,
Ladies and Gentlemen,
    I would like to thank the United Kingdom, Kuwait, Germany, and Norway for co-hosting this timely conference, together with the United Nations, and for

recognizing that conflict-related sexual violence is a human rights, justice, and humanitarian concern that is central to resolving the conflict in Syria, and the related cross-border refugee crisis.

As you know, sexual violence has been systematically used by all parties throughout the conflict in Syria, as a tactic of war, terrorism, and torture, against women, men, girls and boys, including minorities on the basis of their religion, ethnicity and actual or perceived sexual orientation. Women and girls, particularly, have been vulnerable in the context of house-to-house searches, at checkpoints, in detention facilities, and at border crossings. I hope that if and when we get into a concrete political dialogue on solving the crisis in Syria, we will ensure accountability for gross human rights violation committed against people of Syria, especially conflict-related sexual violence. During my last visit to Syria in April 2015 and to the neighbouring countries hosting Syrian refugees, I heard from many men and women that a very weak link is the lack of adequate services including medical and psychosocial support to victims of sexual violence. Therefore I hope that in the course of our discussions today, partners will be able to commit resources towards addressing this issue.

In that regard, I would like to commend Member States, including neighbouring Jordan, Turkey and Lebanon, as well as many in Europe and beyond, for the support they are providing to Syrian refugees. My appeal today to countries present here is:

(1)   To ensure that in the course of the asylum process, survivors of sexual violence get prioritised and provided with adequate services including medical and psychosocial support.

(2)   To ensure that these victims and survivors are kept together with their families to alleviate their trauma and ensure their quick integration.

(3)   To ensure that unaccompanied children seeking refuge are well documented and protected, so that they do not fall prey to sex traffickers and other criminal gangs.

(4)   And finally, it is crucial that while granting safe haven to refugees, asylum States also provide avenues for justice, to hold the perpetrators of crimes such as sexual violence accountable.

All of these are necessary elements in the fight for a sustainable peace in Syria. My Office stands ready to engage with all of you in this regard. Justice for the victims of sexual violence in Syria may be *delayed*, but—ultimately—it must not be *denied*.

Source: Statement by Under-Secretary-General Zainab Hawa Bangura, United Nations Office of the Special Representative of the Secretary-General for Sexual Violence in Conflict, 2016. http://www.un.org/sexualviolenceinconflict/statement/statement-at-the-side-event-on-inside-syria-at-supporting-syria-and-the-region-conference/.

Comfort Women Call for Reparations

Washington Coalition for Comfort Women Issues

March 8, 2016

The euphemism "comfort women" was used to describe the women forced into sexual slavery by the Imperial Japanese Army during World War II. Many of the estimated 200,000 comfort women were Korean; others came from Japanese-occupied land in China, the Philippines, Indonesia, and Taiwan. For many years, South Korea has called for reparations from Japan for these women. The issue has become more heated, as the remaining survivors are now elderly, and only about 46 remain in South Korea. The Washington Coalition for Comfort Women Issues was founded in 1992 "to advocate for the rights of wartime victims and their lawful reparation."

Official Statement of WCCW, Inc. (Washington Coalition for Comfort Women Issues)

March 8th of 2016, UN Headquarters (written by Jungsil Lee, President of WCCW)

After last year's joint agreement issued by the Republic of Korea and Japan on the issues of the "comfort women," WCCW members have been appalled by the Japanese government's continued denial and whitewashing of the historical facts that had already been acknowledged by their previous officials. Their recent statement proves that the agreement was not sincere and genuine. True reconciliation would not be possible without real and perpetual efforts in a clear and unequivocal manner.

WCCW, an organization whose mission is to advocate for the rights of wartime victims—military sex slaves—and their lawful reparation, expected and hoped for progress in terms of the lawful reparation and official treatment followed by the agreement of two countries, but the recent activities of the Japanese government failed to reveal this hope is headed for the right direction. We support the recent recommendation by CEDAW (Committee on the Elimination of Discrimination against Women).

1. WCCW envisions 'comfort women' issues as a global human rights issue and women's rights movement that stretch over 11 nations who had experienced similar atrocities as well as today's violations of women's rights around the globe. Therefore, we do not narrow down the issue to solely a Korean-Japanese political agenda. Rather, we will continue to advocate, research, and educate the importance of human rights through this history.

2. The agreement made no provisions whatsoever for comfort women survivors from North Korea, China, Taiwan, Philippines, Indonesia, Dutch-Indi, Malaysia, Thailand, Burma, East Timor, Guam, India, and Vietnam. The agreement must include restitution and sincere apology from the Japanese government for all comfort women of all nationalities.

3. WCCW will make sure that these women occupy a prominent place in the annals of history and are provided with legal reparations not only to honor their bravery and endurance but also to commemorate the importance of human dignity. If the agreement is sincere and unequivocal, the world will see that the Japanese government will open their archival records concerning wartime and postwar treatment, create policies to reconcile with the comfort women, and cease to rewrite the past history; the Japanese government will contribute to writing of accurate accounts of the history and will promote educating its own people and the future generation about the war crimes against humanity.

4. WCCW hopes to watch the issue be resolved by a series of gradual, ongoing, and sincere accomplishments toward all victimized nations, not through a single political deal with the expression "finally and irreversibly." Although WCCW promotes a peaceful reconciliation and is eager to see the final and completed resolution, we do not believe that one bilateral agreement cannot and must not cease or delete the whole history of the war or stop activities by human rights advocates and NGOs.

5. WCCW expresses deep regrets to see that the agreement includes the possible removal or relocation of the Girl statue in front of the Embassy of Japan in Seoul that has a huge symbolic value for Koreans, the victims, and importance of civil rights.

6. WCCW would like to see the end of the Japanese government's diplomatic and publicity efforts to humiliate comfort women survivors and to revise the past, or to interfere with people's right to study, research, and speak out about their experiences and opinions. That is precisely the reason that WCCW launched the "Webinar Project" through which we research, archive, and publish the unarguable historical material about comfort women.

WCCW has been so honored to fight for and be the voice for these voiceless women for the last 23 years since 1992. We cannot possibly imagine their sufferings, but we have learned from and been inspired by the survivors. We sincerely hope that these women will finally find what they have been seeking: peace and dignity.

Source: Jungsil Lee, "Official Statement of WCCW, Inc. (Washington Coalition for Comfort Women Issues)," March 8, 2016. United Nations Headquarters. http://www.comfort-women.org/.

Eudy Simelane and "Corrective Rape": Eudy Simelane Memorial Lecture

by Edwin Cameron

University of KwaZulu-Natal

April 7, 2016

Eudy Simelane was a South African football player, coach, and LGBT-rights activist. In April 2008, she was abducted, gang-raped, and stabbed repeatedly. Her body was later found in a creek. The crime is considered to be a hate crime and an example of "corrective rape." Edwin Cameron of the Constitutional Court of South Africa delivered the inaugural Eudy Simelane Memorial Lecture at the University of KwaZulu-Natal in 2016.

It is nearly eight years since Eudy Simelane's death. Tonight we gather to mark cruelty, hatred and injustice. We mark the cruelty of a world that denied this beautiful, talented person her life, a world whose hatred suppressed her voice and extinguished her capacity for love and vigour and energy: a world that hated and despised her because she was herself—an openly, proud lesbian.

But we also gather with a positive purpose—to pay tribute to extraordinary courage and a beautiful life. We gather to celebrate Eudy's life as someone who embraced her own sexual orientation; who lived openly in her own township, KwaThema, as a lesbian, who played a beautiful, brave game of soccer—and whose courage made it easier for those who followed her to live their lives as themselves.

My theme tonight is not the destruction of Eudy's life—but the hope her life engendered.

So the evening, and this lecture, have both bitter and sweet in them. We hang our heads in grief at an unspeakable act of cruelty and violent destruction, and the terrible loss it inflicted—not only on Eudy's friends and family, but on all of us. But we also raise our heads in pride at Eudy's courage and her truthfulness, to herself and to humankind. And we honour her life of achievement and integrity.

In the eight years since Eudy's tragic death, much has changed—the debate about lesbians, gays, bisexuals, transgender, intersex and queer (LGBTIQ) people has come electrically alive in Africa. One is almost tempted to say: her death and her suffering were not in vain.

This is in large part because attacks on people like Eudy have drawn attention to an inescapable truth: that sexual and gender diversity exists in Africa—and that it is an ineradicable part of the beauty of this continent.

And increasingly, African LGBTIQs are standing up. They are speaking out. They are becoming visible.

The revolution started shortly after Eudy's death, with an act of astonishing courage on the part of two Malawian men. In late December 2009, Steven Monjeza and Tiwonge Chimbalanga declared their intention to get married. The response was heartless, and extreme. They were arrested, imprisoned, paraded in front of a jeering public, and held without bail. Eventually, to rousing cheers, they were given the maximum sentence of *14 years* in prison.

All this for love—on a continent that has suffered famine, flood, malgovernance, dictatorships, military coups, corruption, genocide and civil wars. As

Archbishop Tutu has said, amidst these pressing problems, the least of Africa's concerns should be same-sex love. . . .

. . . I defy those who say that the Constitution has achieved nothing for gays and lesbians. Has it achieved enough? No. Certainly not. But we do wrong if we under-estimate the beneficial impact of constitutional equality on LGBTI self-esteem, self-regard, inner dignity, social assertiveness and constitutional agency.

. . . South Africa has served as a beacon to the rest of the world, including Africa, on LGBTI rights. Again, we would do wrong to under-estimate the effect on the rest of Africa of our attainment of constitutional equality. Our rights have been a significant catalyst for other African LBGTI communities.

Still, there remains a huge continuing disjunct—between what is promised and what has been attained. . . .

For LGBTIs, there remains widespread homophobia and prejudice. This finds expression in trivial condonations of horror—as when, in one of the *Spud* movies, the John Cleese character jokes smugly that he would like to give all lesbians "a thorough rogering". This has its counterpart in enacted hatred, violence and murder against lesbians. The two are connected. Spoken hatred too often leads to its enactment in terrible deeds of destruction. . . .

The genie of African LGBTI pride can never be put back in the bottle. Eudy Simelane's life was not in vain. Though we mourn the senselessness of the violence that took her young life, we know that what she believed in, what her life entailed and represented, will triumph in our continent and in our time.

Source: Edwin Cameron, "Eudy Simelane Memorial Lecture. Inaugural Lecture on Behalf of The Other Foundation and The Ujamaa Centre," pp. 1, 2, 11, 12, 15. University of KwaZulu-Natal, Pietermaritzburg, South Africa, April 7, 2016. http://ujamaa.ukzn.ac.za/Libraries/manuals/Cameron_Eudy_Simelane _Memorial_Lecture_Thursday_7_April_2016_updated.sflb.ashx. Reprinted with permission from Edwin Cameron.

A Rape Victim Speaks: *The People v. Brock Allen Turner*
June 2, 2016

On January 18, 2015, two witnesses saw Brock Turner sexually assaulting an unconscious woman who was lying on the ground near a dumpster at Stanford University. When they yelled, Turner ran, but the two witnesses pinned him down and held onto him until police officers arrived. Both Turner and his victim had attended a fraternity party, and both were intoxicated. Turner was convicted on three felony counts of sexual assault. On June 2, 2016, Judge Aaron Persky sentenced Turner to six months in jail, plus three months of probation. Turner was released after serving half of his sentence. Many people criticized the sentence as too lenient, and prosecutors had sought a six-year prison sentence. The day after Turner was sentenced, the victim gave BuzzFeed, an online news and entertainment site, permission to publish her courtroom statement. The following are excerpts from this statement.

Your honor,

If it is all right, for the majority of this statement I would like to address the defendant directly.

You don't know me, but you've been inside me, and that's why we're here today.

On January 17, 2015, it was a quiet Saturday night at home. My dad made some dinner and I sat at the table with my younger sister who was visiting for the weekend. . . . I planned to stay at home by myself, watch some TV and read, while she went to a party with her friends. Then, I decided it was my only night with her, I had nothing better to do, so why not, there's a dumb party ten minutes from my house, I would go, dance weird like a fool, and embarrass my younger sister. . . .

The next thing I remember I was in a gurney in a hallway. I had dried blood and bandages on the back of my hands and elbow. I thought maybe I had fallen and was in an admin office on campus. I was very calm and wondering where my sister was. A deputy explained I had been assaulted. I still remained calm, assured he was speaking to the wrong person . . . When I was finally allowed to use the restroom, I pulled down the hospital pants they had given me, went to pull down my underwear, and felt nothing. . . .

I felt pine needles scratching the back of my neck and starting pulling them out of my hair . . . my gut was saying, help me, help me. . . .

I was asked to sign papers that said "Rape Victim." . . . I stood there naked while the nurses held a ruler to the various abrasions on my body . . . I had multiple swabs inserted into my vagina and anus, needles for shots, pills, had a Nikon pointed right into my spread legs. . . .

After a few hours of this, they let me shower. I stood there examining my body beneath the stream of water and decided, I don't want my body anymore. I was terrified of it, I didn't know what had been in it, if it had been contaminated, who had touched it. I wanted to take off my body like a jacket and leave it at the hospital with everything else . . .

For two weeks after the incident, I didn't get any calls or updates about the night or what happened to me. . . .

One day, I was at work, scrolling through the news on my phone, and came across an article. . . . This is how I learned what happened to me. . . .

At the bottom of the article, after I learned the graphic details of my own sexual assault, the article listed his swimming times. . . .

Alcohol is not an excuse. . . . Having too much to drink was an amateur mistake that I admit to, but it is not criminal. . . . Regretting drinking is not the same as regretting sexual assault. We were both drunk, the difference is I did not take off your pants and underwear, touch you inappropriately, and run away. . . .

Source: *People of the State of California v. Brock Allen Turner,* Case #B1577162 (2015), Exhibit Sixteen, Superior Court of California, County of Santa Clara, Palo Alto Courthouse. The victim's complete statement is available at https://www .buzzfeed.com/katiejmbaker/heres-the-powerful-letter-the-stanford-victim -read-to-her-ra?utm_term=.dl6gVXpw#.yidKYgD1.

Holding Colleges and Universities Accountable for Underreporting Sexual Violence on Campus

U.S. Senate Committee on Health, Education, Labor, and Pensions

July 1, 2016

On July 1, 2016, 31 U.S. senators sent a letter to the Department of Education and the Department of Justice, urging them to evaluate colleges and universities that receive federal fund to make certain that they are complying with new regulations on the reporting of sexual violence on campuses and the institution of measures that help provide for students' safety. These measures were included in the Violence Against Women Reauthorization Act of 2013 (VAWA), which also amended the Jeanne Clery Disclosure of Campus Security Policy and Campus Crime Statistics Act (the Clery Act). The acts require that higher institutions report incidents of sexual assault and put training programs into effect for faculty and students. In addition, under the law, schools must provide students with information about their rights.

The Honorable John B. King, Jr.
Secretary
U.S. Department of Education
400 Maryland Avenue, SW
Washington, D.C. 20202

The Honorable Loretta Lynch
Attorney General
U.S. Department of Justice
950 Pennsylvania Avenue, NW
Washington, D.C. 20530

Dear Secretary King and Attorney General Lynch:
    Gender-based violence including sexual assault on our college and university campuses is a serious and growing public health epidemic, and threatens

the ability of students across the nation to learn in a safe environment. According to the Department of Justice (DOJ), one in five female undergraduates have been sexually assaulted while in college. Several other surveys support this finding, including a report from the Centers for Disease Control and Prevention (CDC), which found that 20 percent of women are sexually assaulted in their lifetime. On college campuses, sexual violence disproportionately affects women and impedes their ability to participate fully in campus life. Educational equity for women and all students requires fair, responsive, fully developed campus sexual assault policies, knowledgeable administrators, with the shared goal of ending sexual violence on campuses.

The Violence Against Women Reauthorization Act of 2013 (VAWA) amended the Jeanne Clery Disclosure of Campus Security Policy and Campus Crime Statistics Act (Clery Act) in response to growing concerns about sexual violence on college campuses. These changes require eligible institutions of higher education to take proactive, robust, and preventive measures to make campuses safer and hold schools accountable. July 1st, 2016 marks one year since these regulations went into effect, and while the Administration has taken strong steps to implement these regulations, we are frankly concerned that schools are not doing enough. Failure to fully adhere to these reforms puts women, and all students, nationwide at risk—and the Departments of Education and Justice have a critical role to play in ensuring the protections laid out in VAWA are fully put into practice.

The VAWA reforms, in part, required colleges and universities to include the number of incidents of sexual assault, domestic violence, dating violence, and stalking as part of the required reporting of crime statistics to the Department of Education (ED). Unfortunately, this new data showed that in 2014, while nearly 11,600 schools reported, only nearly nine percent reported any occurrences of sexual assault, dating violence, domestic violence, or stalking and nearly 91 percent reported having no incidents of sexual assault. Further, 91 percent of schools reported no incidents of domestic violence or dating violence. These directly conflict with the DOJ and CDC data on sexual assault, and strongly suggest that schools are either not taking the reporting obligation seriously or are not creating an environment where students feel comfortable coming forward to report, and are vastly underreporting these crimes. This discrepancy demonstrates the need for the Department of Education to reinforce schools' obligation and to examine where schools are falling short in creating trusted systems for reporting and documenting and reporting data on gender-based violence, in order to provide targeted technical assistance and support.

Furthermore, recognizing the need to improve schools' proactive work to prevent these crimes in the first place, the VAWA reforms also focused on increasing student awareness and requiring schools to focus on prevention of gender-based violence. Under the reforms, schools were required to:

- Detail policies to prevent domestic violence, dating violence, sexual assault, and stalking;
- Institute procedures that the institution will follow once an incident has been reported;
- Delineate procedures for survivors to follow when a crime occurs;
- Provide written notification about existing services and accommodations for survivors;
- Train officials who investigate a complaint or conduct an administrative proceeding regarding any of these crimes in a manner that protects the safety of survivors and promotes accountability; and
- Implement primary prevention education programs to promote awareness of crimes, provide ongoing awareness and prevention training for students and faculty. This includes making students aware of the definition of consent in the jurisdiction, safe and positive options for bystander intervention to prevent harm, and information on risk reduction to recognize to warning signs of abusive behavior.

Requiring schools to develop and implement prevention strategies is one of the most successful ways to reduce sexual violence in the campus community. Yet, primary prevention is only one piece of the puzzle when it comes to reducing rates of gender-based violence. Prevention complements work on risk reduction, accountability through our criminal justice process, and victim services.

As we mark the one-year anniversary of these reforms, we are concerned that a significant number of schools may be out of compliance. To that end, we request that you evaluate how schools are complying with these reforms and clarify what steps can be taken by schools to prevent gender-based violence on their campuses. Specifically, we ask that you:

- Clarify university obligations under the Clery Act through guidance articulating a clear and final timeline for compliance that addresses schools needing assistance with compliance;
- Work with schools to provide model training for faculty and staff to ensure that school officials are informed and prepared to respond to violence;
- Issue a best practices guide that includes model policies for improving campus safety and preventing and responding to these crimes based on evidence-based measures for school action as required under the statute; and
- Provide oversight review to ensure institutional compliance with reporting obligations under the Clery Act.

The Departments of Education and Justice have been strong partners in our joint efforts to make colleges and universities safe and supporting environments for students to learn, and we appreciate everything you have done to ensure safer campuses for all students. However, we still have more work to do. We look forward to your ongoing partnership in this work and to more progress in the future.

Signed:
Patty Murray (D-WA)
Tammy Baldwin (D-WI), Michael Bennet (D-CO), Richard Blumenthal (D-CT), Cory Booker (D-NJ), Barbara Boxer (D-CA), Sherrod Brown (D-OH), Maria Cantwell (D-WA), Ben Cardin (D-MD), Bob Casey (D-PA), Richard J. Durbin (D-IL), Dianne Feinstein (D-CA), Al Franken (D-MN), Kirsten Gillibrand (D-NY), Martin Heinrich (D-NM), Mazie K. Hirono (D-HI), Tim Kaine (D-VA), Patrick Leahy (D-VT), Edward Markey (D-MA), Claire McCaskill (D-MO), Barbara A. Mikulski (D-MD), Chris Murphy (D-CT), Jack Reed (D-RI), Bernie Sanders (I-VT), Brian Schatz (D-HI), Jeanne Shaheen (D-NH), Debbie Stabenow (D-MI), Tom Udall (D-NM), Elizabeth Warren (D-MA), Sheldon Whitehouse (D-RI), and Ron Wyden (D-OR).

Source: U.S. Senate Committee on Health, Education, Labor, and Pensions. Washington, D.C., 2016. Accessed December 20, 2017. https://www.help.senate .gov/imo/media/doc/20160701%20VAWA%20Clery%20Anniversary%20 Letter.pdf.

Testimony of Amita Swadhin, Child Rape Survivor and Advocate for Sexual Assault Survivors

Confirmation Hearings for Jeff Sessions for Attorney General

January 11, 2017

Child rape survivor and advocate for sexual assault survivors Amita Swadhin testified against the confirmation of former U.S. Senator Jeff Sessions for Attorney General. Swadhin argued that Sessions does not appear supportive of survivors of sexual violence; she also noted that he has voted against legislation that would support LGBTQ+ people. Sessions was confirmed. An excerpt from Swadhin's testimony follows.

Good morning, my name is Amita Swadhin, I am a resident of Los Angeles, California, born in Ohio to two immigrants from India, and raised in New Jersey. . . .

In October, millions of sexual assault survivors were triggered when hot mic tapes were released of President-elect Trump describing forcibly kissing women and grabbing women by the genitals.

I was one of those survivors. I am a victim of violent crime, in the form of eight years of rape and over a decade of psychological, verbal and physical abuse by my father, beginning when I was four years old. In addition to direct violence from my father, I grew up watching him abuse my mother in a text-book case of domestic violence and marital rape, until she finally found the courage and support to leave him when I was 15 years old.

I am here on behalf of survivors of rape and sexual assault to urge you not to confirm Senator Sessions as Attorney General. In the wake of President-elect Trump's comments about grabbing women by the genitals becoming public, Senator Sessions was quoted stating he doesn't characterize that behavior as sexual assault. Let me be clear—Senator Sessions stated he does not character-ize non-consensual genital grabbing as sexual assault. . . . While he criticized President-elect Trump's inappropriate language, at no point did Senator Sessions condemn the behavior President-elect Trump had admitted to engaging in.

As a publicly out survivor of child sexual abuse, many people, mainly in my father's family and community of friends and colleagues, have dismissed my story as a private family matter or have diminished the impact of this violence on my present-day life. I live with Complex Post Traumatic Stress Disorder, and struggle every day to be well. It directly and negatively impacts me when people disbelieve or attempt to discredit me or other survivors. So, to watch our President-elect admit to forcibly kissing women and grabbing them by the genitals, and to hear Senator Sessions say this behavior does not constitute sexual assault, and then to consider him leading the Department of Justice has been incredibly triggering.

I am unfortunately far from alone in my experience. We live in a country in which the crimes of rape, sexual assault, child abuse, domestic violence are happening at epidemic rates, behind closed doors. These are public health issues occurring in the private sphere. According to the US Department of Justice National Crime Victimization Survey, more than 320,000 Americans over age 12 are raped or sexually assaulted each year. According to the Centers for Disease Control, 1 in 4 girls and 1 in 6 boys will be sexually abused before age 18. In 80% of adult sexual assaults and 90% of cases of child sexual abuse, victims know and trust their perpetrators. When survivors attempt to come forward, we are often shamed and disbelieved in the media. For this reason, most victims of violent crime never seek healing or accountability from the state. Most violent crimes remain unreported.

We need a justice department that can be a partner to families and commu-nities. Our Attorney General must be able to demonstrate leadership to victims of violent crime that helps us feel we can trust the state, the courts, and victim service agencies more than we fear our perpetrators. For most survivors of vio-lent crime, this means trusting the state more than you fear the family member, friend or community member who you trusted and who raped or abused you.

My own story demonstrates how difficult this is to achieve. I disclosed my father's abuse to my mother when I was 13 years old. As in many tight-knit immigrant communities, my mother felt pressured to not get divorced, and lacked support from her peers to leave my father, despite him having hit her at community events more than once over the years. So, when I disclosed, she called a therapist for support, which led to state intervention due to mandated reporting. The female police officer who questioned me sat me across from a double mirror, watched me break down in tears during questioning, and stoically told me I clearly needed therapy but that wasn't her job—she was just there to get the facts about what had happened. The two male prosecutors threatened to prosecute my mother for being complicit in my abuse, without knowing any details from me. They also told me I would be harshly cross examined by the defense attorney. They did not connect me to any victim advocates or support services. Because of these reasons, I did not feel comfortable disclosing the extent of the violence I had survived, and my father was given five years' probation and no jail time. He was allowed to continue living in my home for a year and a half after state intervention. Even after my mother finally found the strength to leave him when I was 15, my father was allowed to have unsupervised visits with me and my sister—he convinced social workers that my mother could serve as the visitation supervisor, subjecting all three of us to another year of verbal and physical violence. These events occurred from 1991 to 1994, just before the Violence Against Women Act was created.

Thankfully, we have improved the response of the criminal justice system to victims of intimate violent crime in the past 23 years. VAWA requires the criminal justice system to work with the victim services system. . . . In 1991, the police did not contact victim advocates for me. Today, thanks to VAWA, the law enforcement system is encouraged to provide victims an advocate to support them in breaking their silence and sharing their truth.

Yet despite this progress, most victims of violent crime still do not come forward, particularly survivors living at the intersections of multiple oppressions—survivors of color, disabled survivors, immigrant survivors, and LGBT survivors. We need an Attorney General who will continue the progress we have made since the initial passage of VAWA, someone committed to improving and enforcing our laws to ensure the most vulnerable victims of crime can come forward to seek accountability and to access healing.

Time and again, Senator Sessions' voting record has shown he is not the man for the job. While he voted in favor of the Violence Against Women Act in the bill's early years, when VAWA was expanded in 2013 to ensure LGBT survivors of domestic violence and sexual assault were being served, Senator Sessions voted against the bill. This is not the first time he demonstrated his bias against the LGBT community. In 2006, Senator Sessions voted in favor of a constitutional ban on same-sex marriage. In 2009, he voted against the Matthew Shepard and James Byrd Jr. Hate Crimes Prevention Act, which extends federal hate crime protections to people victimized because of their sexual orientation, gender identity, or disability.

By voting against VAWA specifically when services and protections were strengthened for LGBT survivors, Senator Sessions has shown his personal bias against LGBT Americans is so strong, he is willing to throw all survivors of domestic violence and sexual assault under the bus, stripping away the services and trainings we have created to better support survivors over the past two decades.

As a bisexual woman with a transgender romantic partner, and as an advocate working to support sexual assault survivors in the LGBT community, the prospect of Senator Sessions as Attorney General is personally and professionally alarming. National data shows LGBT people, and particularly transgender women of color, are disproportionately victimized by rape and sexual assault, intimate partner violence and homicide. One in two transgender people will be raped or sexually assaulted in their lifetime. Furthermore, the majority of hate violence homicide victims are transgender women. In fact, only 11 days into the new year, two transgender women of color have already been murdered— Mesha Caldwell, an African American transgender woman from Mississippi, and Jamie Lee Wounded Arrow, a two-spirit Oglala Lakota woman from South Dakota.

We must trust the Attorney General to enforce and apply our laws fairly, per our Constitution's provisions on equal protection. . . .

Source: Testimony of amita Swadhin, Senate Judiciary, Confirmation Hearings for Jeff Sessions as Attorney General, January 11, 2017. https://www.judiciary .senate.gov/imo/media/doc/01-11-17%20Swadhin%20Testimony.pdf.

A Gymnast Speaks Out against Sexual Abuse

Testimony of Jamie Dantzscher before the U.S. Senate Judiciary Committee

March 28, 2017

On March 28, 2017, U.S. gymnasts testified before a Senate Judiciary Committee. The purpose of the hearing was to discuss the need to protect young athletes from sexual assault and abuse. The gymnasts' testimony was in support of Senate Bill 534, "To prevent the sexual abuse of minors and amateur athletes by requiring the prompt reporting of sexual abuse to law enforcement authorities." As of November 2017, the bill had passed the Senate, but it has not been signed into law.. The bill came amid reports that the company USA Gymnastics had not acted in a timely manner to address allegations of sexual abuse perpetrated by a gymnastics team doctor, Larry Nassar. An excerpt from the testimony of Jamie Dantzscher, a bronze medalist in the 2000 Olympics, follows. Dantzscher notes that children do not often understand they are being abused, and they are "taught to submit to authority." In a Michigan court in November 2017, Nassar pleaded guilty to seven counts of first-degree criminal sexual conduct. He previously pleaded guilty to possession of child pornography, for which he was sentenced to 60 years in prison.

. . . When I was 11 years old, I started training as an elite gymnast at a gym in West Covina, California. I needed to work with more experienced coaches. This was a big sacrifice for my entire family because it was a 90-minute drive each direction from home. My parents both had to work 5–6 days a week and had six other kids that were all involved in sports as well. My coaches told them they believed the sacrifice would be worth it because I had the talent to go really far. Financially my parents didn't know how they would make it all work, but they decided that it was worth the effort in hopes that I would have the opportunity to get a college scholarship one day.

Gymnastics started becoming very intense at this point. I started training 25–30 hours per week including two workouts per day during the summer. My coaches were very serious and even scary at times when they would yell at me.

My body was always sore and I always seemed to be tired, but I was learning new skills that I had only seen on TV before so I thought that's just the way it had to be to accomplish my dream.

I made the USA Junior National Team for the first time when I was just 12 years old. It was in Palm Springs, California. What I remember most about that meet was that Kerri Strug was competing as a senior. I competed at the same meet with so many girls I had seen on TV! I was so excited! I made the USA National Team every year after that all the way up to the Olympics.

It was then that I was introduced to the US National Team Physician, Dr. Larry Nassar.

What I have only recently come to understand is that the medical treatment he performed for my back pain and other in injuries was sexual assault. Dr. Nassar abused me at the USA National Training Center in Texas, he abused me in California and at meets all over the world. Worst, he abused me in my hotel room in Sydney at the Olympic Games.

When I first spoke out about my abuse at the hands of Dr. Nassar, I thought I was the only one. I was disbelieved and even criticized by the some in the Gymnastics community for bringing this disturbing issue to light.

Children often don't speak up when they are abused. They suffer in silence. They are taught to submit to the authority of adults. This is especially true in the hyper-competitive world of elite gymnastics. Women do speak up and that is why I am here today.

USA Gymnastics failed its most basic responsibility to protect the athletes under its care. They failed to take action against coaches, trainers, and other adults who abused children. And they allowed Dr. Nassar to abuse young women and girls for more than 20 years.

USA Gymnastics failed its most basic responsibility to protect the athletes under its care. They failed to take action against coaches, trainers, and other adults who abused children. And they allowed Dr. Nassar to abuse young women and girls for more than 20 years.

The federal law that governs our Olympic program traditionally defines the responsibilities of USA Gymnastics. That law should now specify that USA Gymnastics must abide by stricter policies to prevent sexual abuse in order for it to maintain its certification.

It is time the law reflects that USA Gymnastics' highest priority should be protecting their athletes from sexual abuse by male coaches and doctors and that is exactly what USA Gymnastics failed to prevent.

I am grateful to this Committee for inviting me to add my voice to those who are supporting this important new legislation. It will require USA Gymnastics and other Olympic sports organizations to immediately report child abuse to law enforcement authorities and will provide victims with greater opportunities to seek justice.

Generations of young athletes will thank you for your leadership. So do I.

Source: Testimony of Jamie Dantzscher, United States Senate Judiciary Committee, March 28, 2017. https://www.judiciary.senate.gov/imo/media/doc/03 -28-17%20Dantzscher%20Testimony.pdf.

United Nations Secretary-General António Guterres

Report of the Secretary-General on Conflict-Related Sexual Violence

April 2017

In his introduction to this report, United Nations Secretary-General António Guterres discusses the issues involved in eradicating sexual violence, including detecting and preventing abuses by peacekeeping personnel. He also points out that social norms within various societies that blame victims or permit marital rape, also permit sexual violence to flourish during conflict.

Recognizing that the United Nations has individuals among its ranks who engage in egregious acts of sexual exploitation and abuse, I have pledged to dramatically improve the way the United Nations prevents and responds to sexual exploitation and abuse by our own personnel and those deployed under the auspices of the United Nations. . . . I have also called on Member States to join me in a unified effort to detect, control and prevent incidents of sexual exploitation and abuse in order to make zero tolerance a reality. (p. 4)

In 2016, sexual violence continued to be employed as a tactic of war, with widespread and strategic rapes, including mass rapes, allegedly committed by several parties to armed conflict, mostly in conjunction with other crimes such as killing, looting, pillage, forced displacement and arbitrary detention. The strategic nature of the violence was evident in the selective targeting of victims from opposing ethnic, religious or political groups, mirroring the fault lines of the wider conflict or crisis. Patterns of sexual violence have also been seen in the context of urban warfare, during house searches, operations in residential areas and at checkpoints. Moreover, since 2014, the United Nations has intensified its focus on the use of sexual violence as a tactic of terrorism by a range of violent extremist groups. For these actors, sexual violence advances not only such objectives as incentivizing recruitment, terrorizing populations into compliance, displacing civilians from strategic areas, eliciting operational intelligence and forcing conversions through marriage, but also entrenches an ideology based on suppressing women's rights and controlling their sexuality and reproduction. It is further used to generate revenue, as part of the shadow economy of conflict and terrorism, through sex trafficking, sexual slavery, enforced prostitution and the extortion of ransoms from desperate families. In some circumstances, women and girls are themselves treated as the "wages of war", being gifted as a form of in-kind compensation or payment to fighters, who are then entitled to resell or exploit them as they wish. The past year has also seen the use of women and girls held in sexual slavery as human shields and suicide bombers, denoting their status as expendable "resources" in the machinery of terrorism. In the context of mass migration, women and children affected by conflict, displacement or violent extremism are particularly at risk of falling prey to traffickers owing to the collapse of protective political, legal, economic and social systems. (pp. 5–6)

To change conduct at the level of individuals and institutions alike, it is critical to challenge the underlying social norms that prescribe and proscribe behaviour and perpetuate victim-blame. This entails bridging the formal and informal sphere to ensure that legal and policy approaches and community-driven responses are mutually-reinforcing. There is a discernible trend of outdated and incomplete definitions of sexual violence at the level of national law, which often fail to criminalize rape in marriage, ignore coercive circumstances, and exclude males from the scope of protection, leading to permissive attitudes in wartime about sexual violence in the context of forced marriage, slavery or detention. These practices tend to be justified as "legitimate" by certain belligerent and extremist groups, and can become "normalized" and more deeply entrenched in the post-conflict phase. Similarly, legislative immunity for members of the armed and security forces can translate in wartime to a "licence to rape". Male control over women's production and reproduction can pave the way for sexual violence being deemed an acceptable and effective military strategy: a reward, an entitlement and a form of group bonding. This indicates a need for both government officials and traditional leaders to make clear through their public pronouncements and behaviour that the prohibition of sexual violence is categorical and that the stigma of culpability rests squarely with the perpetrator. Transitional justice can provide an opportunity to transform both inadequate laws and harmful social norms, by ensuring that the gravity of sexual violence is registered on the historical record and in the public memory. (p. 6)

Source: "Report of the Secretary-General on Conflict-Related Sexual Violence" (S/2017/249), April 15, 2017, pp. 4, 5, 6. Office of the Special Representative of the Secretary-General on Sexual Violence in Conflict. http://www.stoprapenow.org/uploads/advocacyresources/1494280398.pdf. Reprinted with permission.

Sexual Abuse at an Elite School

Report to the Board of Trustees of Choate Rosemary Hall

April 2017

In October 2016, Choate Rosemary Hall, an elite boarding school in Connecticut, announced to alumni, parents, and staff that it had hired Nancy Kestenbaum, an investigator and prosecutor, to investigate allegations of sexual misconduct and assault between adult staff members and children. The abuses detailed in a report issued in April 2017 go back decades. In recent years, there have been several highly publicized cases in which Catholic priests, coaches, and teachers have been accused of sexual abuse of children in their charge. In 2016, the Boston Globe Spotlight team investigated and reported on abuse in over 110 private New England schools, including Choate Rosemary Hall. In this excerpt from the Choate report, Kestenbaum summarizes the school's response to incidents of sexual misconduct.

We have paid particular attention to Choate's responses to the incidents we describe in our report. Many of the Choate graduates who reported incidents to us did not tell any adult at the school at the time of the incidents. Some did not report because they did not recognize the conduct as abusive at the time and/or did not want the school to find out. Others expressed the view that the culture at the time made it difficult to report and that, at the time, they could not identify an administrator whom they believed would be sympathetic to a report. In other instances, the school was informed, but not until many years later. We also learned of situations when administrators or faculty learned of sexual misconduct in real time. In nearly all the incidents we describe in this report, when a faculty or staff member who was still employed by Choate was found to have violated school policy, that individual was required to leave, usually by way of resignation.

Our interviews and school records showed that sometimes the school moved quickly and decisively. In other cases, it was slower to respond and allowed the faculty member to remain at the school, sometimes with restrictions on his or her activity, for a considerable length of time. When a faculty member was a long-term and admired teacher, action sometimes came more slowly. On at least one occasion, a faculty member remained until his voluntary retirement, some ten years after a student reported an incident of sexual misconduct.

Our investigation further showed that when reports of sexual misconduct were substantiated by the Choate administration, sexual misconduct matters were handled internally and quietly. Even when a teacher was terminated or resigned in the middle of the school year because he or she had engaged in sexual misconduct with a student, the rest of the faculty was told little and sometimes nothing about the teacher's departure and, when told, was cautioned to say nothing about the situation if asked. Individuals we interviewed cited the impact on affected students and their parents' concerns for privacy, as well as protection of the faculty members in question and potential risks to the school, as reasons why the school followed this approach. Some of the former students and parents with whom we spoke were satisfied with how the school responded at the time, although some, looking back, felt that more communication about the issues might have benefitted both teachers and students or thought that the school should have notified government authorities. Others said that they felt that the school had not responded as it should have. In a few instances, the school entered into settlement agreements with the student or graduate, some of which are confidential.

Our mandate was factual reporting, not legal analysis, and we have not analyzed whether Choate or any individuals affiliated, or previously affiliated, with the school violated any laws.

Source: Nancy Kestenbaum, Covington & Burling LLP, "Report to the Board of Trustees of Choate Rosemary Hall." April 2017, pp. 5–6. http://www.choate.edu /uploaded/Documents/eNotify/Report_to_the_Board_of_Trustees_of_Choate _Rosemary_Hall.pdf?1492107268673.

Exoneration for the Groveland Four

Florida Senate

April 14, 2017

In 1949, a 17-year-old white woman, Norma Padgett, said she was raped by four black men in Groveland, Florida. Despite a complete lack of evidence, four young men—Ernest Thomas, Charles Greenlee, Samuel Shepherd, and Walter Irvin—were arrested. Ernest Thomas was shot and killed while trying to evade arrest. The other three were beaten in the county jail to obtain confessions. Mobs, stirred up by Sheriff Willis V. McCall, burned black-owned homes in the area, creating a situation so intense that the governor sent in the National Guard. The three men were found guilty. Samuel Shepherd and Walter Irvin, both World War II army veterans, were sentenced to death, while 16-year-old Charles Greenlee was sentenced to life imprisonment. McCall shot Shepherd and Irvin while transporting them for retrial, claiming they had tried to escape. Shepherd was killed; Irvin survived by pretending to be dead. In 2015, college student Josh Venkataraman started a petition to exonerate the men. The petition received nearly 10,000 signatures. In April 2017, the Florida House of Representatives voted unanimously to pardon the men. The following excerpt, from the concurrent Florida Senate bill, acknowledges the injustice and offers an apology to the men's families.

Senate Concurrent Resolution

A concurrent resolution acknowledging the grave injustices perpetrated against Charles Greenlee, Walter Irvin, Samuel Shepherd, and Ernest Thomas, who came to be known as "the Groveland Four"; offering a formal and heartfelt apology to these victims of racial hatred and to their families; and urging the Governor and Cabinet to perform an expedited clemency review of the cases of Charles Greenlee, Walter Irvin, Samuel Shephard, and Ernest Thomas, including granting full pardons.

. . . we hereby acknowledge that Charles Greenlee, Walter Irvin, Samuel Shepherd, and Ernest Thomas, who came to be known as "the Groveland Four," were the victims of gross injustices and that their abhorrent treatment by the criminal justice system is a shameful chapter in this state's history.

BE IT FURTHER RESOLVED that we hereby extend a heartfelt apology to the families of Charles Greenlee, Walter Irvin, Samuel Shepherd, and Ernest Thomas for the enduring sorrow caused by the criminal justice system's failure to protect their basic constitutional rights.

BE IT FURTHER RESOLVED that the Legislature urges the Governor and Cabinet to expedite review of the cases of Charles Greenlee, Walter Irvin, Samuel Shephard, and Ernest Thomas as part of the Governor's and Cabinet's constitutional authority to grant clemency, including granting full pardons.

BE IT FURTHER RESOLVED that a copy of this resolution be provided to the Governor, the Attorney General, the Chief Financial Officer, the Commissioner of Agriculture, and the families of the Groveland Four as a tangible token of the sentiments expressed herein.

Source: "CS/SCR 920: Groveland Four," Florida Senate, 2017. https://www.flsenate.gov/Session/Bill/2017/920/BillText/c1/PDF.

Prison Rape Elimination Act Data Collection Activities

June 2017

The Prison Rape Elimination Act, passed in 2003, requires the collection of data on rape in federal, state, and local correctional institutions. The collection, analysis, and review take place nationwide. Below are some of the activities and findings of the National Survey of Youth in Custody (NSYC) for 2017.

The Prison Rape Elimination Act of 2003 (PREA; P.L. 108-79) requires the Bureau of Justice Statistics (BJS) to carry out, for each calendar year, a comprehensive statistical review and analysis of the incidence and effects of prison rape. PREA further specifies that the review and analysis shall be based on a random sample, or other scientifically appropriate sample of not less than 10% of all prisons, and a representative sample of municipal prisons.

In 2016, more than 7,600 prisons, jails, community-based facilities, and juvenile correctional facilities nationwide were covered by PREA. The act requires the Attorney General to submit—no later than June 30 of each year—a report that lists institutions in the sample and ranks them according to the incidence of prison rape. BJS has developed a multiple-measure, multiple-mode data collection strategy to fully implement requirements under PREA.

The National Survey of Youth in Custody (NSYC) provides facility-level estimates of youth reporting sexual victimization in juvenile facilities. To collect this information, the youth use audio computer-assisted self-interviewing (ACASI) technology with a touchscreen-enabled laptop and an audio feed to maximize confidentiality of responses and minimize literacy issues. The first NSYC (NSYC-1) was conducted from June 2008 to April 2009, and the second (NSYC-2) was conducted from February 2012 to September 2012. The third data collection (NSYC-3) will begin in late 2017.

In previous surveys, a large number of juveniles have been interviewed, including more than 9,000 during 2008–09 in 195 facilities and 8,700 in 2012 in 326 facilities. These surveys have found that juveniles have high rates of sexual victimization (9.5% in 2012) when compared to incarcerated adults in prisons (4.0% during 2011–12) and jails (3.2% during 2011–12). Because of these higher rates of sexual victimization, NSYC-3 will be the first in the series of upcoming PREA collections to be conducted by BJS in 2017 since the release of the PREA standards in 2012. In addition to ranking facilities as required under the act, NSYC-3 will measure the impact of the PREA standards and other efforts on the prevalence of sexual victimization, type of incidents, reporting behaviors of victims, and response by correctional staff when incidents occur.

In June 2016, BJS released Facility-level and Individual-level Correlates of Sexual Victimization in Juvenile Facilities, 2012 (NCJ 249877, BJS web), which used NSYC-2 data to examine how the environment of a juvenile facility impacts youth sexual victimization. The report also considered critical youth-level predictors. Overall, facilities with higher rates of sexual assault housed more youth who had submitted written complaints against staff, did not have enough staff to monitor the facility, and had higher levels of gang fights. However, the report found that a juvenile's individual characteristics—including victimization history, sex, gender, and offense history—were more important than facility factors in predicting sexual victimization.

Among facility-level findings—

- Rates of youth-on-youth sexual assault in female-only juvenile facilities (5.3%) were more than three times greater than those in male-only facilities (1.5%).
- Youth-on-youth sexual assault was lowest (1.1%) in facilities where almost all youth in the facility reported that they first learned sexual assault was not allowed within the first 24 hours of arrival.
- Youth-on-youth sexual assault was most prevalent (4.5%) when facilities had a high concentration of youth with histories of sexual abuse (24.0% or more of youth), a concentration of lesbian, gay, or bisexual (LGB) youth (5.0% in facilities with 18% or more of LGB youth), and a greater-than-average proportion of youth held for violent sexual assault (3.3%).
- Sexual assault by another youth (4.0%) was more common in facilities that held greater concentrations of youth with a history of psychiatric conditions (76% or more of youth).
- Staff sexual misconduct was reported by 5.9% of youth in facilities with multiple living units, compared to 2.1% of youth in facilities with single units.
- Staff sexual misconduct was most prevalent in detention centers (7.4%) and training/long-term secure facilities (7.3%). It was lowest in residential treatment centers (3.1%) and nonstate-operated facilities (3.1%).

In male-only juvenile facilities, 5.7% of youth reported staff sexual misconduct, compared to 1.4% in female only facilities.

- Facilities with a change in staffing levels during the previous 12 months (7.1%) had higher rates of staff sexual misconduct than facilities with no change (3.1%).
- Rates of staff sexual misconduct were highest in facilities where youth perceived the facility staff to be unfair (10.3%), youth had the fewest positive perceptions of staff (9.7%), and youth worried about physical assault by other youth (8.2%) or staff (11.2%).
- In facilities where the majority of youth reported gang fights, the rate of staff sexual misconduct (10.6%) was more than double the facility average (5.2%).
- In preparation for NSYC-3, BJS engaged in the following activities during 2016–17 to assess the prior NSYC-1 and NSYC-2 surveys and to develop new items:
- From January to April 2016, BJS conducted an item-by-item assessment of the NSYC-1 and NSYC-2 questionnaires to determine the basis for additional items and revisions to past items in the sexual victimization and facility characteristics surveys.

- In April 2016, BJS convened a national workshop of juvenile correctional facilities' administrators and other stakeholders (as required under Section 4 of PREA) to solicit their views on potential revisions for the next data collection.
- In April 2016, BJS issued a competitive solicitation to obtain a collection agent through a cooperative agreement to administer the NSYC-3. It was awarded to Westat (Rockville, MD) in August 2016.
- In August 2016, BJS conducted a cognitive test of new and revised items in the NSYC-3 survey among 20 youth in three state-operated facilities. A total of 68 questions were tested.
- In August and November 2016, BJS also tested new items on sexual orientation, sexual preference, and gender identity. Given the higher rates of sexual victimization reported by lesbian, gay, and bisexual (LGB) youth in previous NSYC surveys, these tests were designed to further refine the questions and response items. The tests were conducted with 20 male and female adjudicated youth in three juvenile correctional facilities during the cognitive test if time permitted, and with 15 youth not held in a facility who were lesbian, gay, bisexual, and transgender (LGBT) or had a close family member or friend who were LGBT.
- In October and November 2016, BJS completed an expert review of the facility characteristics survey with members of the Council of Juvenile Correctional Administrators (CJCA). Expert reviewers from seven states reviewed the wording of the questions and provided feedback on their ability to provide the data being requested by the survey. Additional input on measures related to the use of restrictive housing were obtained from CJCA's PREA committee.
- In April 2017, BJS conducted a pilot test of the NSYC-3 collection protocols and revised survey instruments. The test was completed in six facilities with 150 completed youth interviews and six completed facility surveys.
- In May 2017, BJS conducted a cognitive test of the youth survey's Spanish language version. This test, which represents the final test before national collection, was conducted in two state-operated juvenile facilities that held a large number of Spanish-speaking youth.
- National data collection is scheduled to begin in late 2017 once the survey has been approved by the Office of Management and Budget. The first report from NSYC-3 is expected in early 2019.

Source: U.S. Department of Justice, Bureau of Justice Statistics, "PREA Data Collection Activities, 2017." NCJ 250752, June 2017. https://www.bjs.gov /content/pub/pdf/pdca17.pdf.

Resources

Selected Bibliography

Allen, Beverly. *Rape Warfare: The Hidden Genocide in Bosnia-Herzegovina and Croatia.* Minneapolis: University of Minnesota Press, 1996.

Baker, Carrie. N. *The Women's Movement Against Sexual Harassment.* New York: Cambridge University Press, 2008.

Bevacqua, Maria. *Rape on the Public Agenda: Feminism and the Politics of Sexual Assault.* Boston: Northeastern University Press, 2000.

Brownmiller, Susan. *Against Our Will: Men, Women and Rape.* Repr. ed. New York: Ballantine, 1993.

Buchwald, Emilie, Pamela Fletcher, and Martha Roth. *Transforming a Rape Culture.* Rev. ed. Minneapolis, MN: Milkweed Editions, 2005.

Chang, Iris. *The Rape of Nanking: The Forgotten Holocaust of World War II.* New York: BasicBooks, 1997.

Ehrlich, Susan. *Representing Rape: Language and Sexual Consent.* New York: Routledge, 2001.

Finley, Laura L. *Domestic Abuse and Sexual Assault in Popular Culture.* Santa Barbara, CA: ABC-CLIO, 2016.

Freedman, Estelle B. *Redefining Rape: Sexual Violence in the Era of Suffrage and Segregation.* Cambridge, MA: Harvard University Press, 2013.

Horvath, Miranda A. H., and Jessica Woodhams, eds. *Handbook of the Study of Multiple Perpetrator Rape: A Multidisciplinary Response to an International Problem.* London and New York: Routledge, 2013.

McGuire, Danielle L. *At the Dark End of the Street: Black Women, Rape, and Resistance—A New History of the Civil Rights Movement from Rosa Parks to the Rise of Black Power.* New York: Vintage, 2010.

Roiphe, Katie. *The Morning After: Sex, Fear, and Feminism on Campus.* Boston: Little, Brown, 1993.

Sanday, Peggy Reeves. *Fraternity Gang Rape: Sex, Brotherhood, and Privilege on Campus.* 2nd ed. New York: New York University Press, 2007.

Smith, Merril D. *Encyclopedia of Rape.* Santa Barbara, CA: Greenwood Press, 2004.

Weaver, Gina Marie. *Ideologies of Forgetting: Rape in the Vietnam War.* Albany: State University of New York Press, 2010.

Whittier, Nancy. *The Politics of Child Sexual Abuse: Emotion, Social Movements, and the State.* New York: Oxford University Press, 2009.

Films

Feature Films

The Accused (1988). A woman is gang-raped in a tavern. Based on the Big Dan's Tavern case.

Boys Don't Cry (1999). Based on the story of Brandon Teena, born Teena Brandon, who was raped and murdered in Nebraska.

The Color Purple (1985). Based on Alice Walker's Pulitzer Prize–winning novel. The story focuses on a young black woman in the South who raped by her stepfather and husband.

Deliverance (1972). The story of four city men from Atlanta who decide to take a canoe voyage through rural Georgia. One of the men is raped at gunpoint.

Extremities (1986). After a woman is raped, she decides to fight back.

The Girl with the Dragon Tattoo (Swedish version, 2009; English-language remake, 2011). Based on the novel by Stieg Larsson. A computer hacker and an investigative journalist uncover a sex-trafficking ring. Contains two rape scenes.

The Innocents (2016). A French-Polish movie about a Red Cross doctor who helps nuns in a convent after discovering they had been raped by Soviet soldiers toward the end of World War II.

Precious (2009). An illiterate, overweight black teenage girl suffers emotional and physical abuse, including repeated rapes by her father.

Rosemary's Baby (1968). Roman Polanski's horror classic includes a rape scene in which a young woman is drugged and raped while a group of Satanists watches.

Spotlight (2015). The Academy Award–winning drama based on the true story of how the *Boston Globe's* "Spotlight" team uncovered the Catholic Church's cover-up of sex abuse by clergy.

Talk to Her (2001). A young woman in the hospital in a coma is raped by a hospital attendant. In Spanish, with English subtitles.

Virgin Spring (1960). Ingmar Bergman's film based on a 14th-century legend about a spring that emerges after a young girl is raped and killed. In Swedish, with English subtitles.

The Woodsman (2004). The story of a child molester who returns to his hometown after he is released from prison.

Documentaries

Audrie & Daisy (2016). A Netflix documentary that studies sexual assault in high schools.

The Brandon Teena Story (1998). The story of transgender man Brandon Teena, who was raped and murdered in Nebraska.

The Hunting Ground (2015). Documentary about sexual assault on U.S. college campuses.

India's Daughter (2015). After a female student is brutally gang-raped on a bus in India, filmmaker Leslee Udwin interviews one of the rapists and examines Indian society and values.

The Invisible War (2012). A documentary that explores sexual assault within the U.S. military.

Outlawed in Pakistan (2013). Kainat Soomro is gang-raped in Pakistan and then dares to take her case to court.

United States Organizations

American Overseas Domestic Violence Crisis Center
http://www.866uswomen.org/
Provides a toll-free crisis line and resources for U.S. civilians and military personnel living overseas.

Amnesty International, USA
https://www.amnestyusa.org/
Fights injustice and promotes human rights.

Asian Task Force
http://www.atask.org/site/
Aims "to prevent domestic violence in Asian families and communities and to provide hope to survivors."

Bureau of Justice Statistics
https://www.bjs.gov/
Provides statistics on national crime.

Corporate Alliance to End Partner Violence
http://www.caepv.org/
Focuses on how to involve businesses and corporate resources to combat and prevent partner violence.

End the Backlog
http://www.endthebacklog.org/
An initiative of the Joyful Heart Foundation, focused on ending the backlog of untested rape kits.

End Rape on Campus
http://endrapeoncampus.org/
Works to end sexual violence on college campuses.

Grateful Garment Project
http://gratefulgarment.org/
Provides clothing and toiletries to rape survivors to give them dignity after a rape exam.

Human Rights Watch
https://www.hrw.org/
Focuses on fighting human rights abuses globally.

INCITE!
http://www.incite-national.org/
"a nation-wide network of radical feminists of color working to end violence against women, gender non-conforming, and trans people of color, and our communities."

It's On Us
http://www.itsonus.org/
A national campaign to end sexual assault; launched in September 2014 after the White House Task Force to Prevent Sexual Assault.

Joyful Heart Foundation
http://www.joyfulheartfoundation.org/
Strives to end sexual violence through education and advocacy, as well as providing support to survivors; founded by Mariska Hargitay.

Just Detention International
https://justdetention.org/
Seeks to end sexual assault in prisons all over the world: "Rape is not part of the penalty."

Know Your IX
https://actionnetwork.org/fundraising/support-know-your-ix-2
Works to provide legal education "to empower students to stand up for their rights and change their campuses."

Men Can Stop Rape
http://www.mencanstoprape.org/
Focuses on how men can stop sexual harassment and assault.

Men Stopping Violence
http://menstoppingviolence.org/
"To organize men to end male violence against women and girls through innovative trainings, programs, and advocacy."

Mending the Sacred Hoop
http://mshoop.org/
Works to end violence against Native American women and children.

National Alliance to End Sexual Violence
http://endsexualviolence.org/who-we-are/about-naesv
Works "to provide a missing voice in Washington for state coalitions and local programs advocating and organizing against sexual violence and for survivors."

National Center on Domestic and Sexual Violence
http://www.ncdsv.org/
Provides training and resources to end domestic and sexual violence.

National Clearinghouse for the Defense of Battered Women
http://www.ncdbw.org/
"Working for justice for battered women charged with crimes."

National Sexual Violence Resource Center
http://www.nsvrc.org/
Provides resources on sexual violence.

National Human Trafficking Hotline
https://www.acf.hhs.gov/otip/victim-assistance/national-human-trafficking-hotline
A "24/7, confidential, multilingual hotline for victims, survivors, and witnesses of human trafficking."

Rape, Abuse, and Incest National Network (RAINN)
https://www.rainn.org/
"The nation's largest anti-sexual violence organization"; operates the National Sexual Assault Hotline (800-656-HOPE) and provides the Safe Helpline for the U.S. Department of Defense; also provides a wealth of information and statistics on all forms of sexual violence.

Stalking Resource Center
https://victimsofcrime.org/our-programs/stalking-resource-center/help-for-victims
Provides a hotline, services, and information for victims of stalking.

Stop Street Harassment
http://www.stopstreetharassment.org/about/
Dedicated to documenting and ending street crime; runs a national street harassment hotline with RAINN.

TELL (Therapy Exploitation Link Line)
http://www.therapyabuse.org/index.htm
"TELL is a resource, referral, and networking organization that seeks to help victims and survivors of exploitation by psychotherapists and other healthcare providers find the support and resources they will need to understand what has happened to them, take action, and heal."

Unchained at Last
http://www.unchainedatlast.org/
Dedicated to helping women escape arranged or forced marriages, and to preventing arranged marriages through education and advocacy.

Women Under Siege
http://www.womenundersiegeproject.org/
A journalism project originated by Gloria Steinem to investigate "how rape and other forms of sexualized violence are used as tools in genocide and conflict throughout the 20th century and into the 21st."

International Hotlines and Shelters

International Rape Crisis Hotlines
A list of sexual assault hotlines.
http://www.ibiblio.org/rcip/internl.html

Australia
1800Respect: National Sexual Assault, Domestic Family Violence Counseling Service
https://www.1800respect.org.au/
Brisbane: Rape and Incest Survivors Support Centre (BRISSC)
Provides free, confidential support services.
http://www.brissc.org.au/
Sydney: NSW Rape Crisis Centre
Provides 24/7 online and telephone support to women and men
http://www.nswrapecrisis.com.au/

England and Wales
Rape Crisis Centers
https://rapecrisis.org.uk/centres.php
London: The Havens—specialist centers in London for victims and survivors of
sexual assault.
https://www.thehavens.org.uk/

Ireland
Rape Crisis Network Ireland
Provides lists and resources for sexual assault victims.
http://www.rcni.ie/

Japan
Tokyo Rape Crisis Center
Provides counseling and a fund to help women who want to prosecute their rapists.
http://www.tokyo-rcc.org/center-hp-english.htm

Kenya
Coalition on Violence Against Women
Works against violence to women, access to justice, and advocacy.
http://covaw.or.ke/index.html

South Africa
The GBV Prevention Network
http://preventgbvafrica.org/
A network of activists and organizations working together to combat violence against
women.

Turkey
Istanbul: Mor Cati Kadin Siginagi Vakfi (Purple Roof Women's Shelter and
Foundation)
http://www.morcati.org.tr/en/

New Zealand
Rape Prevention Education
http://rpe.co.nz/
Wellington: Sexual Abuse Help
Provides counseling and a 24/7 help line.
http://www.wellingtonhelp.org.nz/

About the Editor and Contributors

Merril D. Smith, editor and contributor, is an independent scholar with a PhD in American history from Temple University. She is the author or editor of several books on this critical topic, including *Encyclopedia of Rape*, *Sex without Consent: Rape and Sexual Coercion in America*, and *Cultural Encyclopedia of the Breast*.

Sydney A. Bender is a doctoral student in the American University School of Public Affairs.

Sarah Boeshart is a PhD candidate in sociology at the University of Florida, where her primary research focus is on lesbian experiences of violence and of representation.

A. S. Catey, PhD, JD, earned his degrees concurrently at the University of Florida in 2011. His work focuses on law, policy, and public health in the United Kingdom, Europe, and the United States. He is a criminal justice policy consultant in Washington, D.C.

Laurence Cobbaert, originally from Belgium, graduated with a bachelor of science degree from Lewis University in December 2015. She is now pursuing a research degree in gender studies and sociology at the University of Adelaide, Australia.

R. Gregg Dwyer is director of the Community and Public Safety Psychiatry Division and the Sexual Behaviors Clinic and Lab, Department of Psychiatry and Behavioral Sciences, at the Medical University of South Carolina. He consults on sexual behavior topics with government entities, including mental health personnel, attorneys general, state police, probation officers, public defenders, and juvenile justice departments, and with private mental health clinicians and attorneys. Dr. Dwyer has also published and reviewed works on sexual behavior.

Michelle Evans is a licensed clinical social worker and a licensed sex offender treatment provider. She is an instructor, writer, and bilingual therapist treating sexual addiction issues, substance abuse issues, and mental health issues. She is also an administrator at Waubonsee Community College, near Chicago.

Laura Finley is associate professor of sociology and criminology at Barry University in Miami. She is the author, coauthor, or editor of 18 books, as well as many book chapters and journal articles. Dr. Finley is also a syndicated columnist with PeaceVoice and a contributor with New Clear Vision. In addition, she is actively involved with a number of local, state, and national groups working on peace, justice, gender equality, and human rights.

Emily D. Gottfried is a clinical forensic psychologist and an instructor in the Community and Public Safety Psychiatry Division at the Medical University of South Carolina. In this capacity, Dr. Gottfried completes forensic evaluations for the courts, including evaluations for the Sexual Behaviors Clinic and Lab. Dr. Gottfried's research interests include the accurate assessment of malingering/feigning during criminal forensic evaluations; improving the validity of evaluations of sexual dangerousness; and examining the correlates of and psychometric properties of the Minnesota Multiphasic Personality Inventory-2-Restructured Form (the MMPI-2-RF) to predict a number of behaviors, suicide risk assessment, and female offenders.

Tuba Inal is senior lecturer of politics at University West, in Sweden. She is the author of *Looting and Rape in Wartime: Law and Change in International Relations.*

Deborah Laufersweiler-Dwyer is an assistant professor of criminal justice, sociology, and political science at Claflin University in Orangeburg, South Carolina.

Sheila M. McMahon is a social worker in a higher-education setting, where she provides support services to student survivors of sexual assault, dating violence, domestic violence, and stalking. As well, she designs and implements evidence-based bystander intervention trainings, consent workshops, and restorative justice circles for undergraduate and graduate students. Her current research focuses on the diverse students' needs for specialized prevention education and strategies for improving campus climate issues pertaining to sexual misconduct and power-based violence.

Trudy Mercadal teaches organizational communication and works in community-organization for development at Florida Atlantic University. Her research interests are human and community rights and alternative pedagogies from the standpoint of race and gender. Her current research projects include investigation into the National Police Archives of Guatemala City.

Victoria M. Nagy is an associate lecturer in criminology at Deakin University. She received her PhD from Monash University in 2012. Her research interests include investigating violent women in British and Australian history, and investigating sexual violence against children and adults terrestrially and virtually. She is the author of *Nineteenth-Century Female Poisoners: Three English Women Who Used Arsenic to Kill*.

Gianina Pellegrini is a peace psychologist and independent scholar. She serves on the board of directors for Partnerships for Trauma Recovery, in Berkeley, California, and is a member-at-large for the American Psychological Association's Division 48: Society for the Study of Peace, Conflict, and Violence.

Paul Reynolds is a reader in sociology and social philosophy at Edge Hill University in Ormskirk, Lancashire, UK. He is also coeditor of the *Journal of the International Network for Sexual Ethics and Politics*.

Emily Knight Shier is a faculty member at the Medical University of South Carolina's Community and Public Safety Psychiatry Division, assisting with forensic court evaluations. She has provided therapy services to adults with sexual offending behaviors, to youth with behavior problems, and to youth who have experienced traumatic events, as well as to youth who have engaged in inappropriate/illegal sexual behaviors and to the families of this last group.

Amanda M. Stylianou is a social worker who focuses on improving services at the intersection of trauma, mental health, and poverty. In her role as senior director of research and program development at Safe Horizon, the United States' leading victim services agency, she works with her team to ensure the organization is providing the most effective and efficient services to clients throughout New York City. Her current research is centered on understanding the needs of victims/survivors of domestic violence and human trafficking and on understanding and evaluating practices in the field.

Index

Page numbers in **bold** indicate the location of main entries.

PTSD, 4
risky behavior, 420–421
secure juvenile facility, 269
statutory rape, 416–417
YouTube, 280
Yugoslavia (former)
wartime rape, 463
See also International Criminal
Tribunal for the former Yugoslavia

Zabinski, Antonina, 237
Zabinski, Jan, 237
Ziering, Amy, 44
Zimbabwe
child rape cases, 16
incest, 203
sexual victimization of men and
boys, 368
The Zookeeper's Wife (film), 237